JAPANISM

— 世界に伝えたい、日本美景 —

山田悠人

JAPANISM

日本の美しさを世界に伝えたい

2013年、ドイツの首都ベルリンに移住し、そこから本格的にフォトグラファーとして写真を撮り始めました。撮影していく中で、それは私の新しい表現方法となり、情熱へと変わっていきました。

久しぶりに日本に帰国したとき、最もインパクトがあり、圧倒されたのが東京の街の活気やネオンの輝きでした。それ以来「自分が生まれ育った東京の素晴らしさを世界に伝えたい」という思いが強まり、帰国するたびに東京の夜景や人々を撮影するようになりました。

遠く離れた外国の地に住むことにより、日本に住んでいたときには当たり前で気付くことができなかった独自の良さや素晴らしさを再認識するきっかけとなりました。それと同時に、写真を撮影する際にもこれまでとは違った視点で日本を見るようになり、生まれ育った東京、そして日本という国に新たな興味が湧いてきました。

2018年には、ベルリンを中心とした廃墟を撮り収めた写真集『SILENT WORLD』を出版しましたが、そのことをきっかけに、継続していた廃墟の撮影を一旦ストップし、新しい被写体として私の好きな日本の美しい風景や文化を世界の人々と共有したいと思い、「日本の美しさを自分の作品を通して世界に伝える」ことをメインテーマに掲げることにしました。

そして4年間にわたり、壮大な日本の至るところで移りゆく四季を通して、数え切れないほどのシャッターを切ってきました。同時に、美しい景色に心を震わせてきました。また、奇跡的な出会いに感謝し、人々に助けられ、無償の優しさに涙することもありました。美しい日本の風景だけではなく、日本人の他者を思いやる優しい心や、地域ごとの伝統を大切にする風習、人々の仕事に対する真摯な姿勢、そして、日本の工芸品や食文化に常に感動を覚えたのです。

日本という国は、過去の歴史、文化、伝統の連続性が創り出した国であると思います。さまざまな場所で撮影をしていると、高速道路から旧街道へ、都会の熱狂が杉林の静寂へと続いているように、過去からの文化や風習などが目に見えない道を通じて現在へと、すべてが繋がっているように強く感じました。睡眠時間を削り、重たい機材を背負い、山に登り、砂丘を歩き、真夏の炎天下、吹雪の中、ときにはフェリーに24時間乗船し、移動に移動を重ねて、奇跡がもたらす一瞬の光景のために、一枚の写真のためだけに、情熱とエネルギー、時間、資産、持てるすべてを費やして撮影してきました。

その集大成として、私の渾身の写真たちが一冊にまとまることを誇りに思います。

この写真集では、日本のすべてを網羅しているわけではありません。しかし、四季折々の広大で多様な近年の日本の姿、そして、その美しさを私の感性とカメラのレンズを通し、表現しています。

私の大好きな日本という国とその美しさをこの写真集を通じて、日本はもとより世界中の皆さまに伝えることができたらとても嬉しく、光栄です。

Communicating the beauty of Japan to the world

In 2013, I moved to Germany's capital city of Berlin, where I officially embarked on my career in photography. In the process of my work, photography became a new form of self-expression that gradually turned into my passion.

When I returned to Japan after being away for some time, what most impressed and overwhelmed me was the vibrancy of Tokyo and the radiance of its neon lights. Since then, my desire to communicate the wonders of the city to the rest of the world has intensified. Every time I returned, I would photograph the nightscapes and the people of Tokyo, where I was born and raised.

Living in a distant foreign country allowed me to rediscover the virtues and splendors of Japan that had been too familiar for me to notice when I was a resident. At the same time, I began to observe my motherland from a different perspective when shooting my photographs. There was a new-found interest in my hometown and the country itself.

In 2018, I published *SILENT WORLD*, a photography collection of abandoned ruins, mainly taken in Berlin. This prompted me to temporarily suspend my urban exploration photography project and turn my aspirations to a new subject. I decided that the focal theme of my new endeavor would be to capture the splendid landscapes and culture of my beloved country and convey its charms to people around the world.

I spent four years shooting countless images throughout the changing seasons in all parts of the magnificent island country. All the while, I was awestruck by the splendor of the landscapes. I am also grateful for the magical encounters and the support I have received. At times, I was moved to tears by those who extended their selfless generosity. I was constantly amazed and touched not only by the exquisite scenic beauty, but also by the caring and kind nature of its people, the regional practices that honor traditional customs, the people's diligence in their undertakings, and the craftsmanship and culinary culture of Japan.

I believe Japan is a country built on a continuum of its history, cultures, and traditions. As I ventured to locations, I strongly sensed that the culture and customs from the past are all connected to the present through unseen paths, just as highways meet with ancient roads, and urban frenzy merges into the tranquility of cedar forests. I have cut back on sleep, hauled heavy equipment on my back, climbed mountains, trudged along dunes, braved the blazing midsummer heat and snowstorms, even set out on 24-hour ferry rides at times, and traveled transit after transit. I invested my passion, energy, time, resources, and everything I had, all for that miraculous moment, all for that single image.

It is my proud privilege to showcase my best photographs in one volume to present the culmination of these efforts.

This book certainly isn't enough to cover Japan in its entirety. Nevertheless, I have endeavored to portray the vast and diverse facets as well as the sheer beauty of modern Japan in each of its four seasons—capturing images through the camera lens and with my keen sensibility. I am deeply delighted and honored to have the opportunity to share my love of Japan and its wonders not only with the people in my native country but also with those around the world.

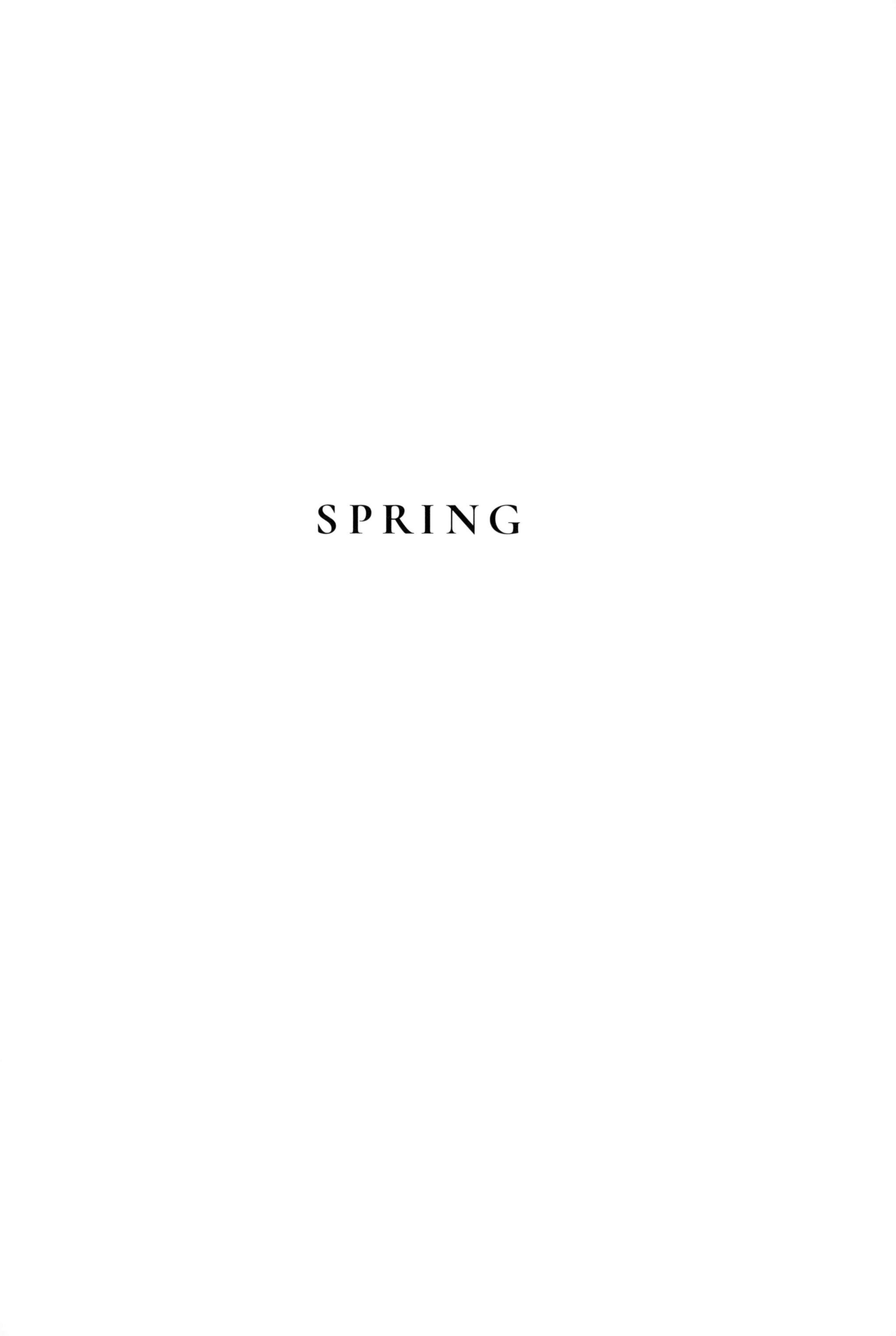

SPRING

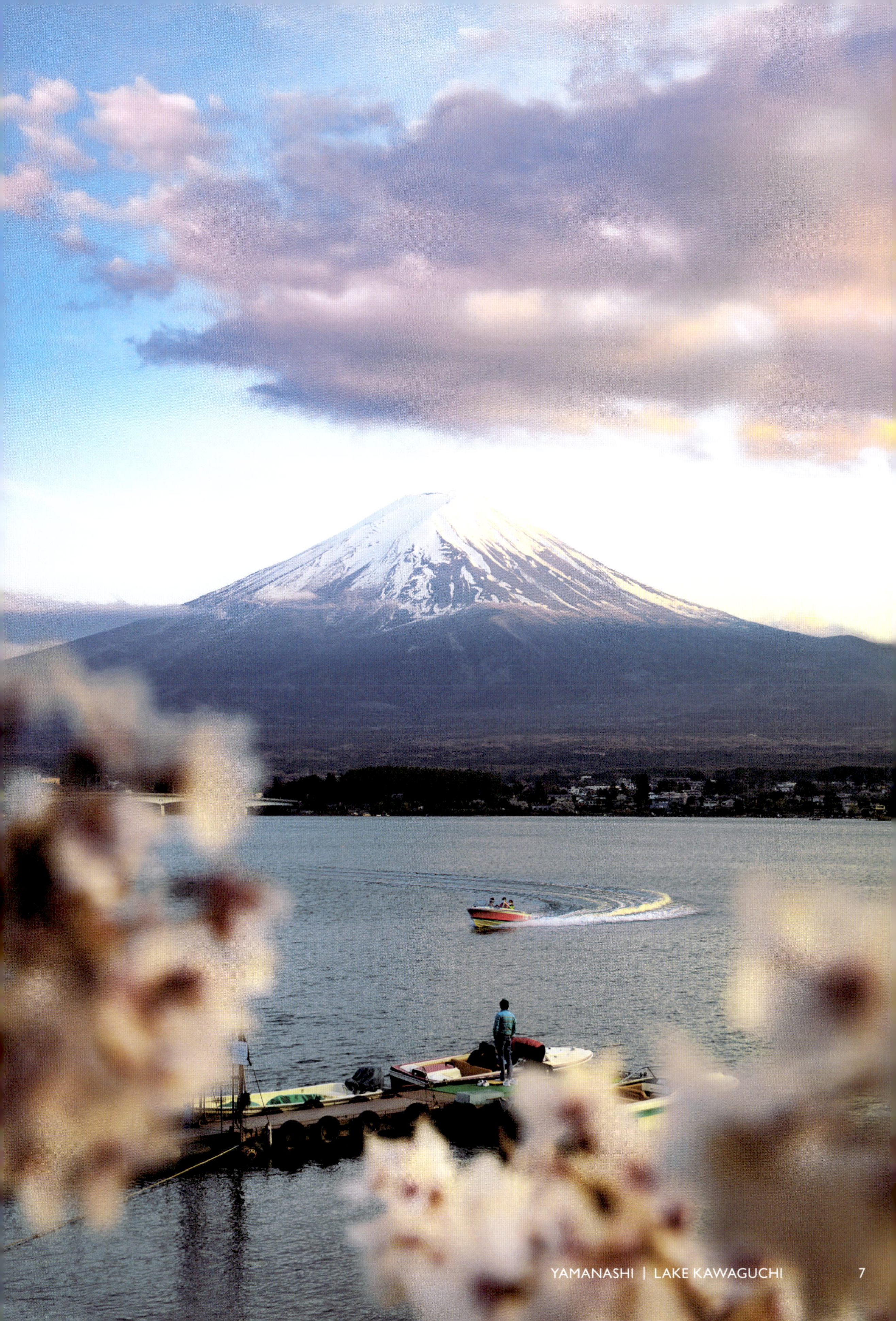

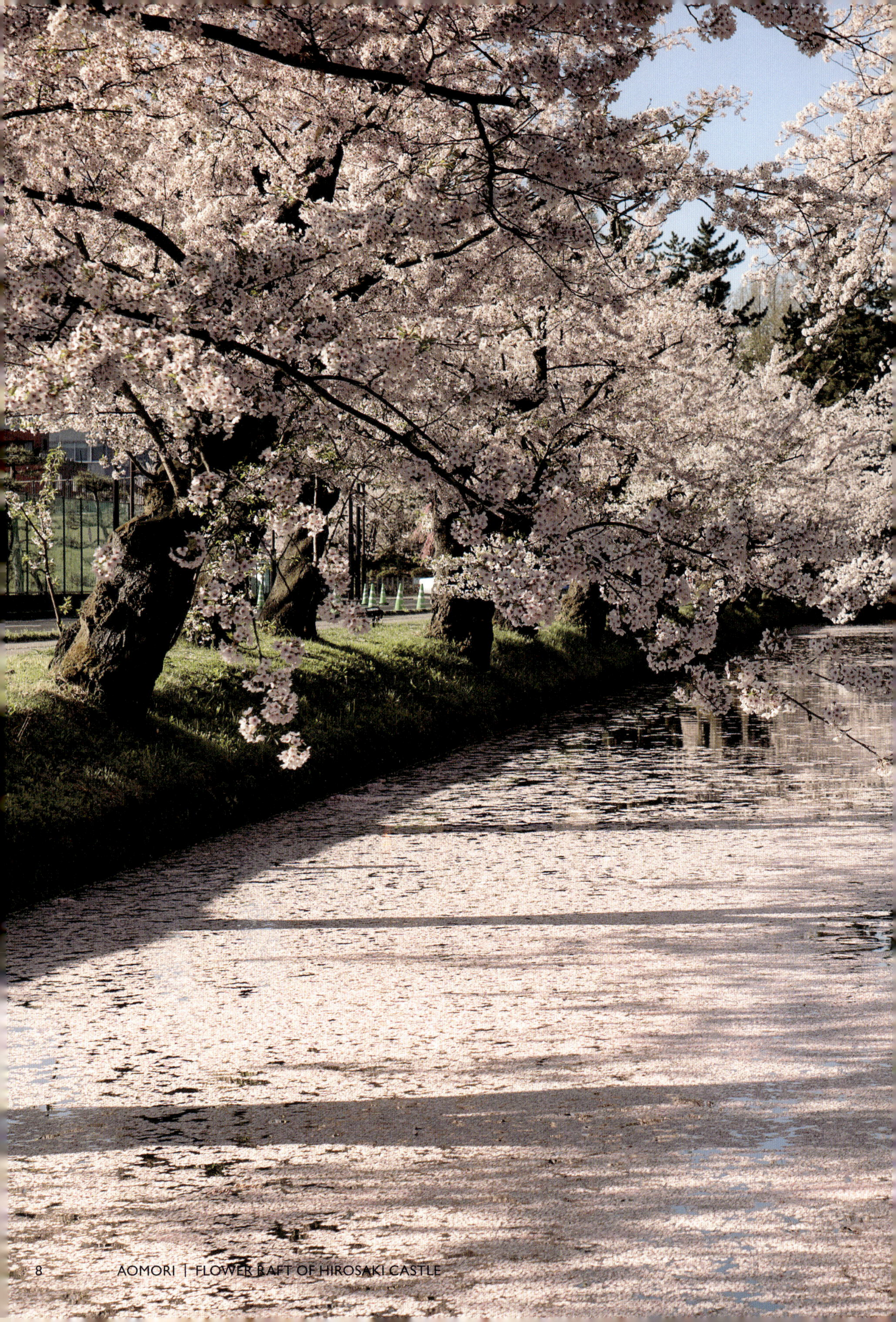

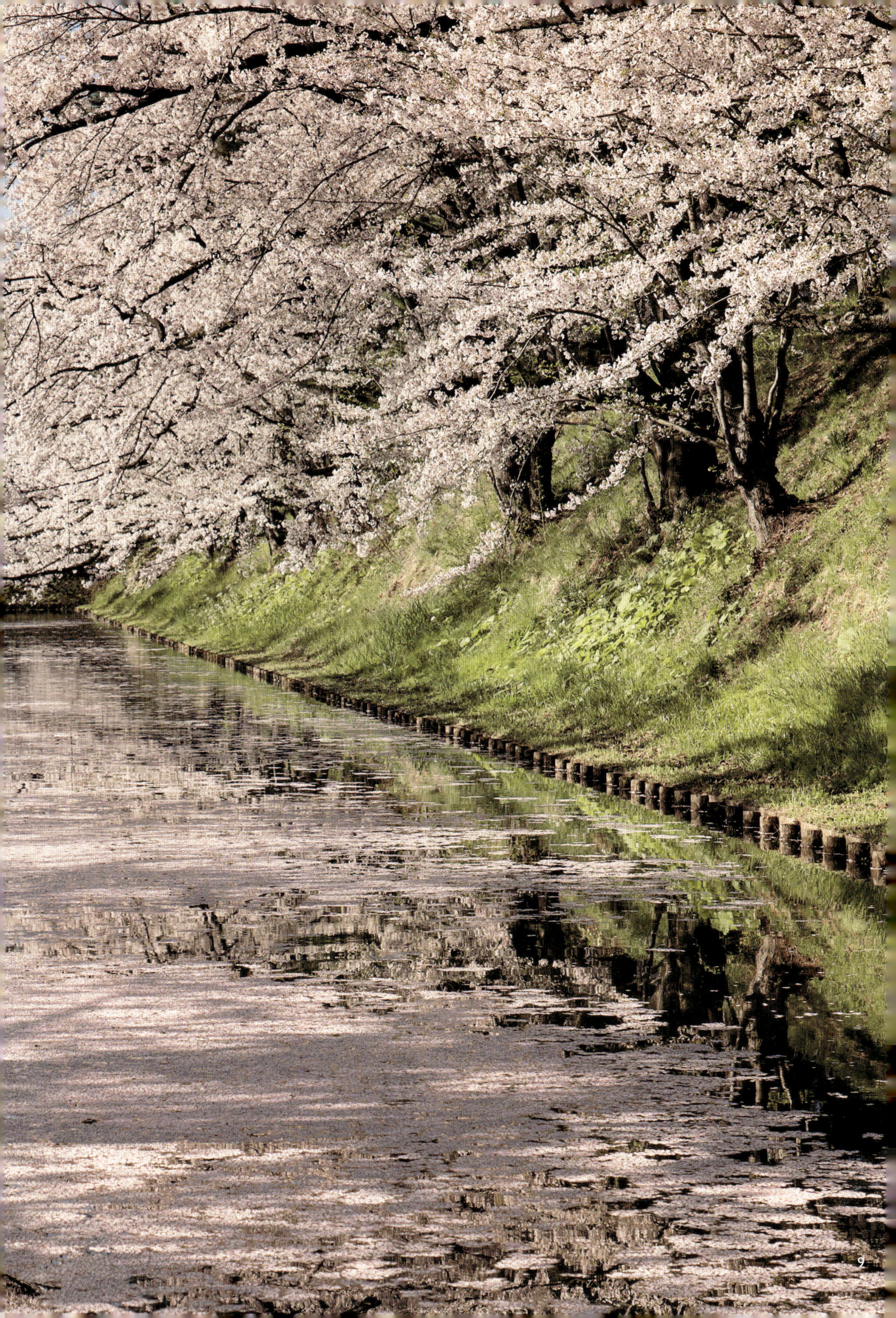

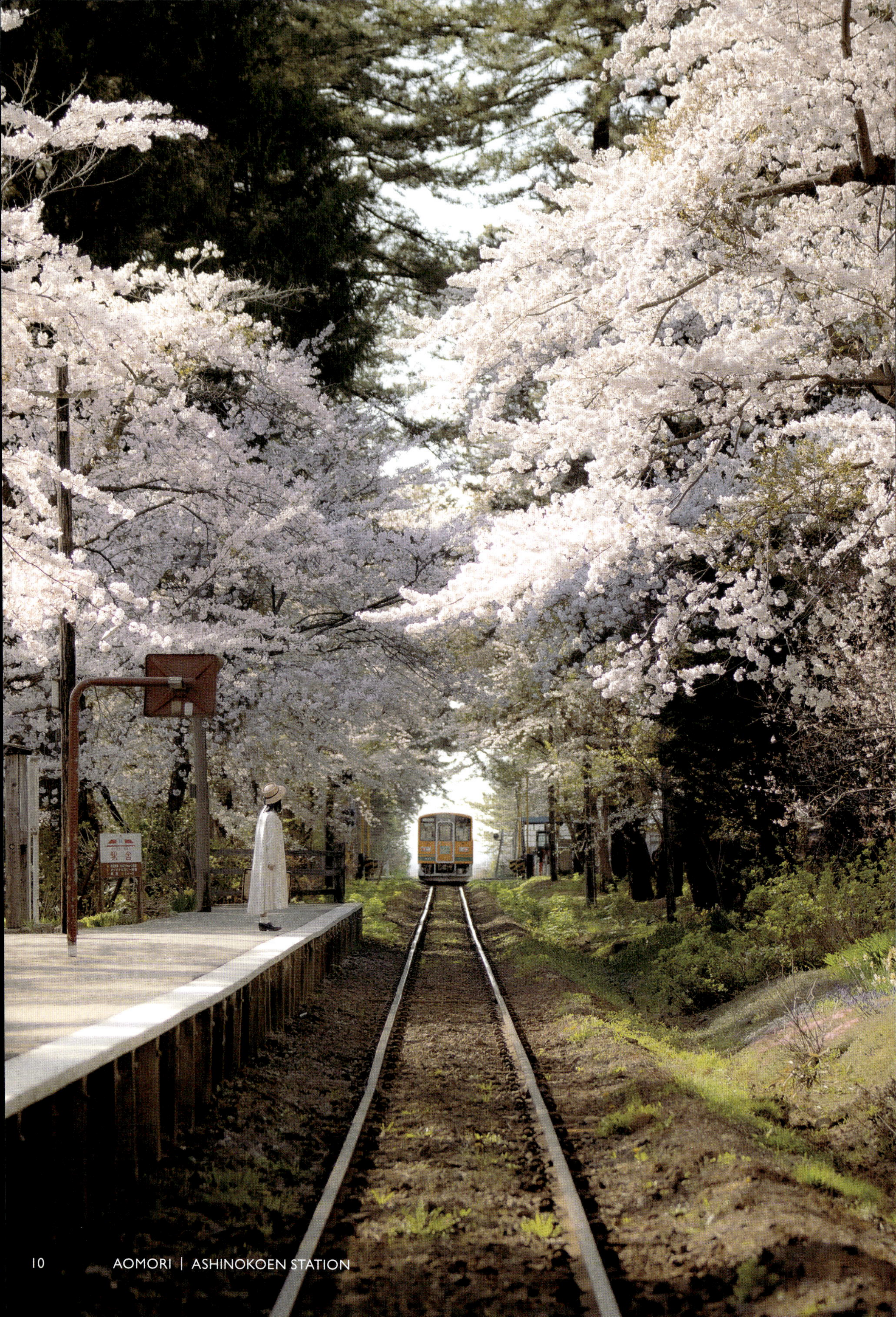

 AOMORI | ASHINOKOEN STATION

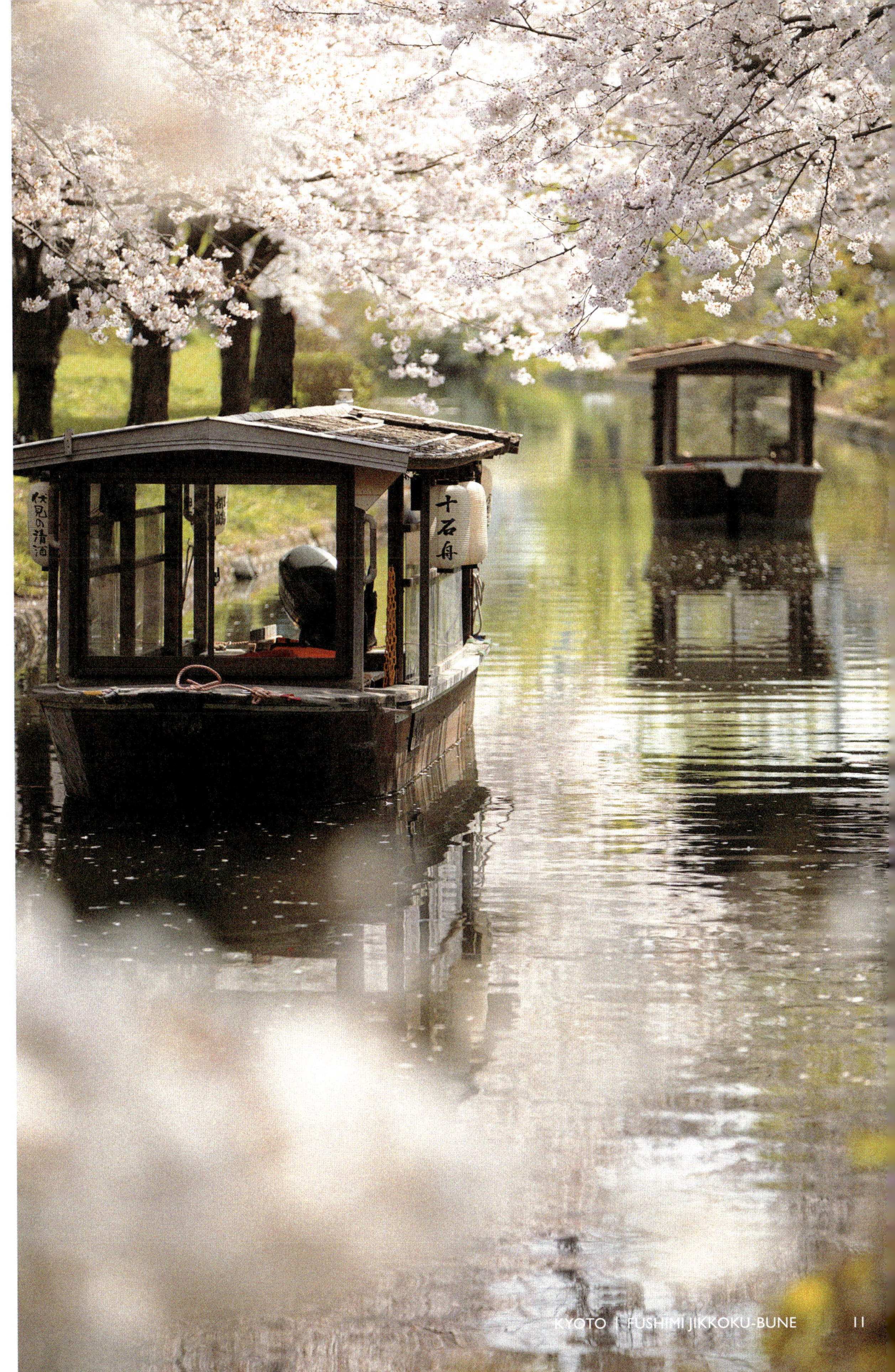

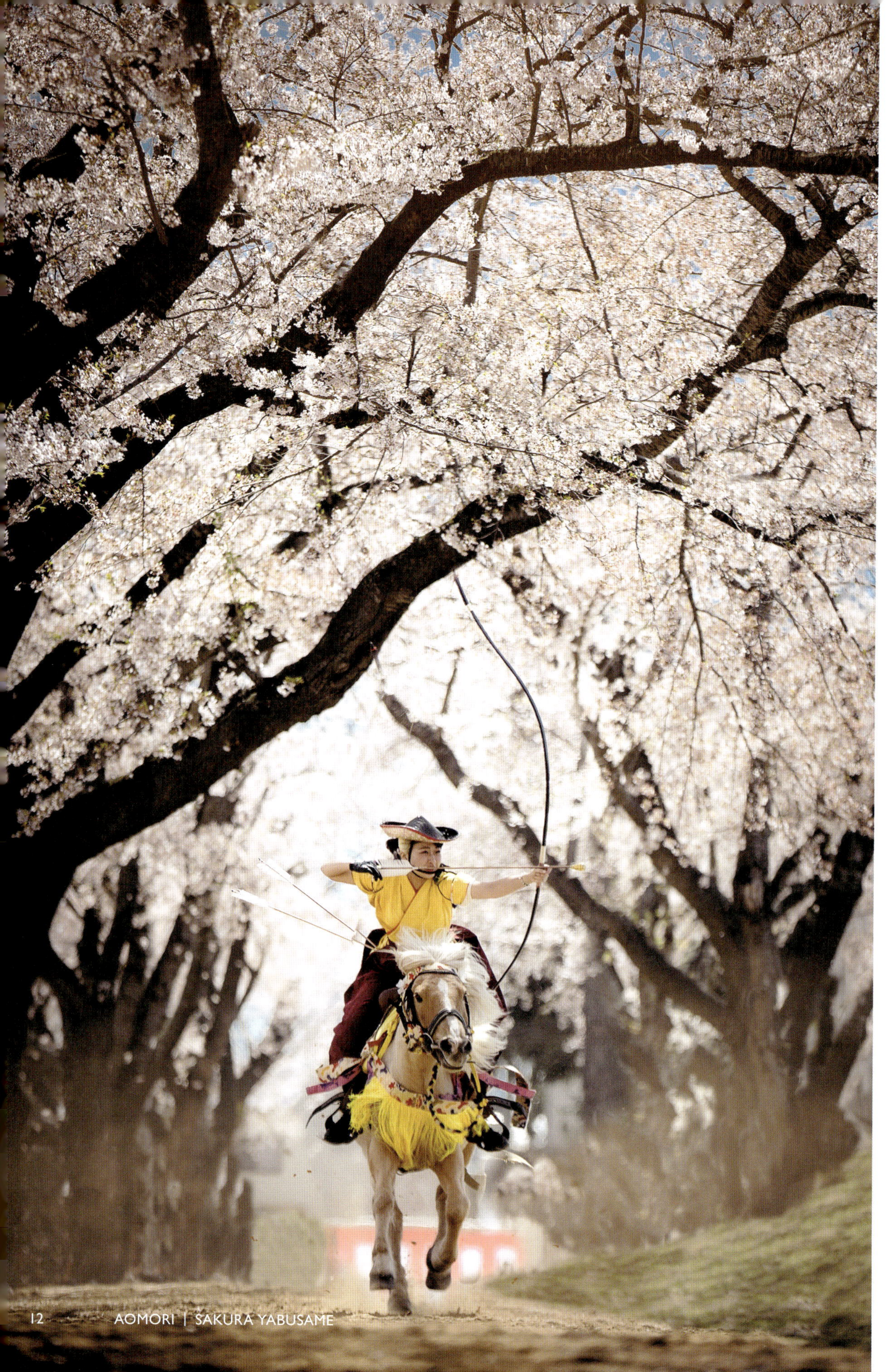

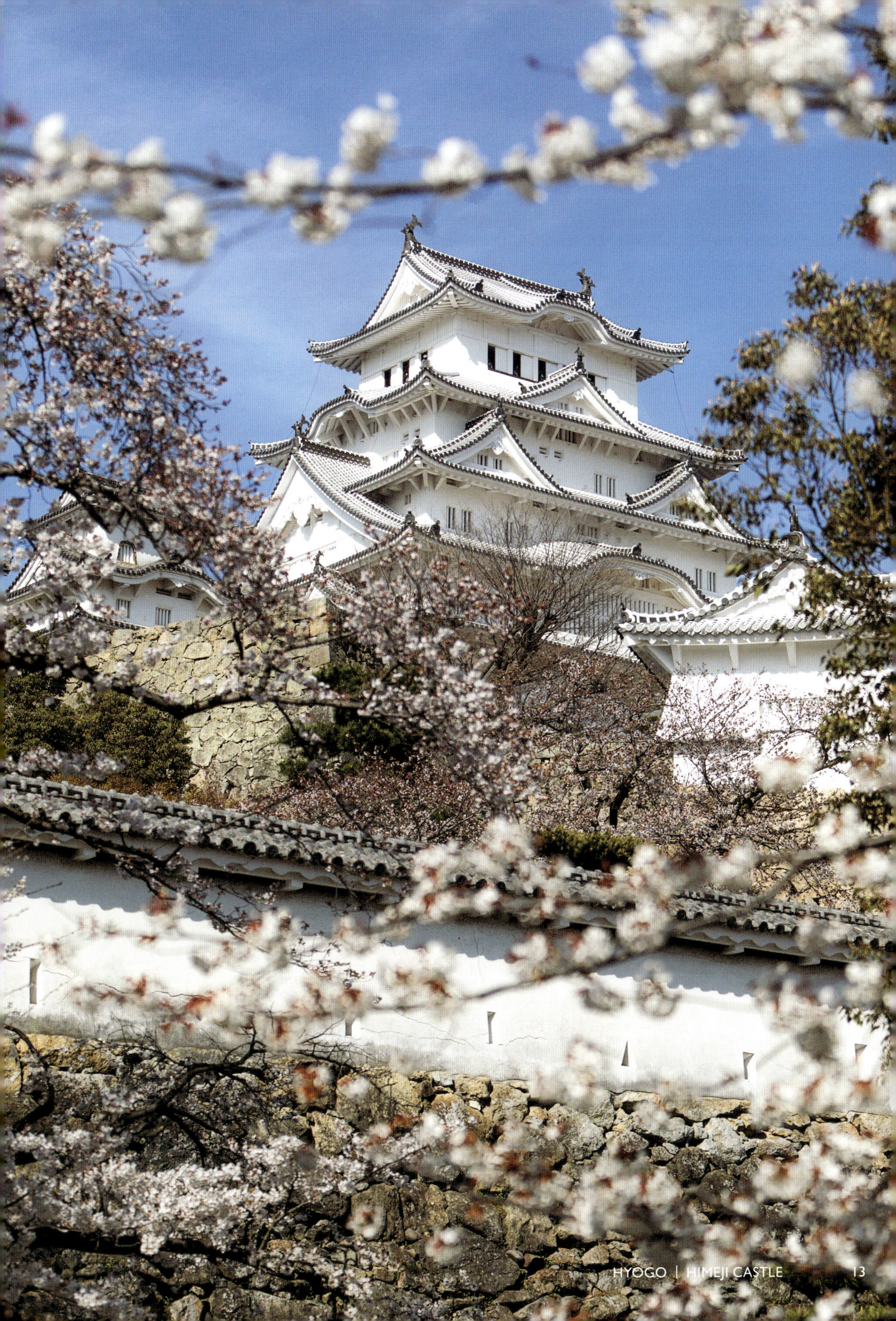

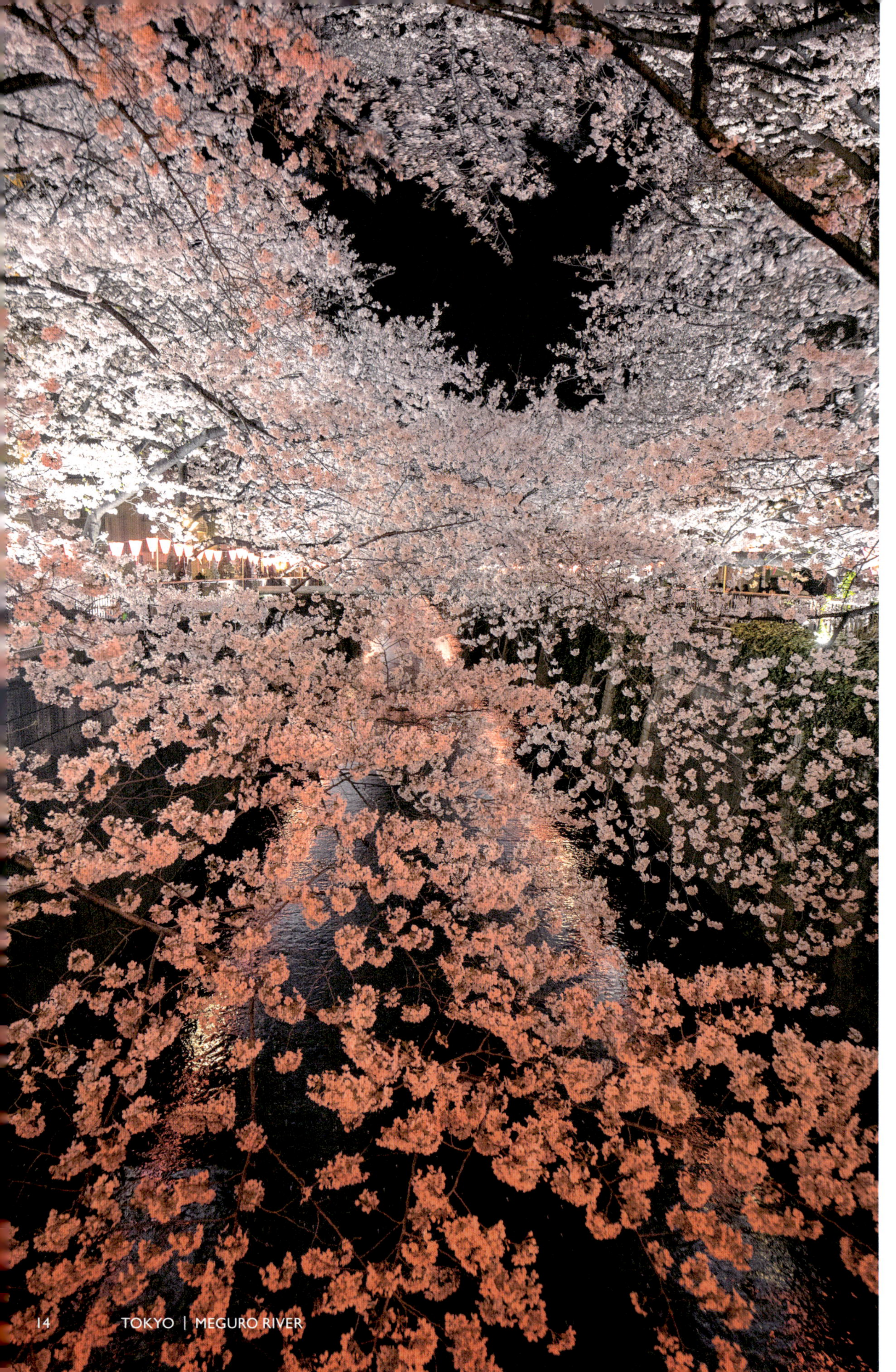

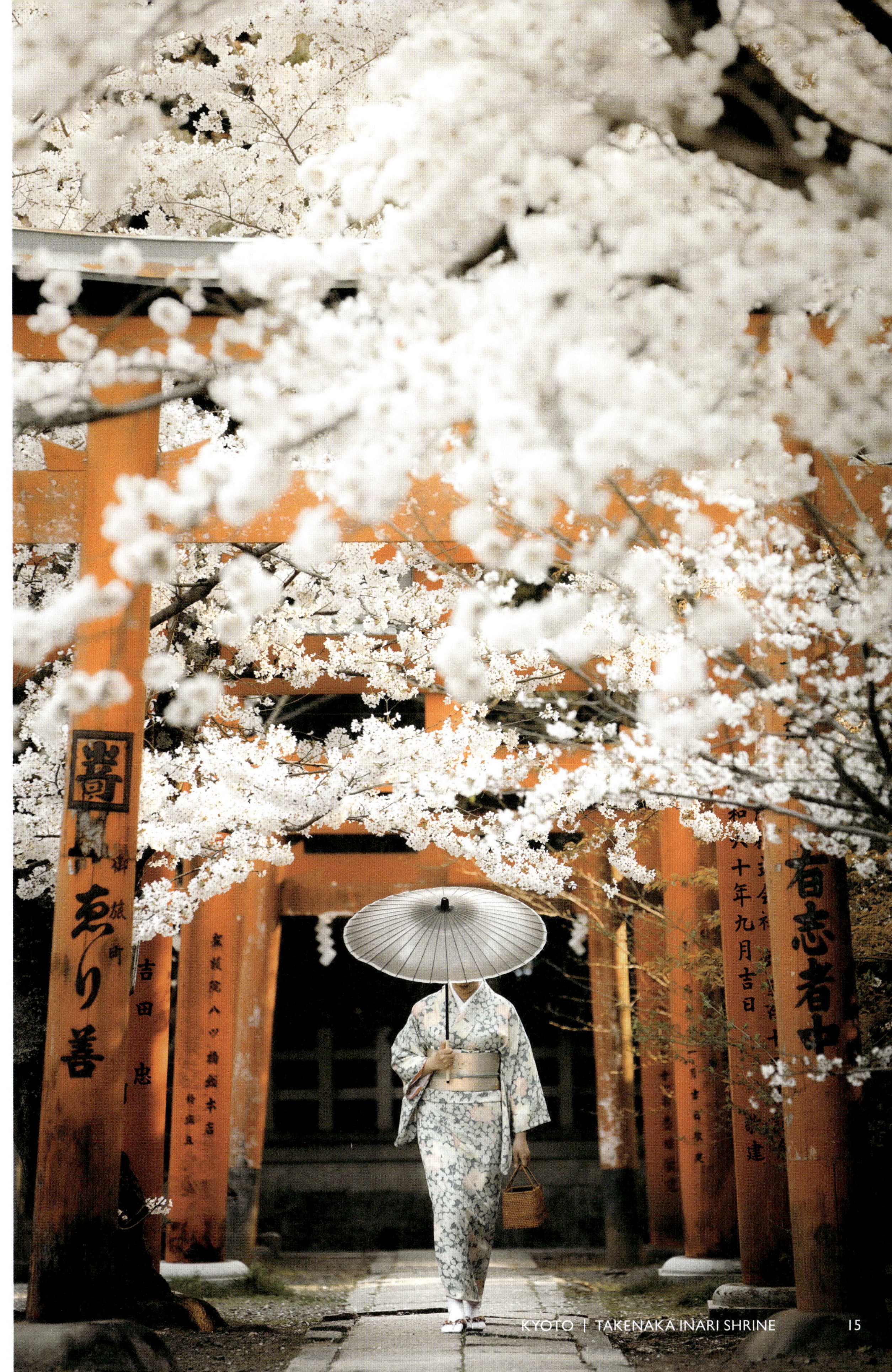

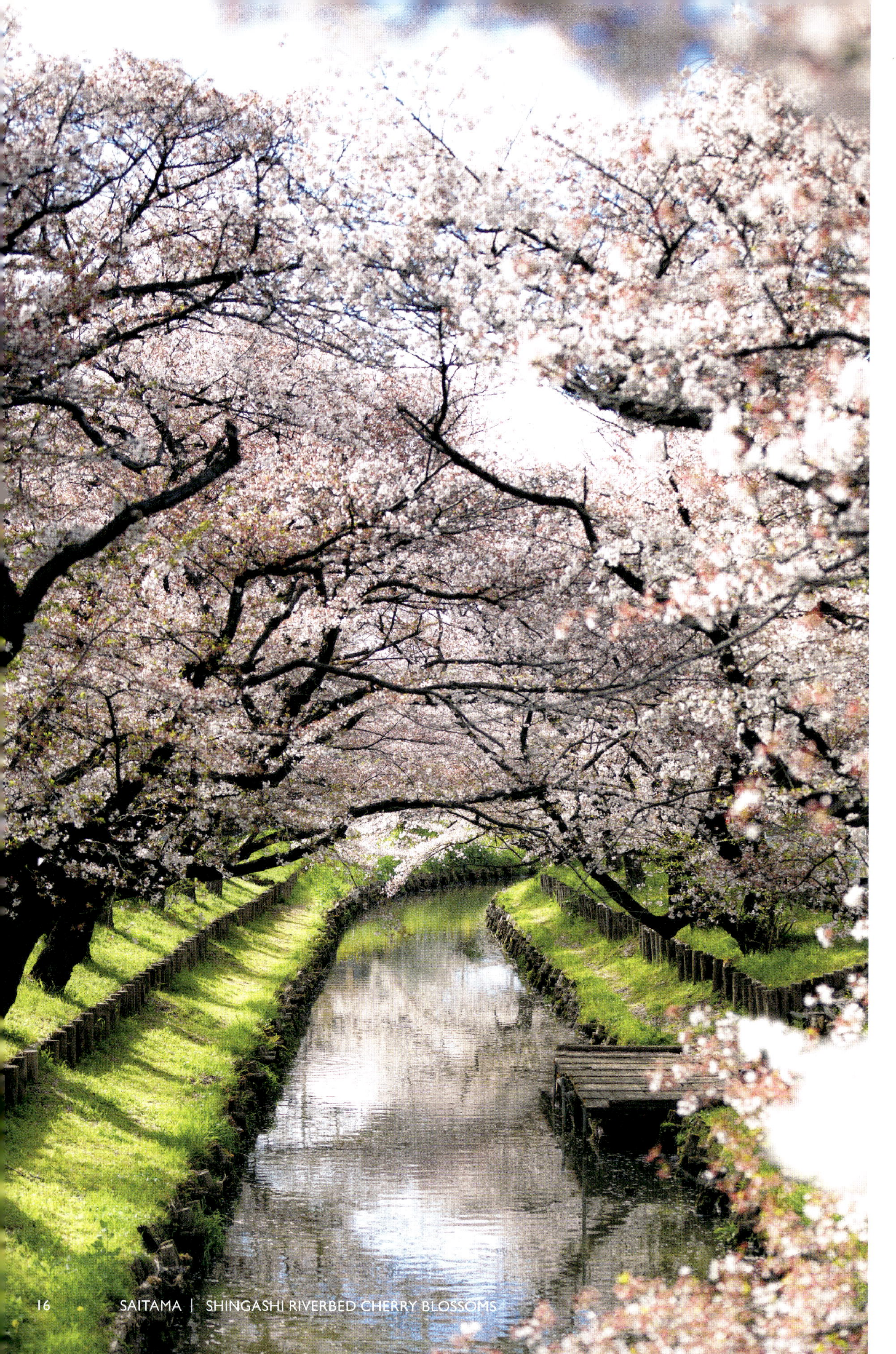

 SAITAMA | SHINGASHI RIVERBED CHERRY BLOSSOMS

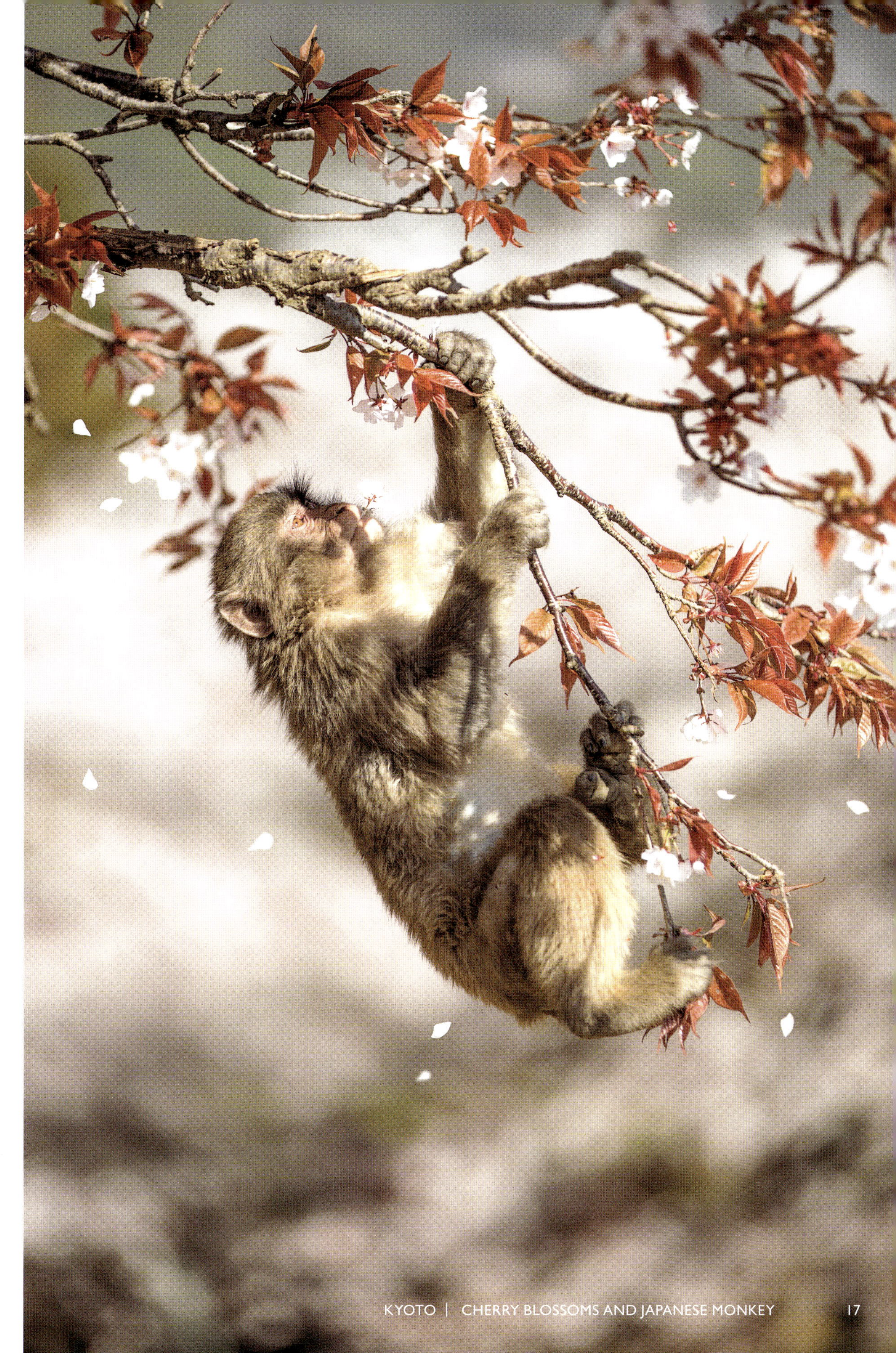

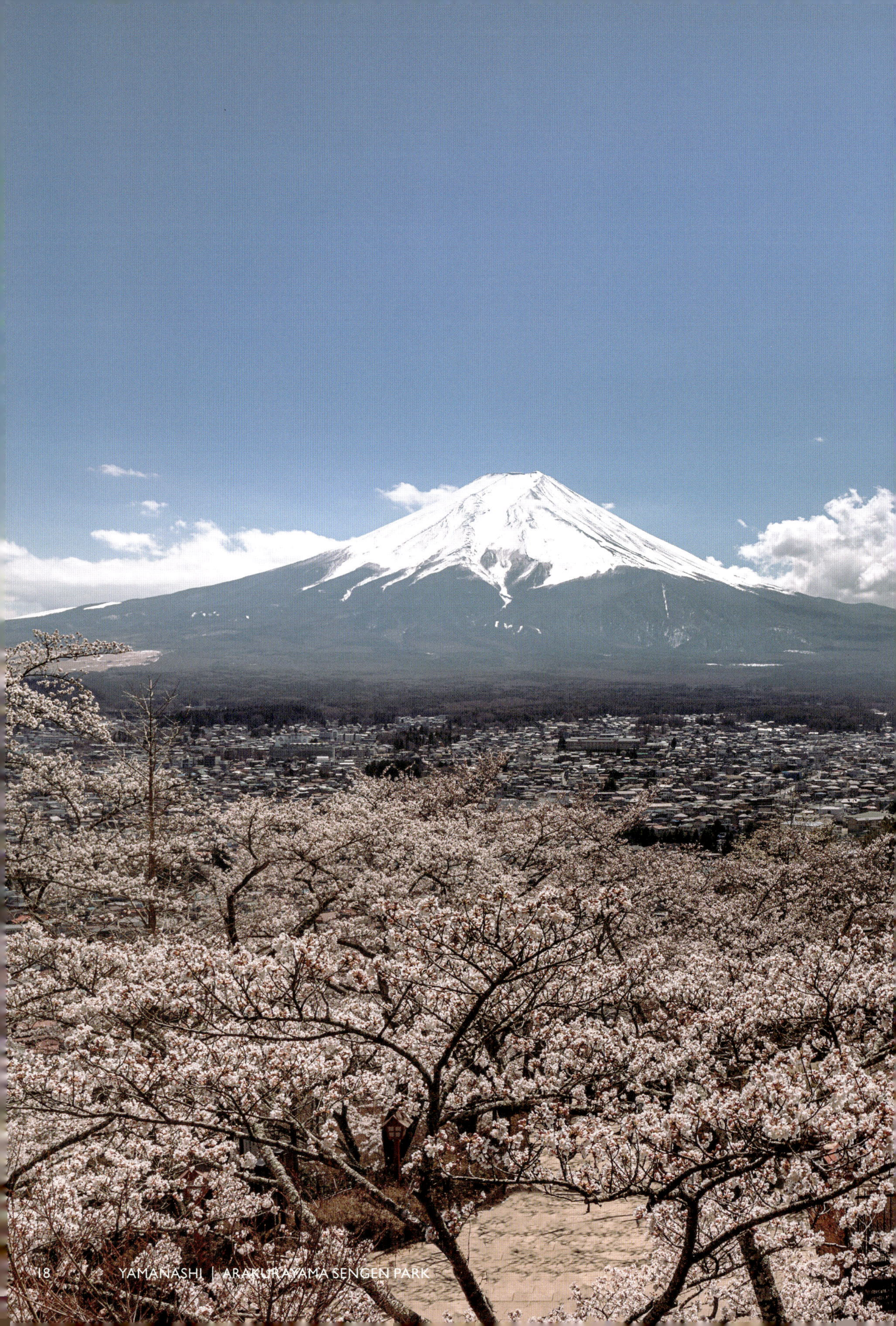

YAMANASHI | ARAKURAYAMA SENGEN PARK

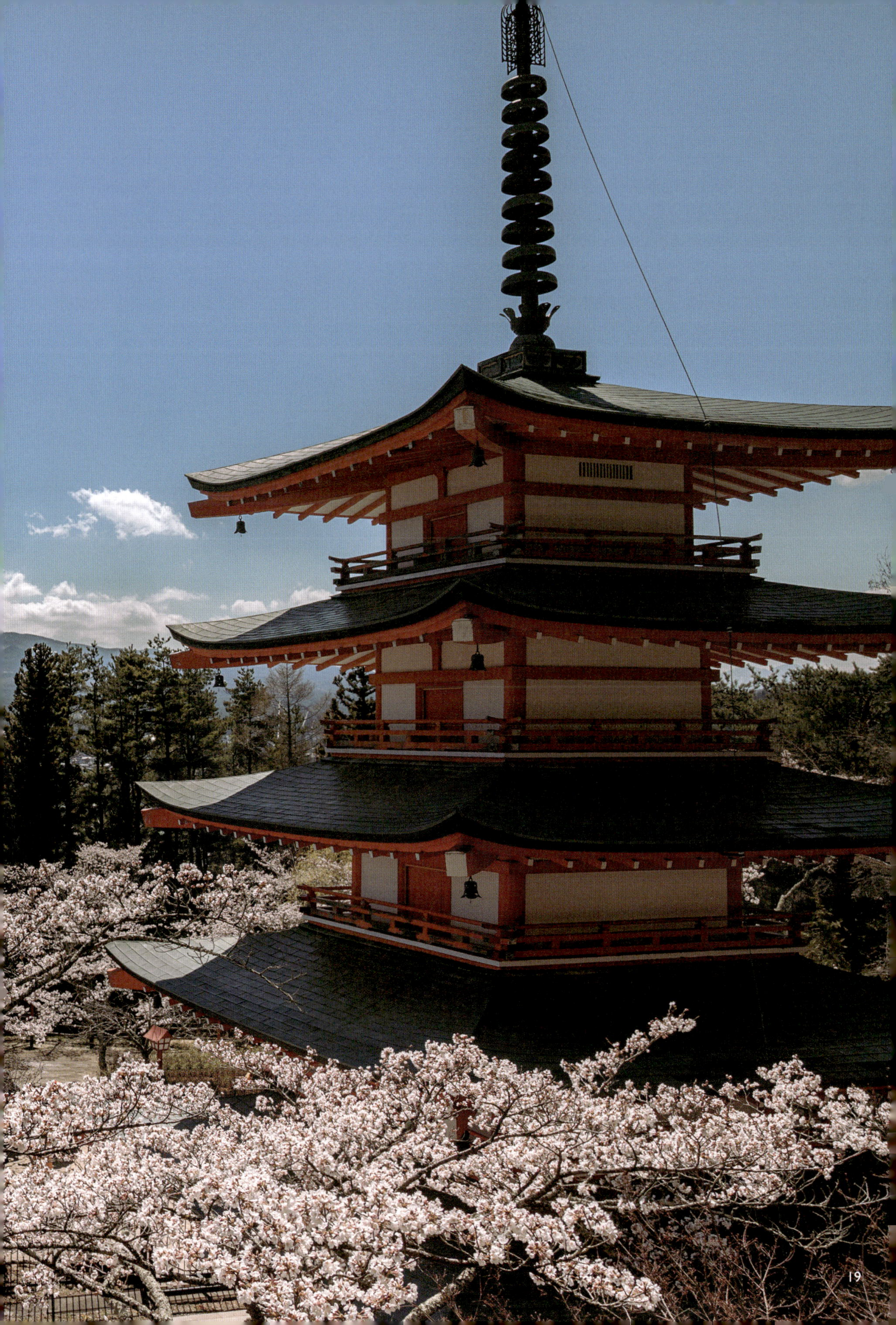

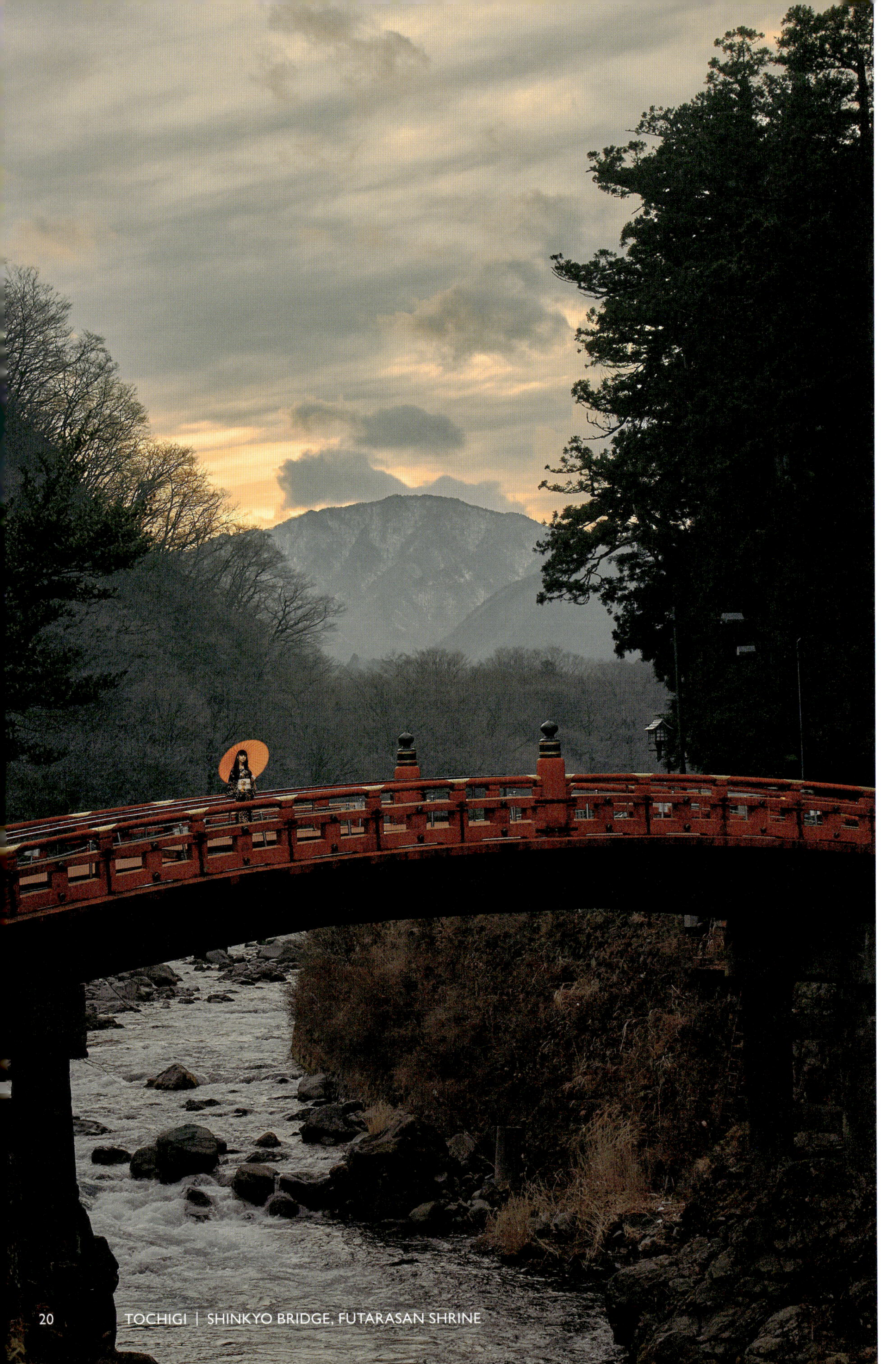

    TOCHIGI | SHINKYO BRIDGE, FUTARASAN SHRINE

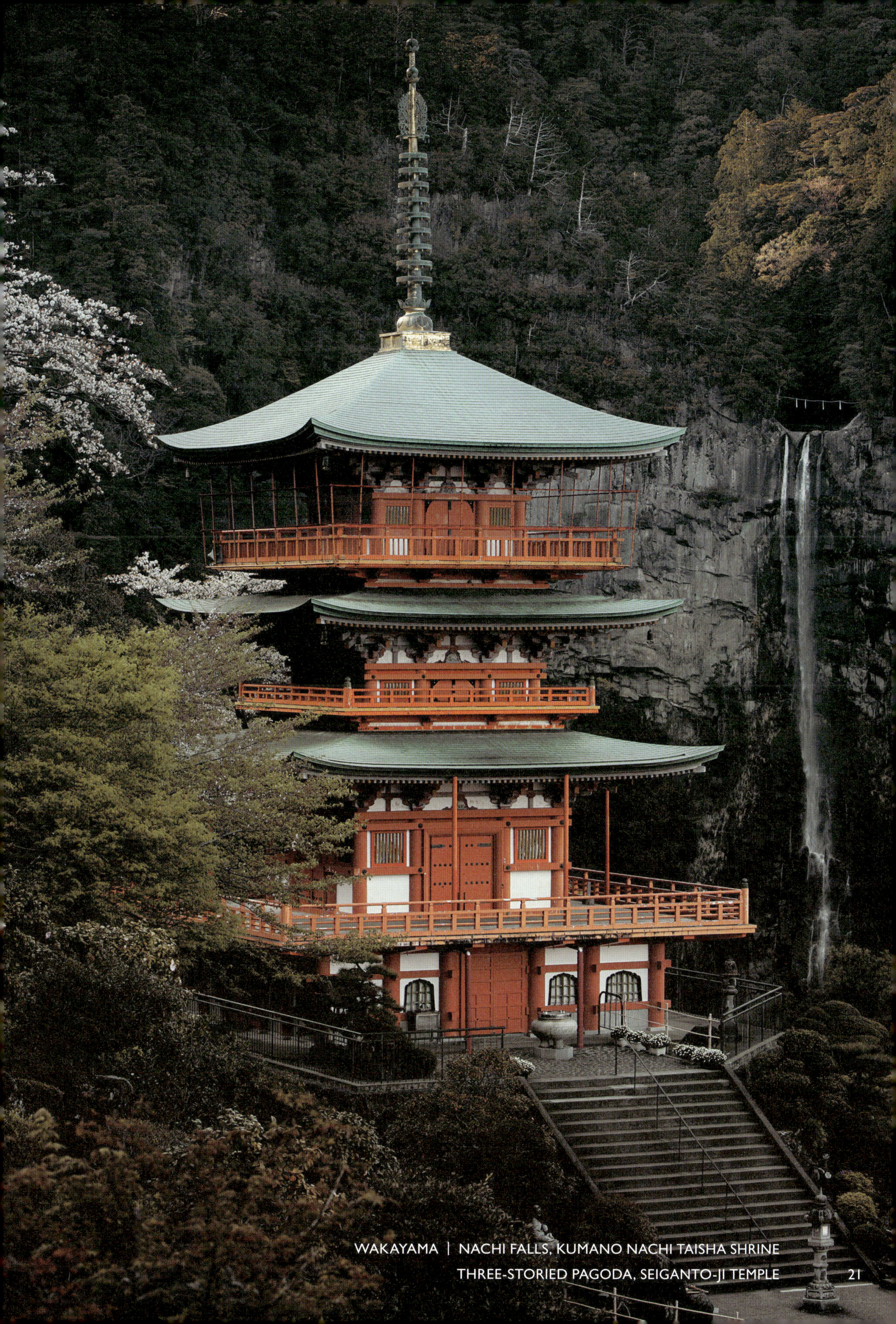

WAKAYAMA | NACHI FALLS, KUMANO NACHI TAISHA SHRINE
THREE-STORIED PAGODA, SEIGANTO-JI TEMPLE

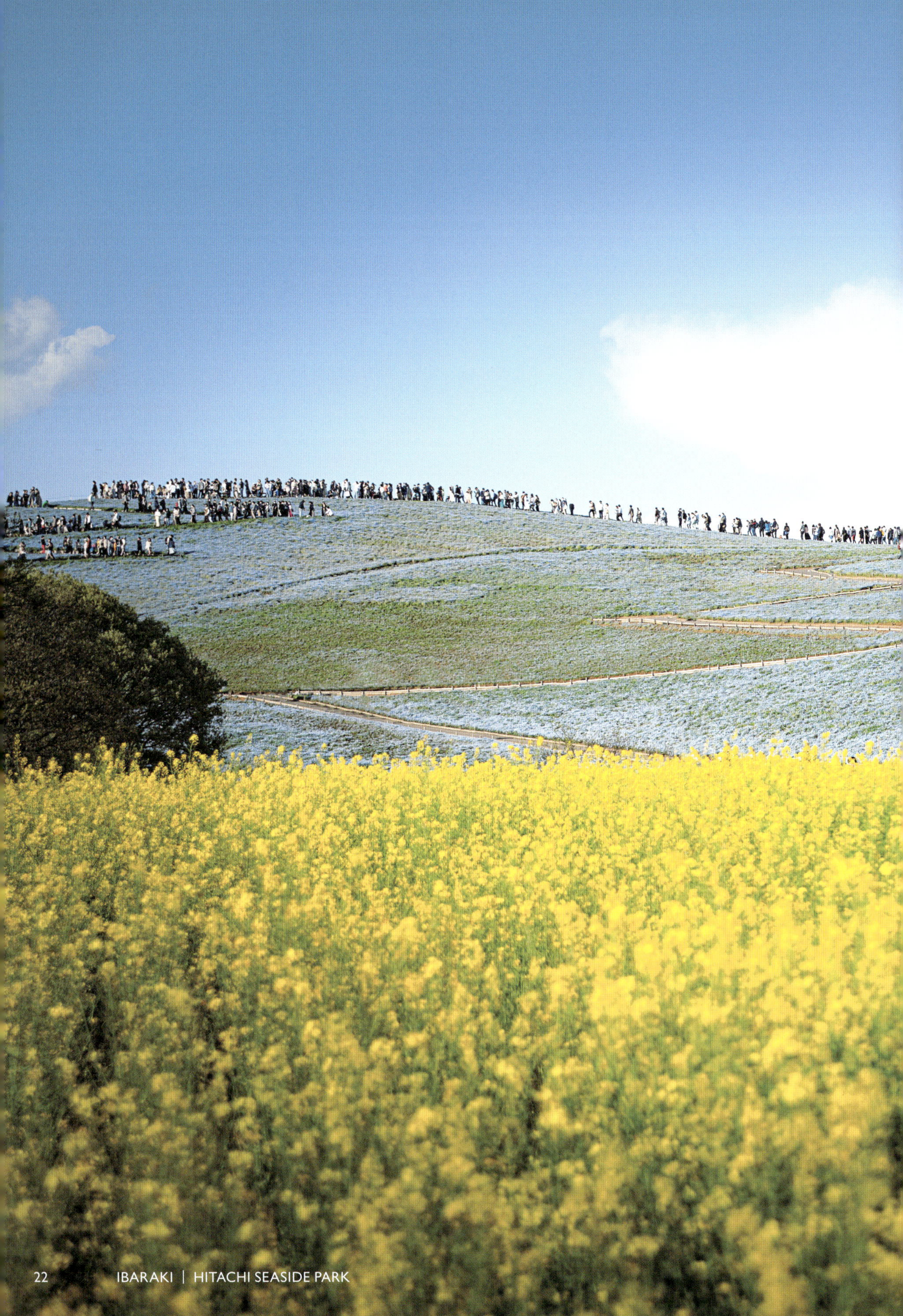

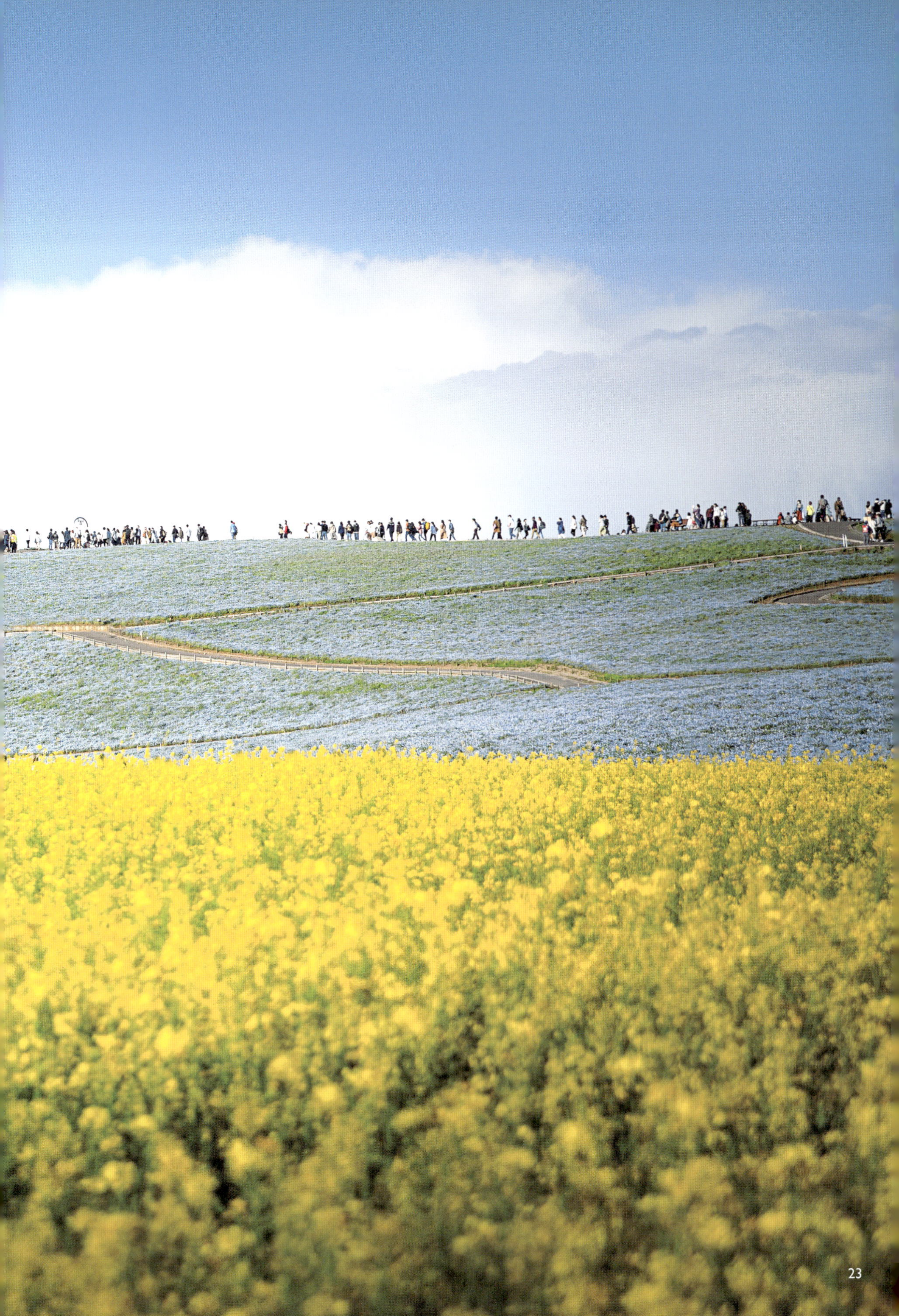

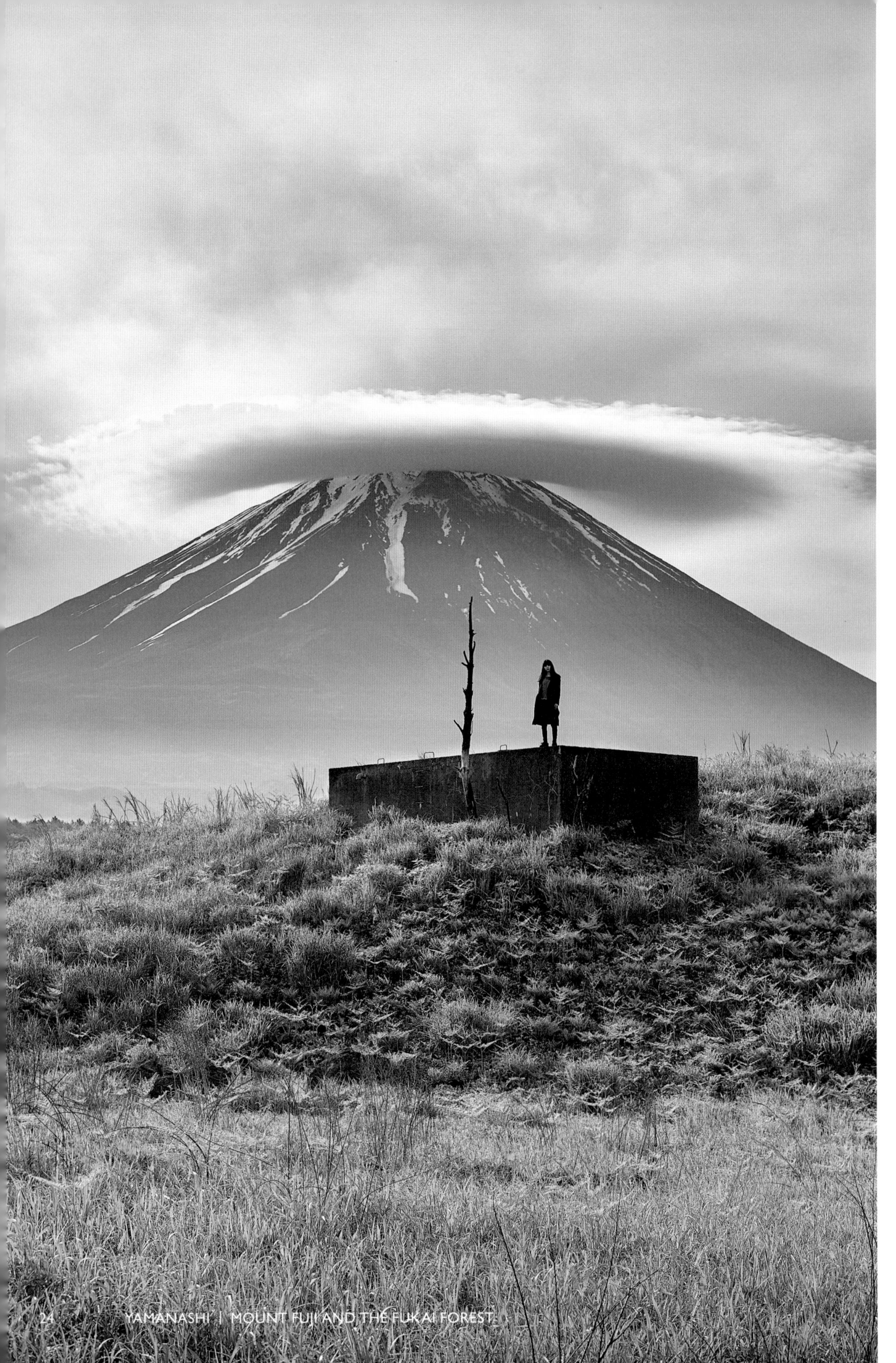

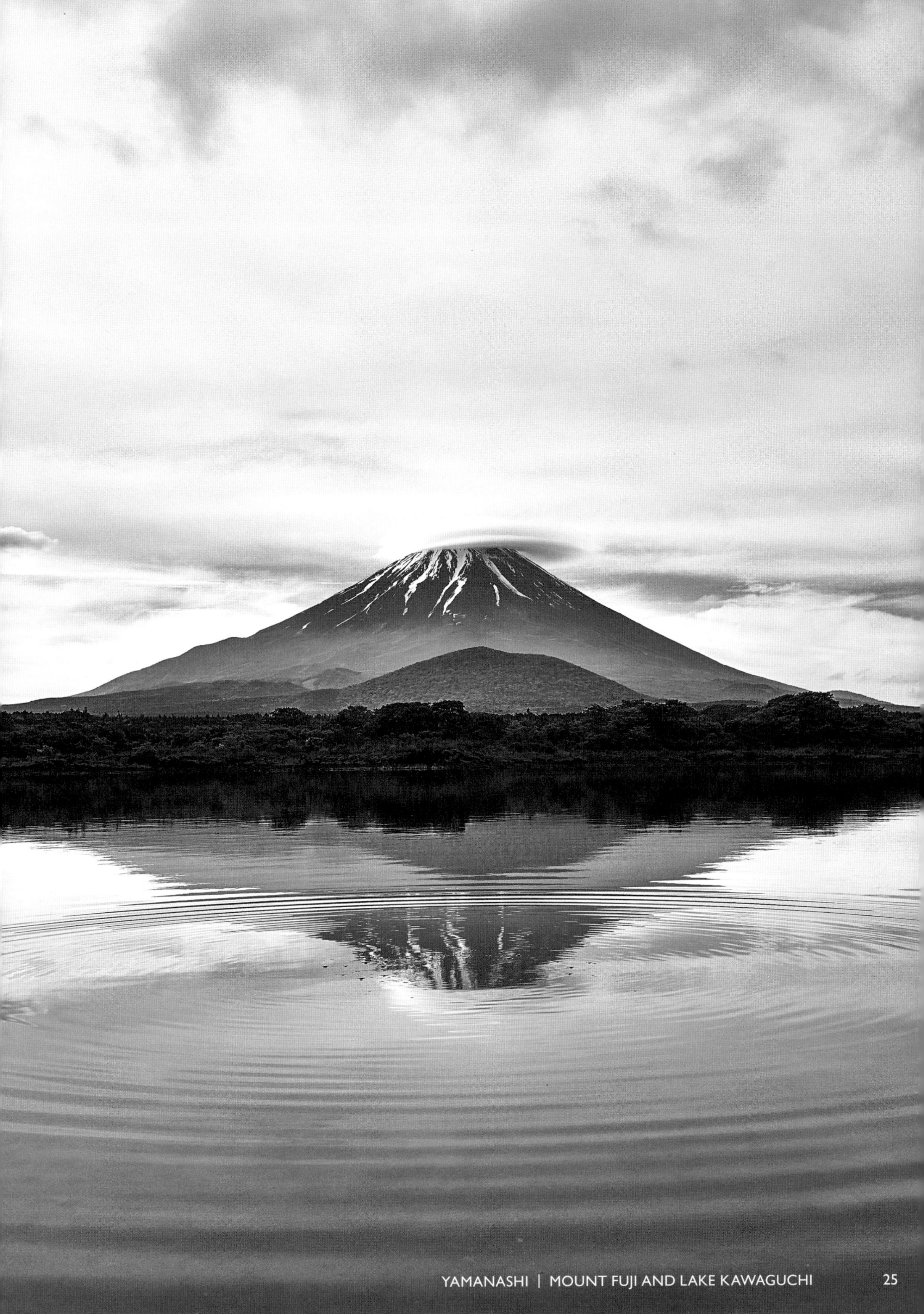

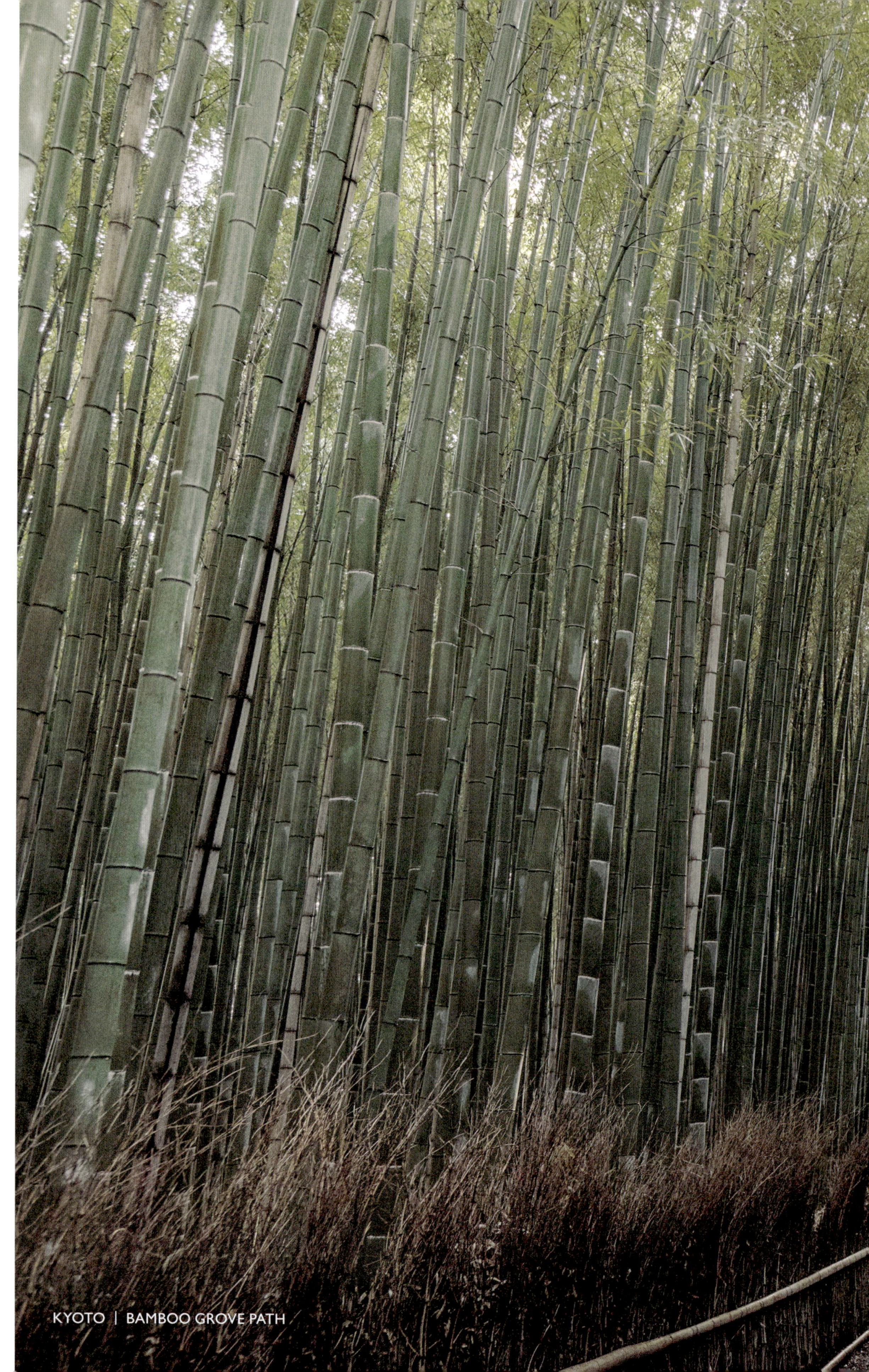

    KYOTO | BAMBOO GROVE PATH

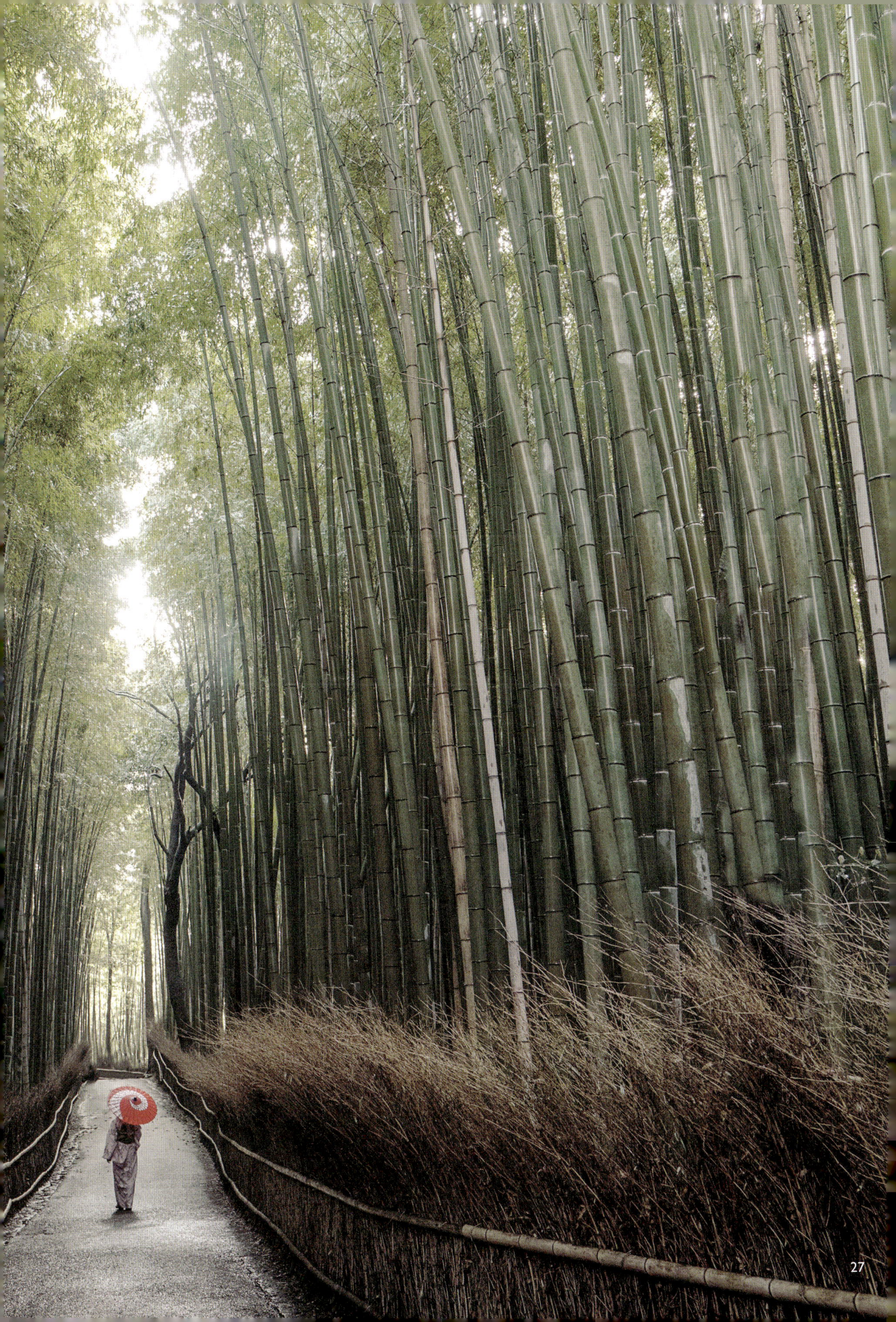

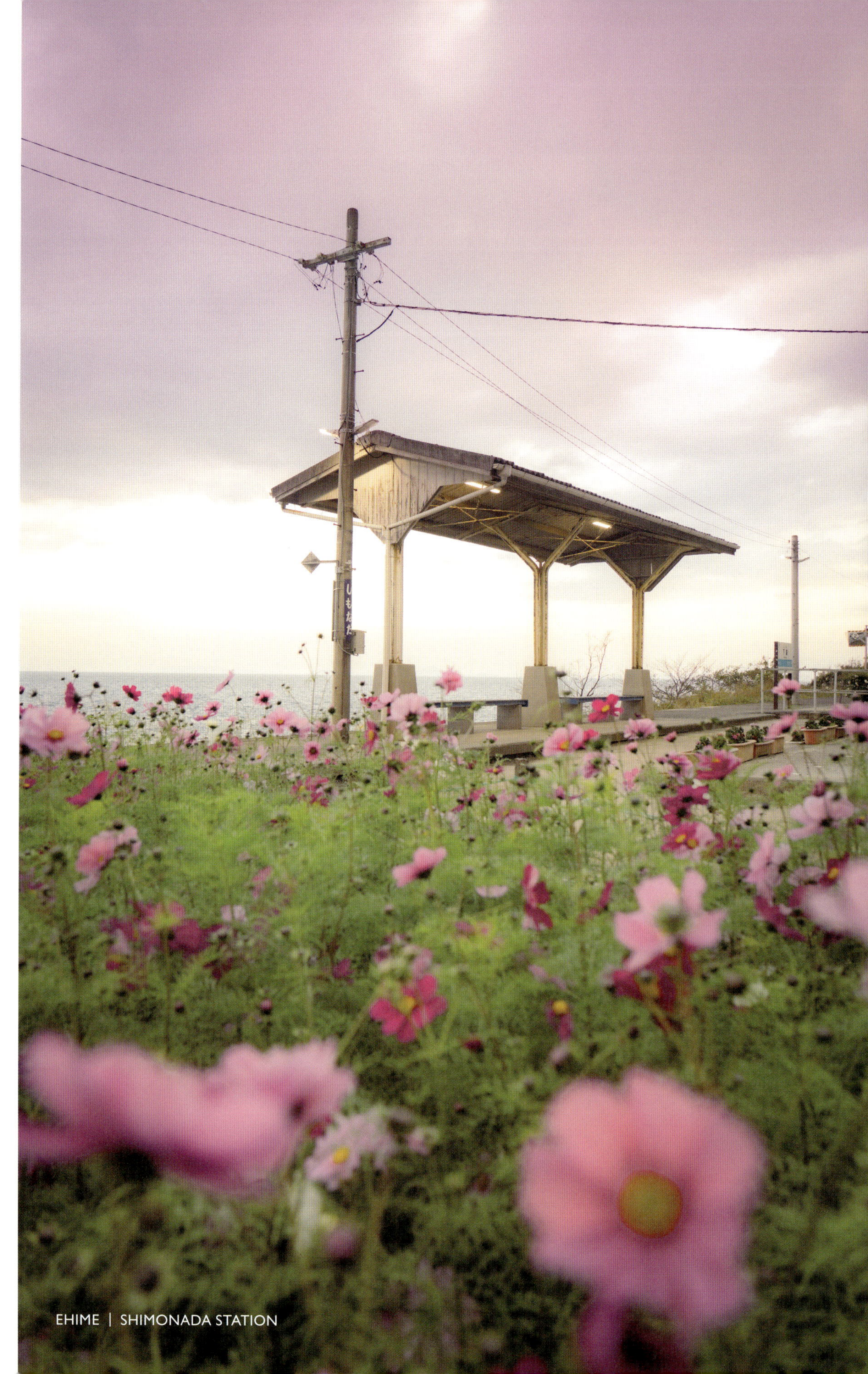

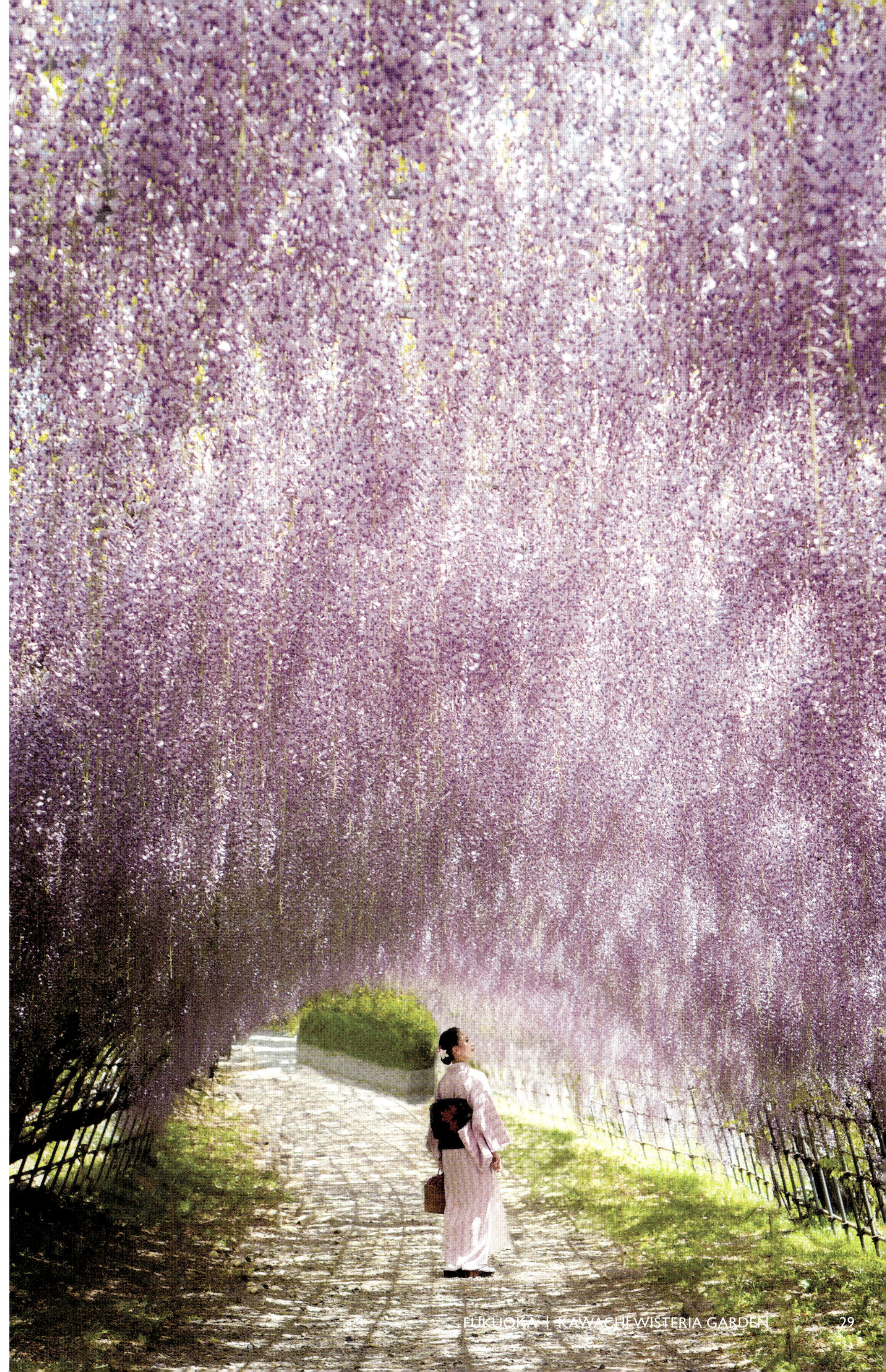

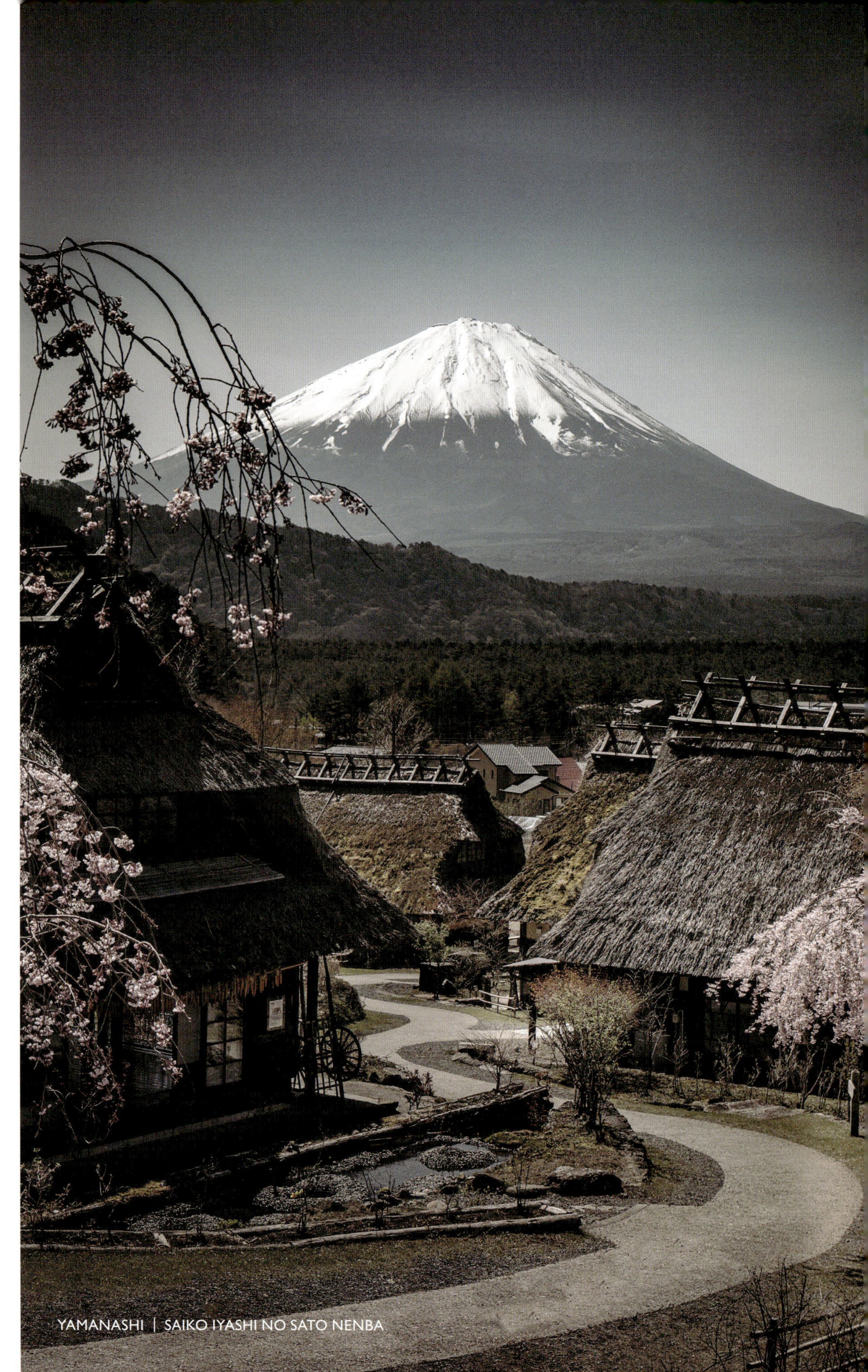

YAMANASHI | SAIKO IYASHI NO SATO NENBA

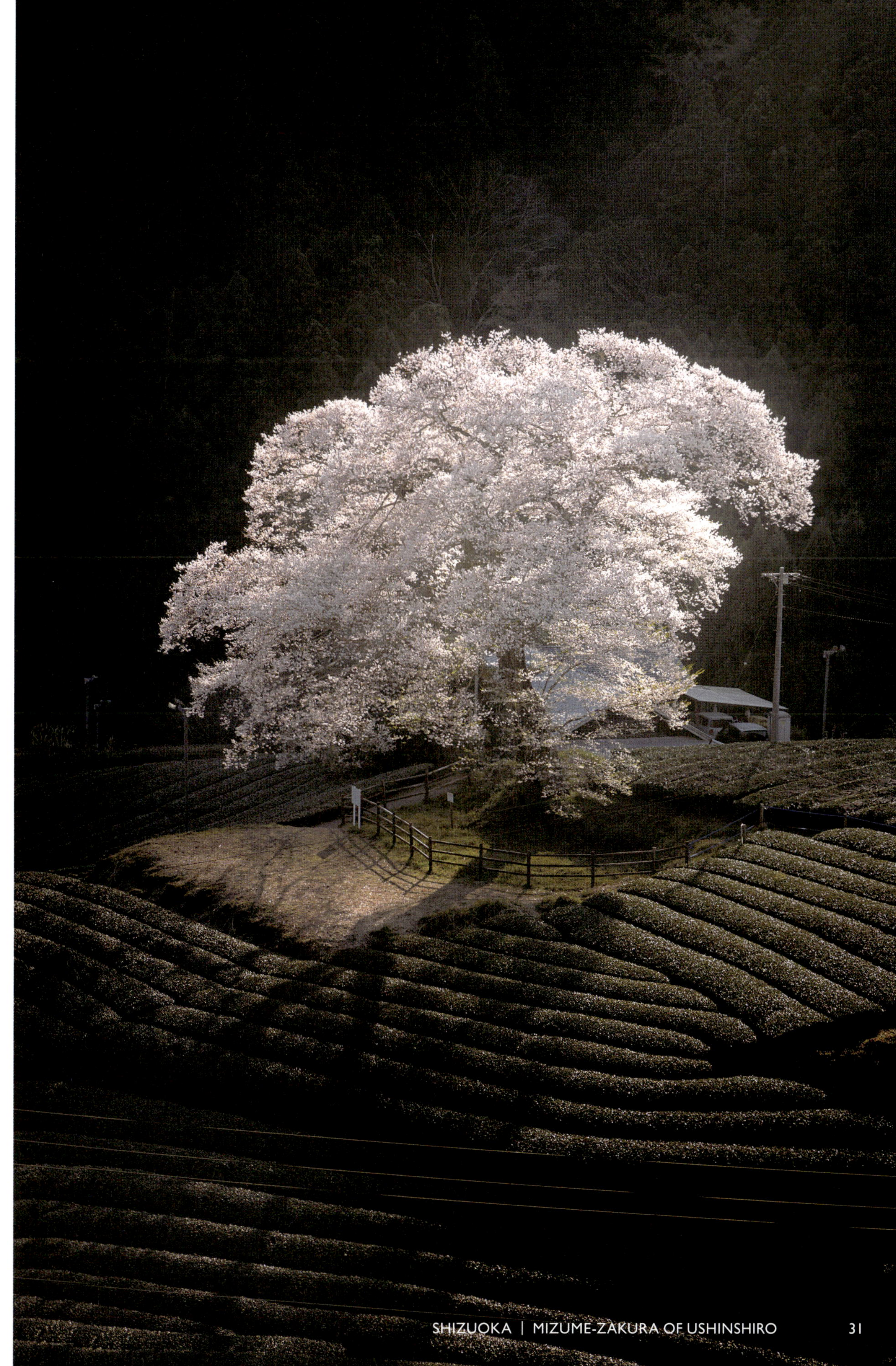

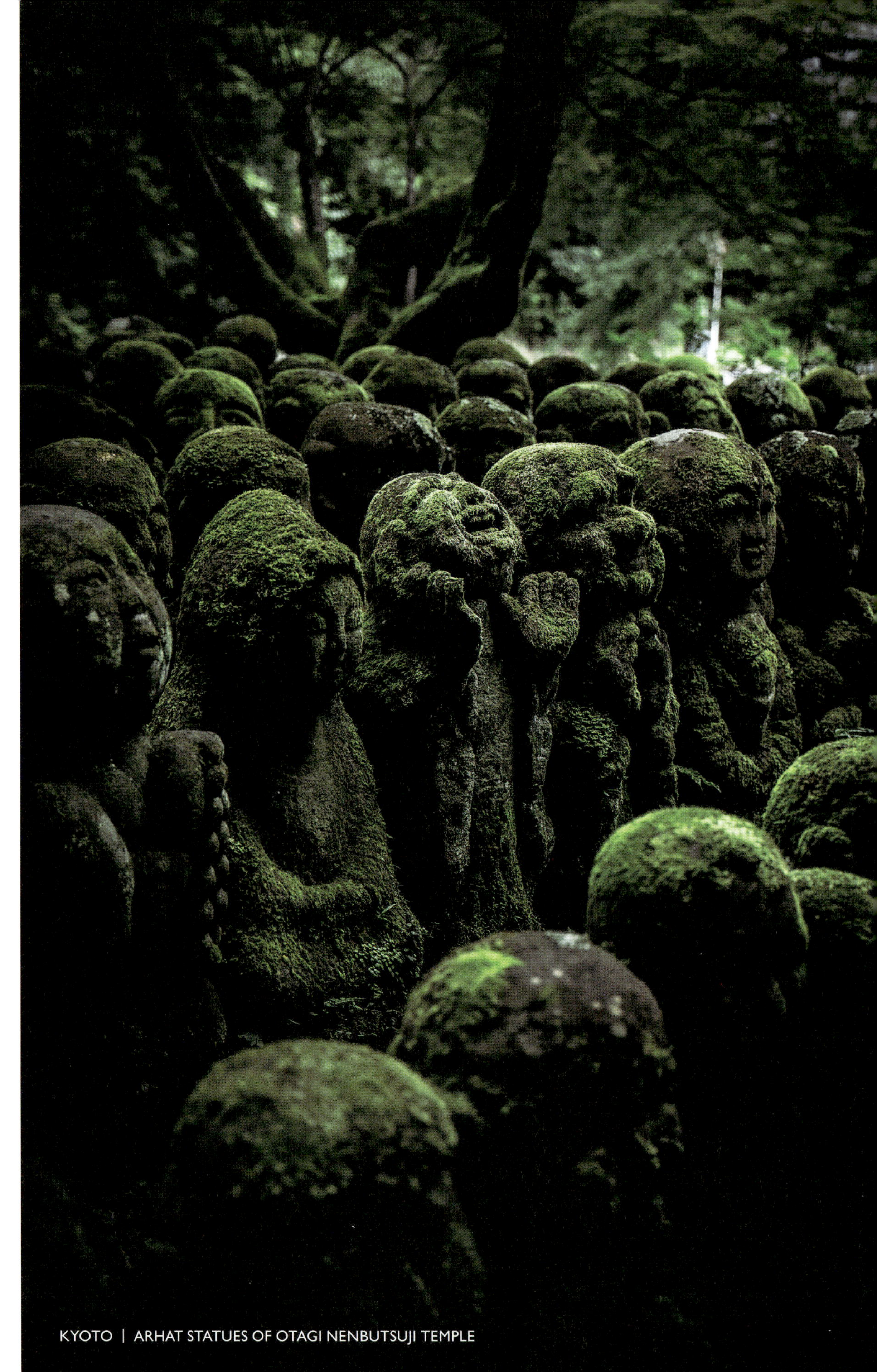

 KYOTO | ARHAT STATUES OF OTAGI NENBUTSUJI TEMPLE

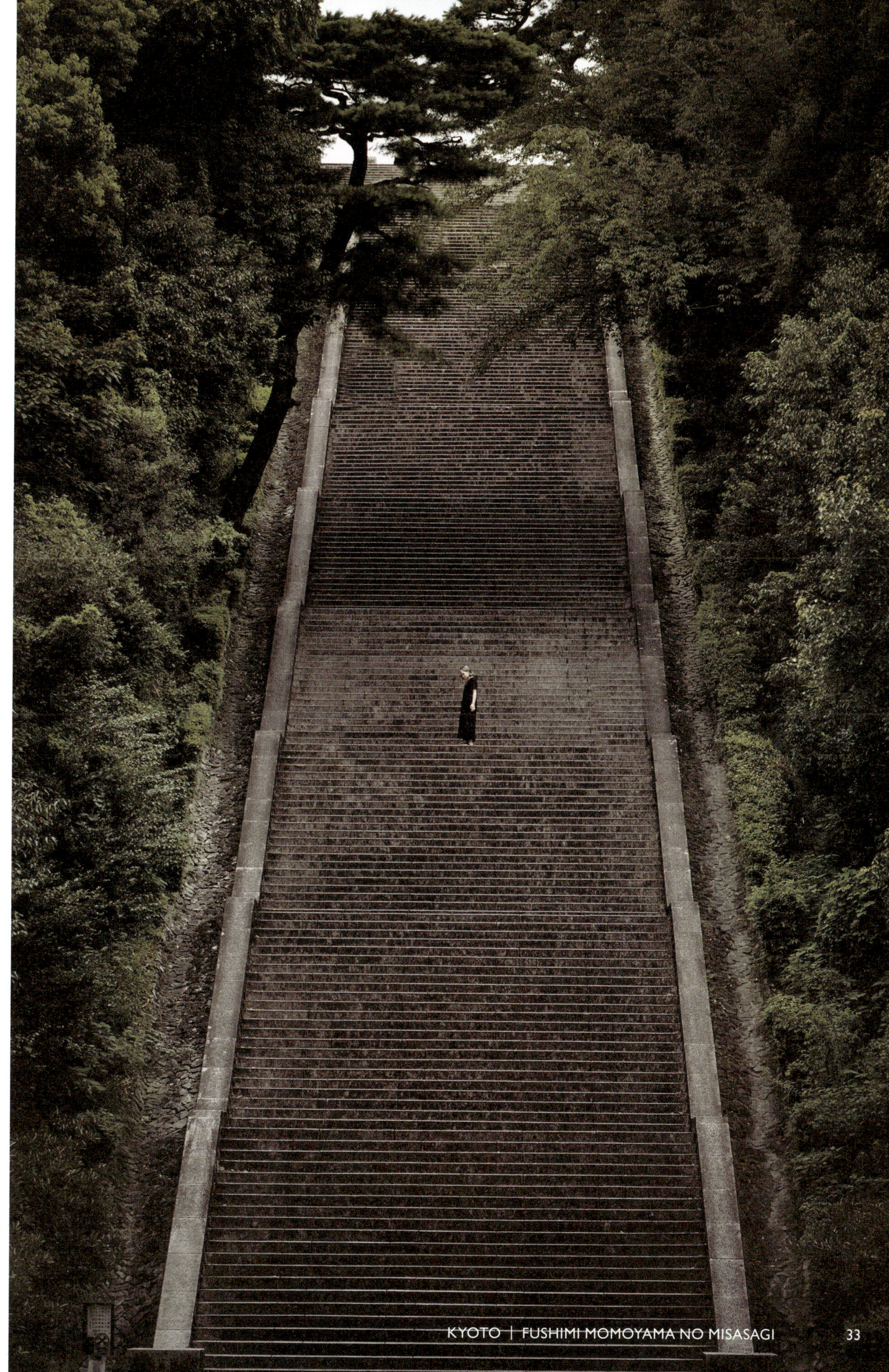

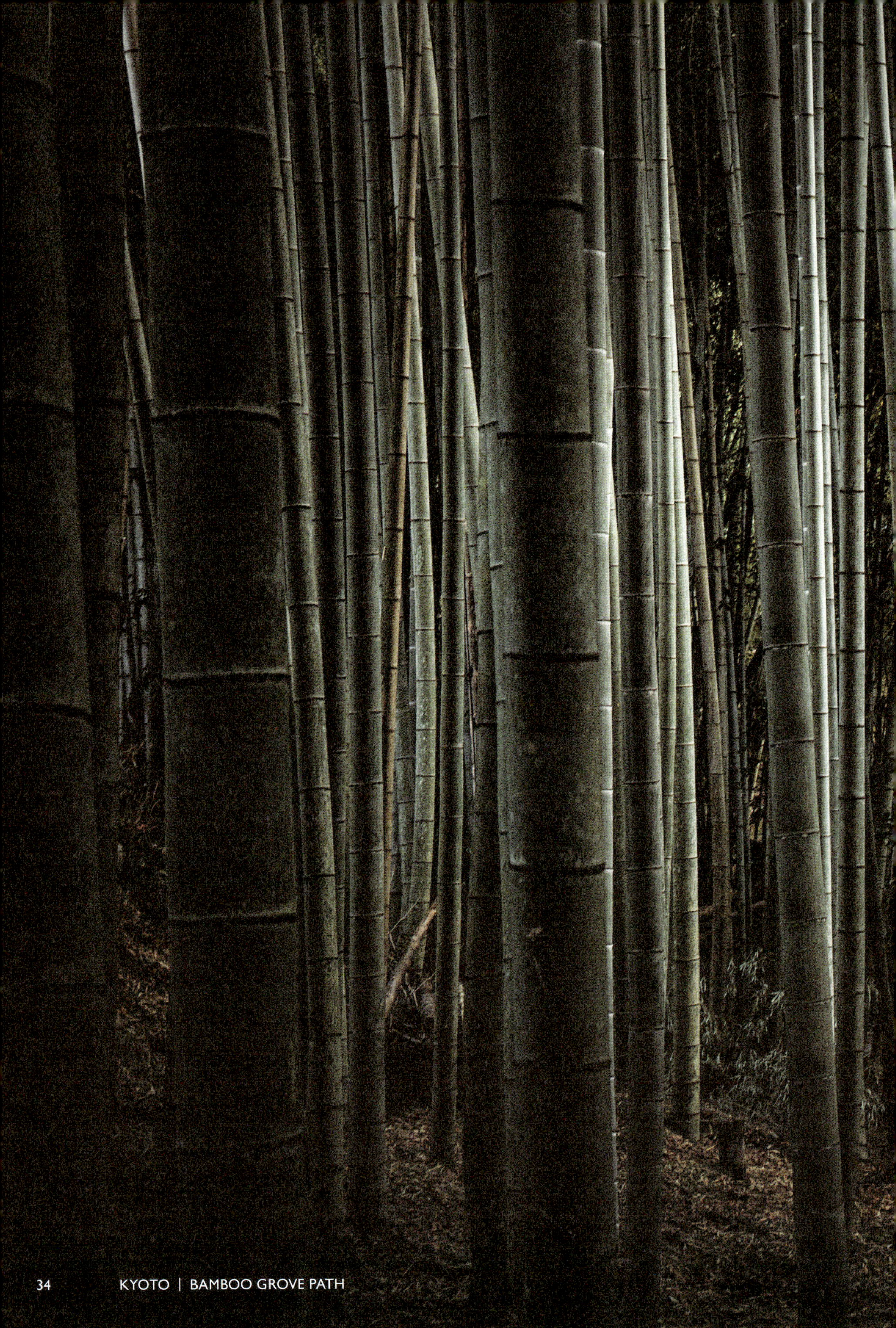

   KYOTO | BAMBOO GROVE PATH

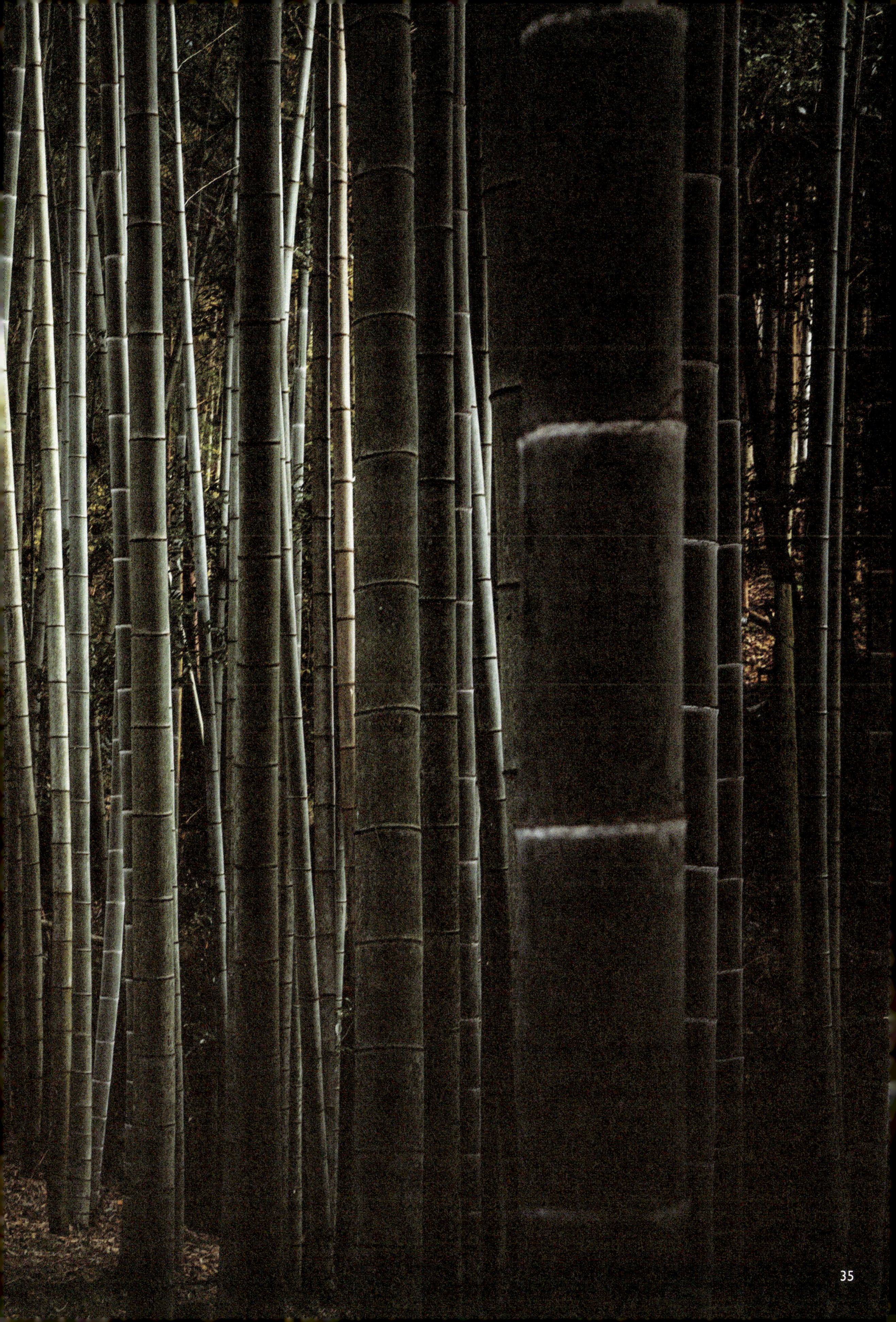

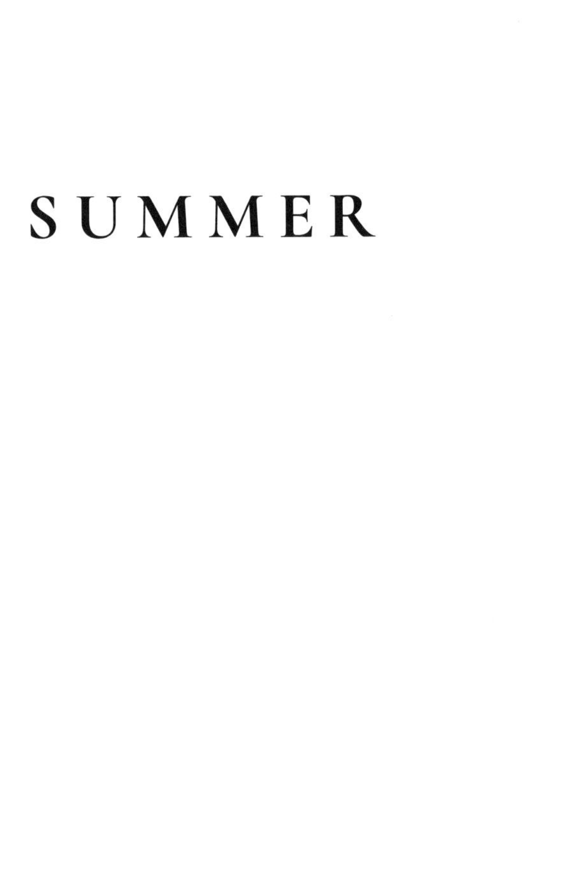

SUMMER

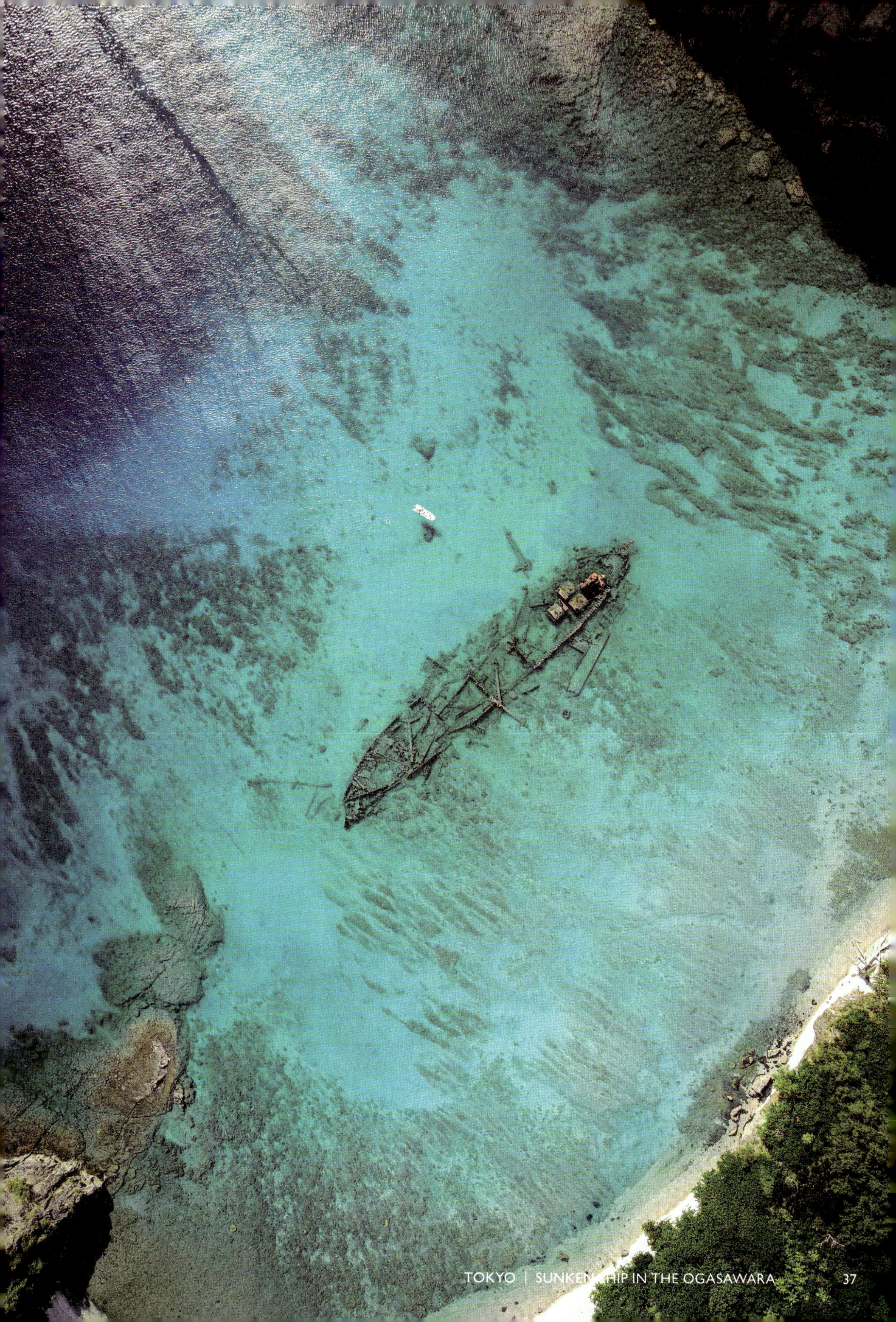

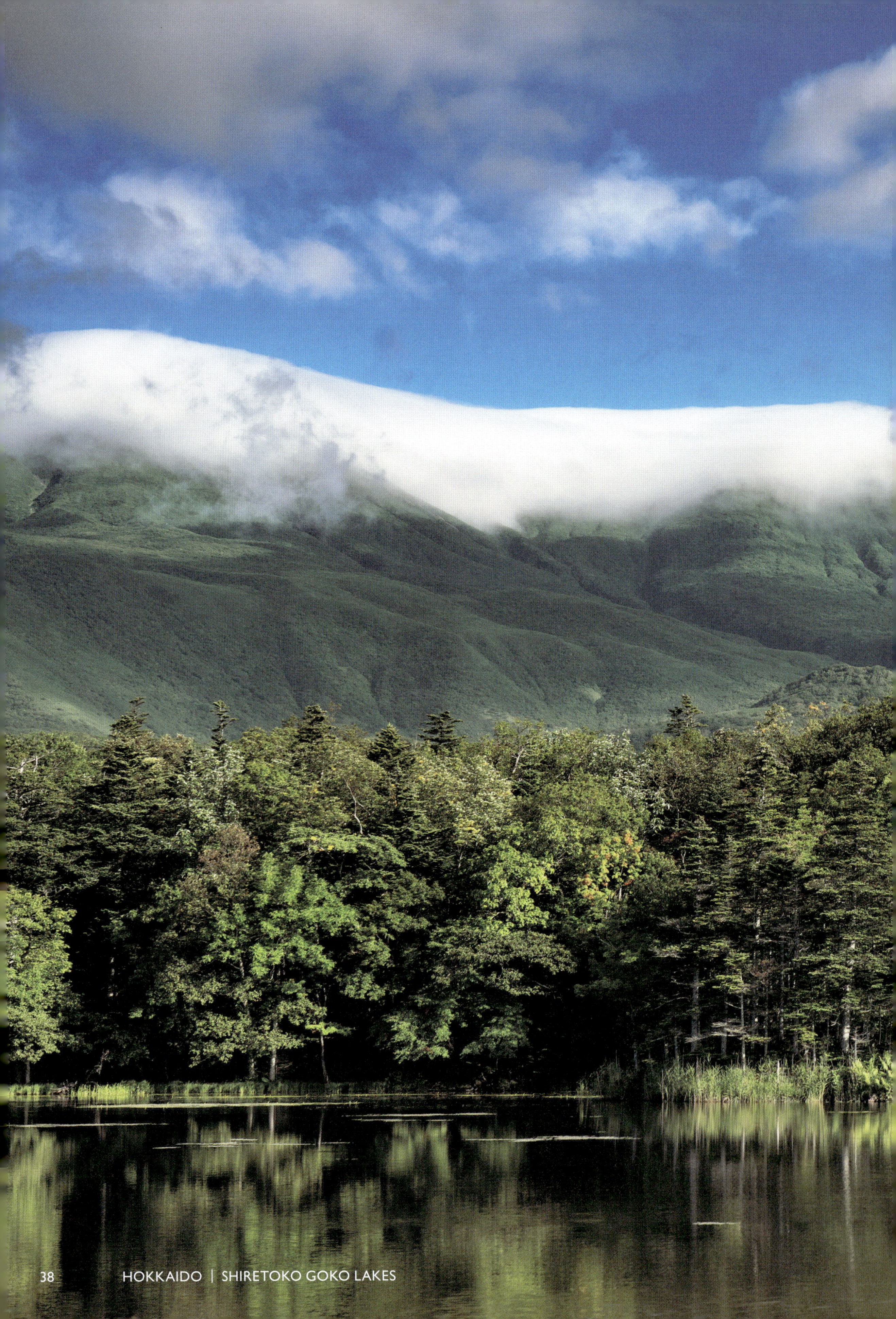

 HOKKAIDO | SHIRETOKO GOKO LAKES

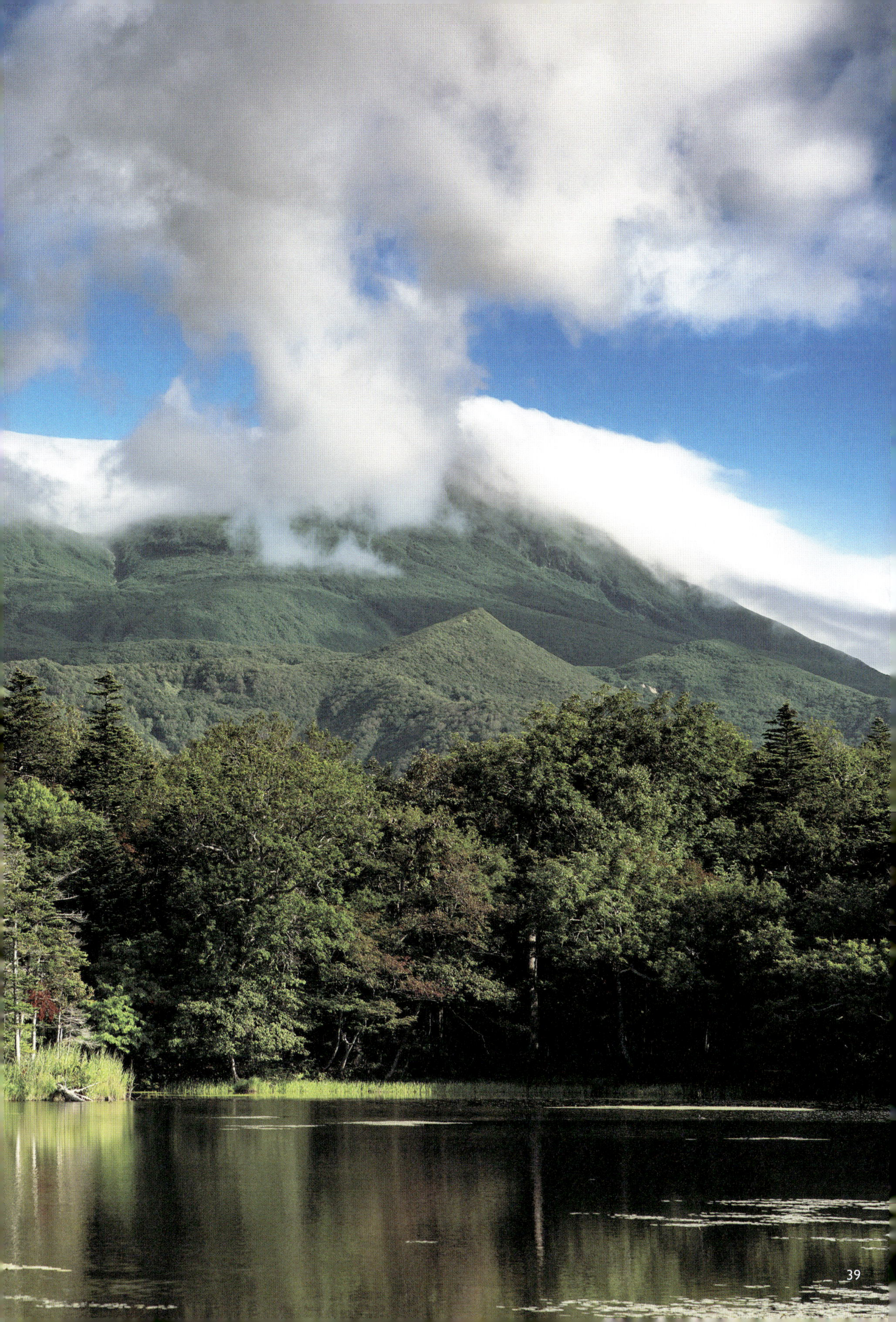

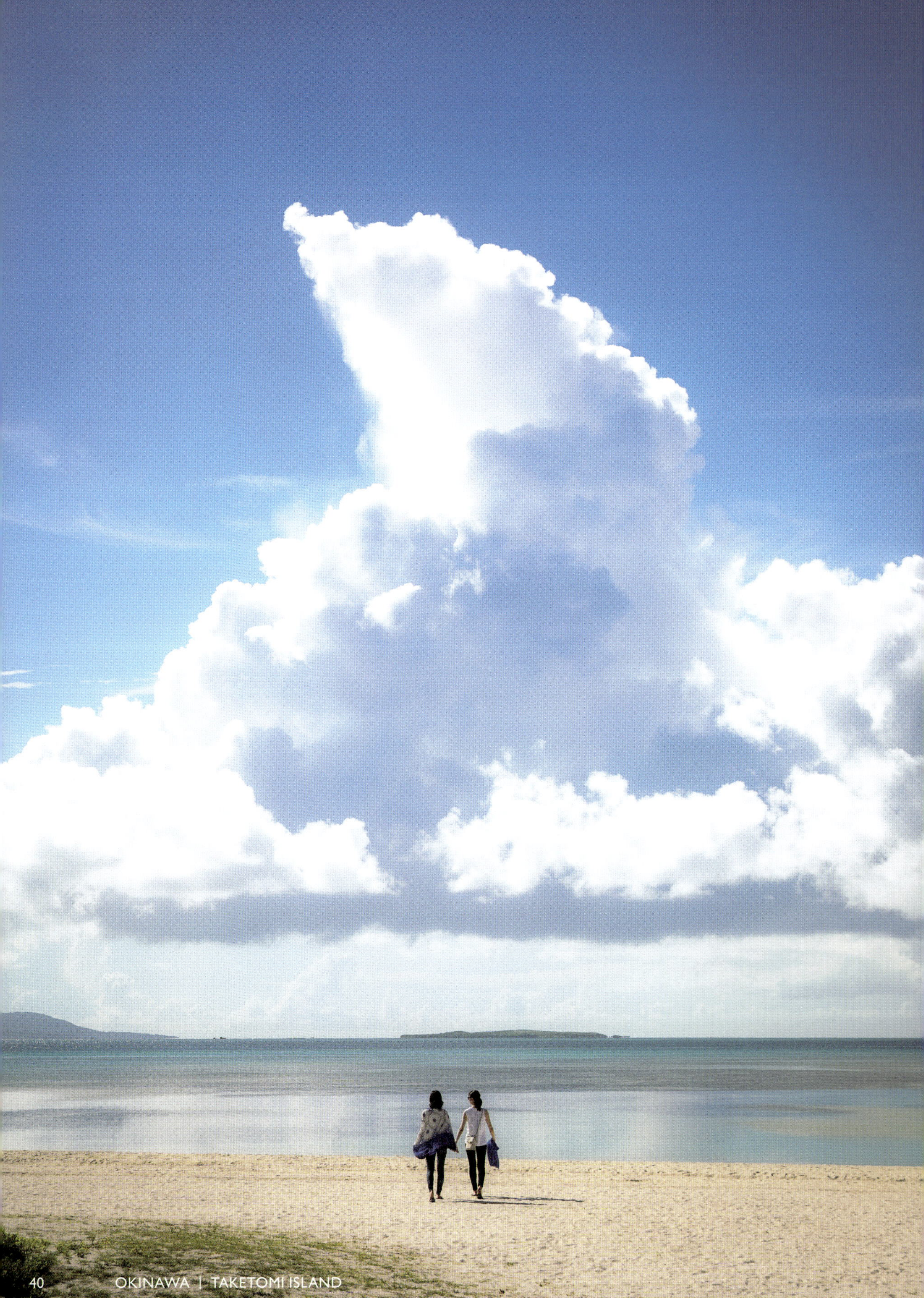

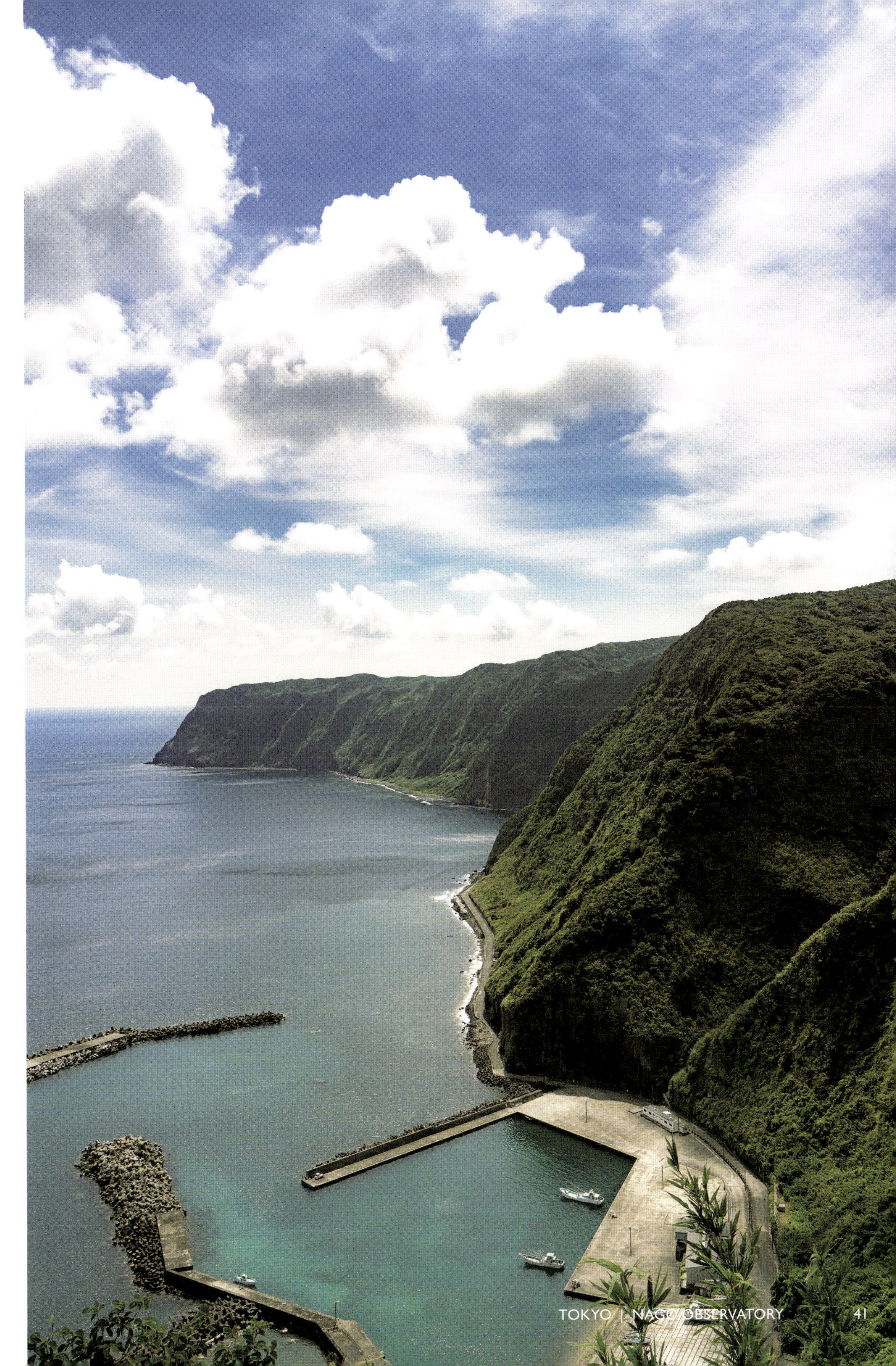

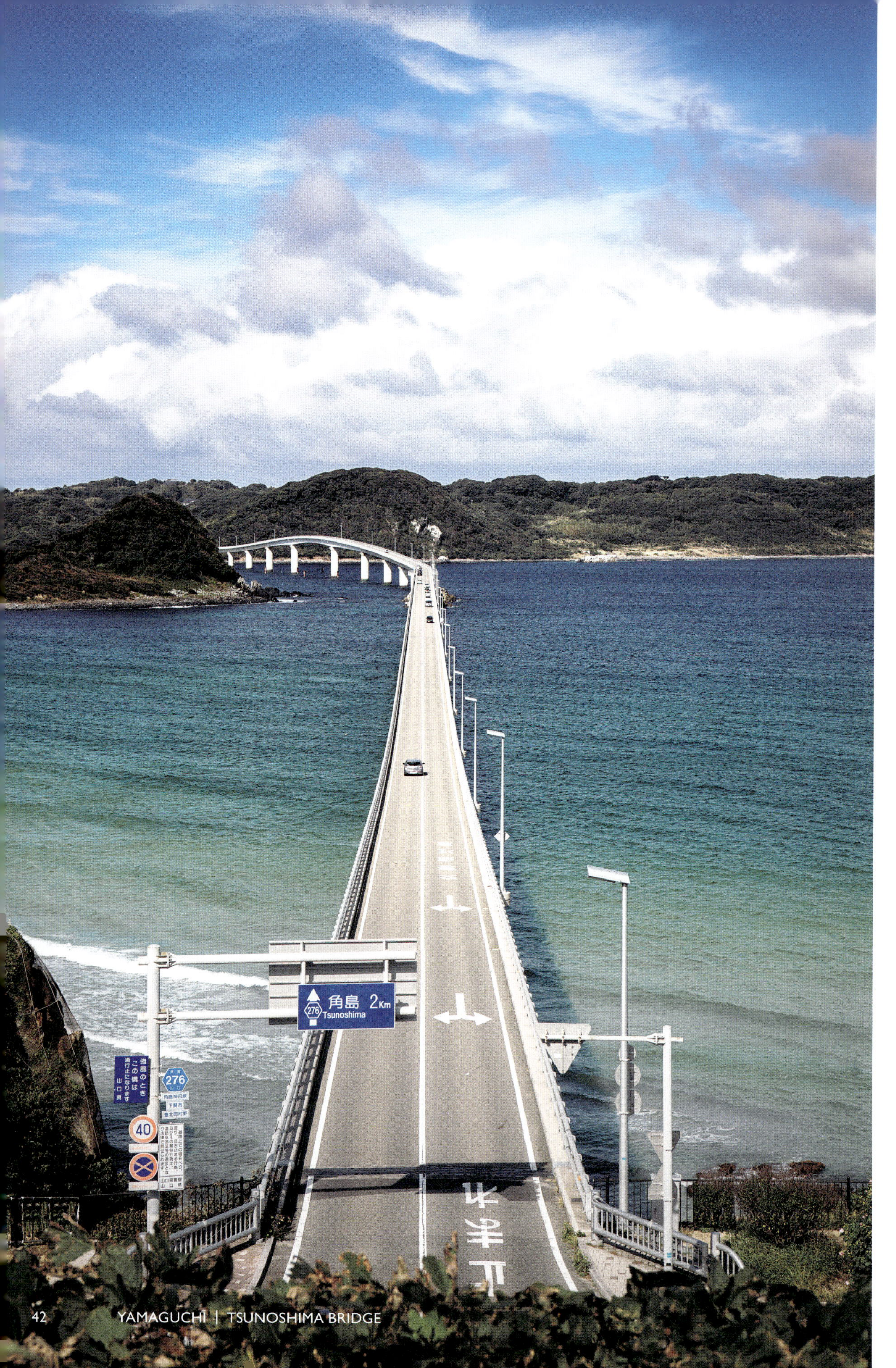
角島 2Km
Tsunoshima
276
強風のとき
この橋は
通行止になります
山口県
276
40

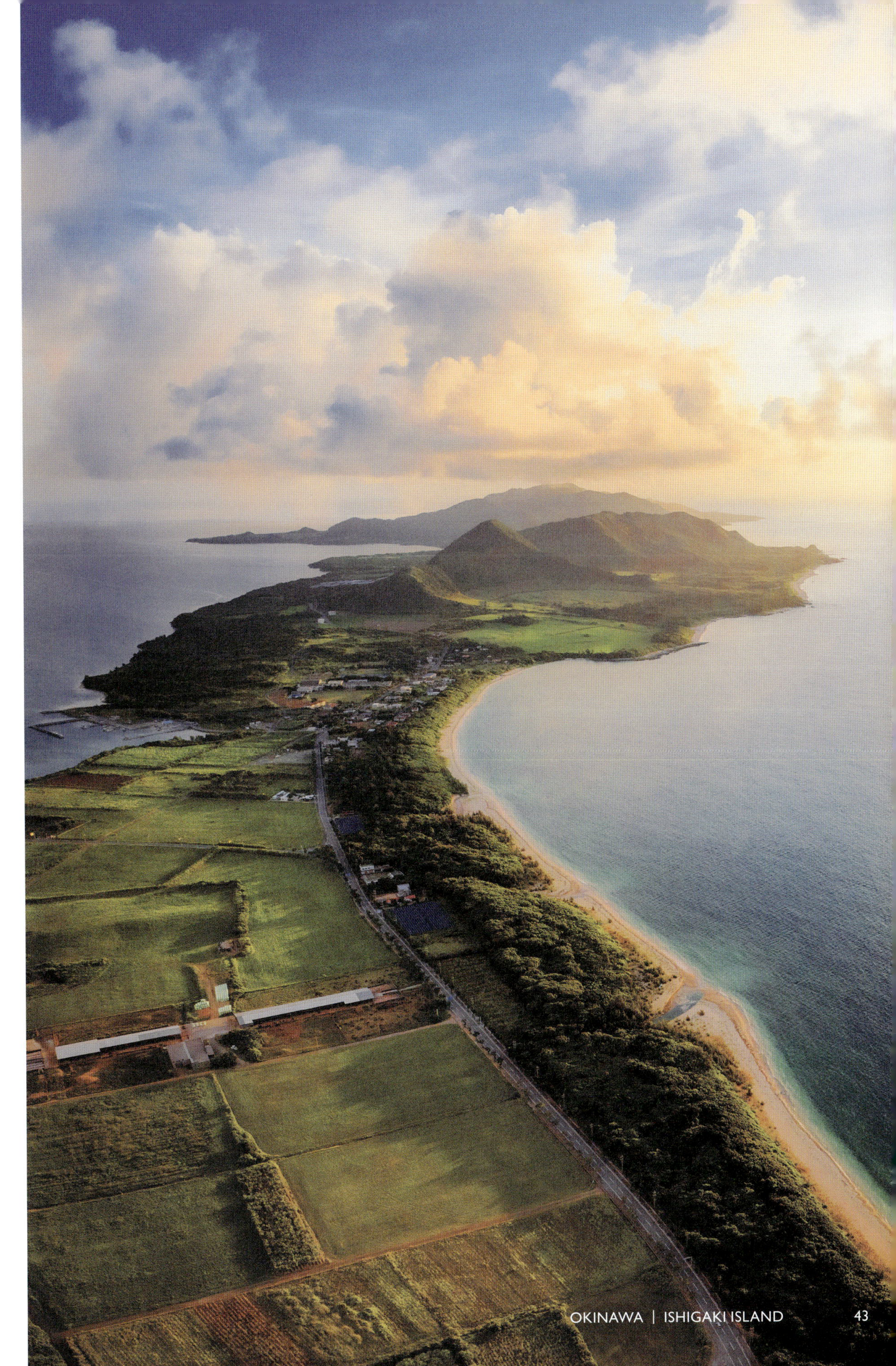

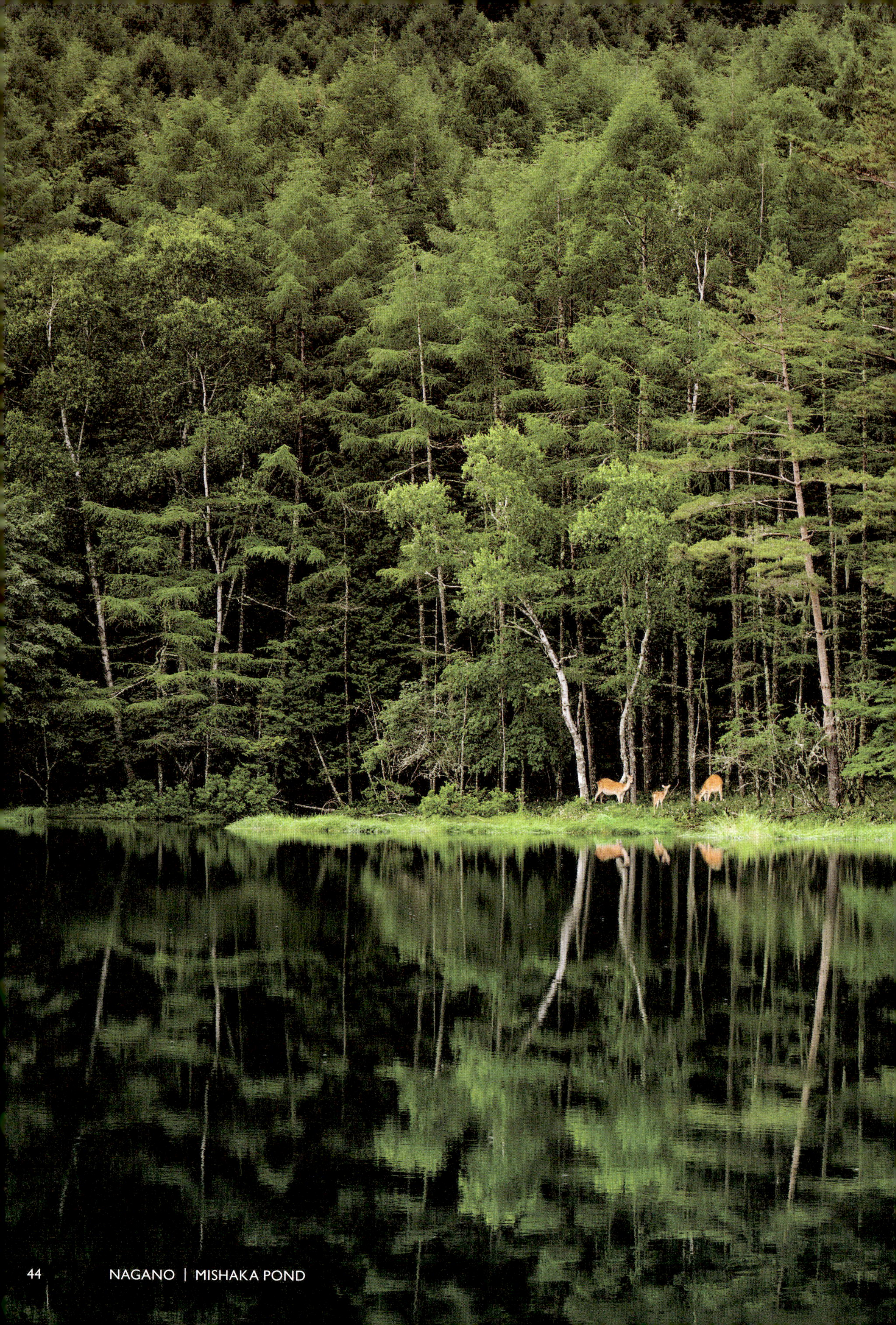

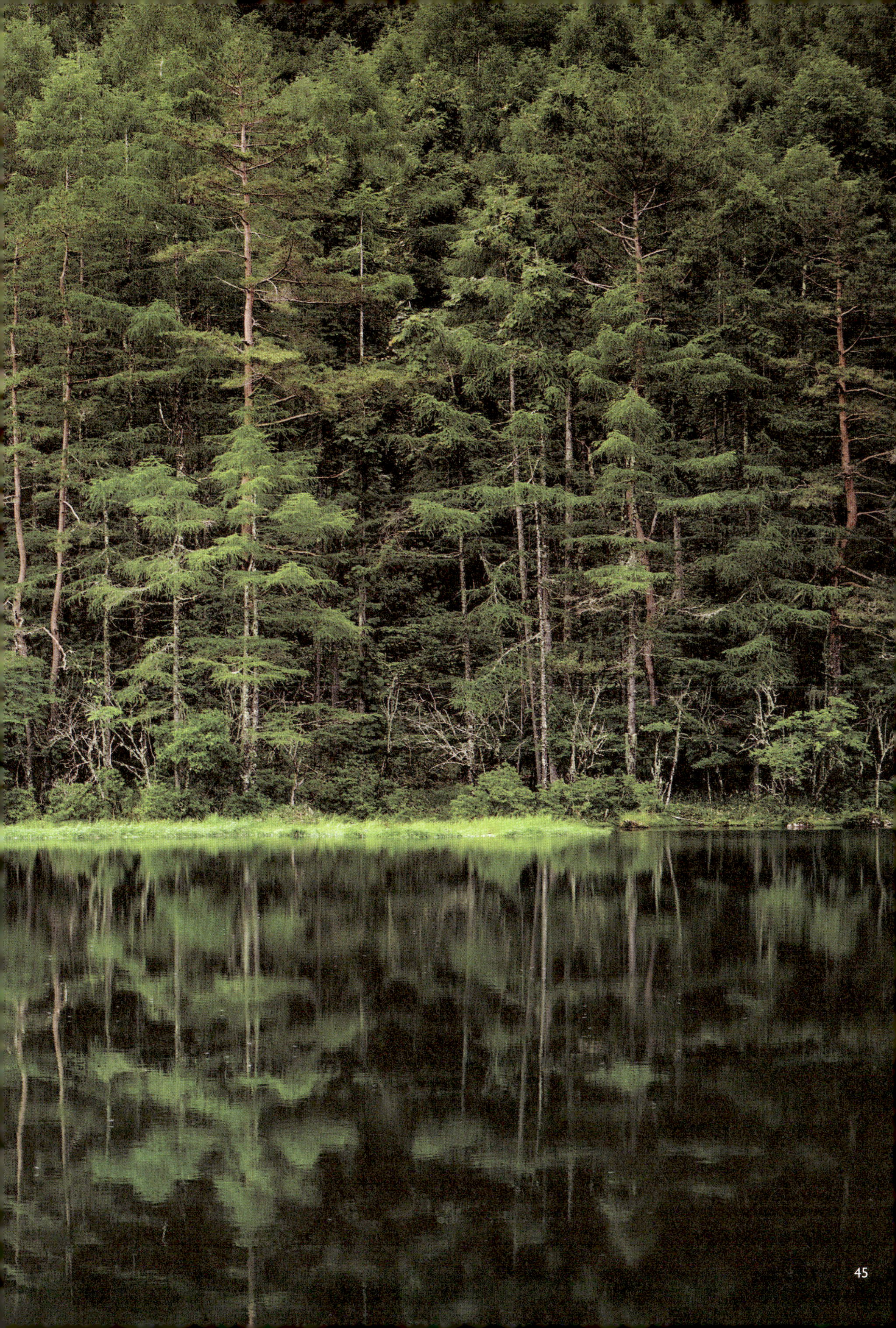

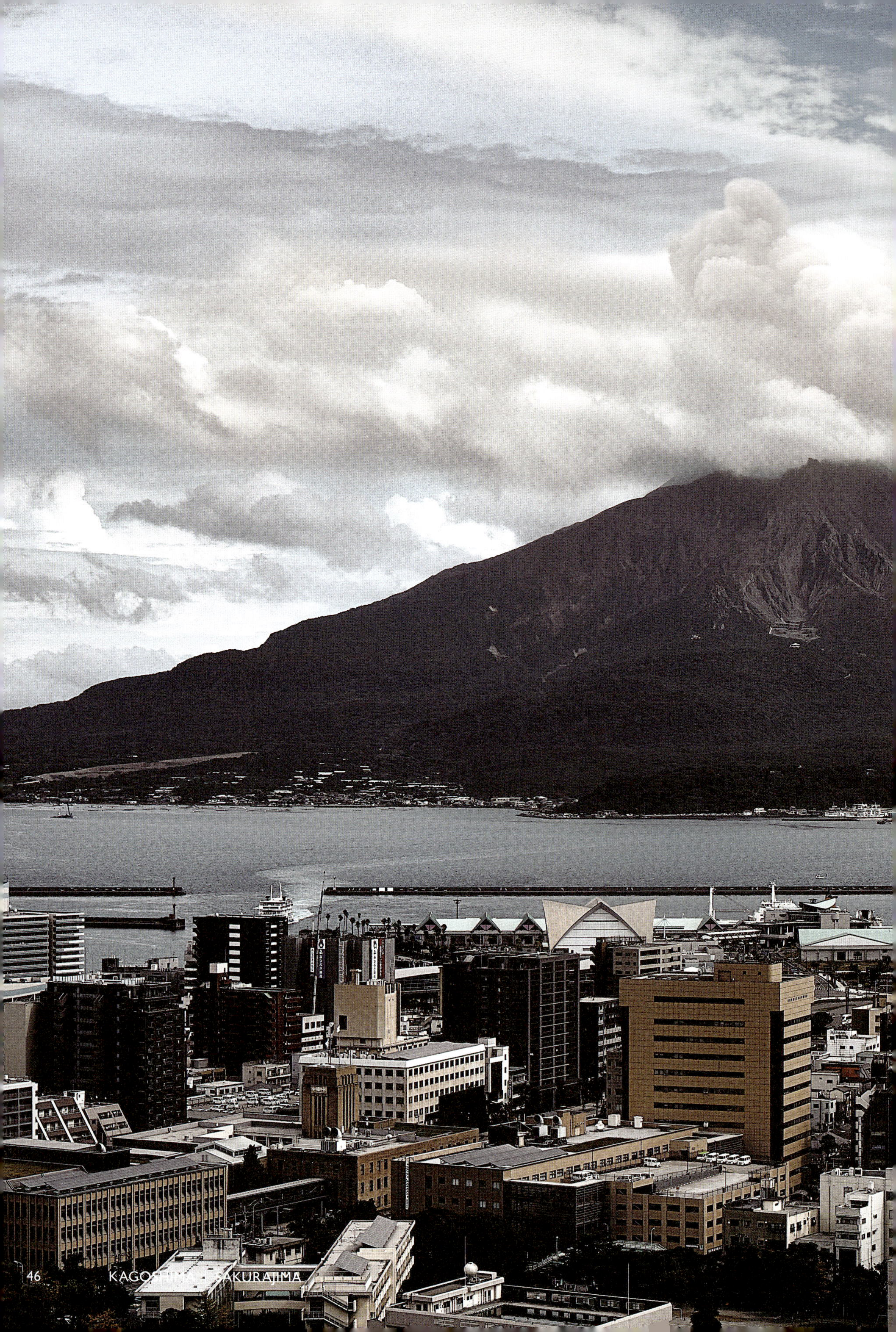

 KAGOSHIMA · SAKURAJIMA

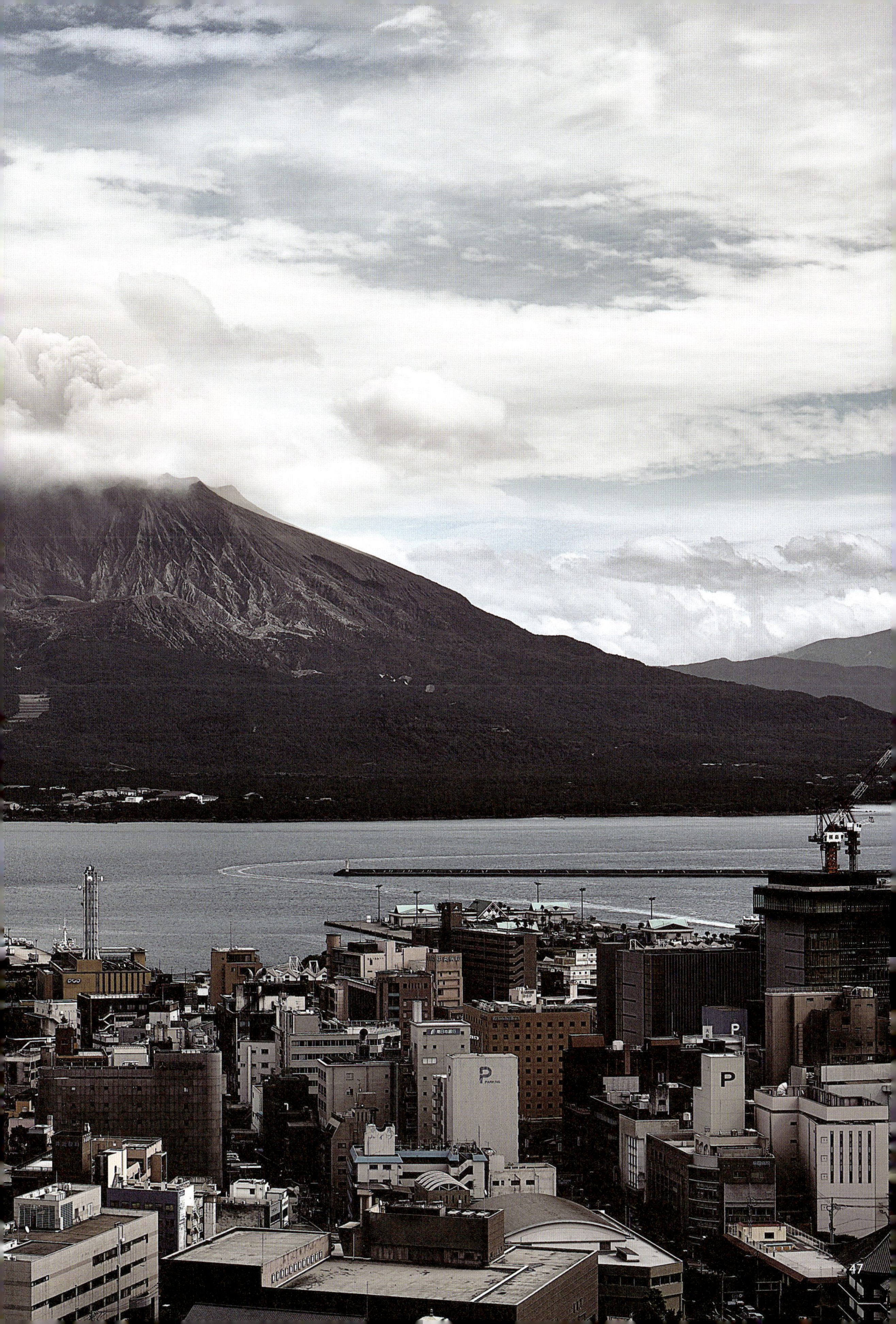

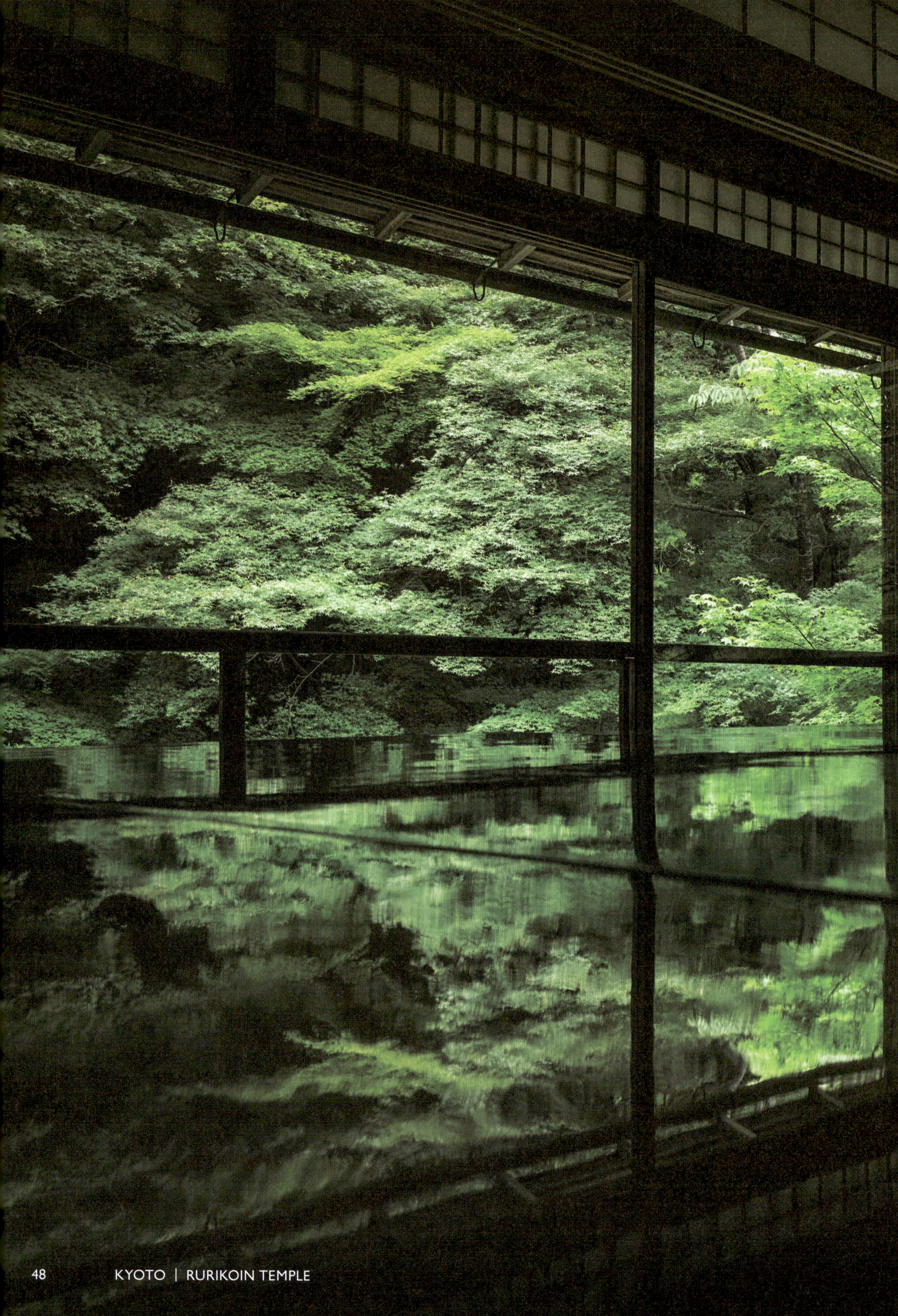

  KYOTO | RURIKOIN TEMPLE

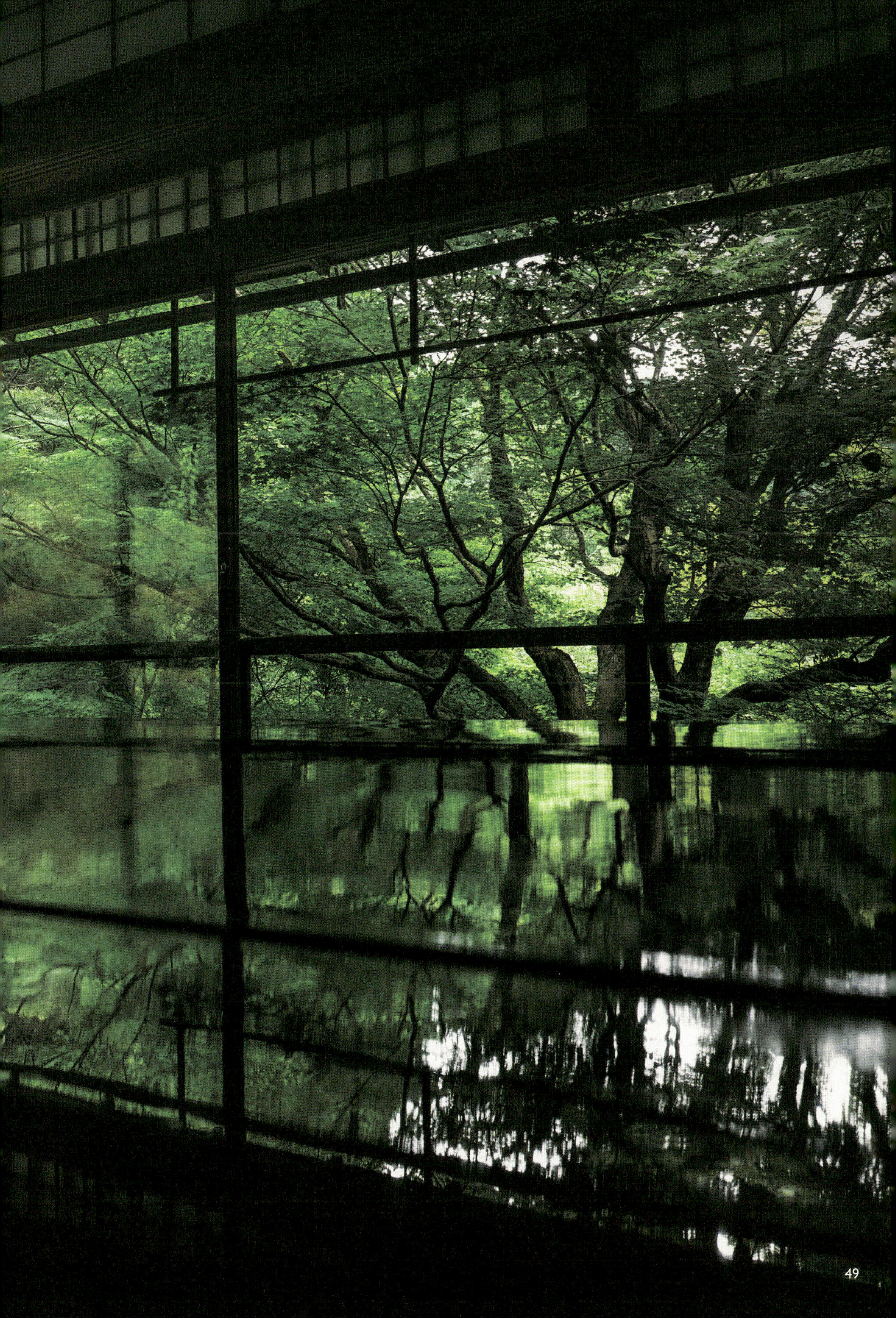

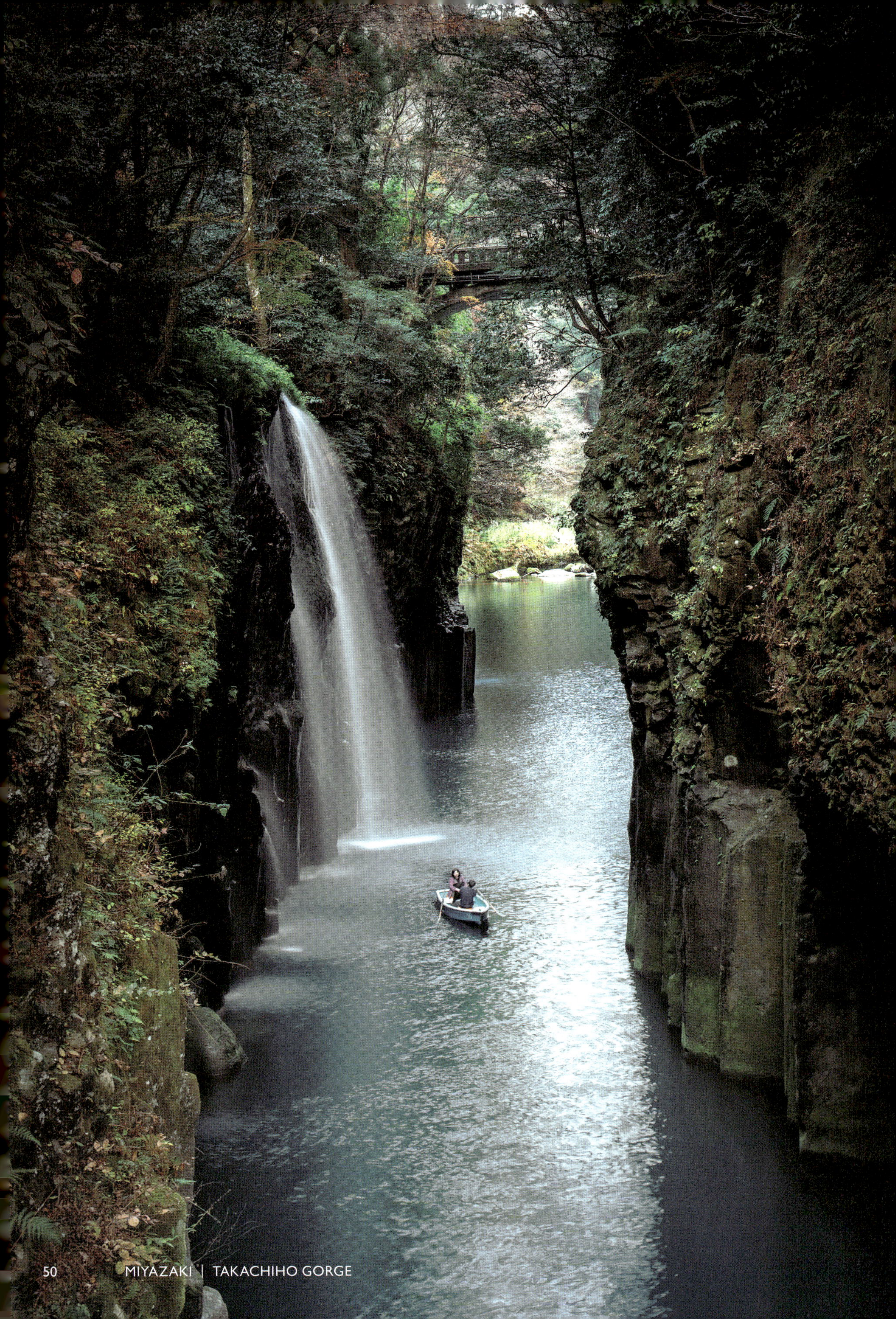

  MIYAZAKI | TAKACHIHO GORGE

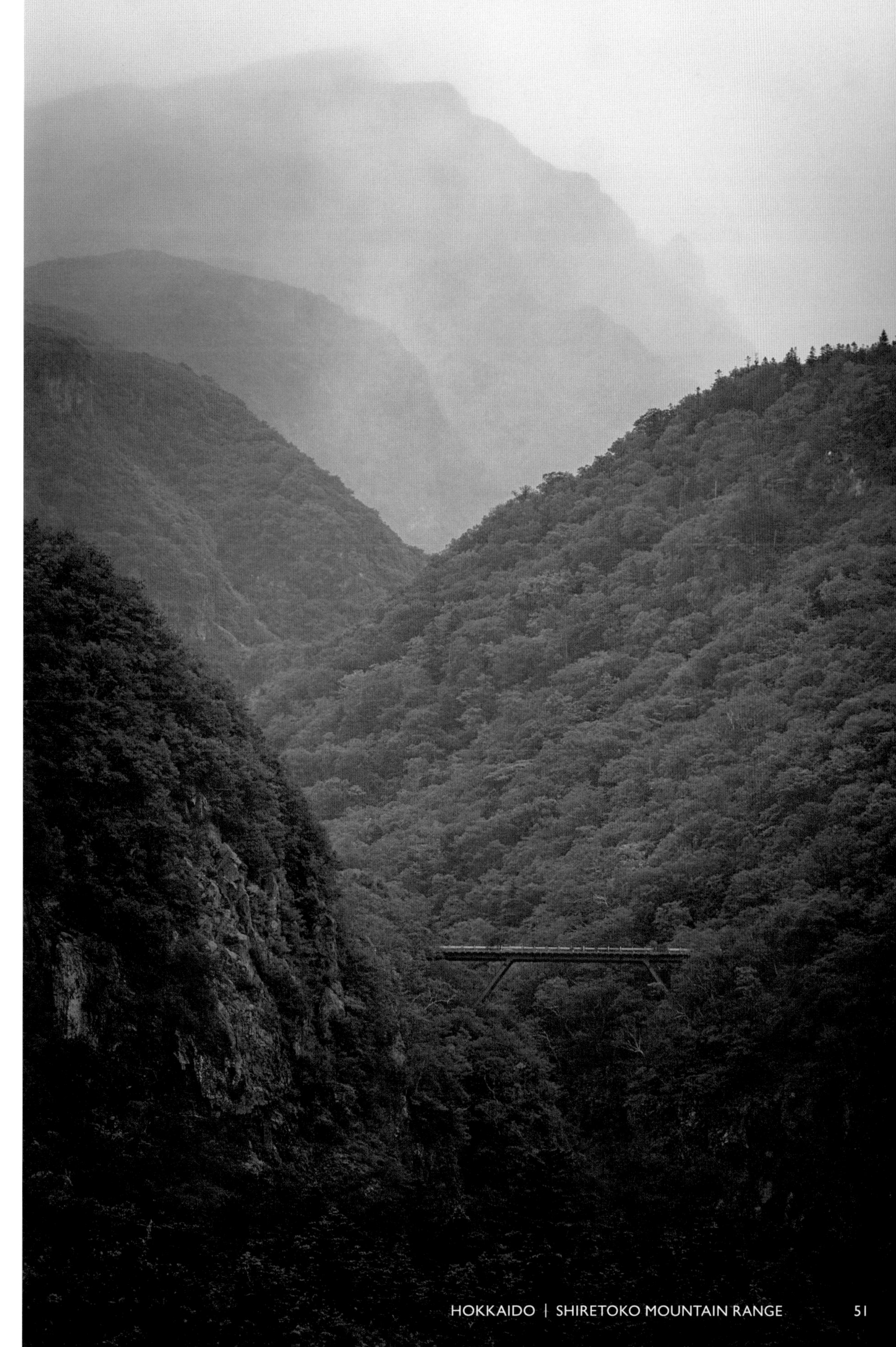

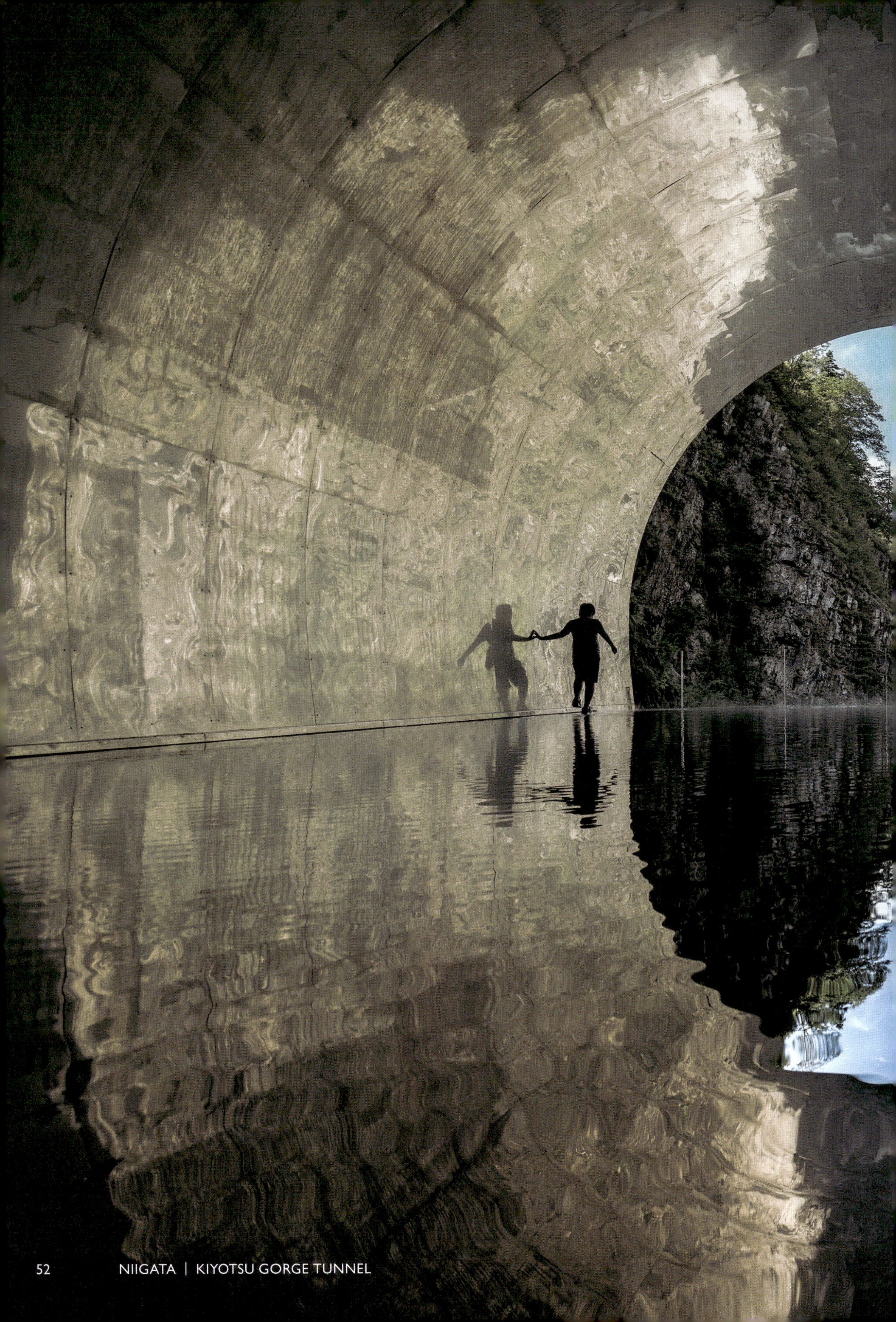

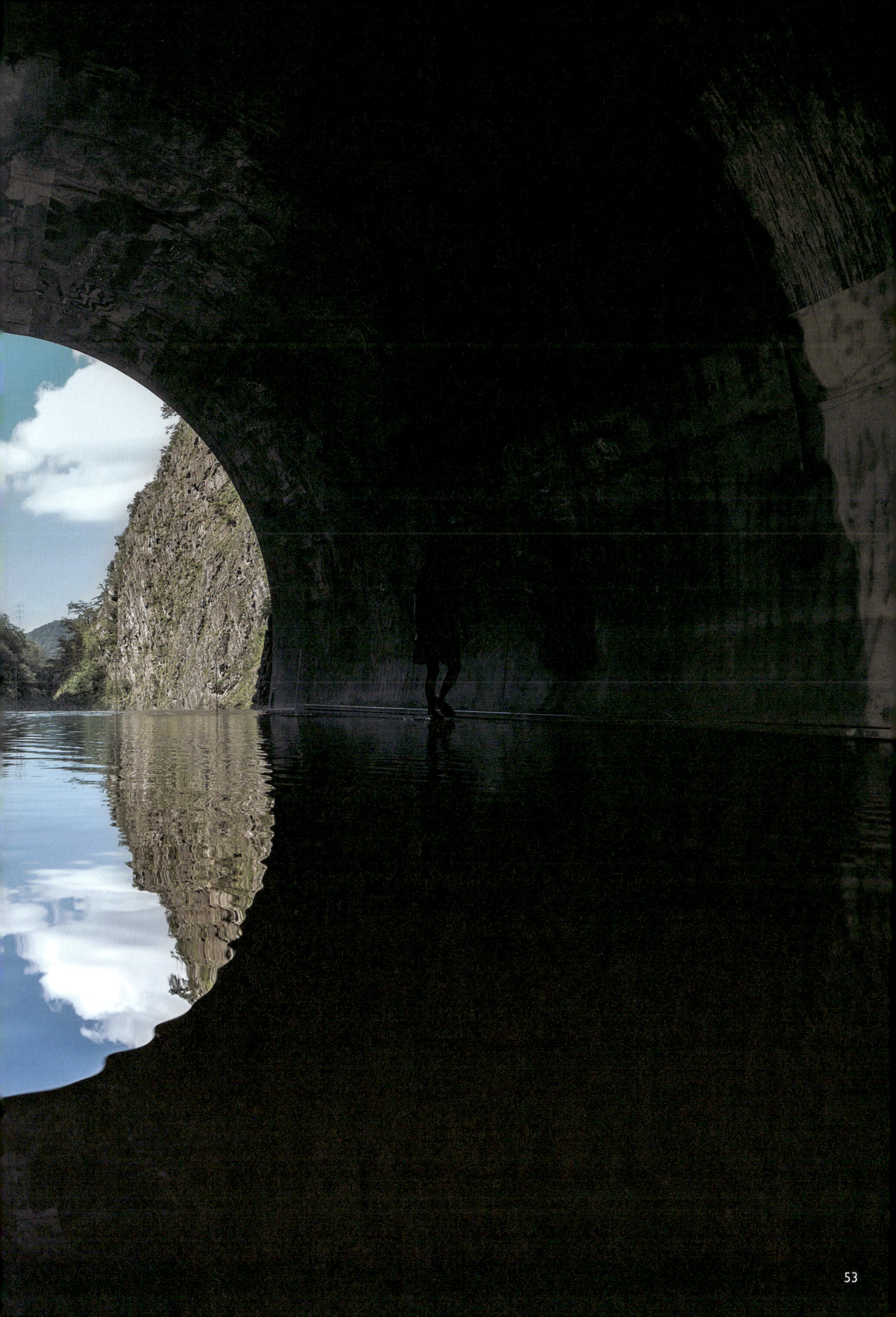

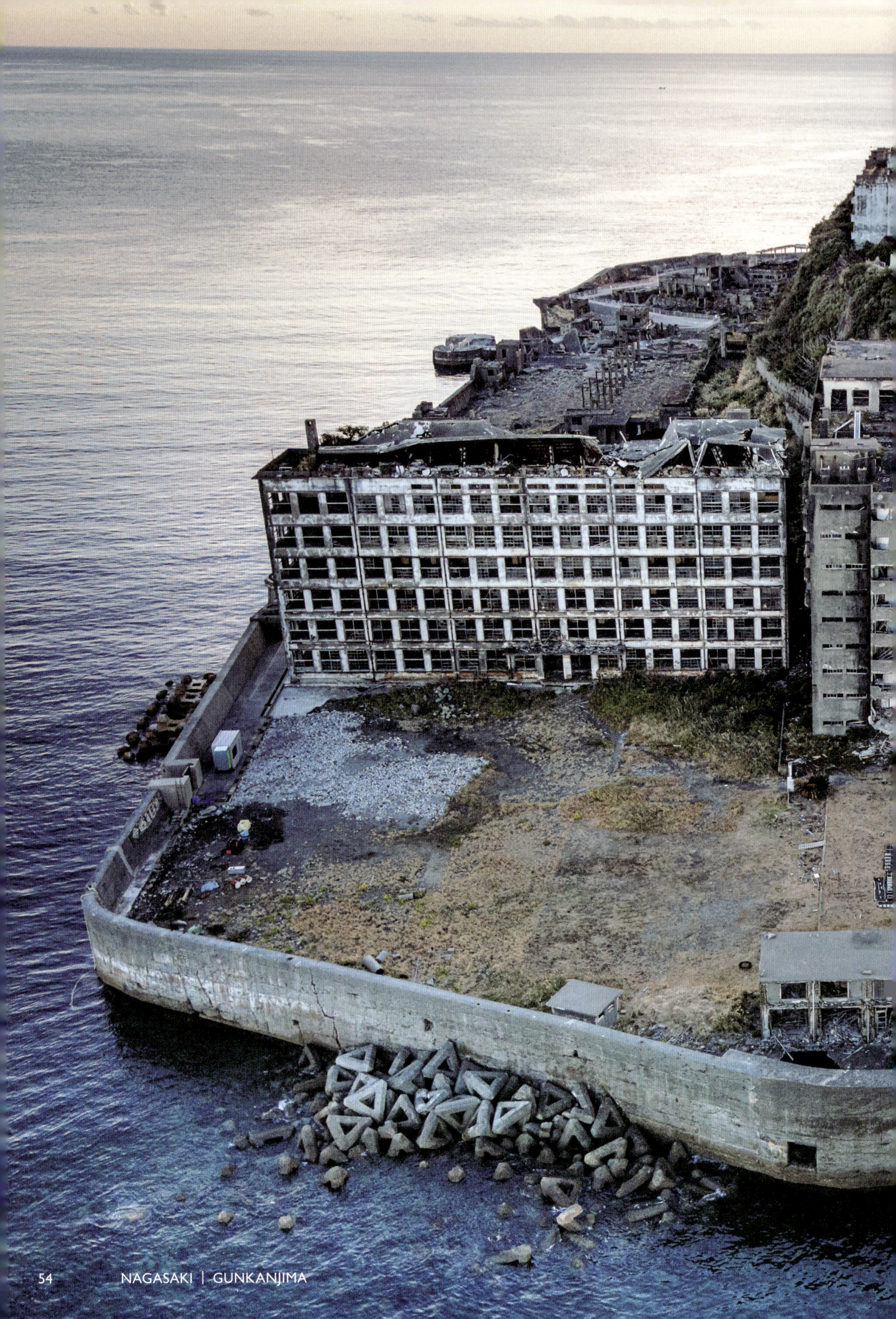

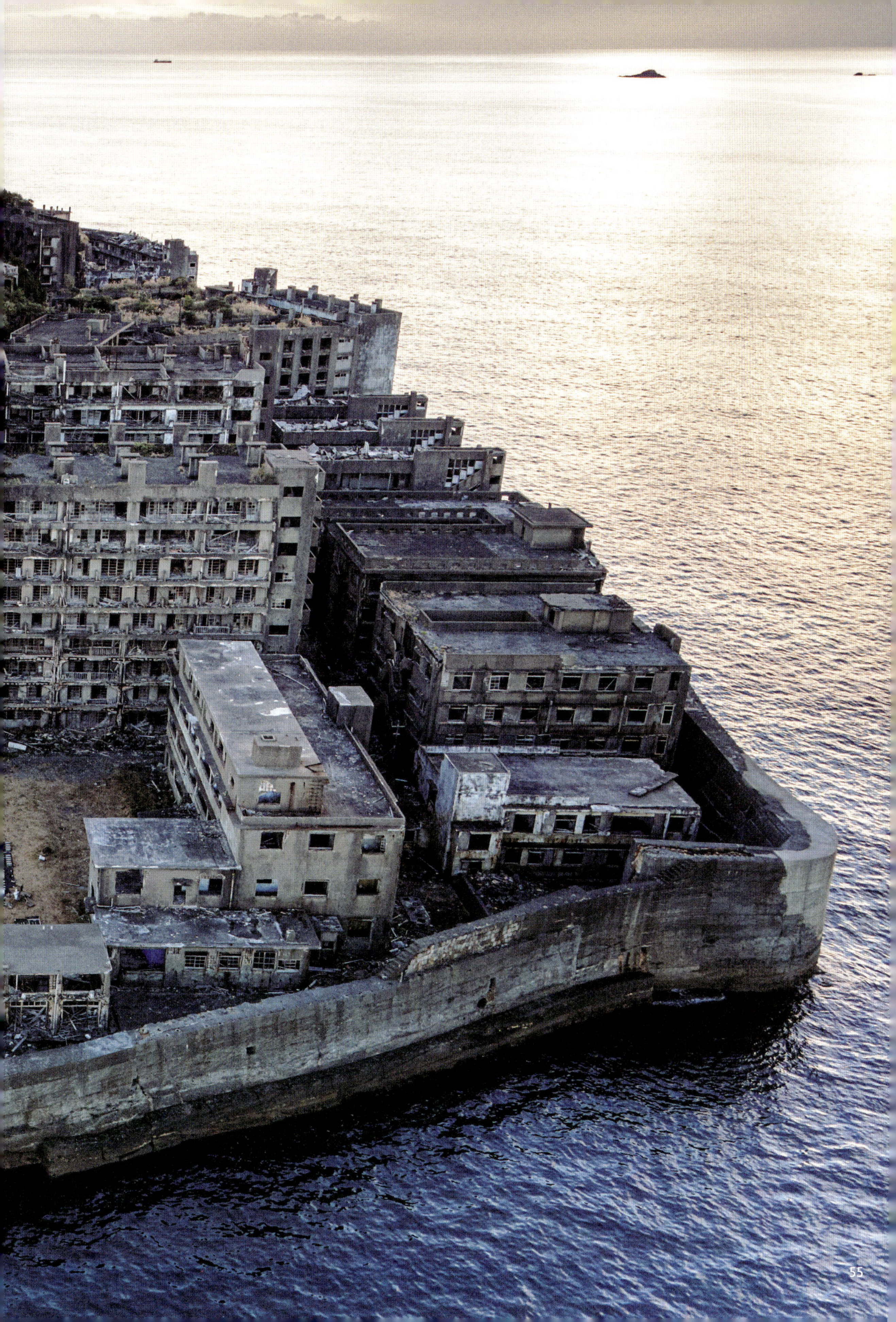

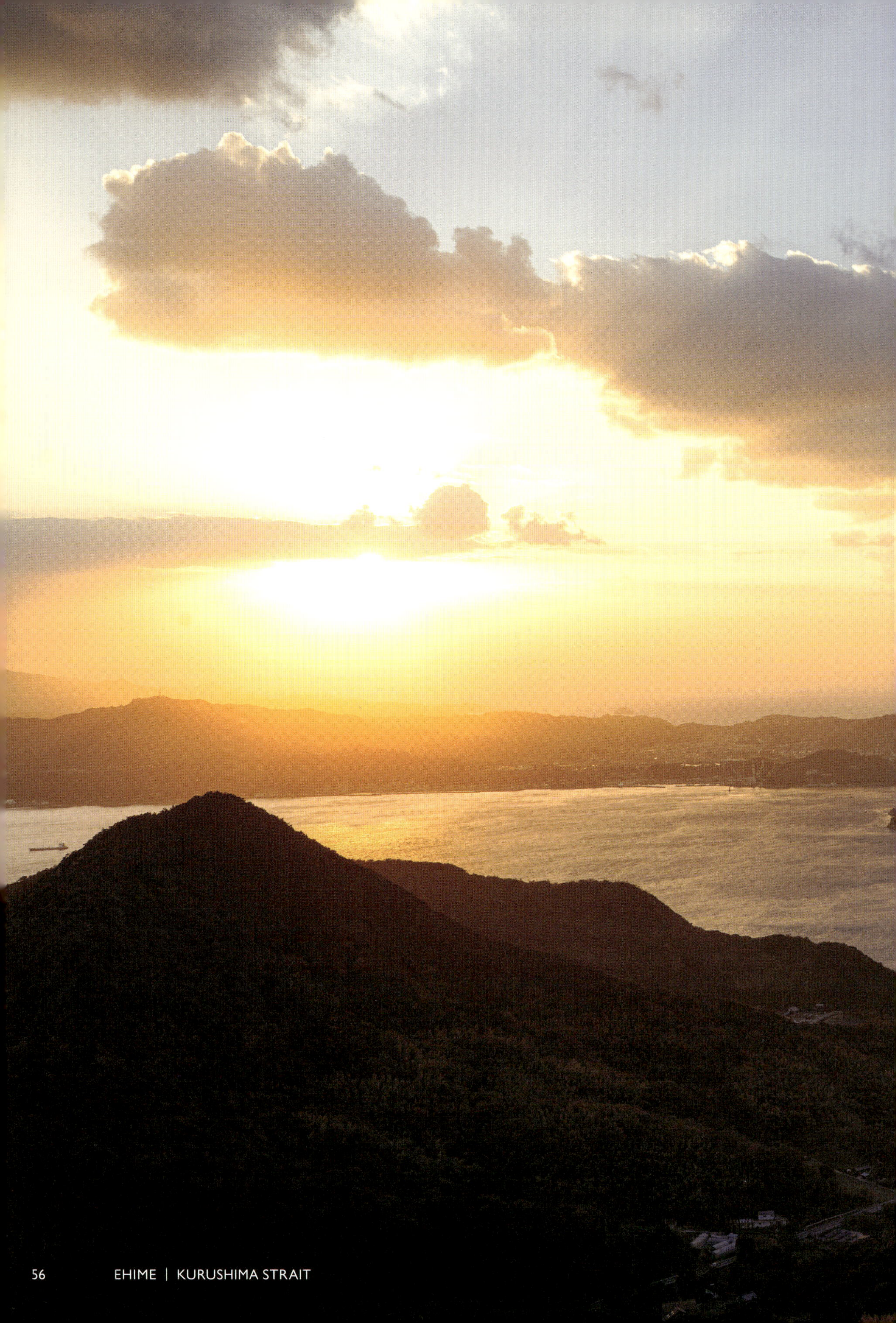

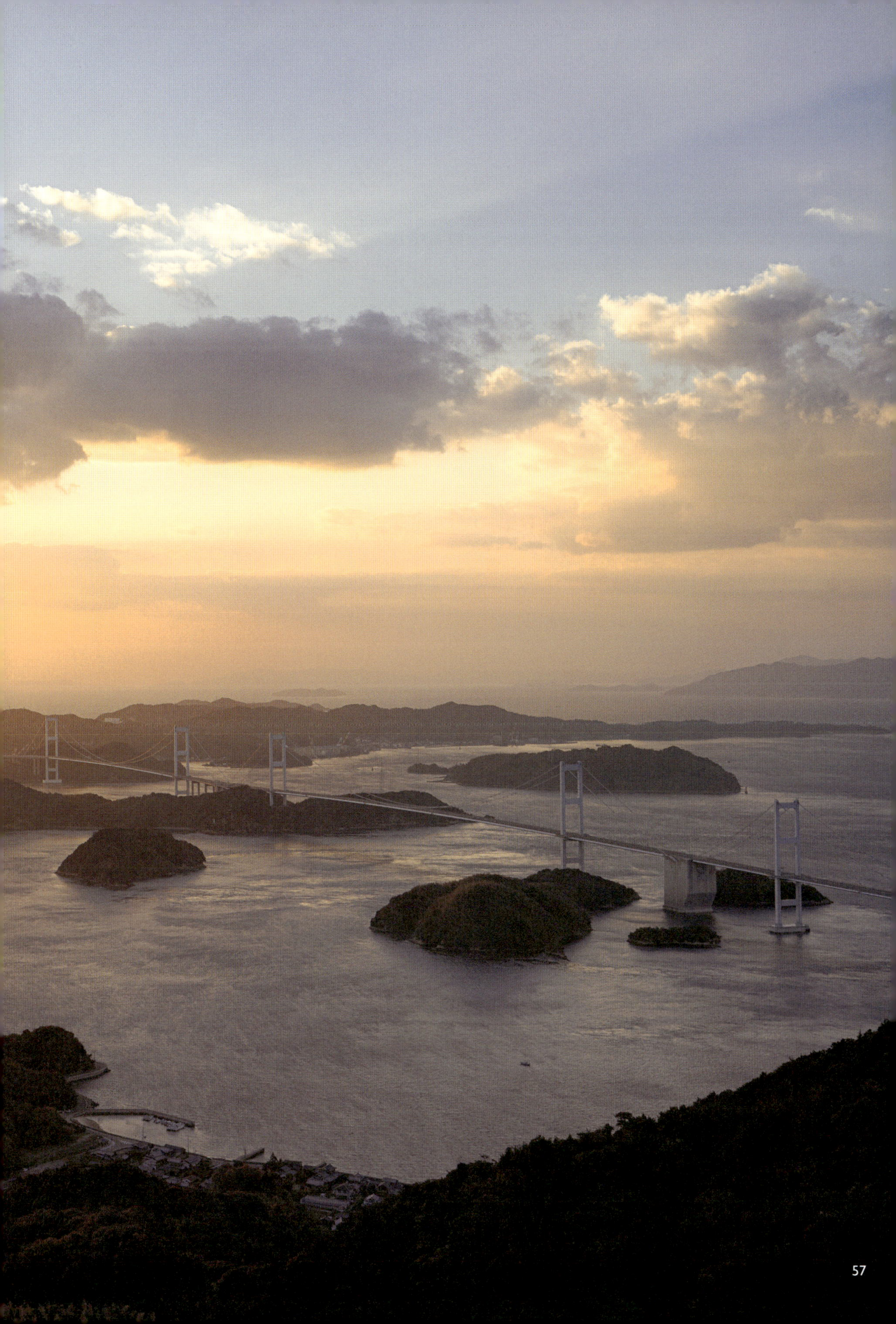

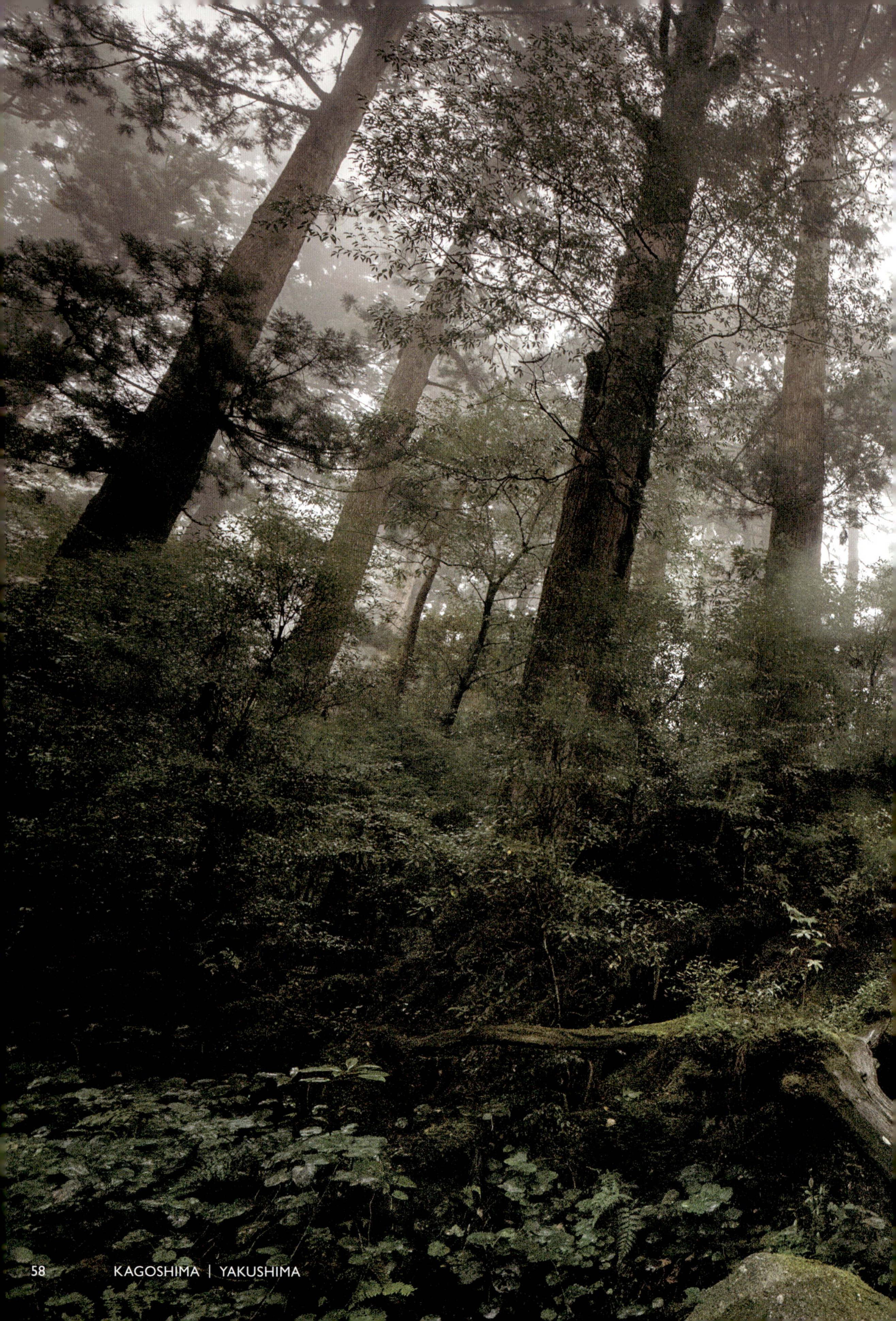

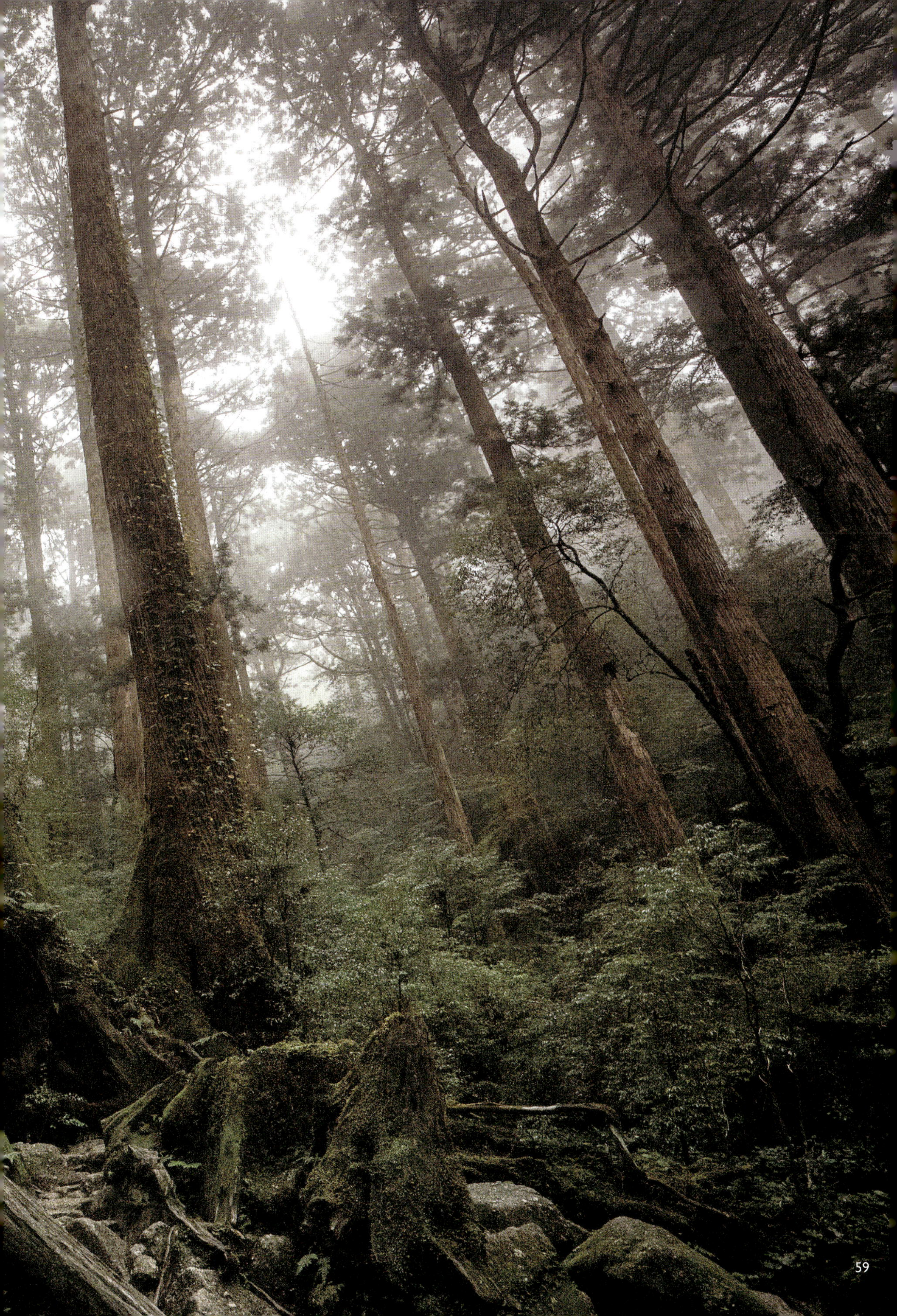

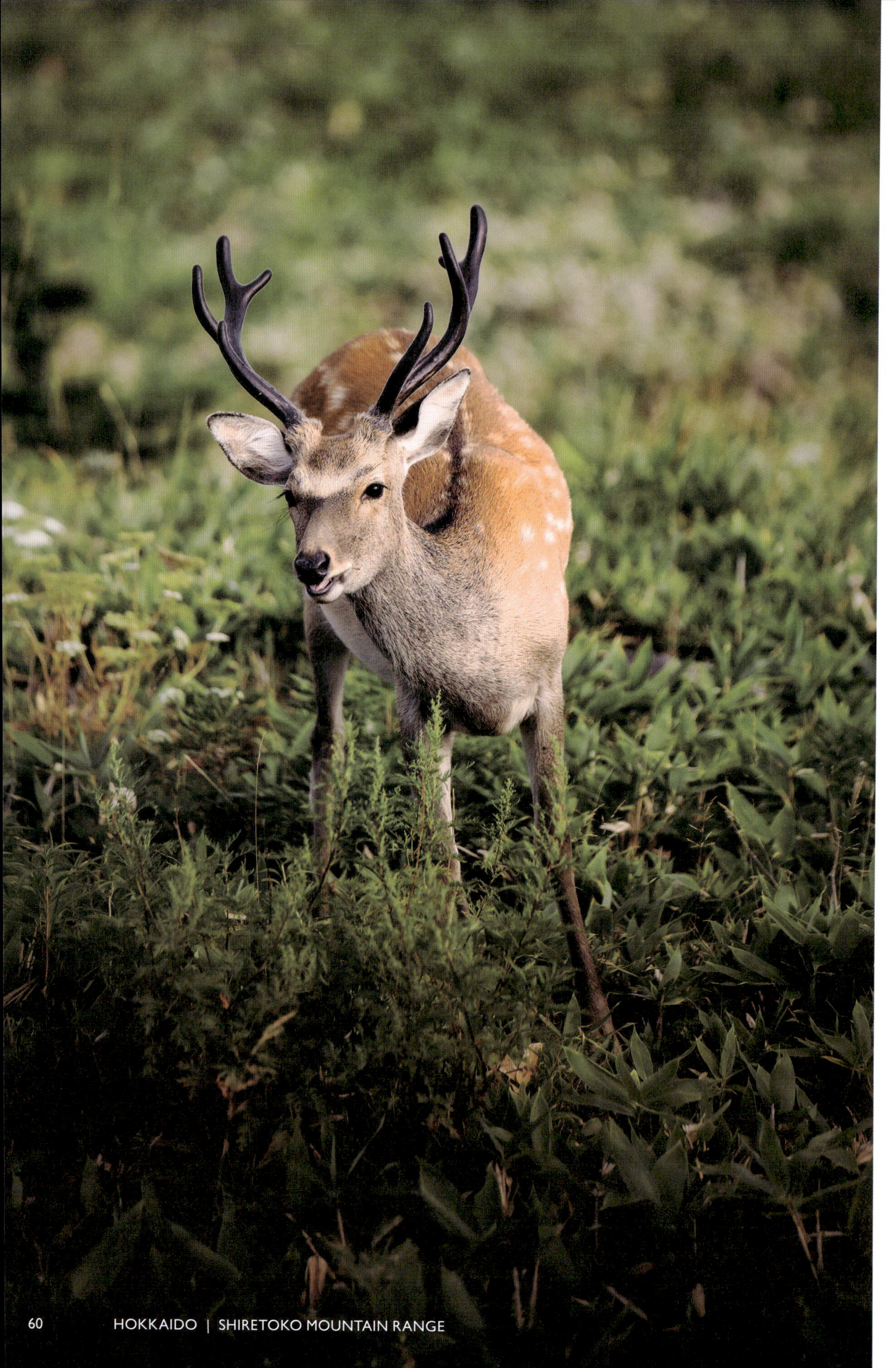

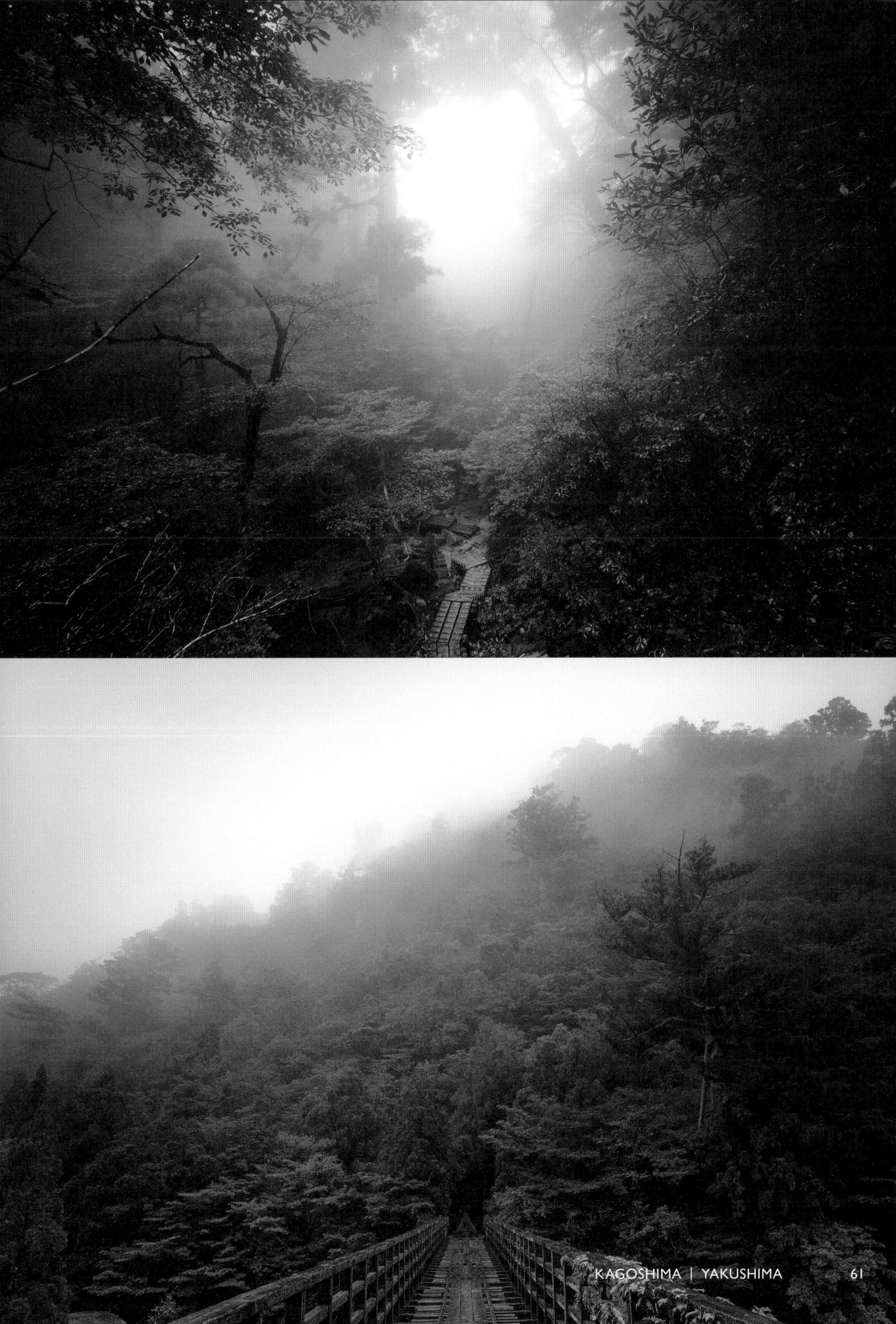

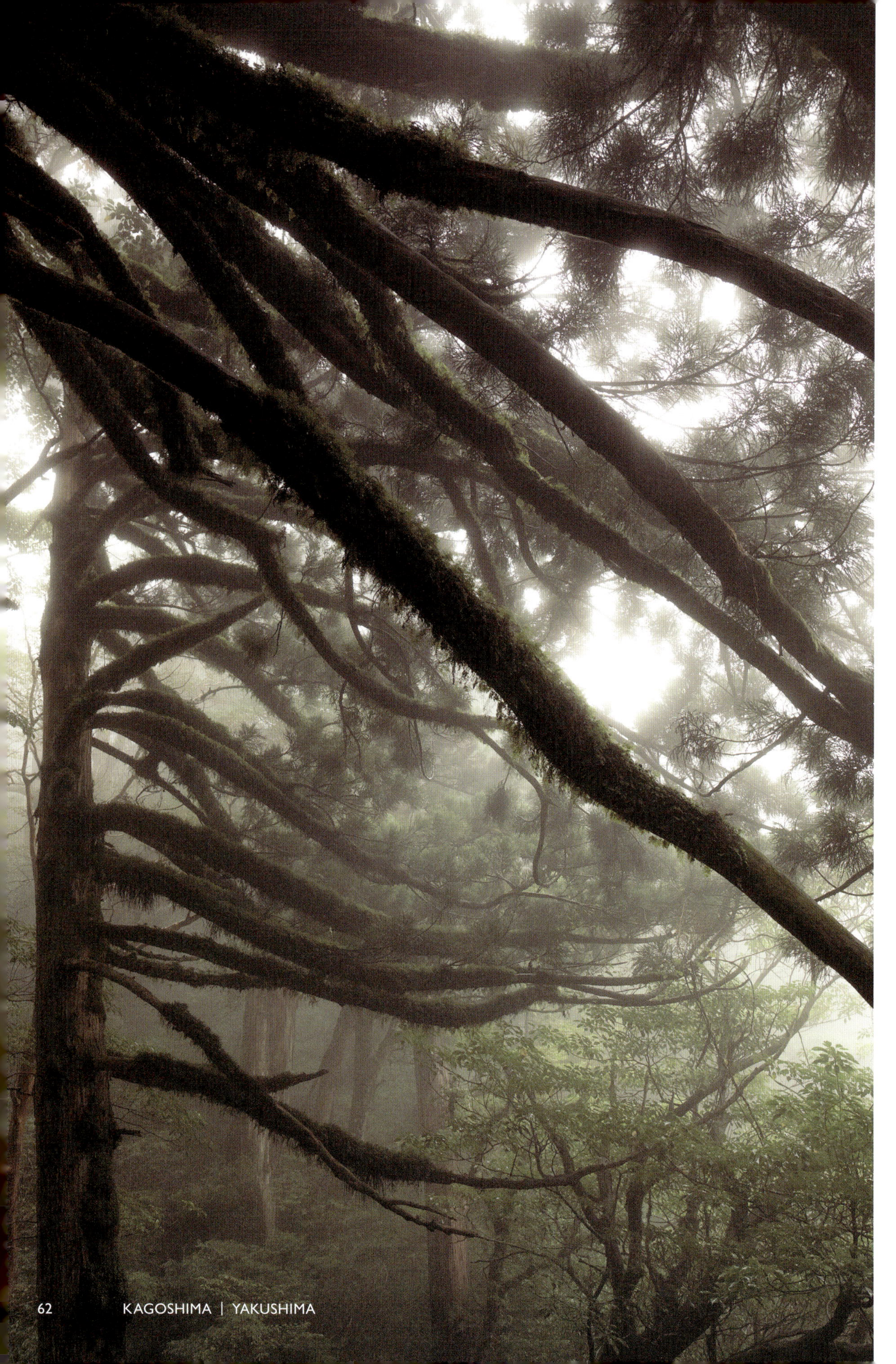

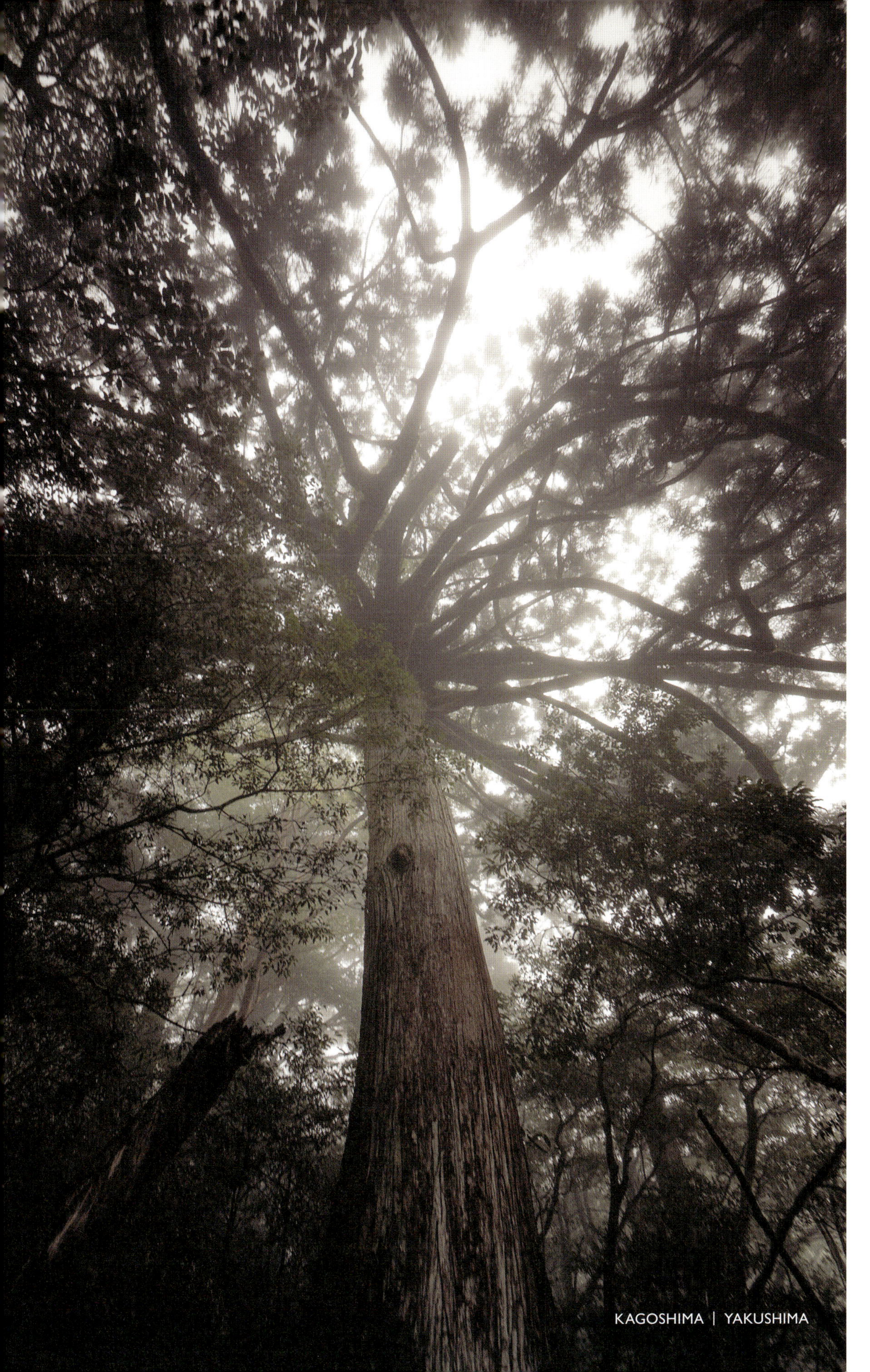

KAGOSHIMA | YAKUSHIMA

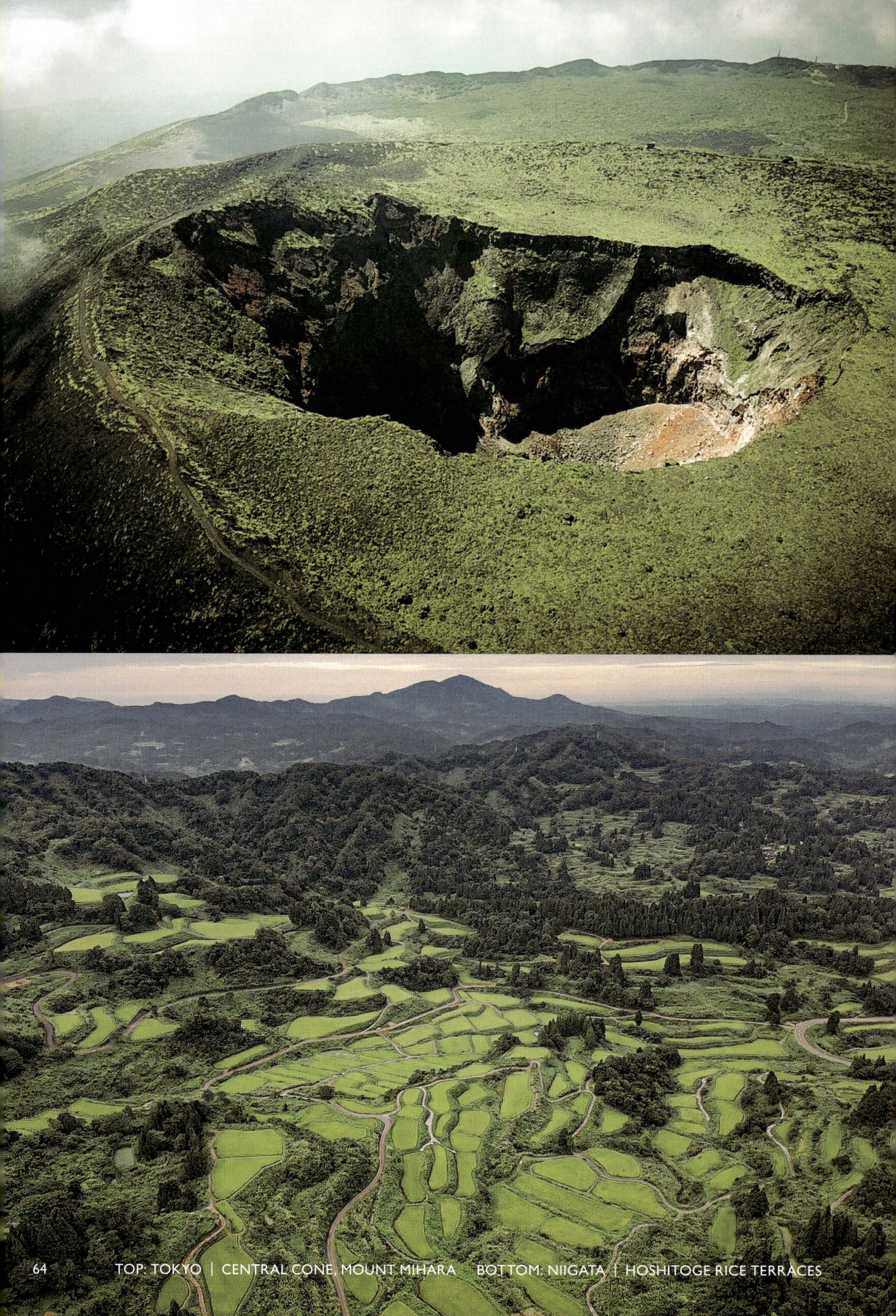

 TOP: TOKYO | CENTRAL CONE, MOUNT MIHARA   BOTTOM: NIIGATA | HOSHITOGE RICE TERRACES

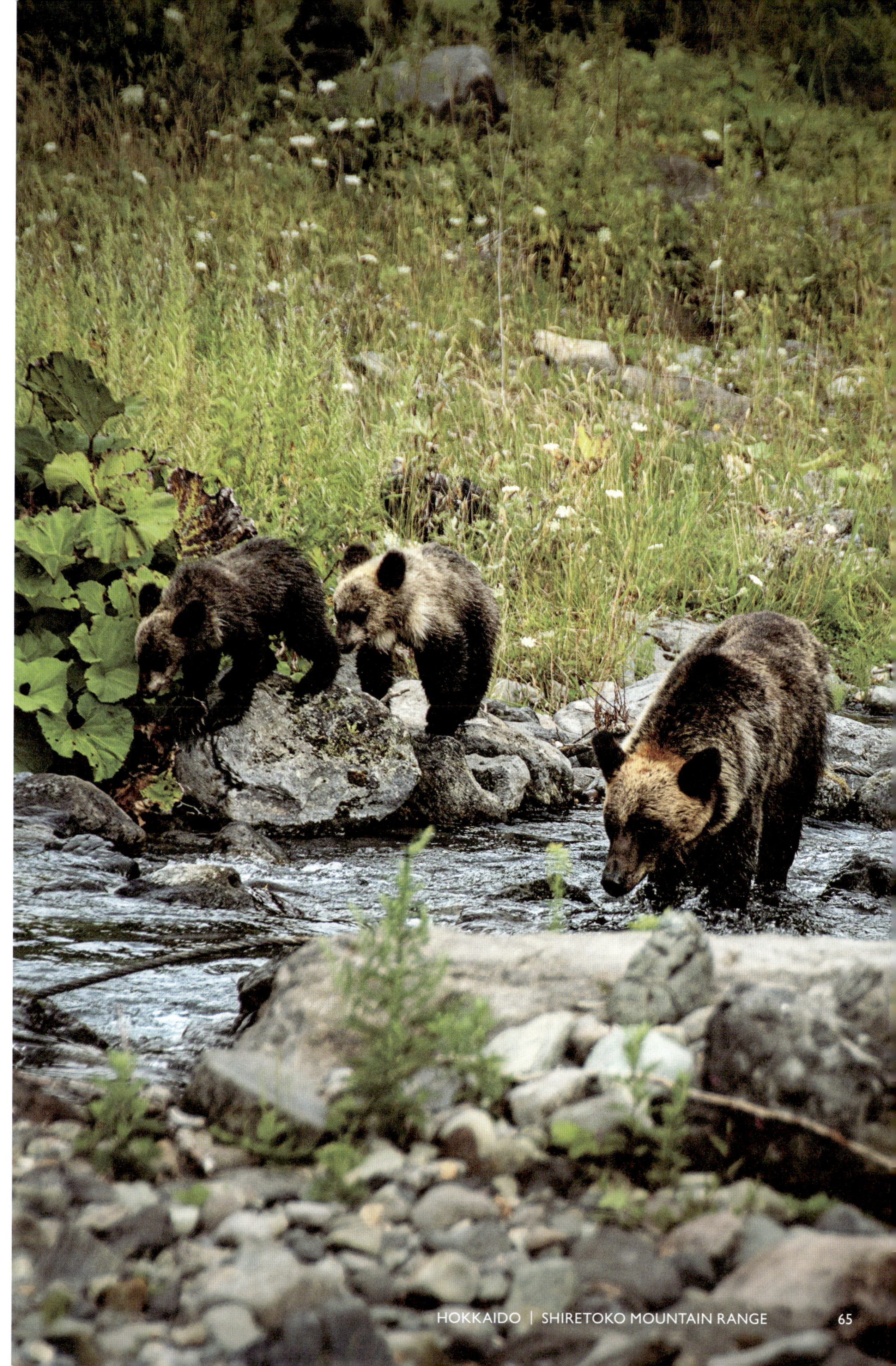

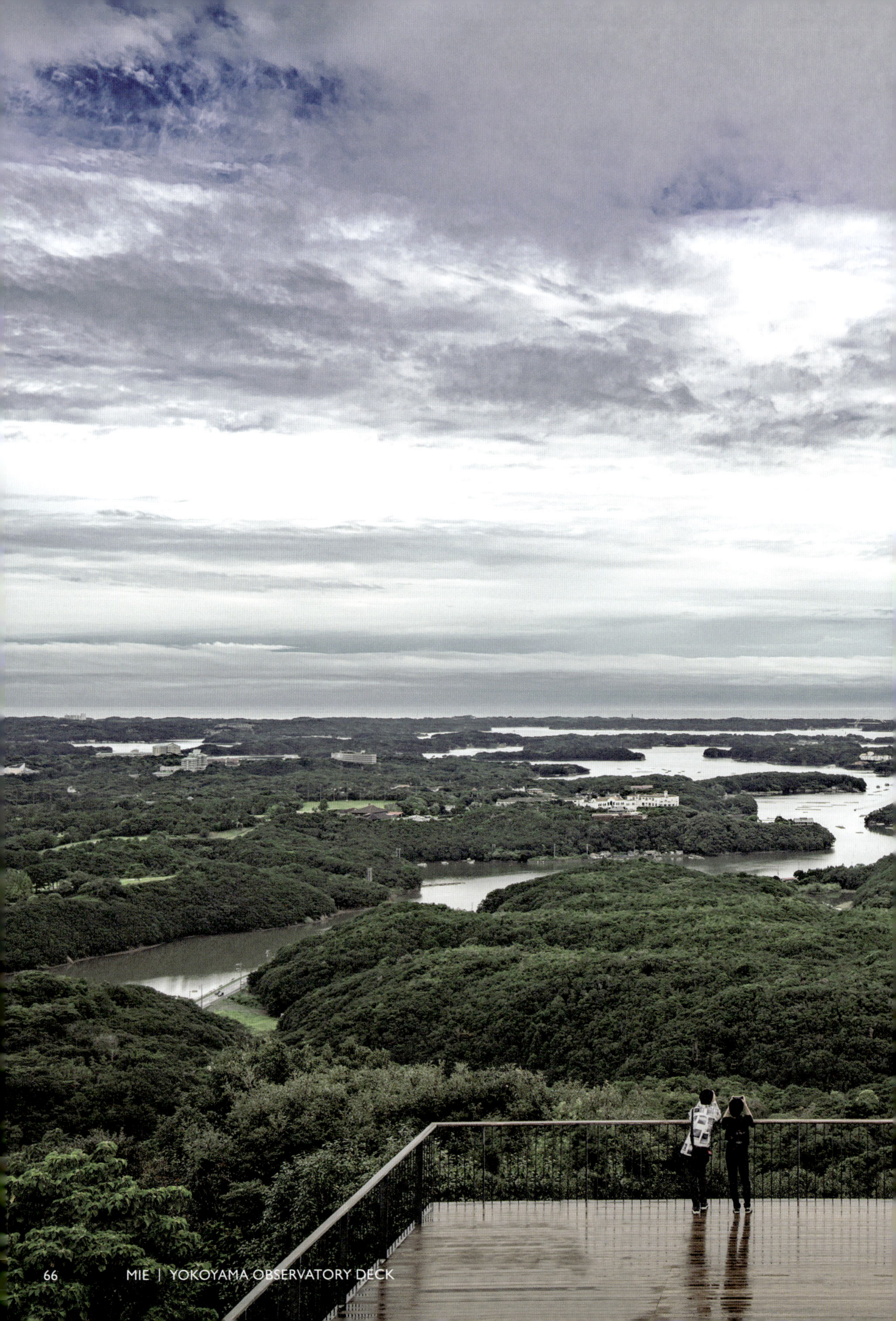

MIE | YOKOYAMA OBSERVATORY DECK

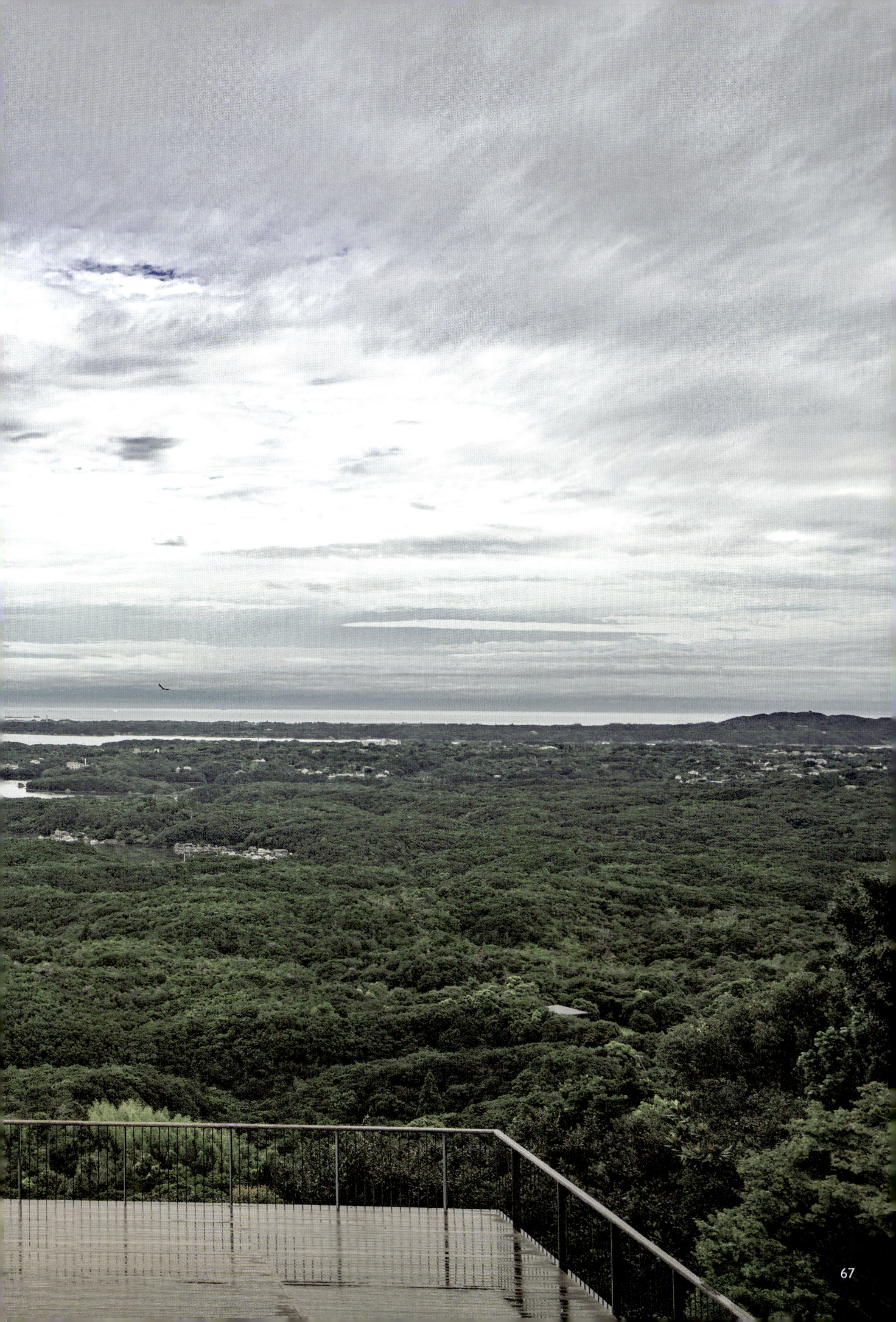

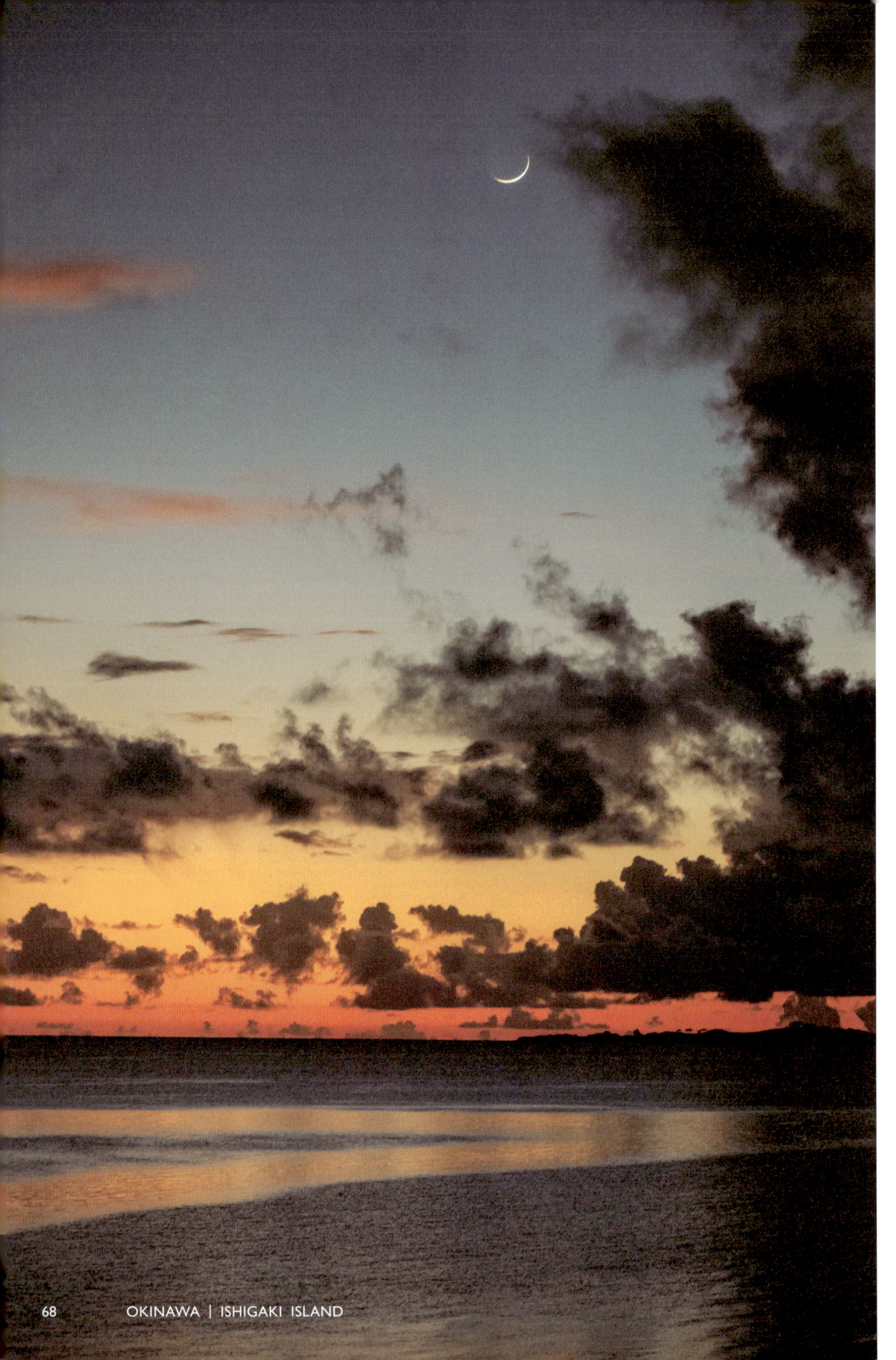

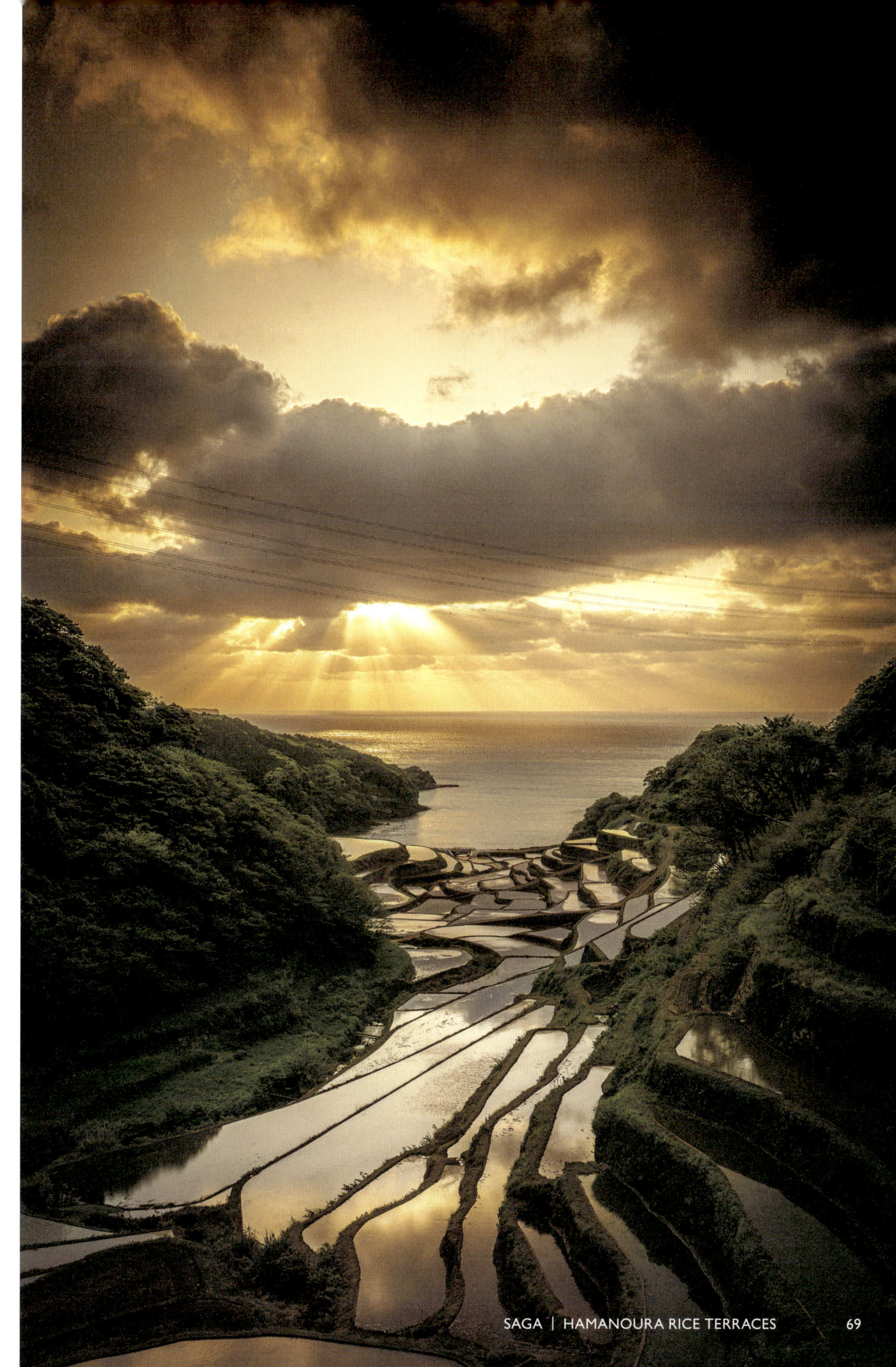

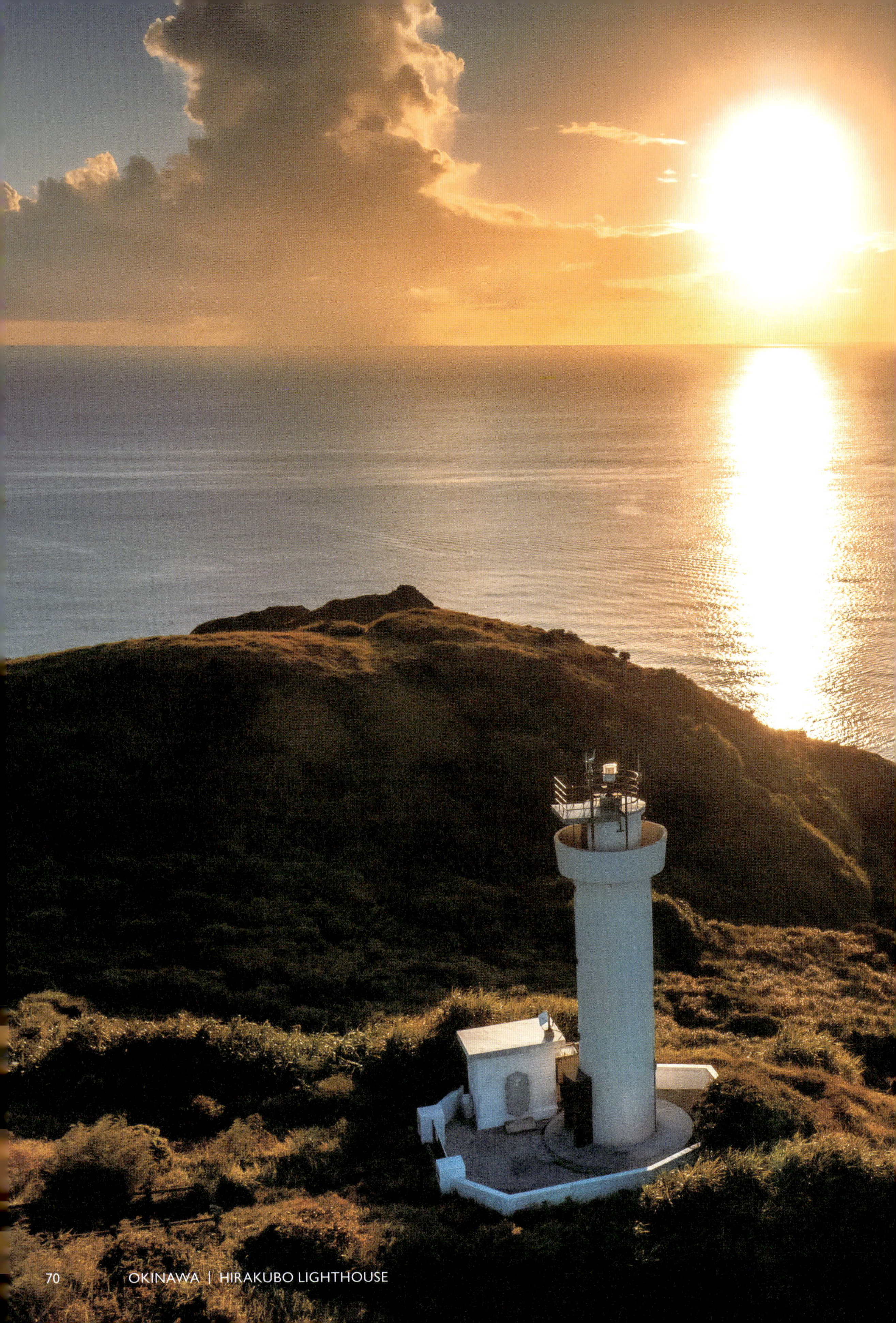

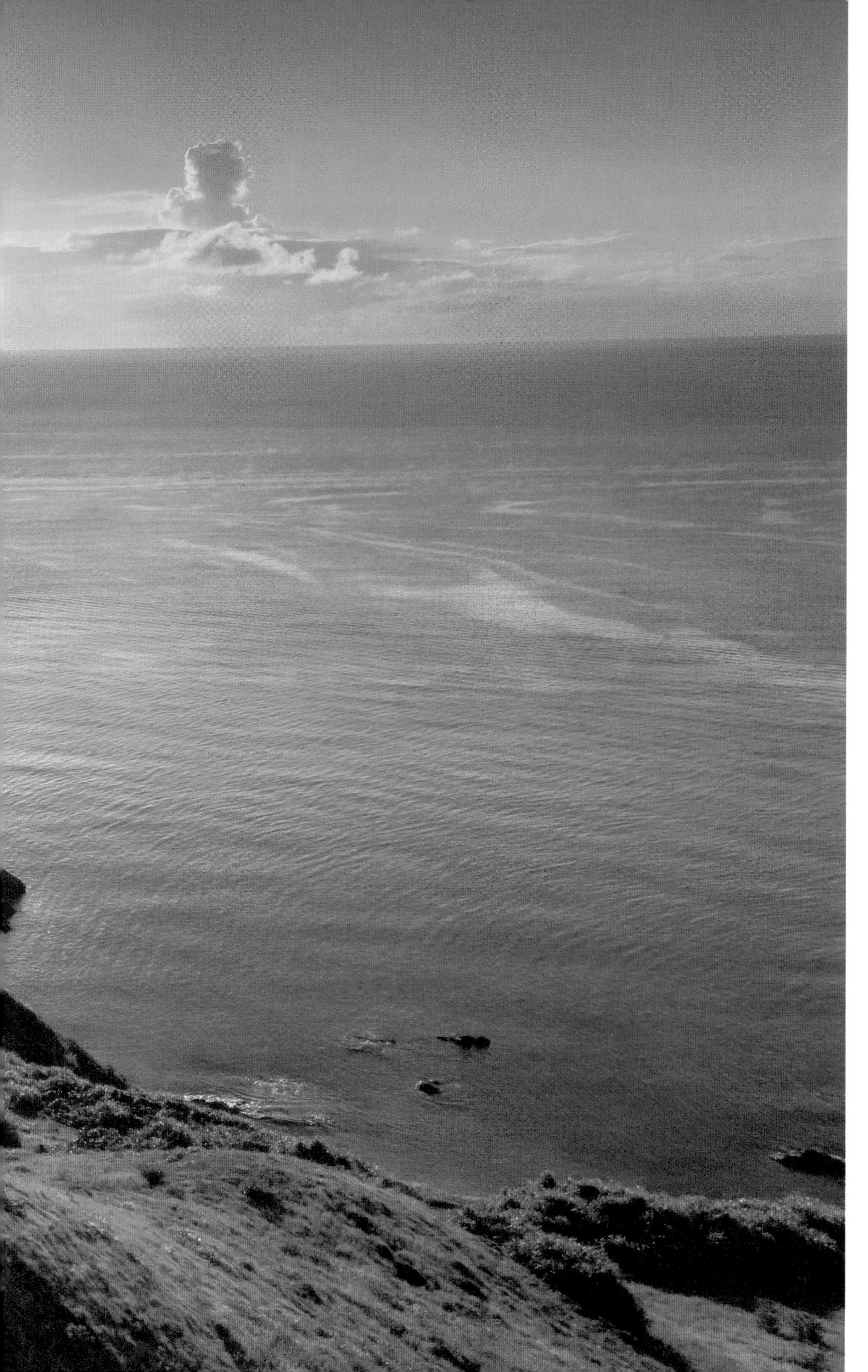

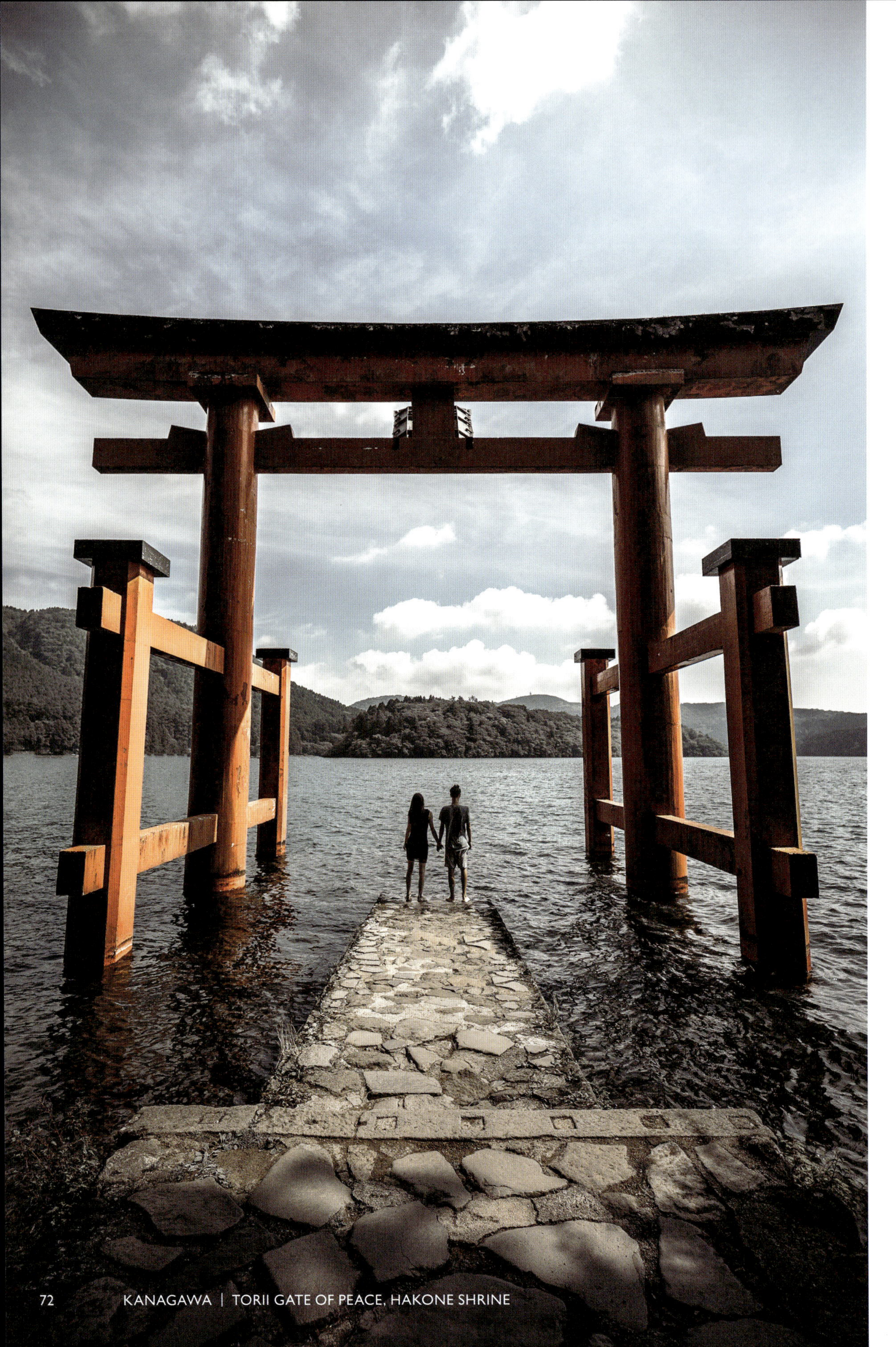

  KANAGAWA | TORII GATE OF PEACE, HAKONE SHRINE

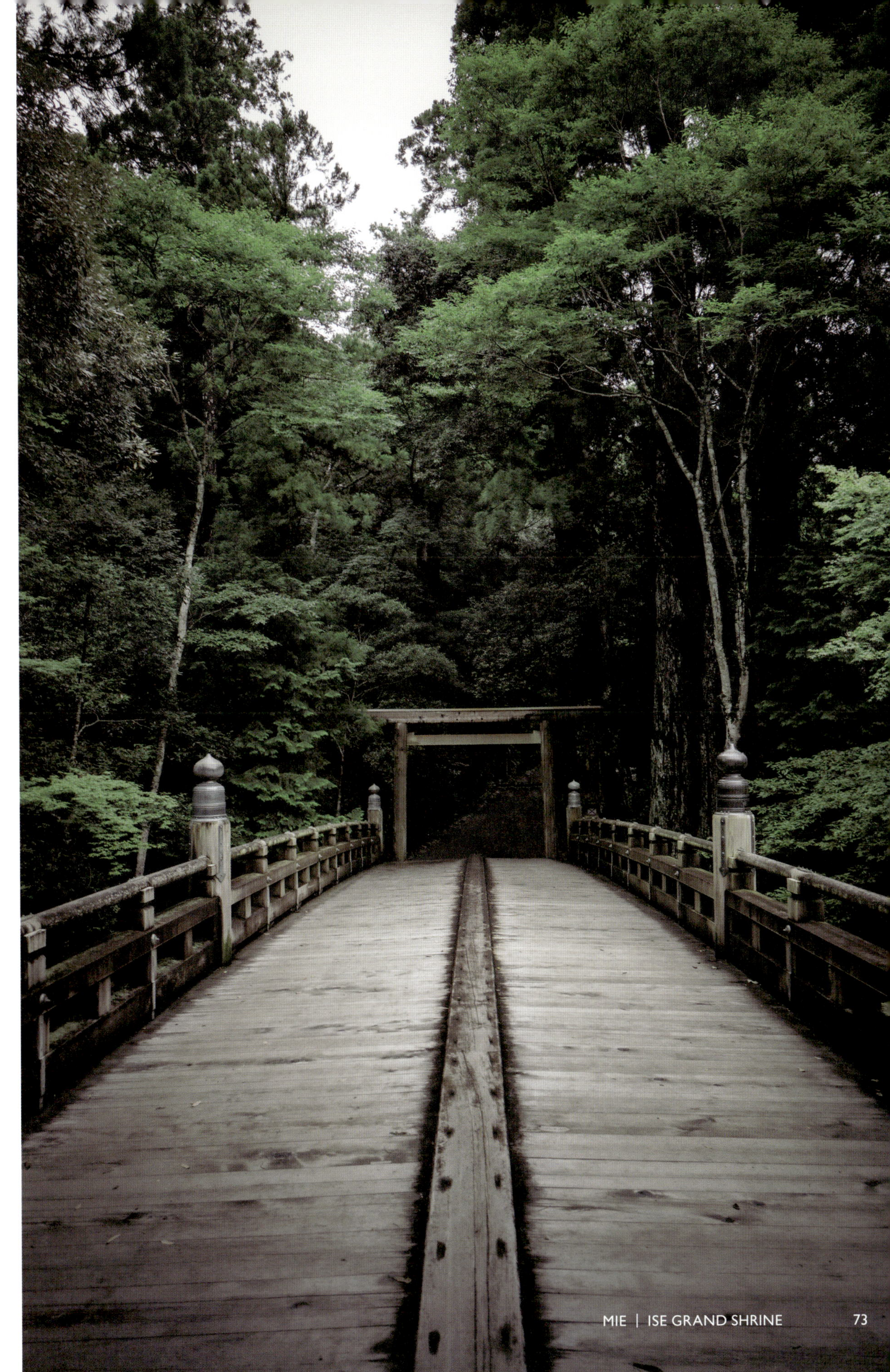

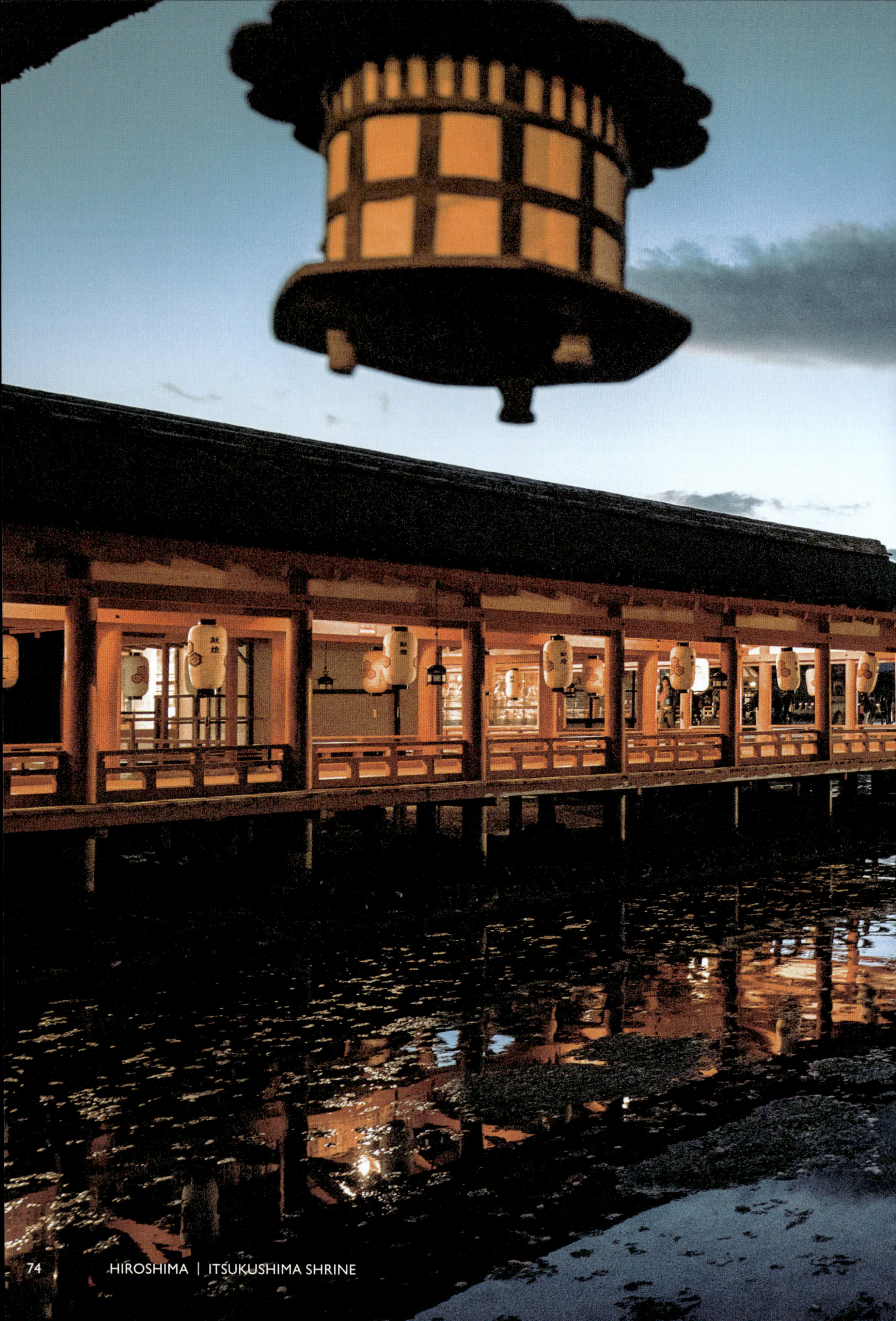

  HIROSHIMA | ITSUKUSHIMA SHRINE

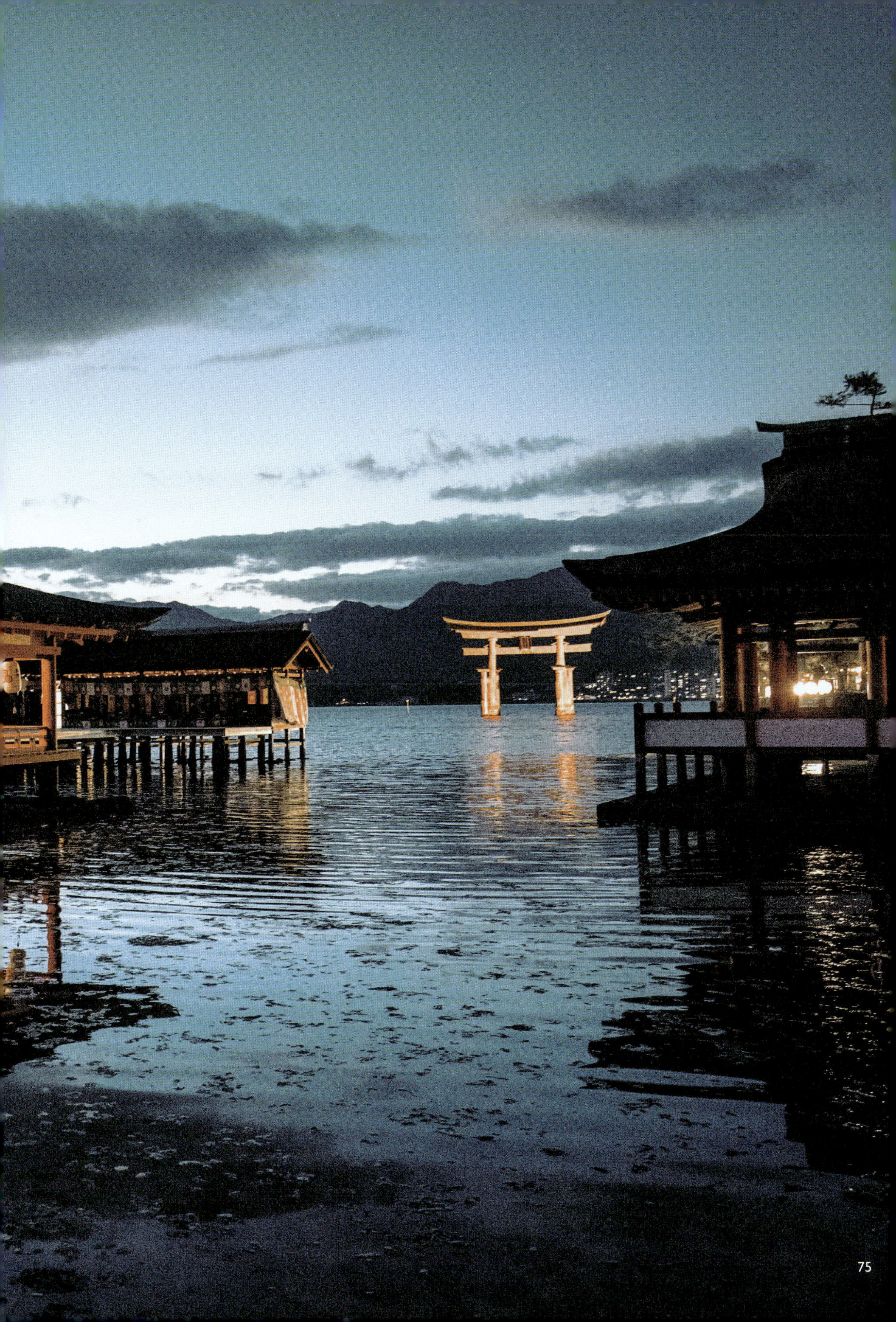

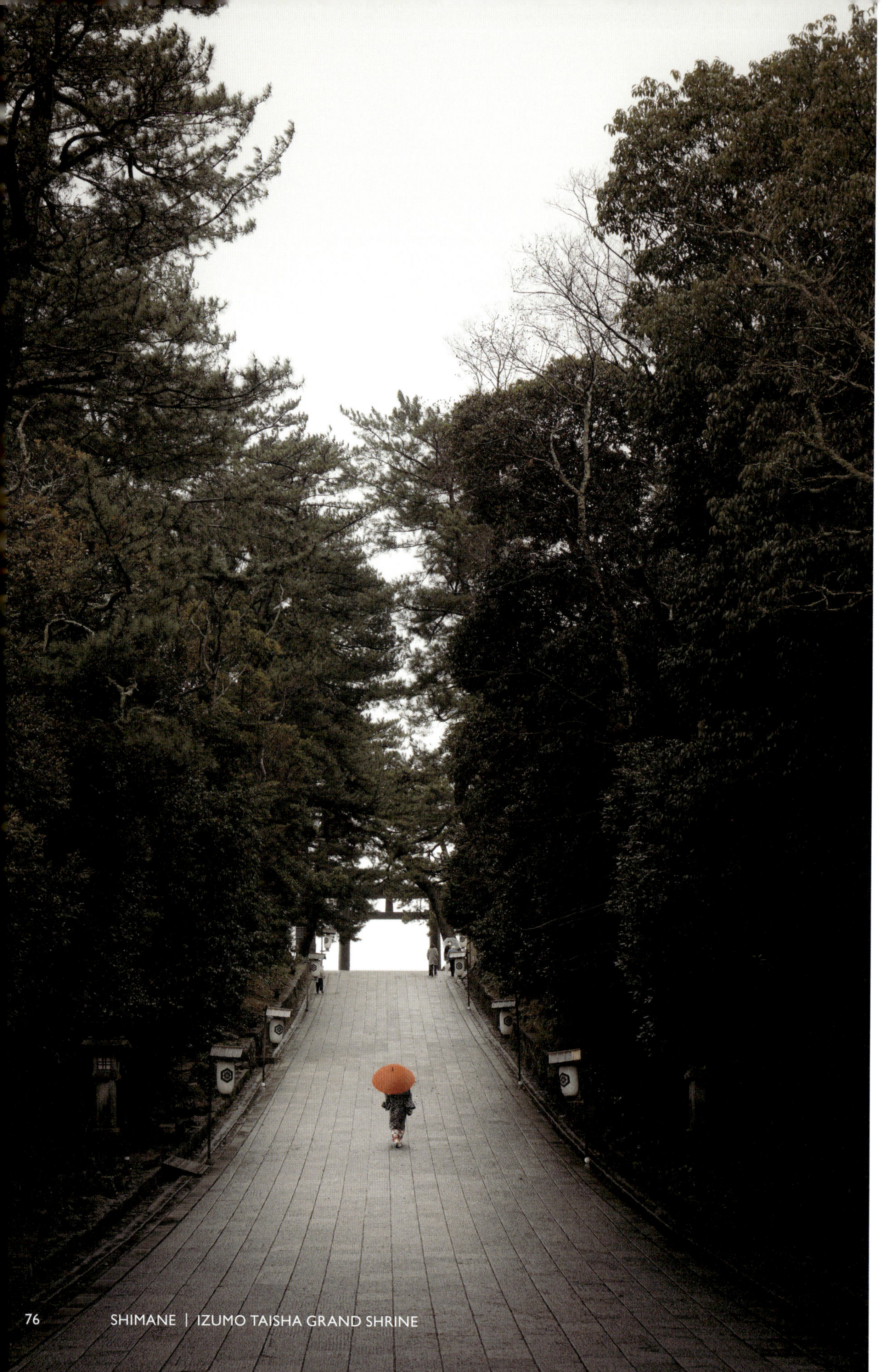

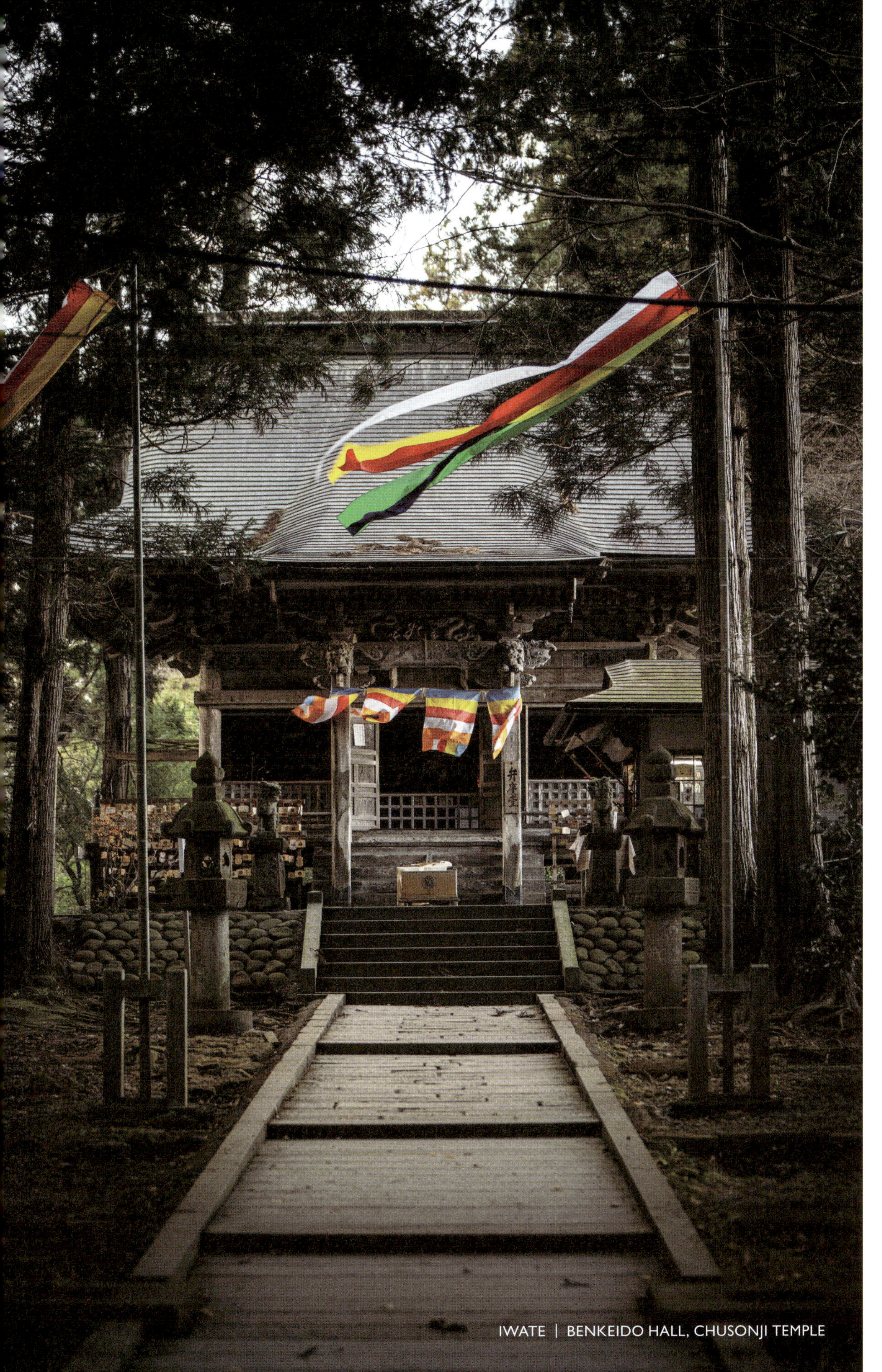

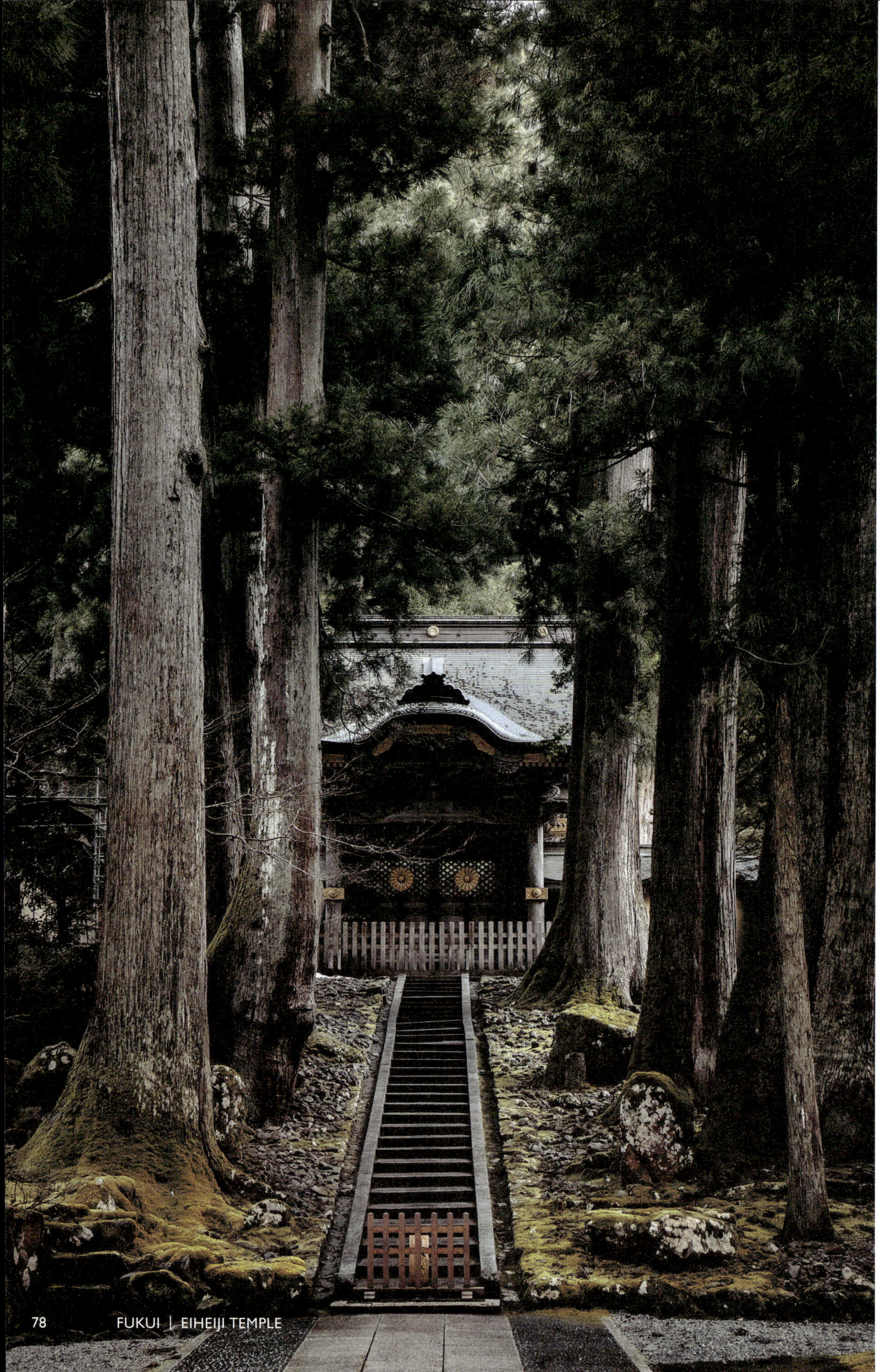

 FUKUI | EIHEIJI TEMPLE

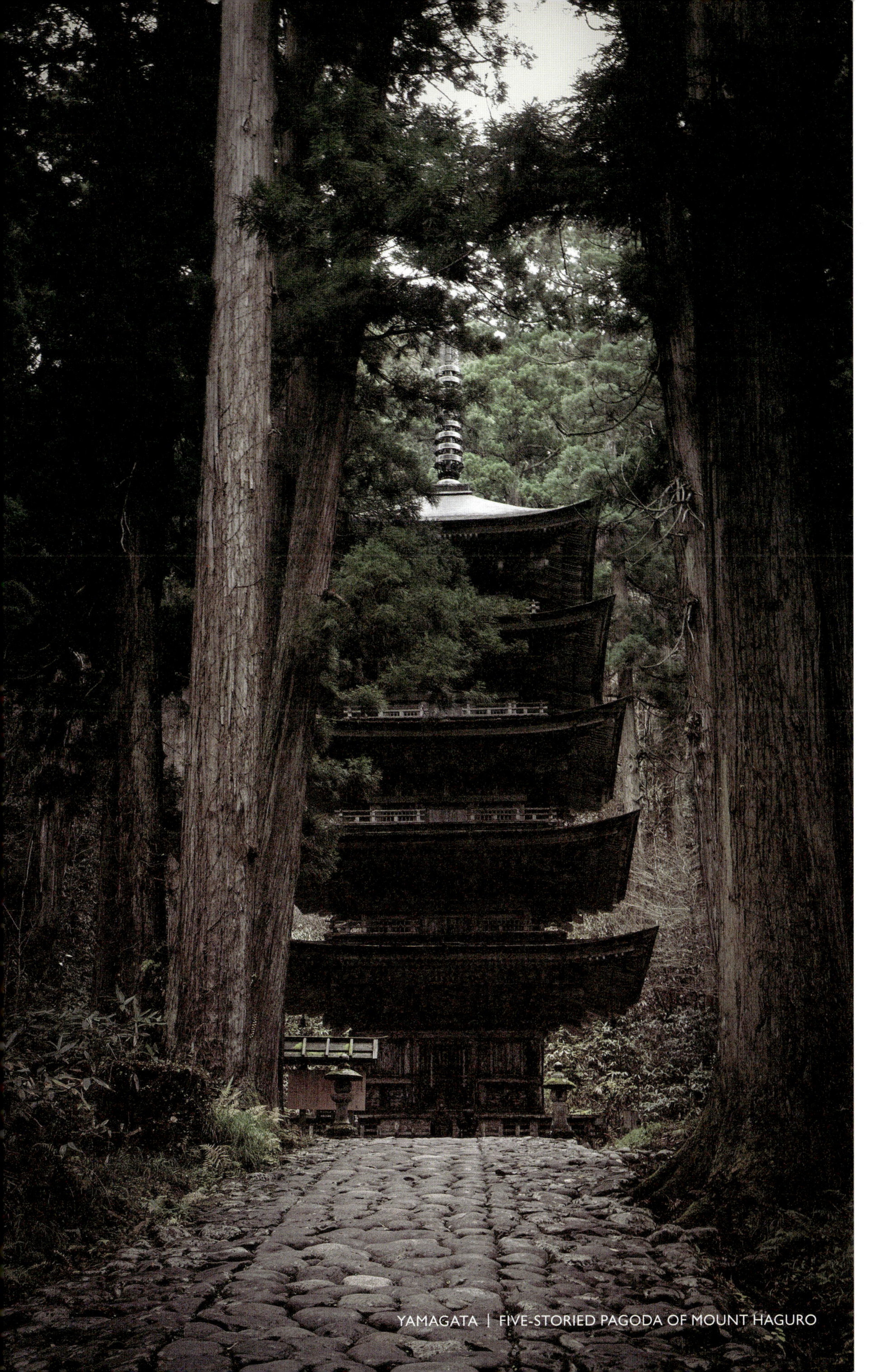

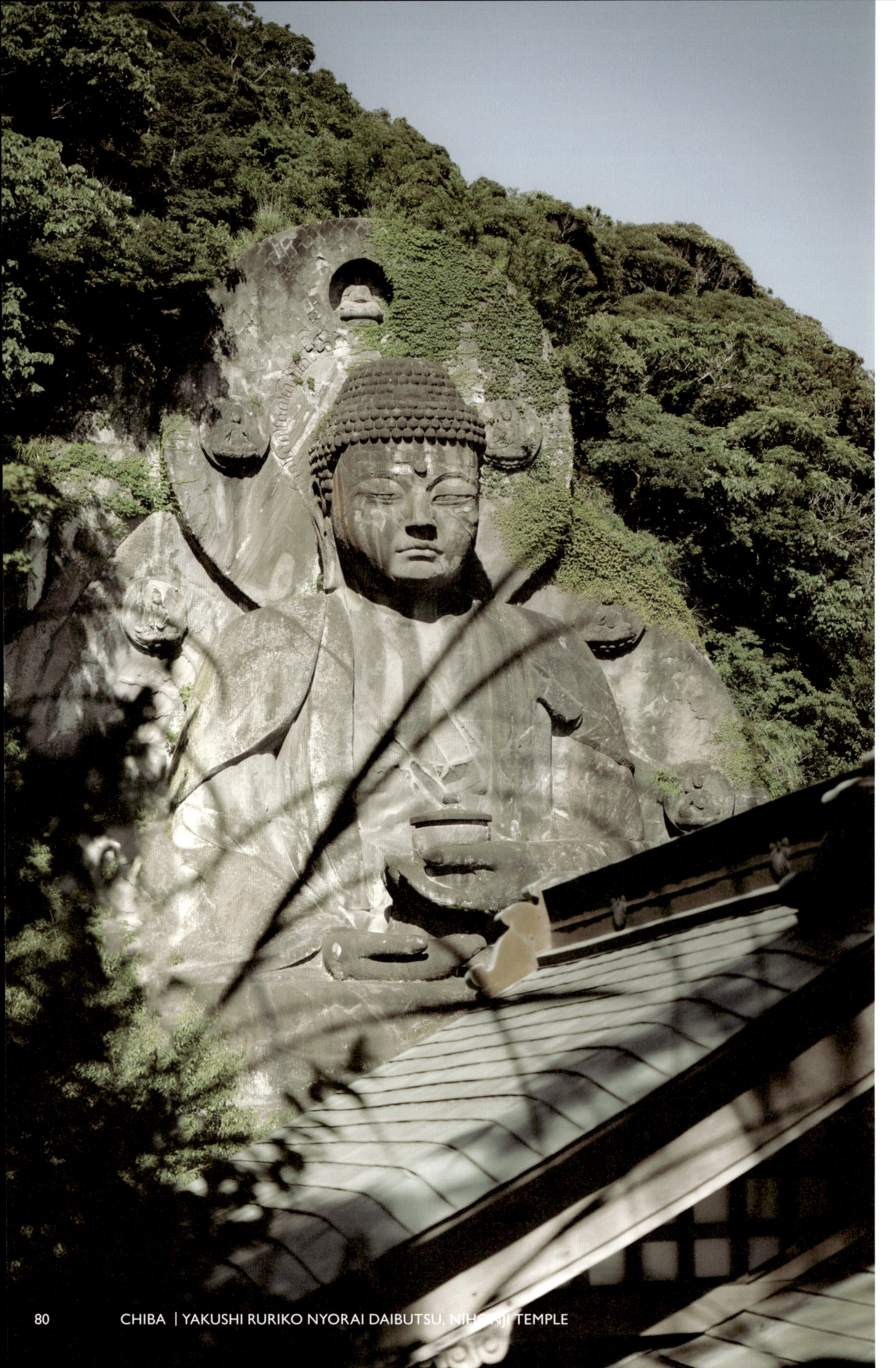

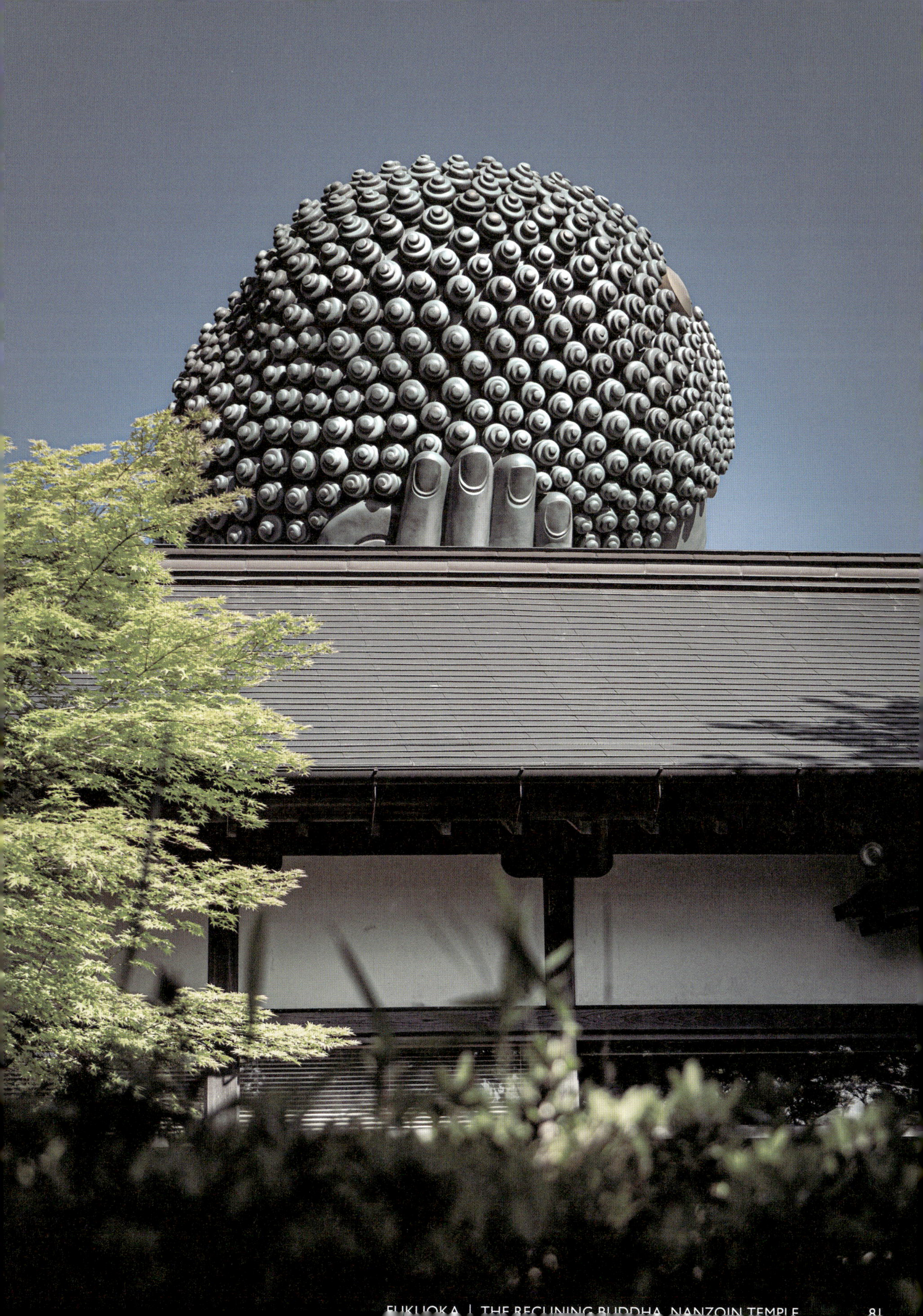

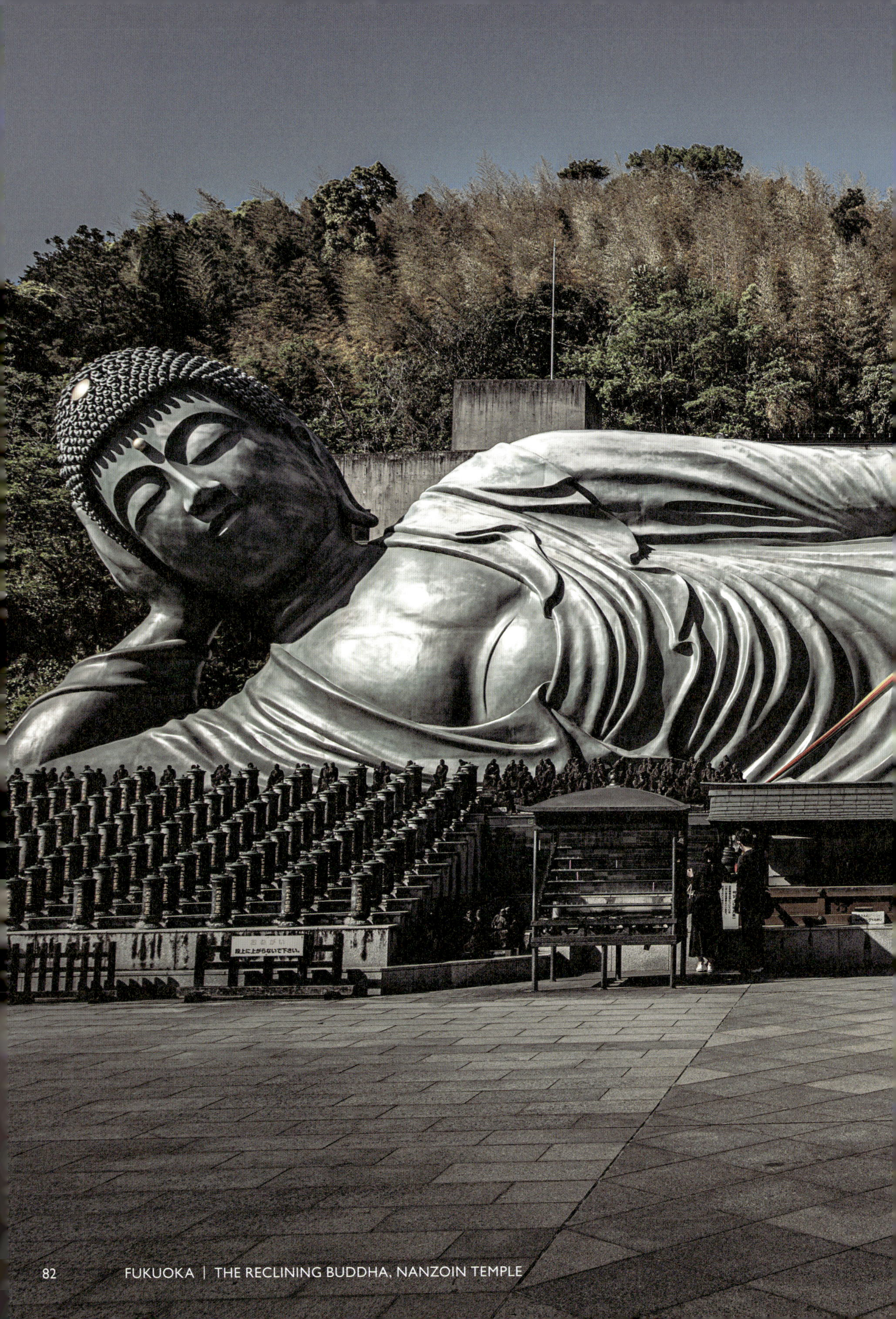

  FUKUOKA | THE RECLINING BUDDHA, NANZOIN TEMPLE

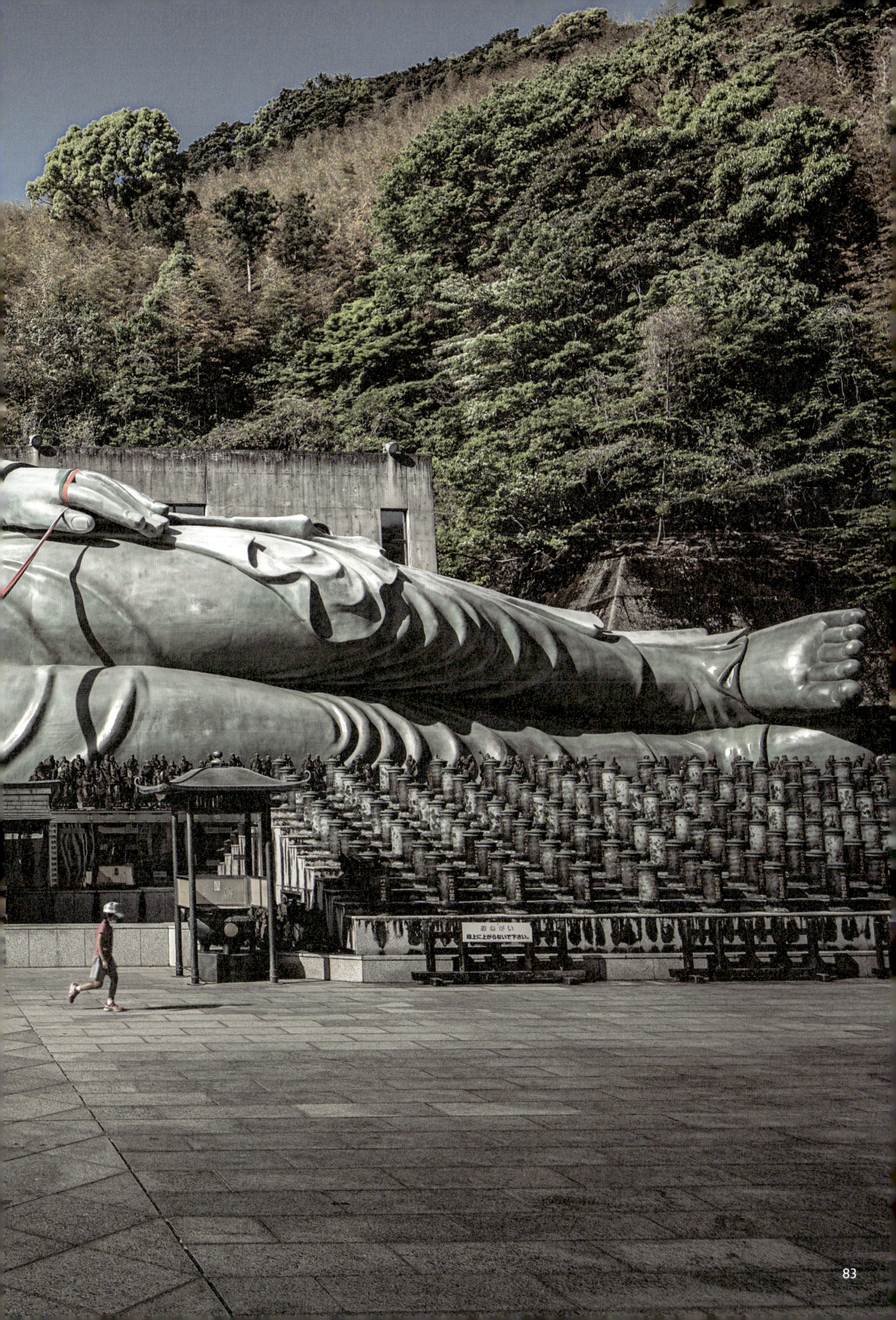
おねがい
壇上に上がらないで下さい。

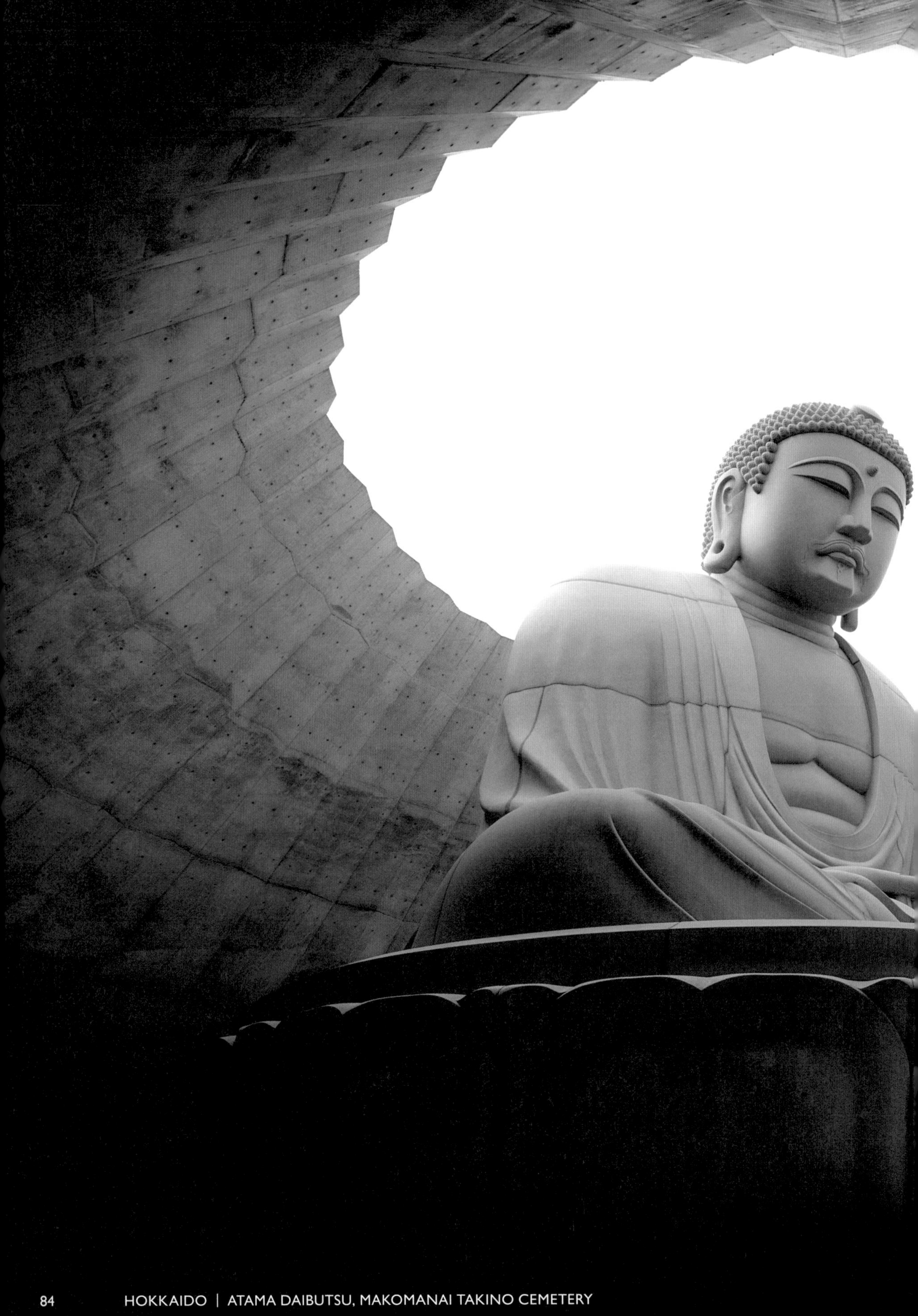

 HOKKAIDO | ATAMA DAIBUTSU, MAKOMANAI TAKINO CEMETERY

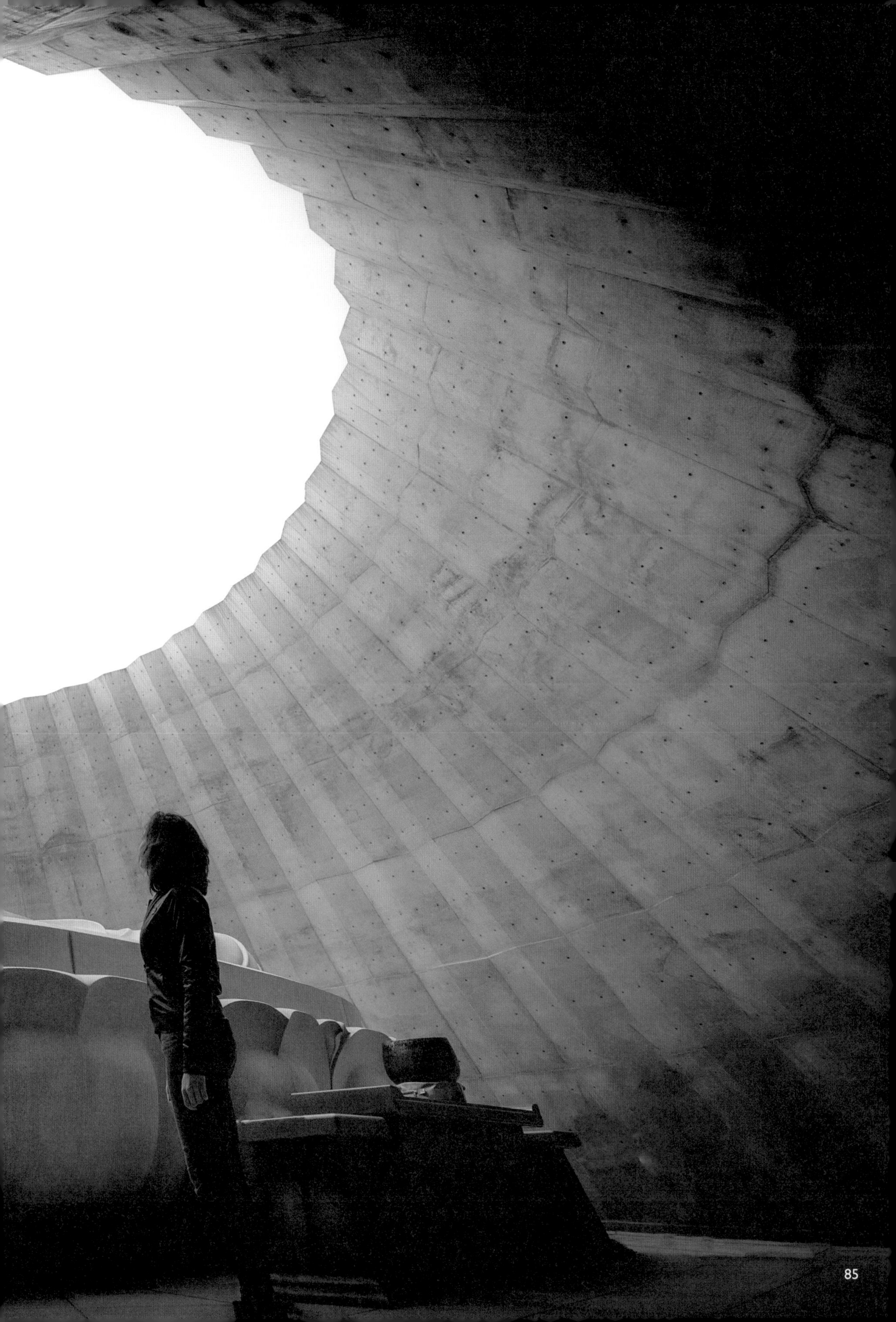

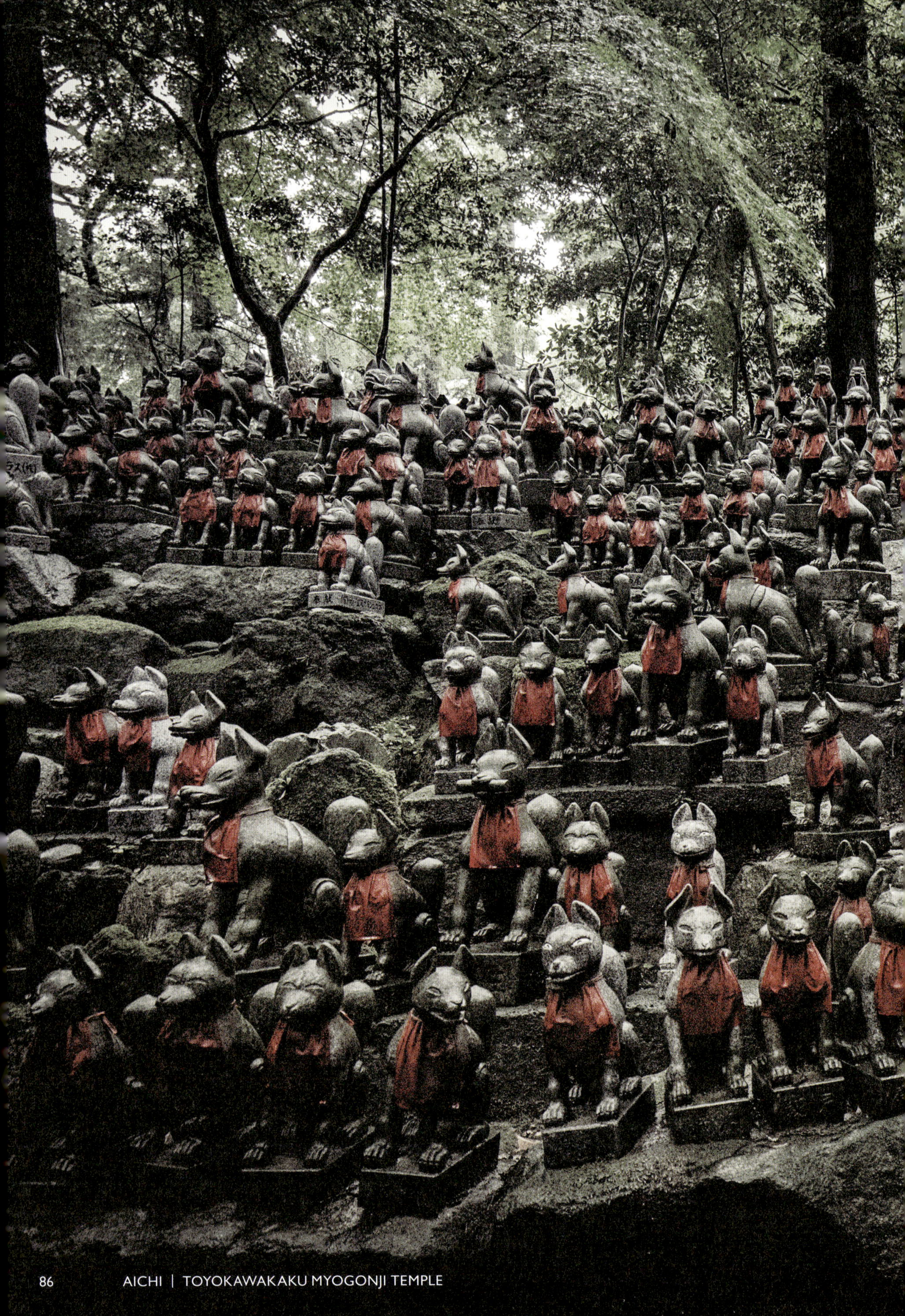

   AICHI | TOYOKAWAKAKU MYOGONJI TEMPLE

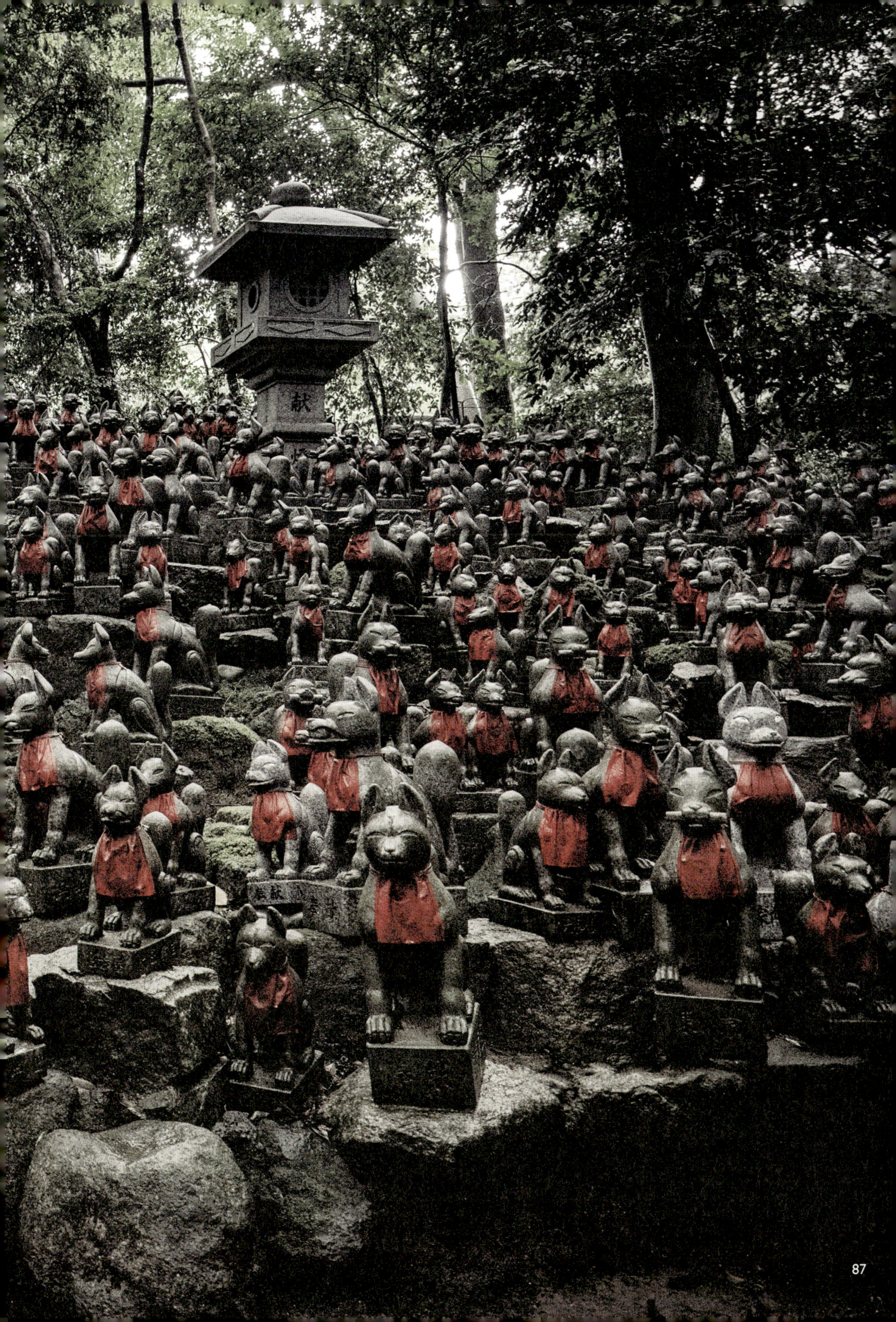

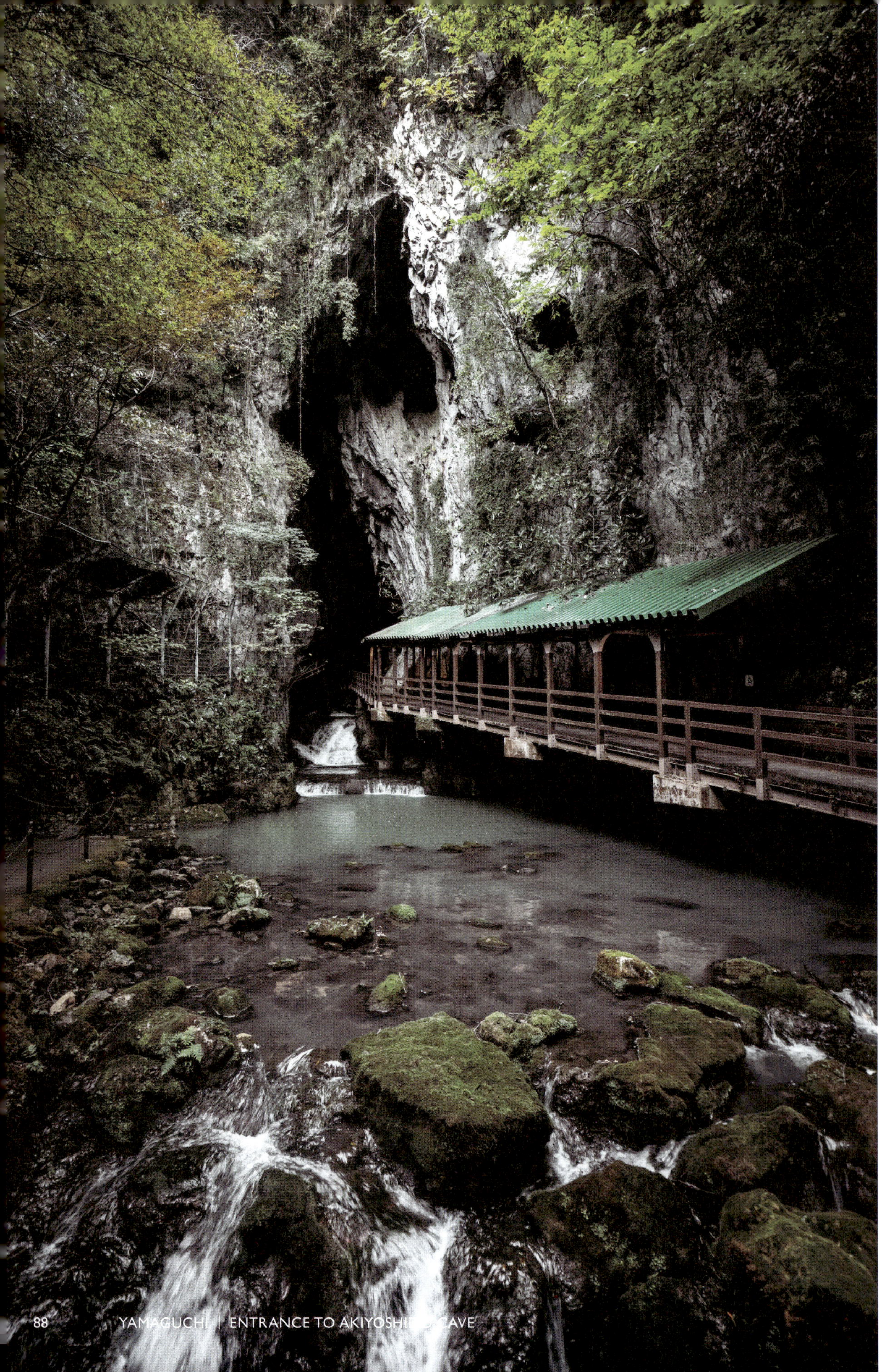

 YAMAGUCHI | ENTRANCE TO AKIYOSHIDO CAVE

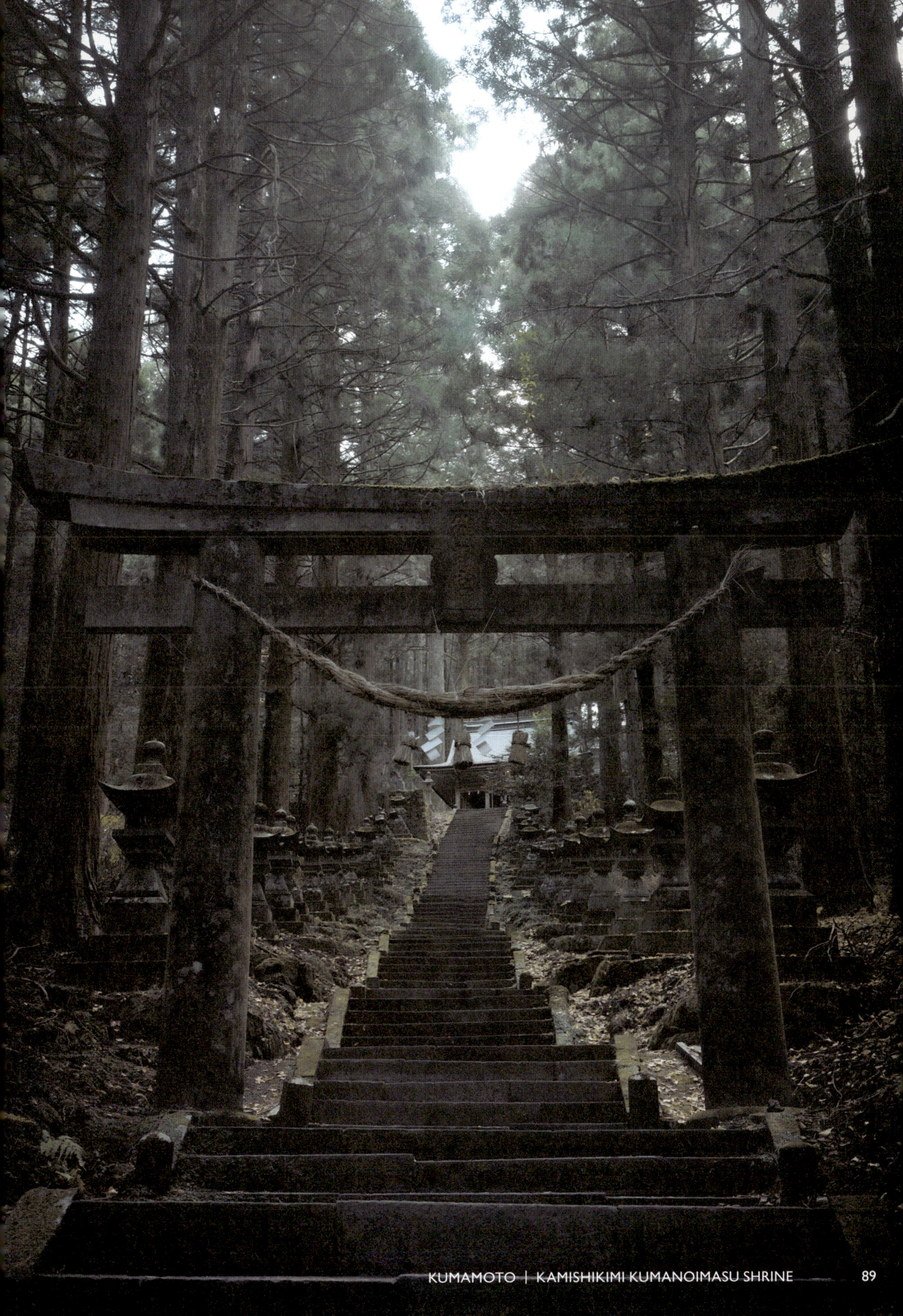

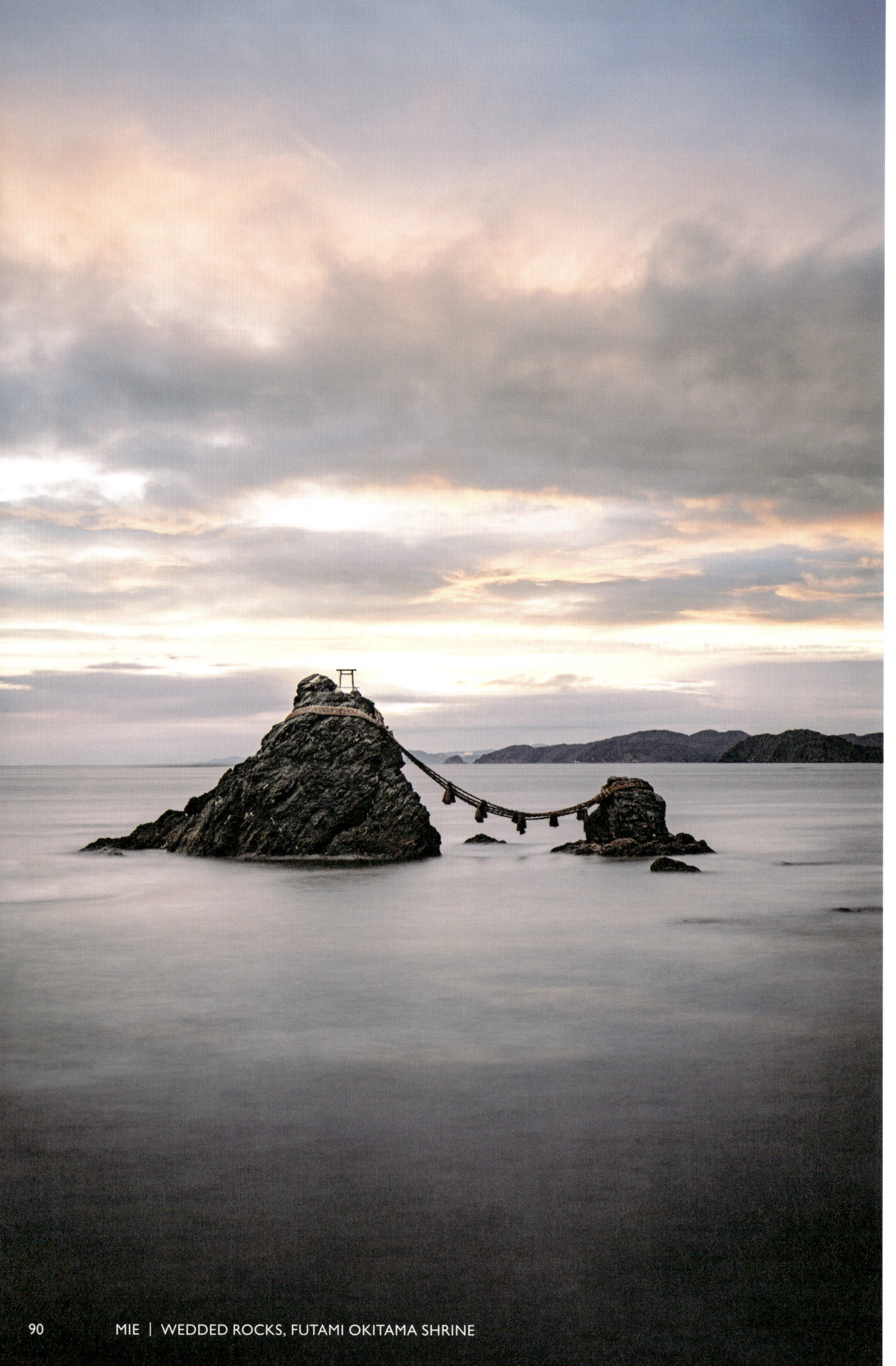

     MIE | WEDDED ROCKS, FUTAMI OKITAMA SHRINE

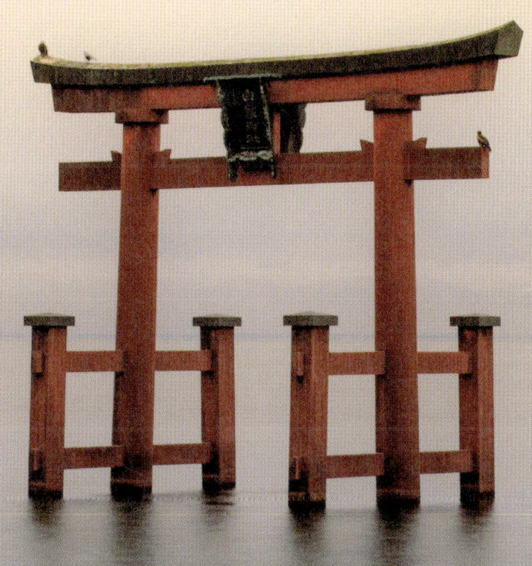

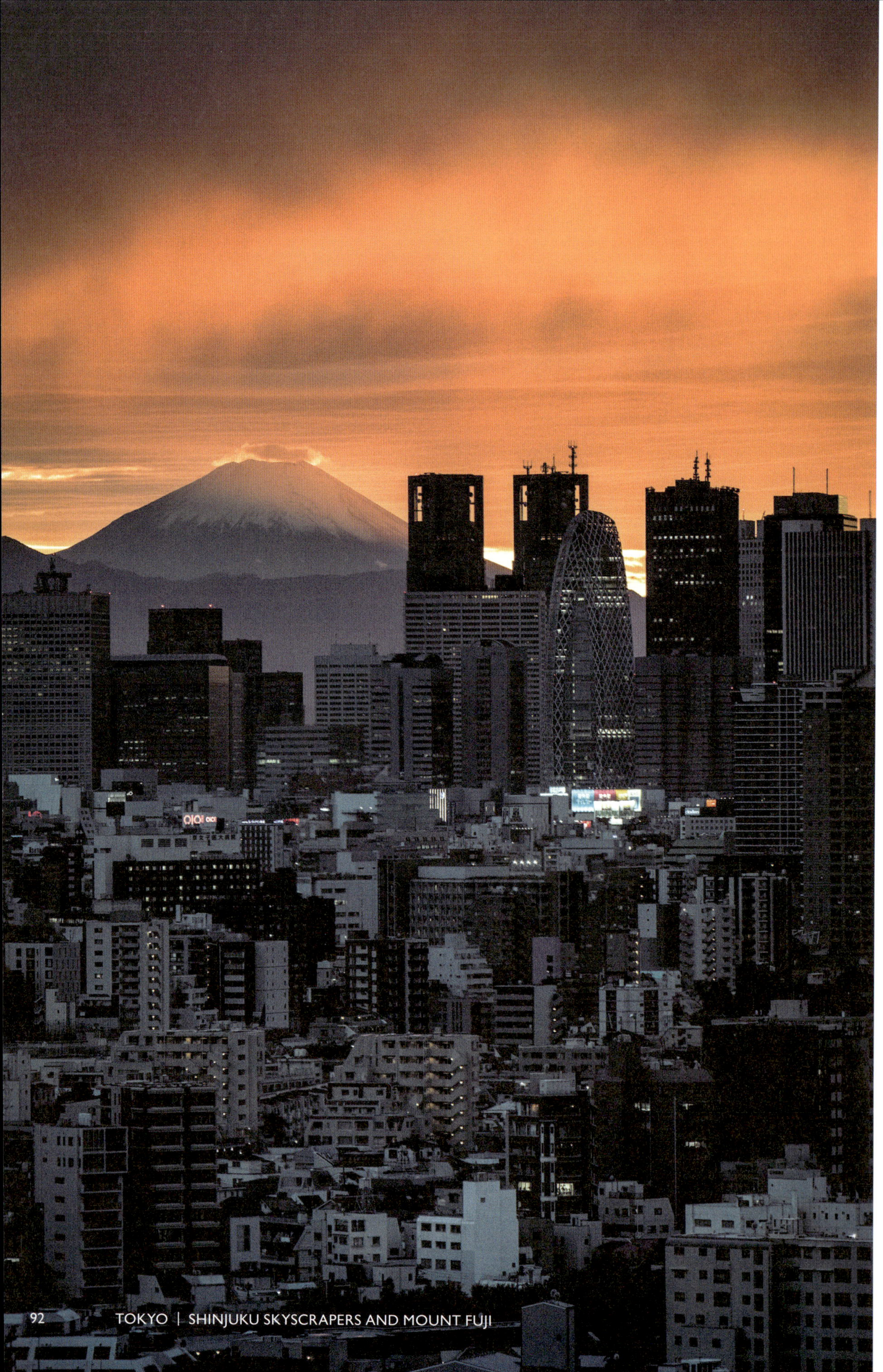

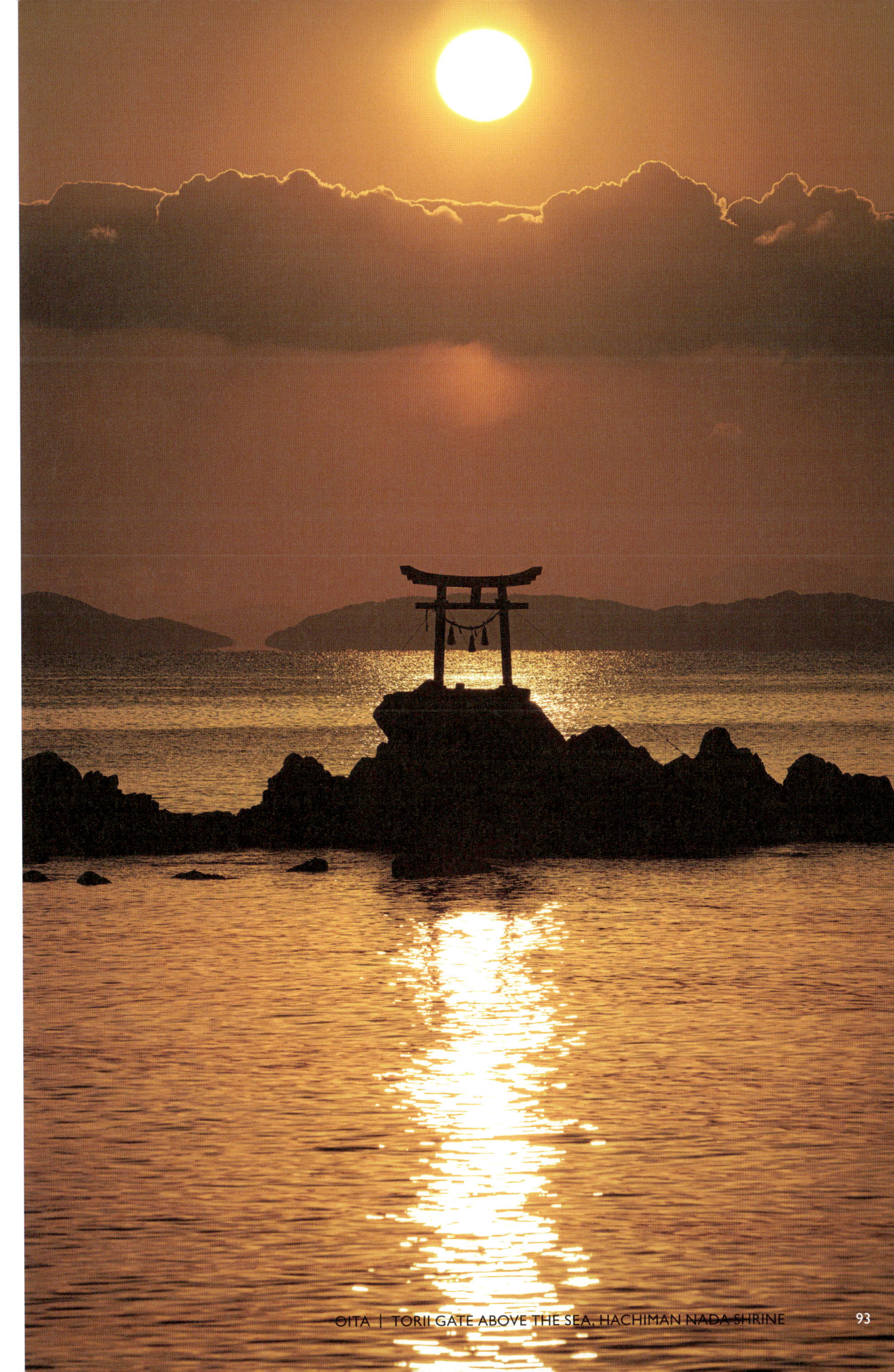

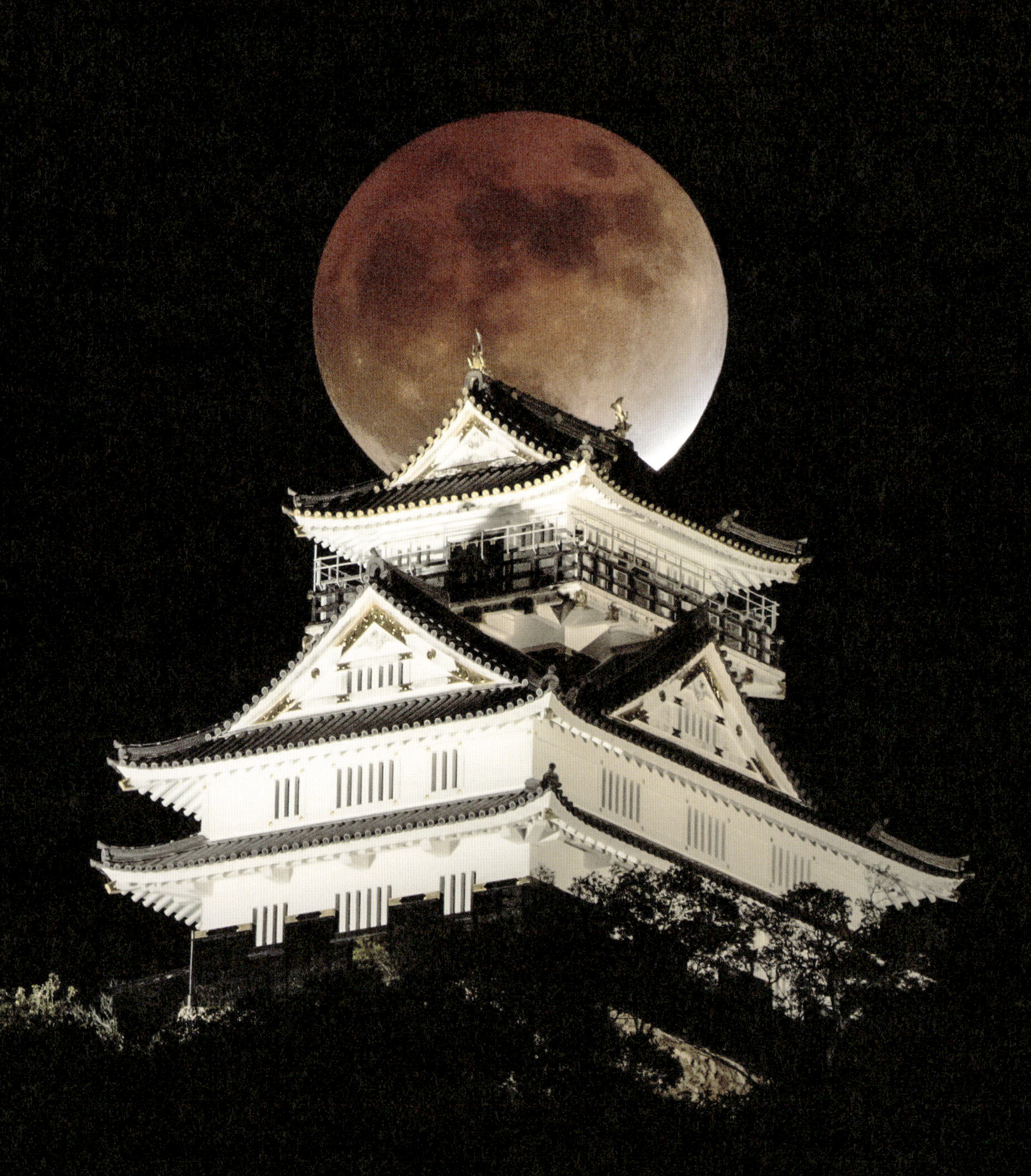

    GIFU | GIFU CASTLE

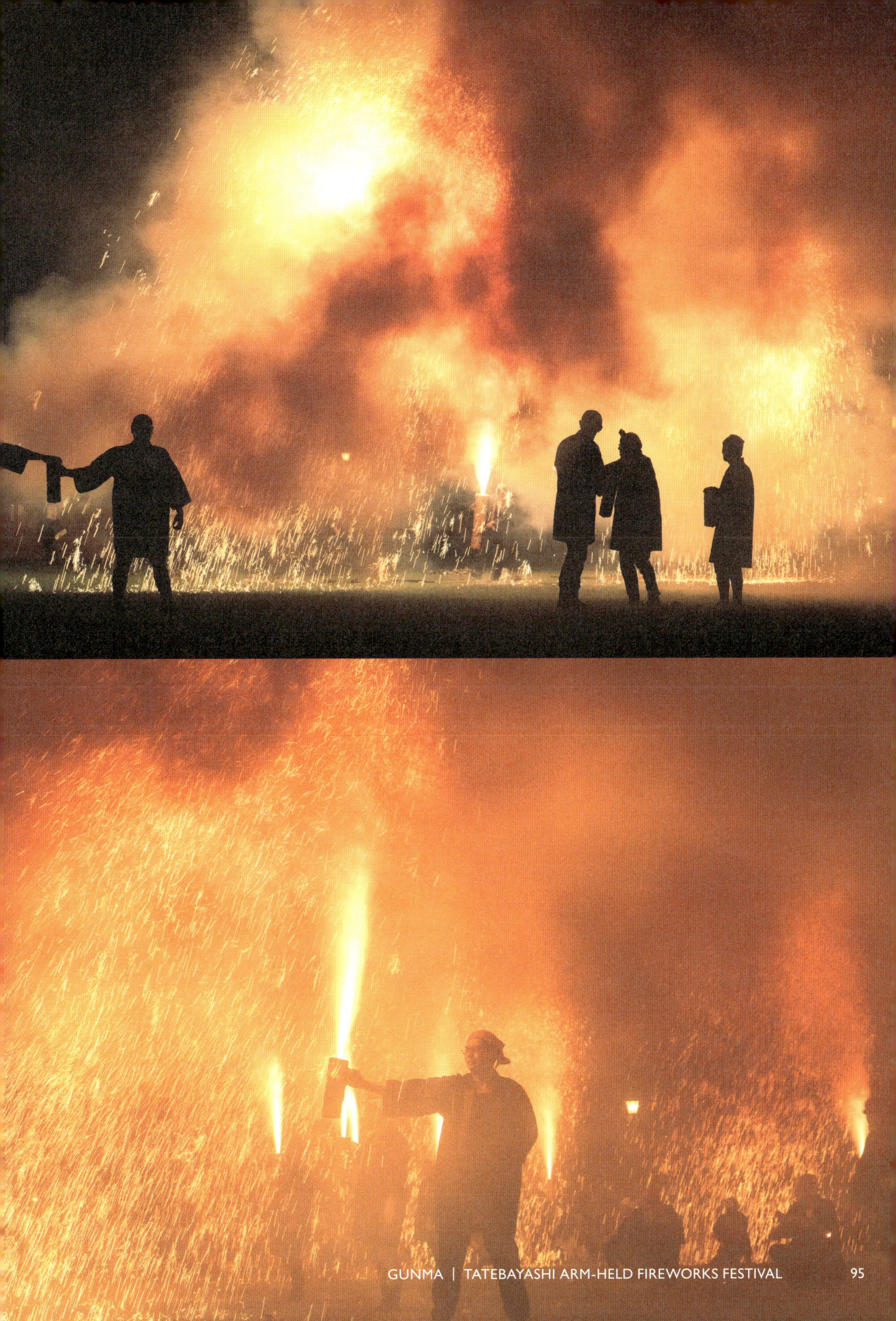

AUTUMN

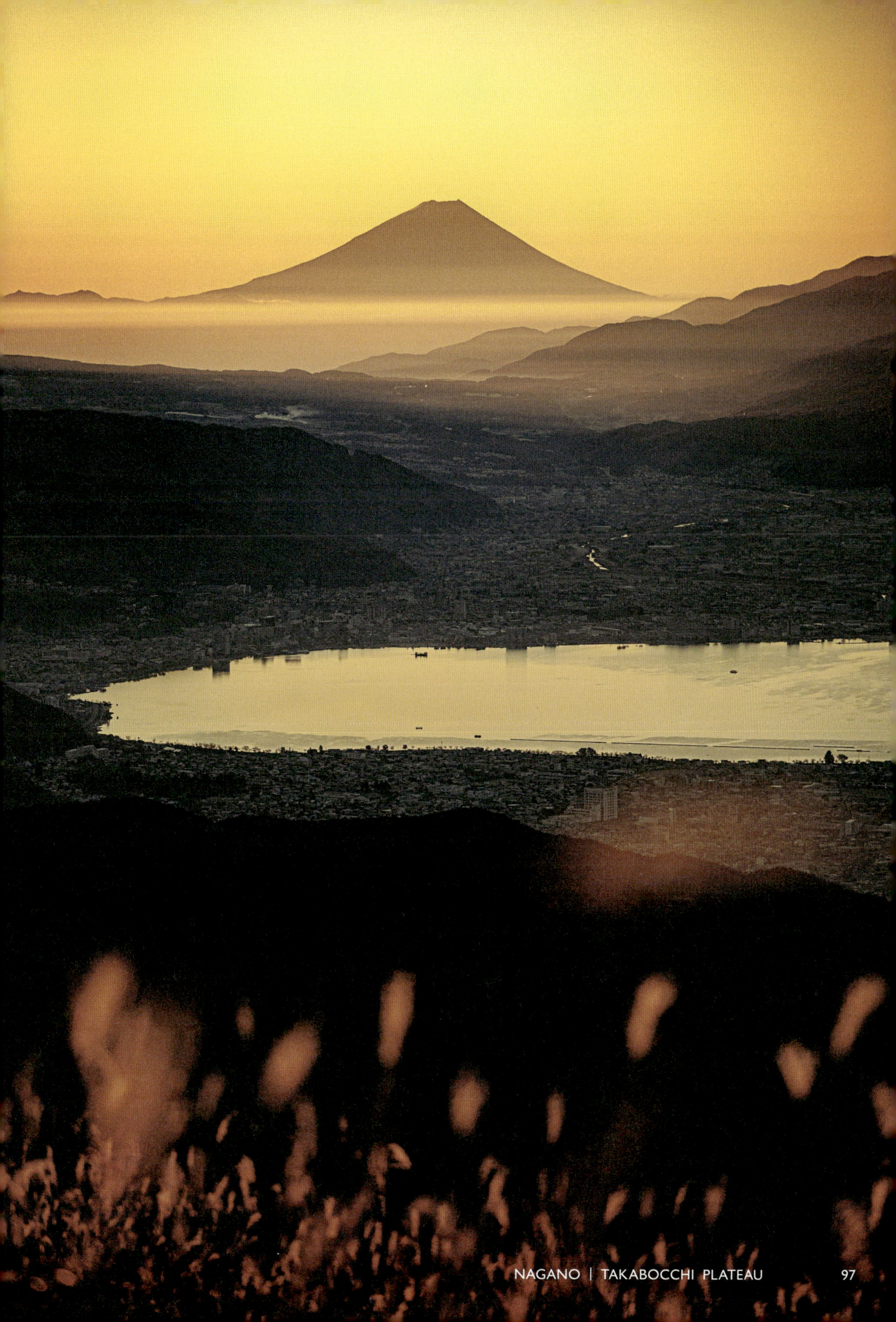

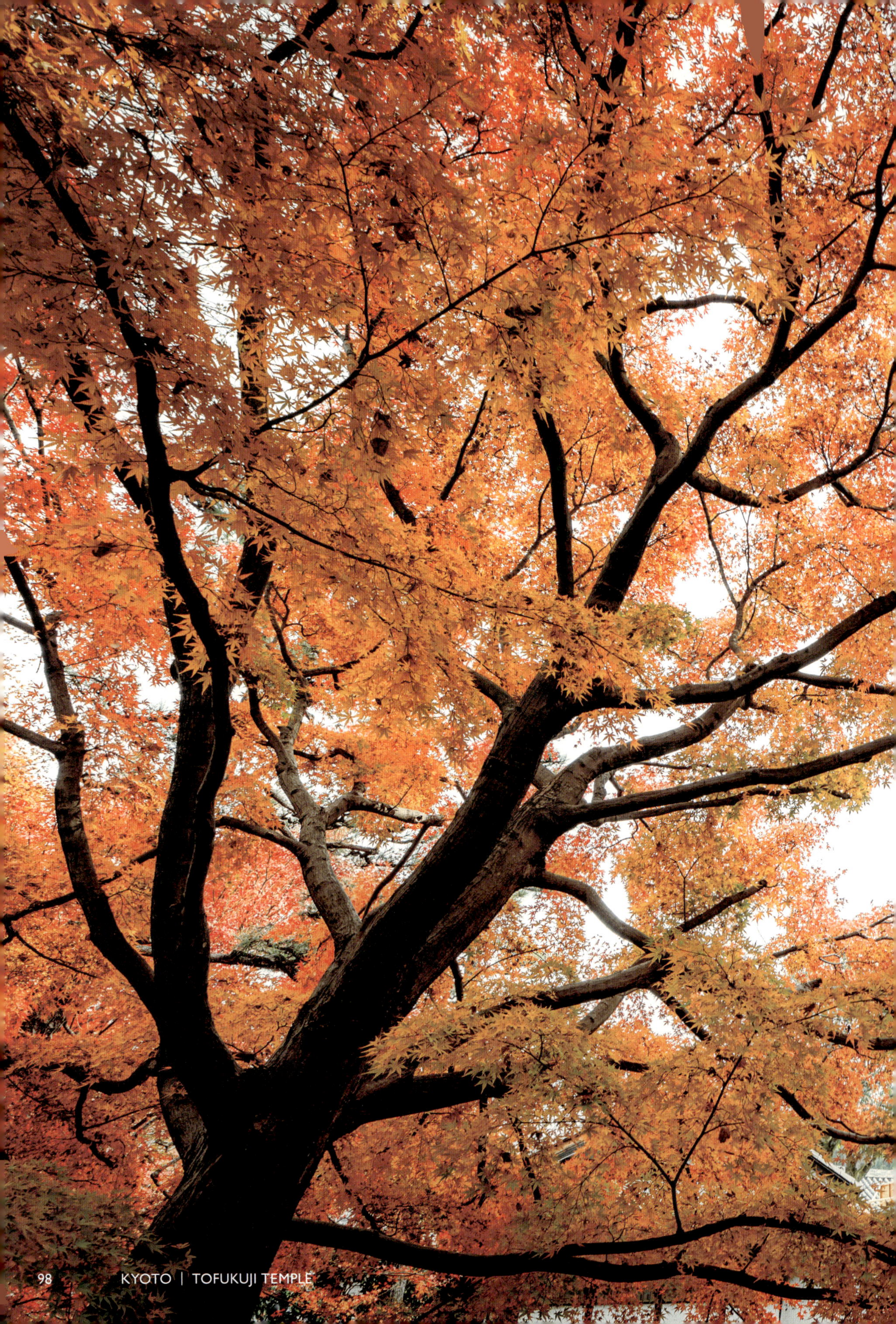

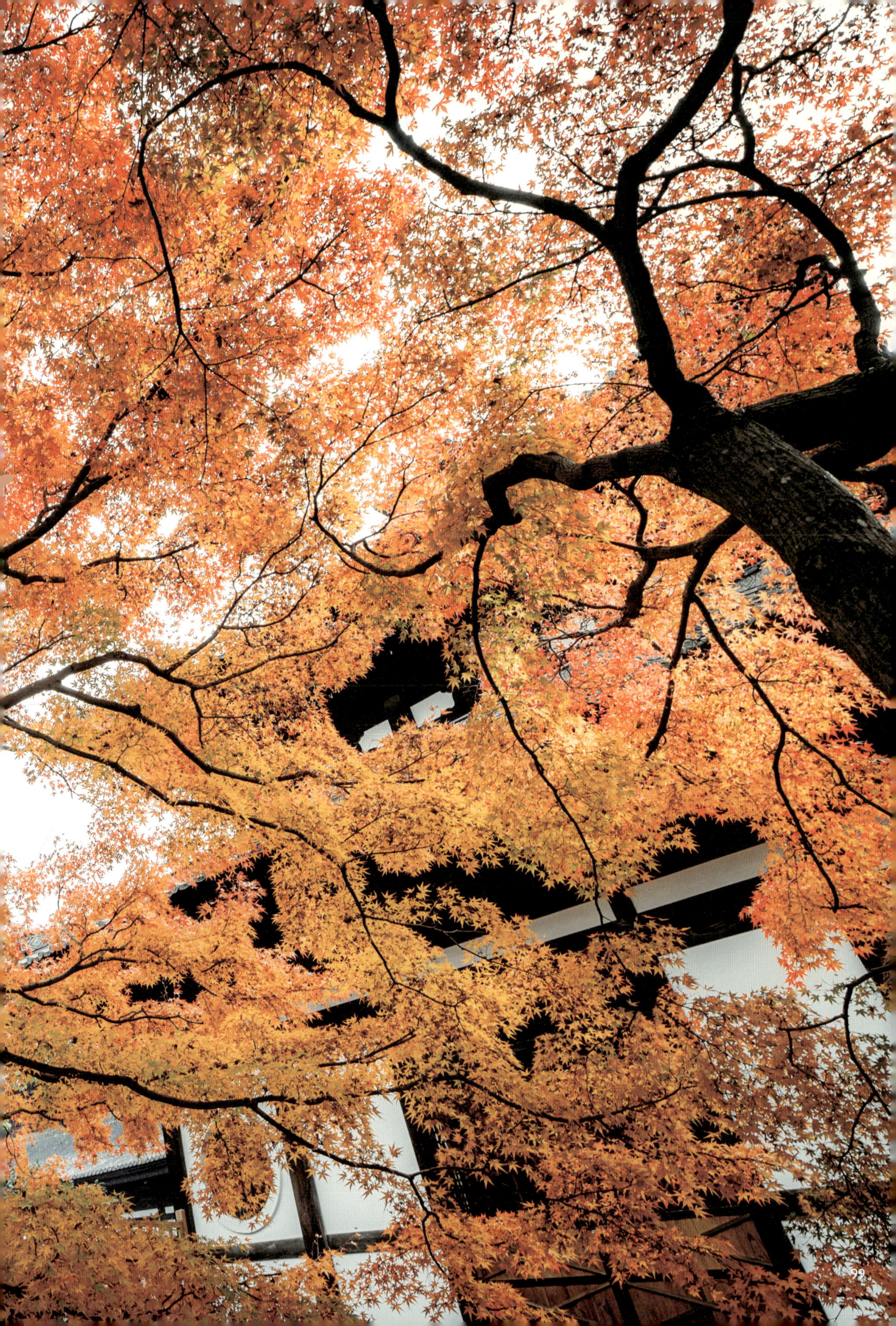

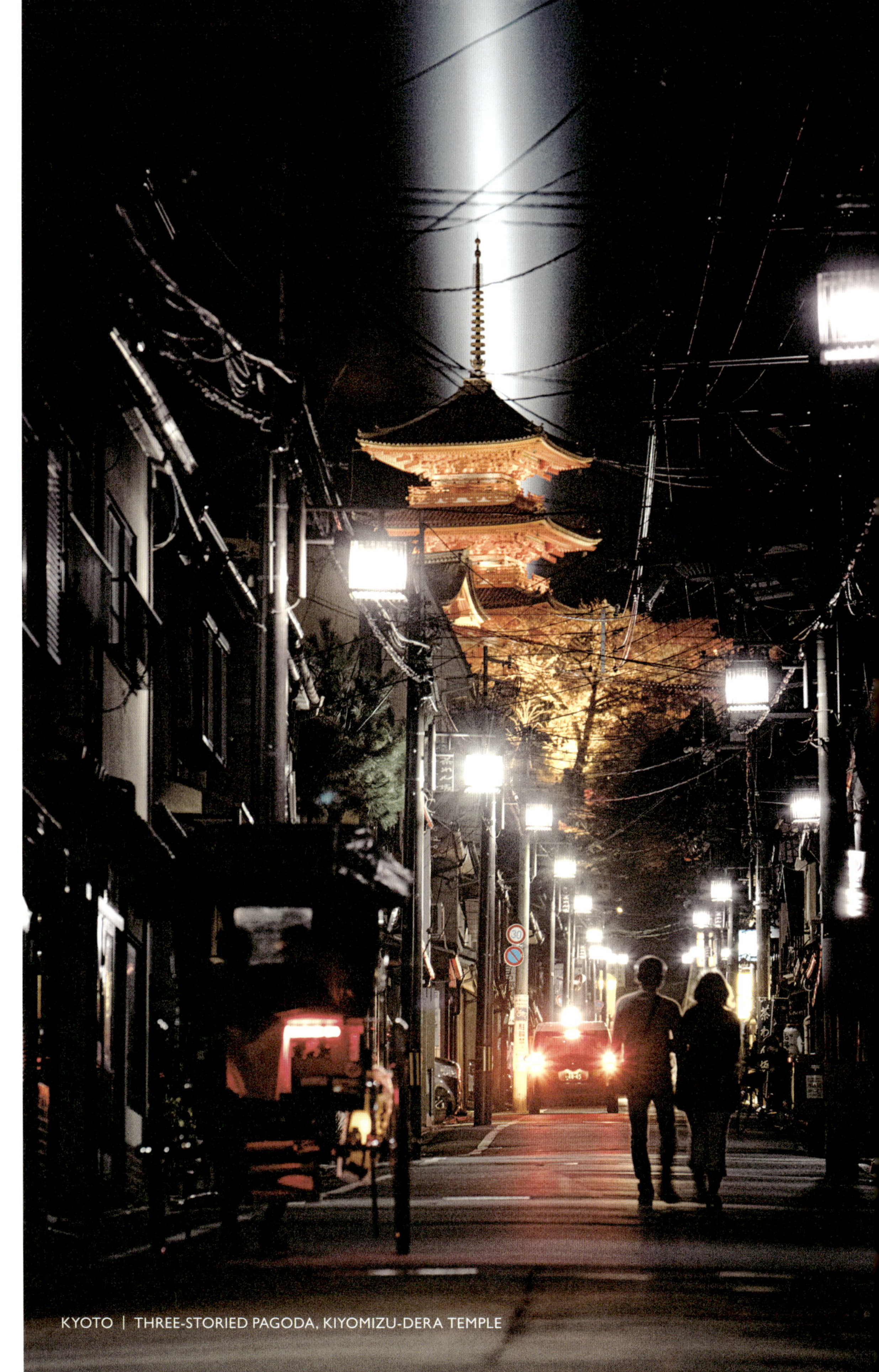

  KYOTO | THREE-STORIED PAGODA, KIYOMIZU-DERA TEMPLE

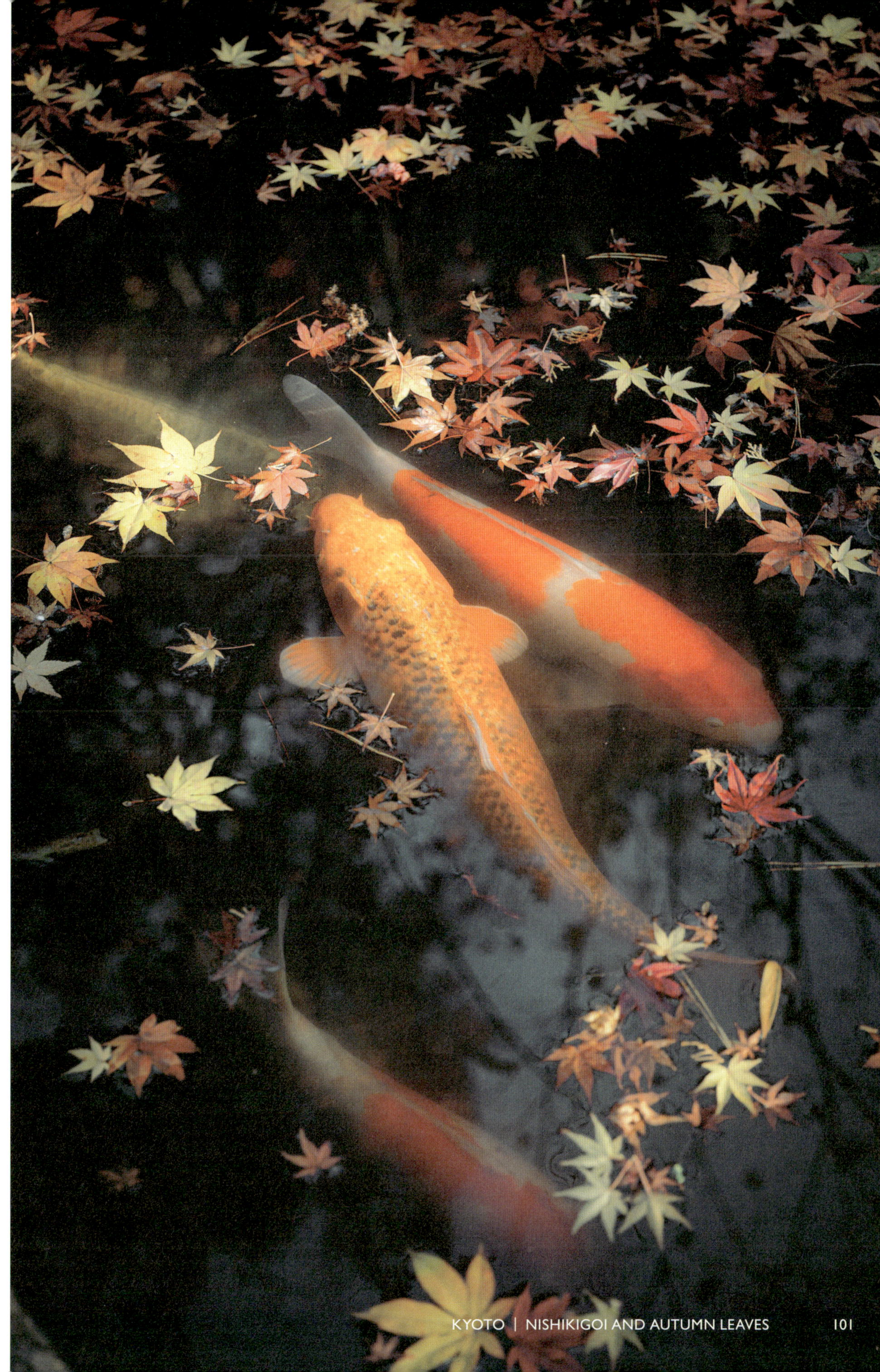

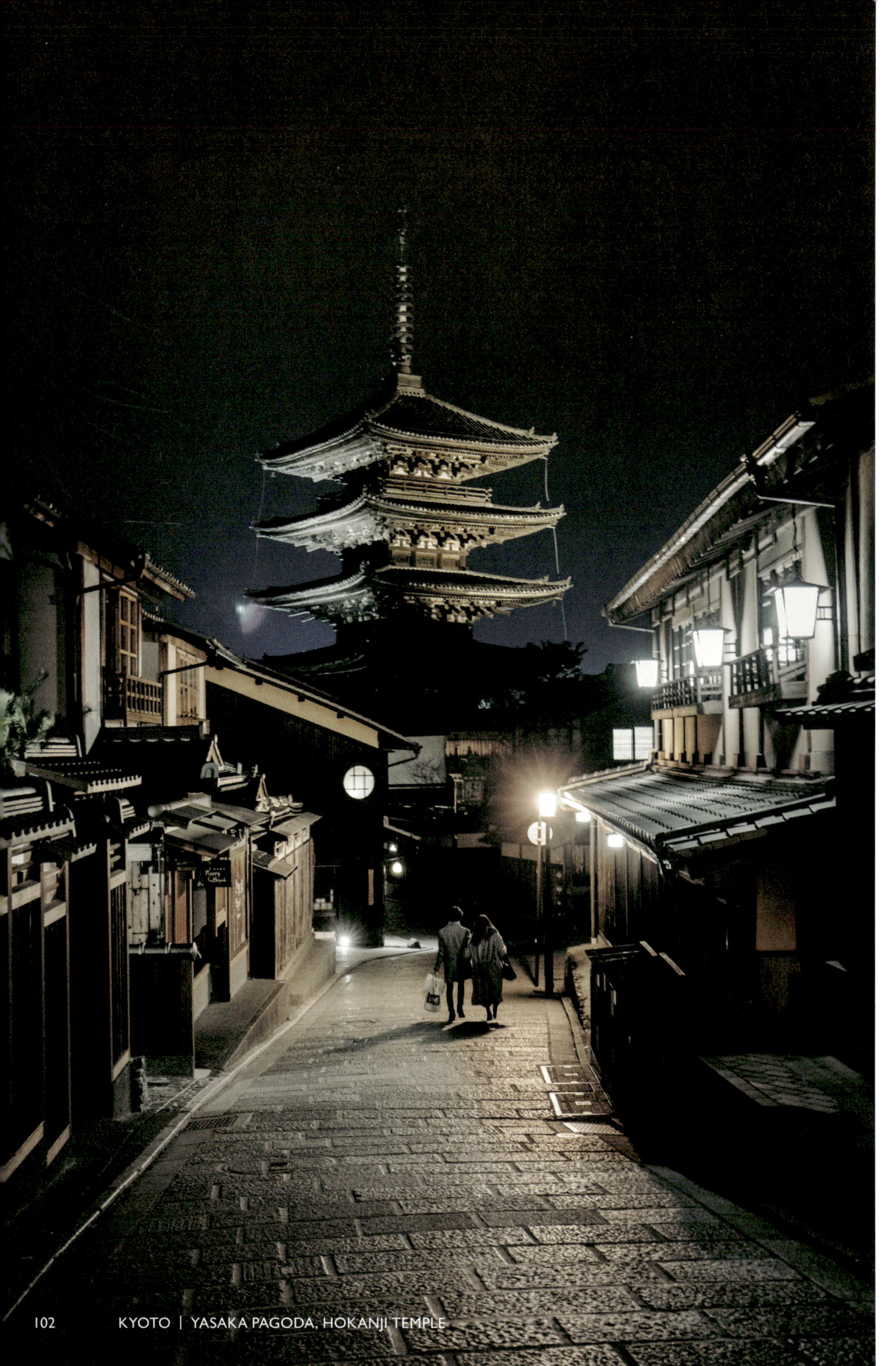

 KYOTO | YASAKA PAGODA, HOKANJI TEMPLE

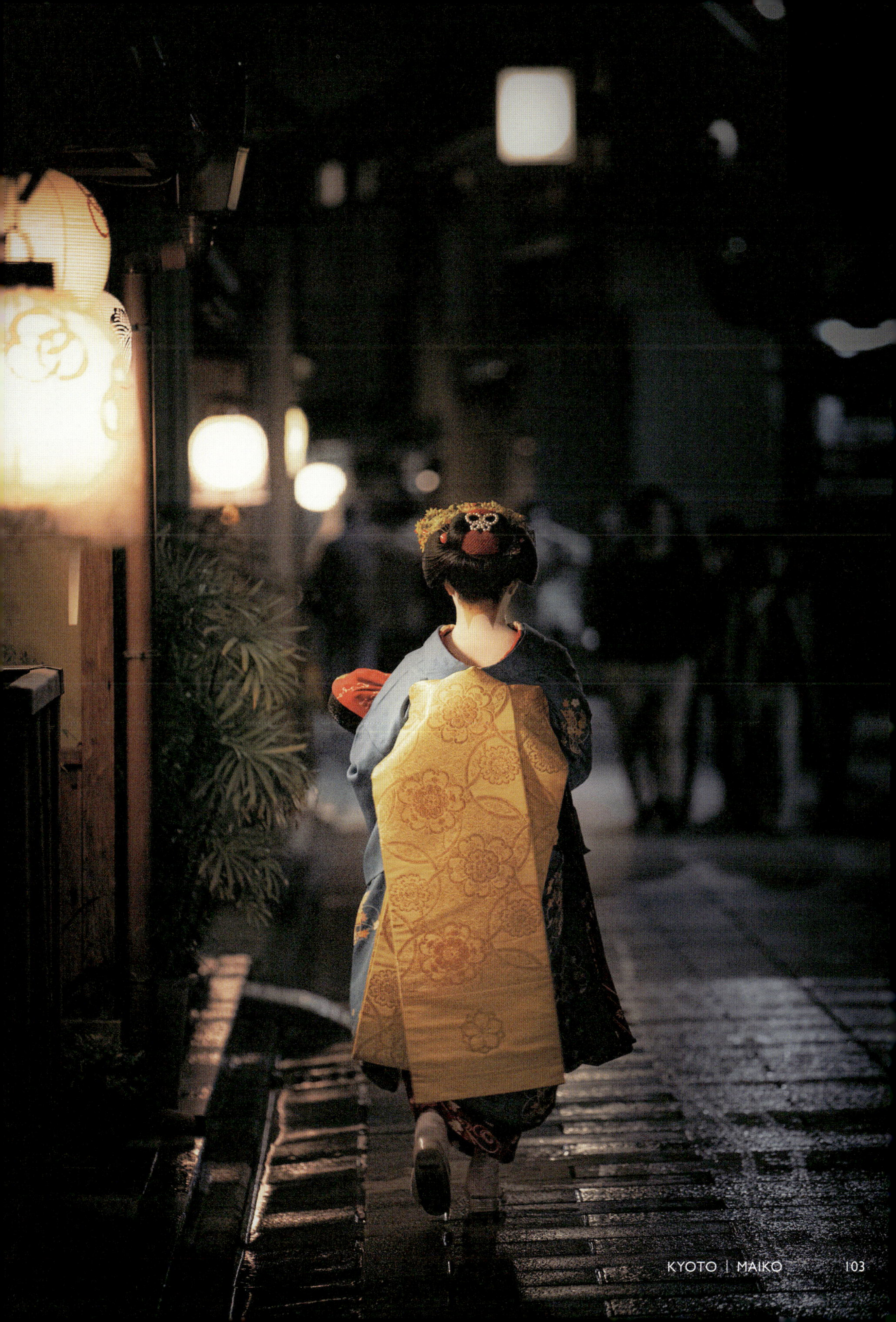

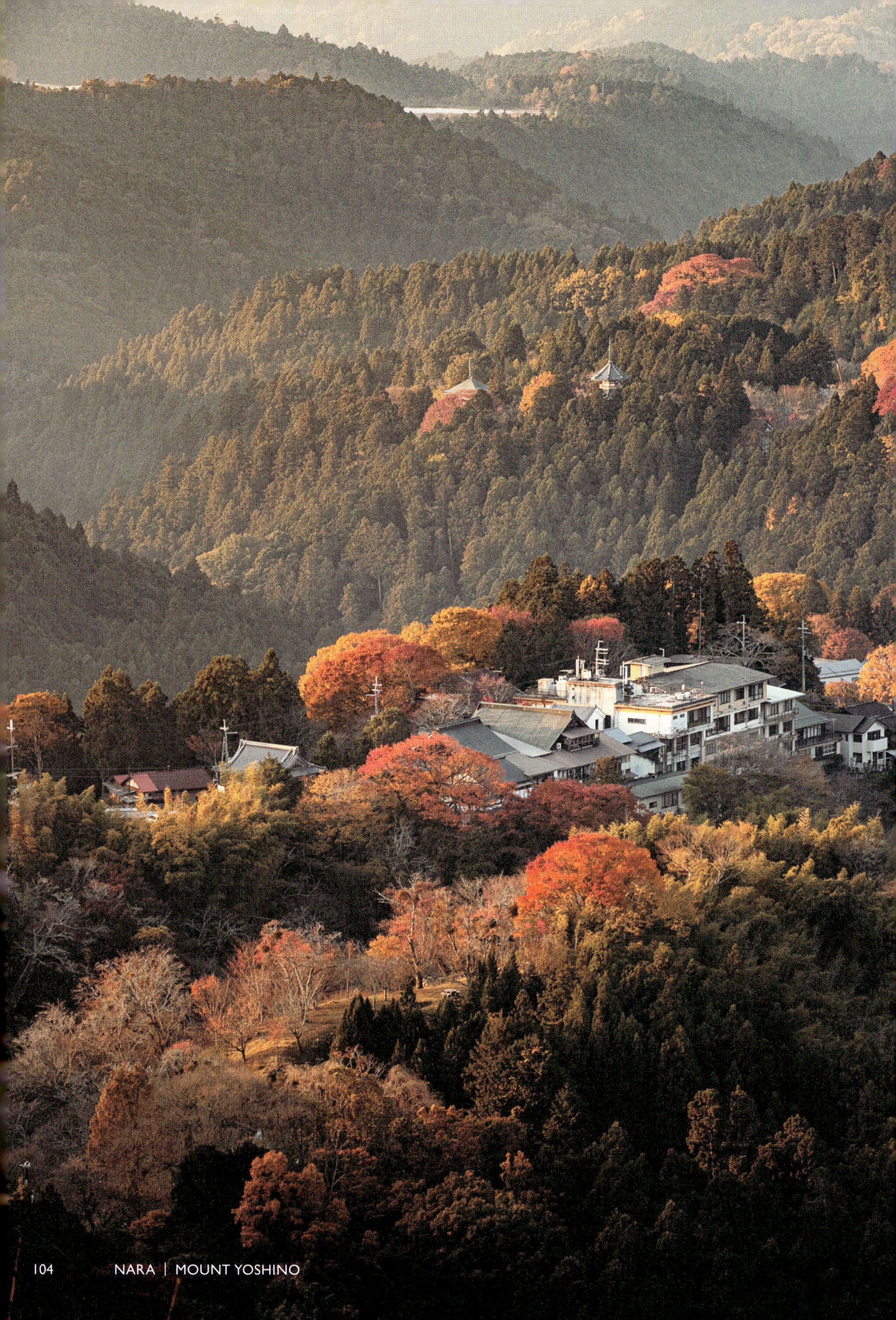

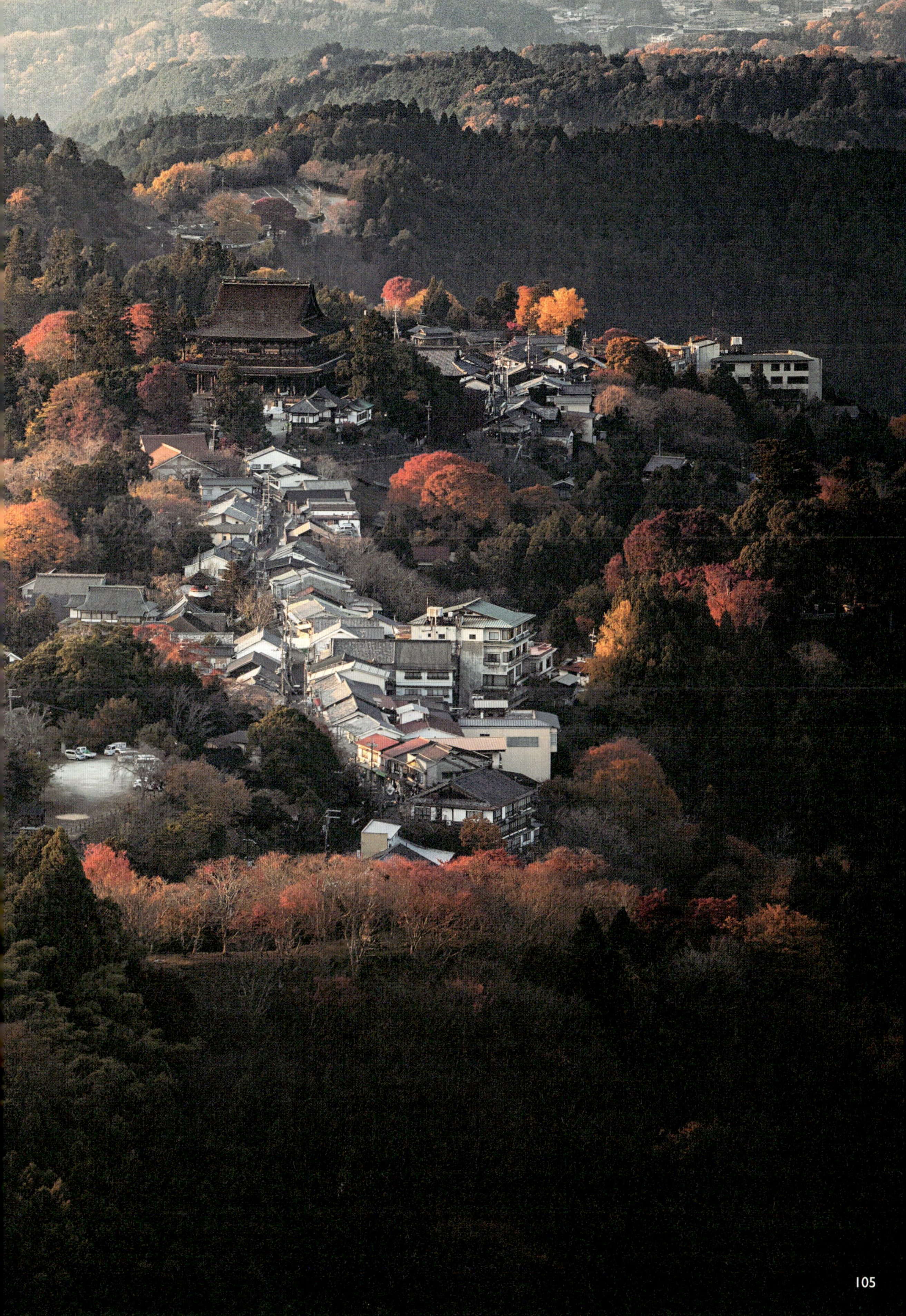

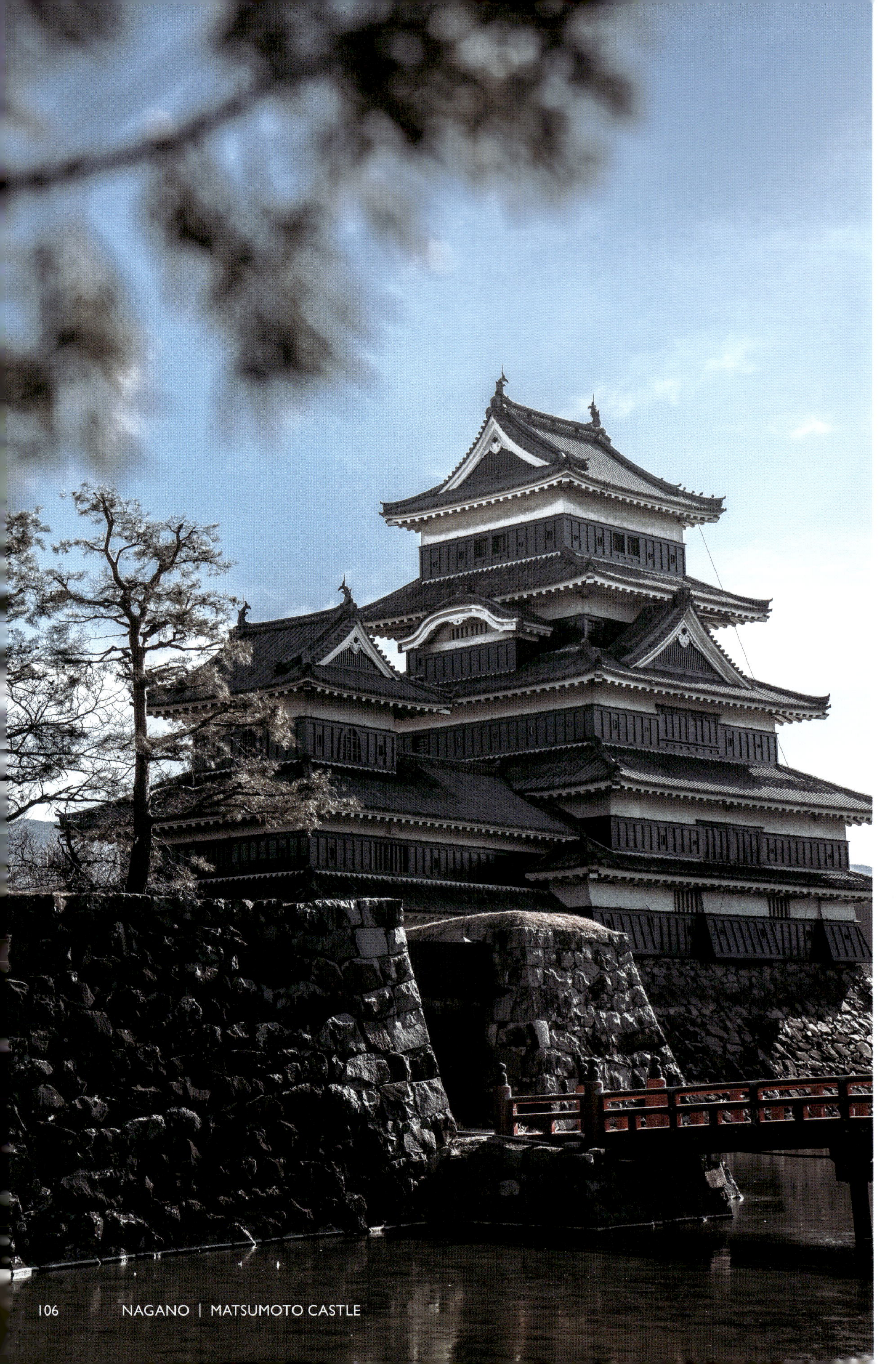

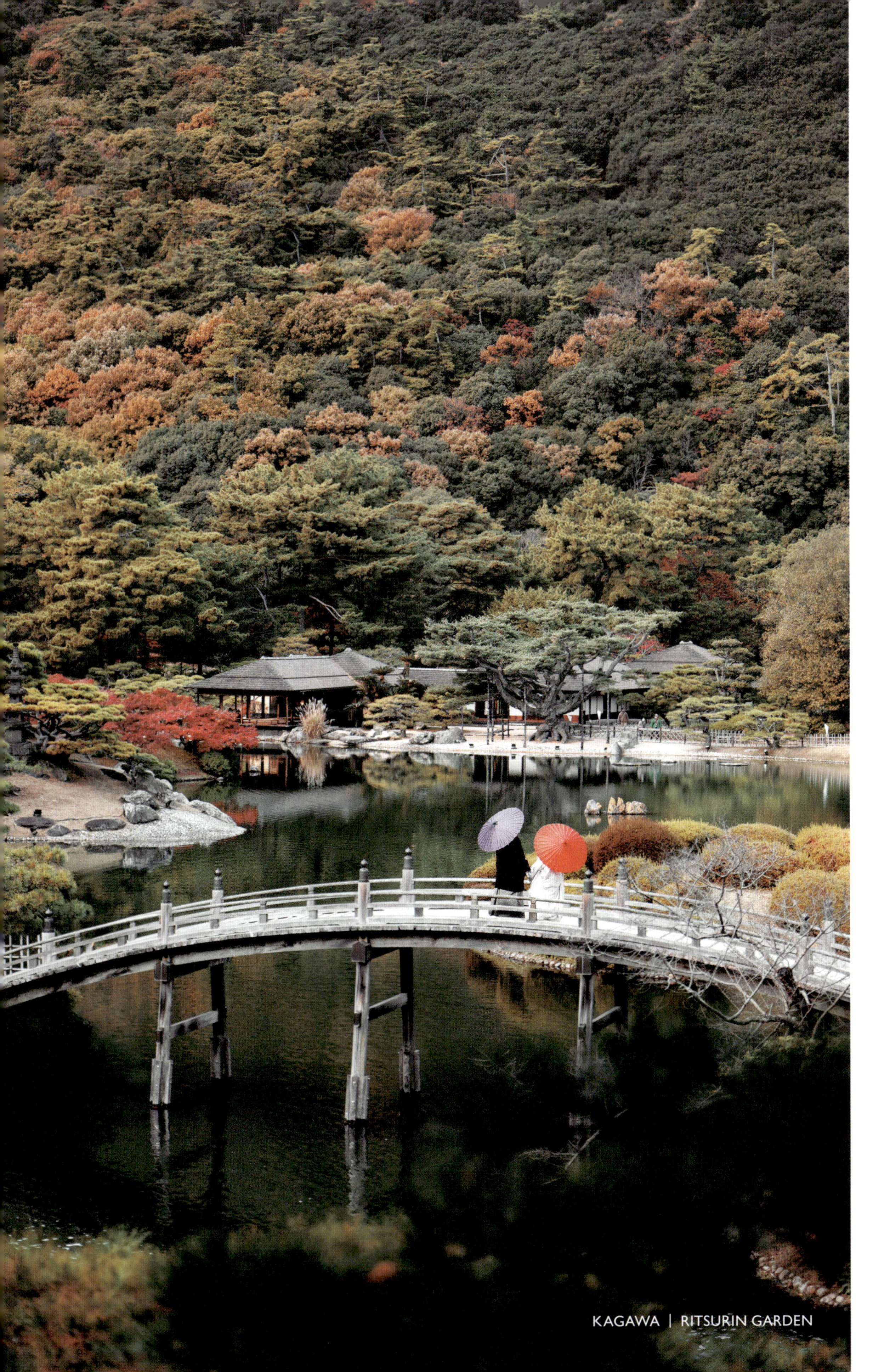

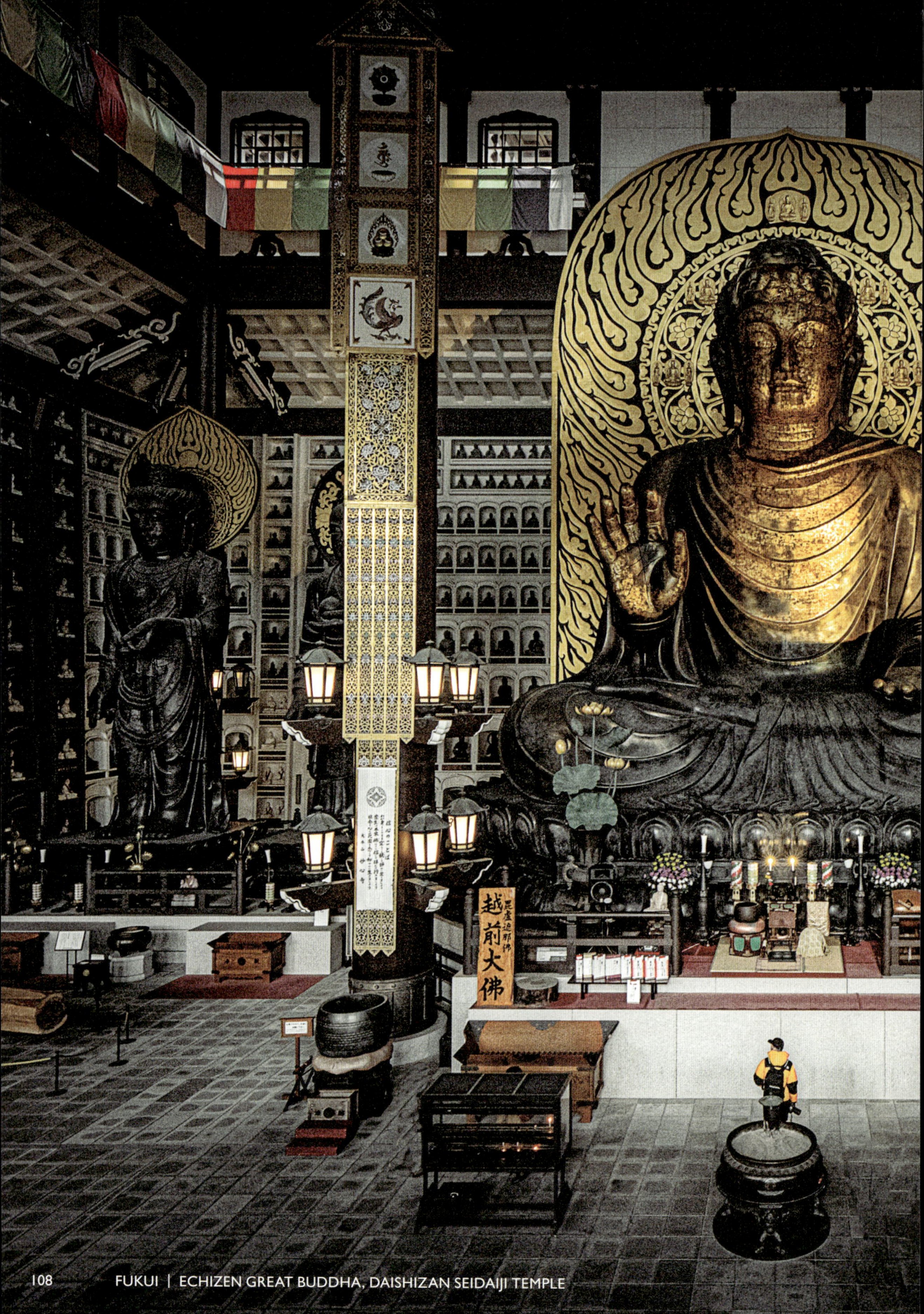

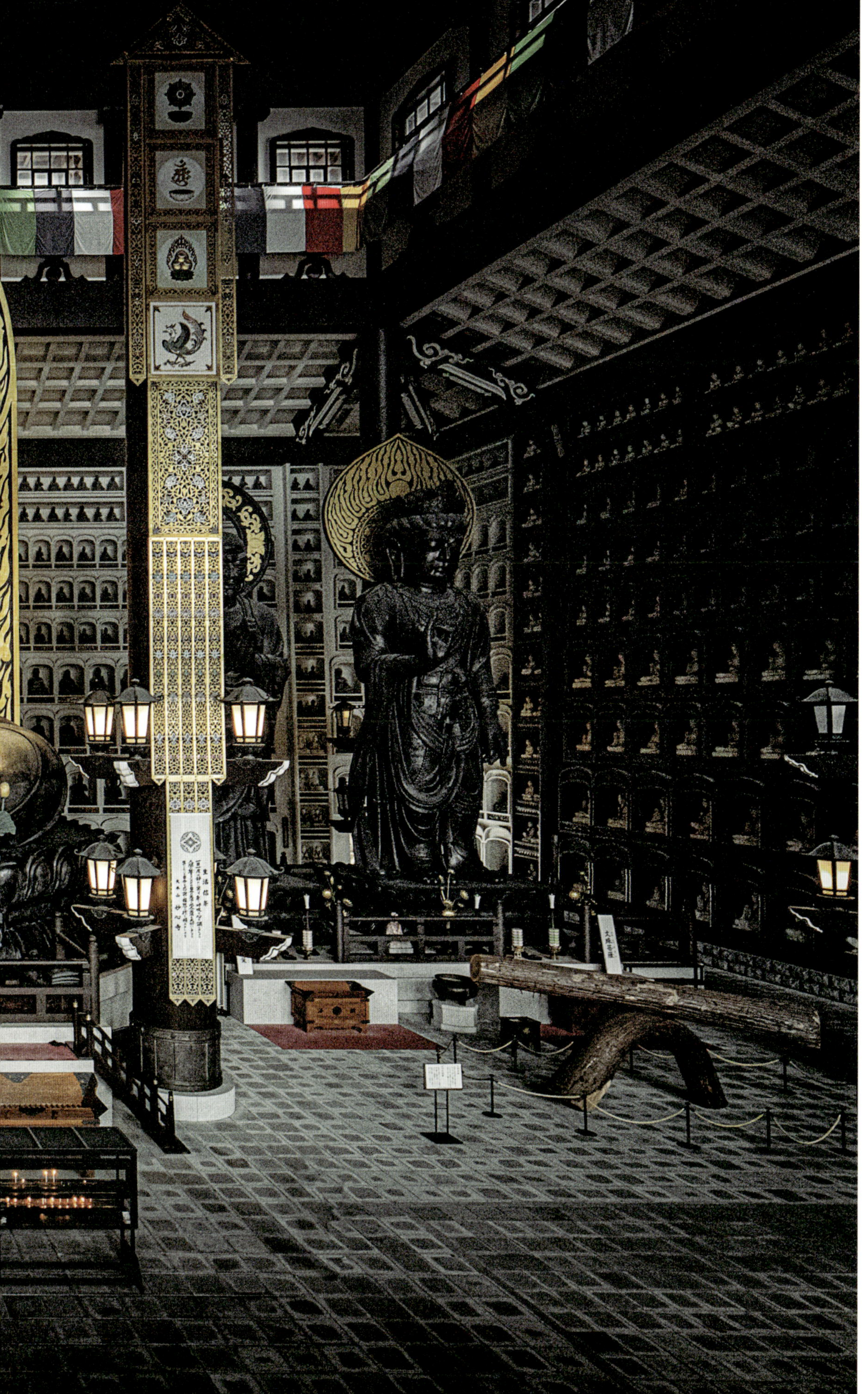

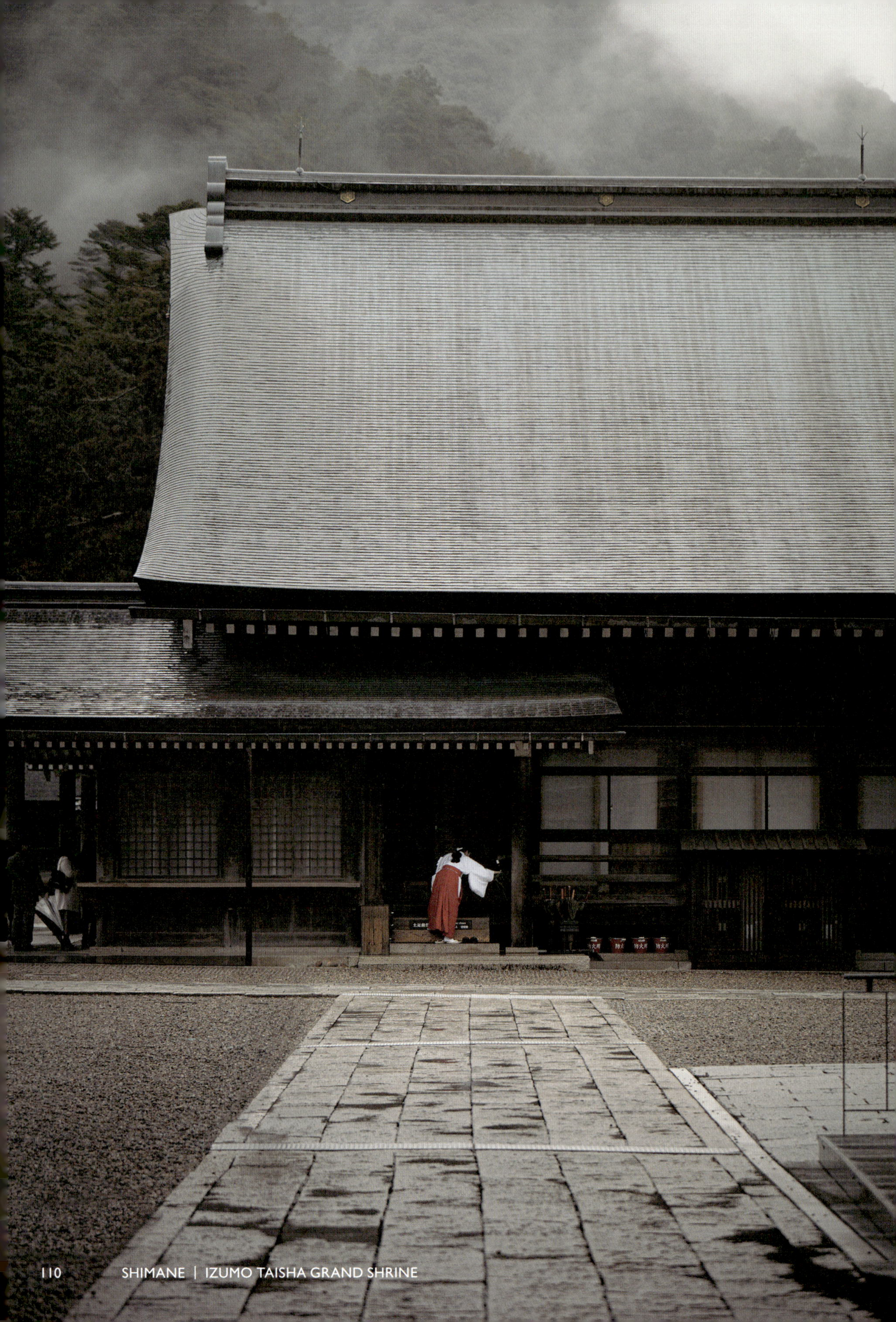

 SHIMANE | IZUMO TAISHA GRAND SHRINE

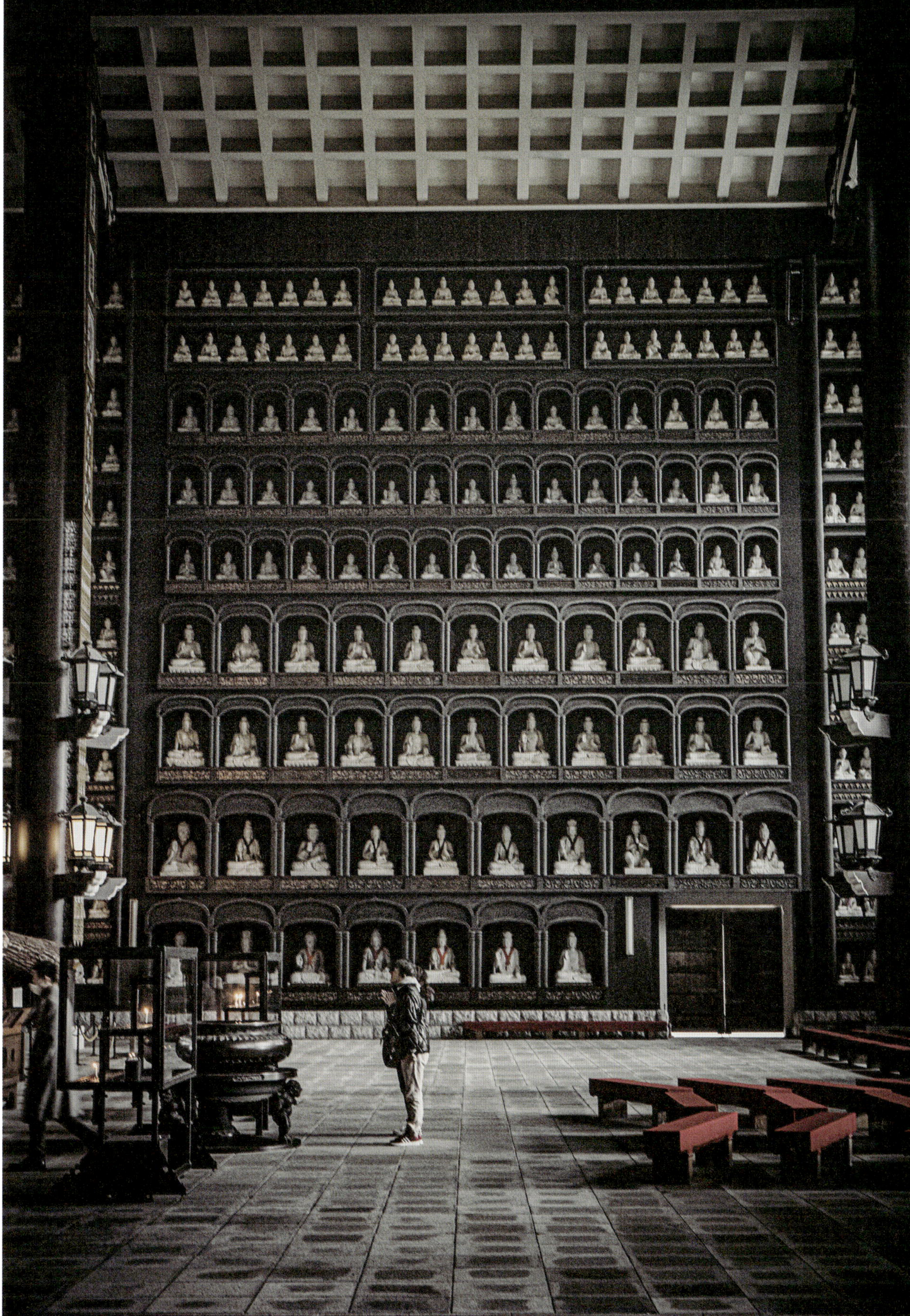

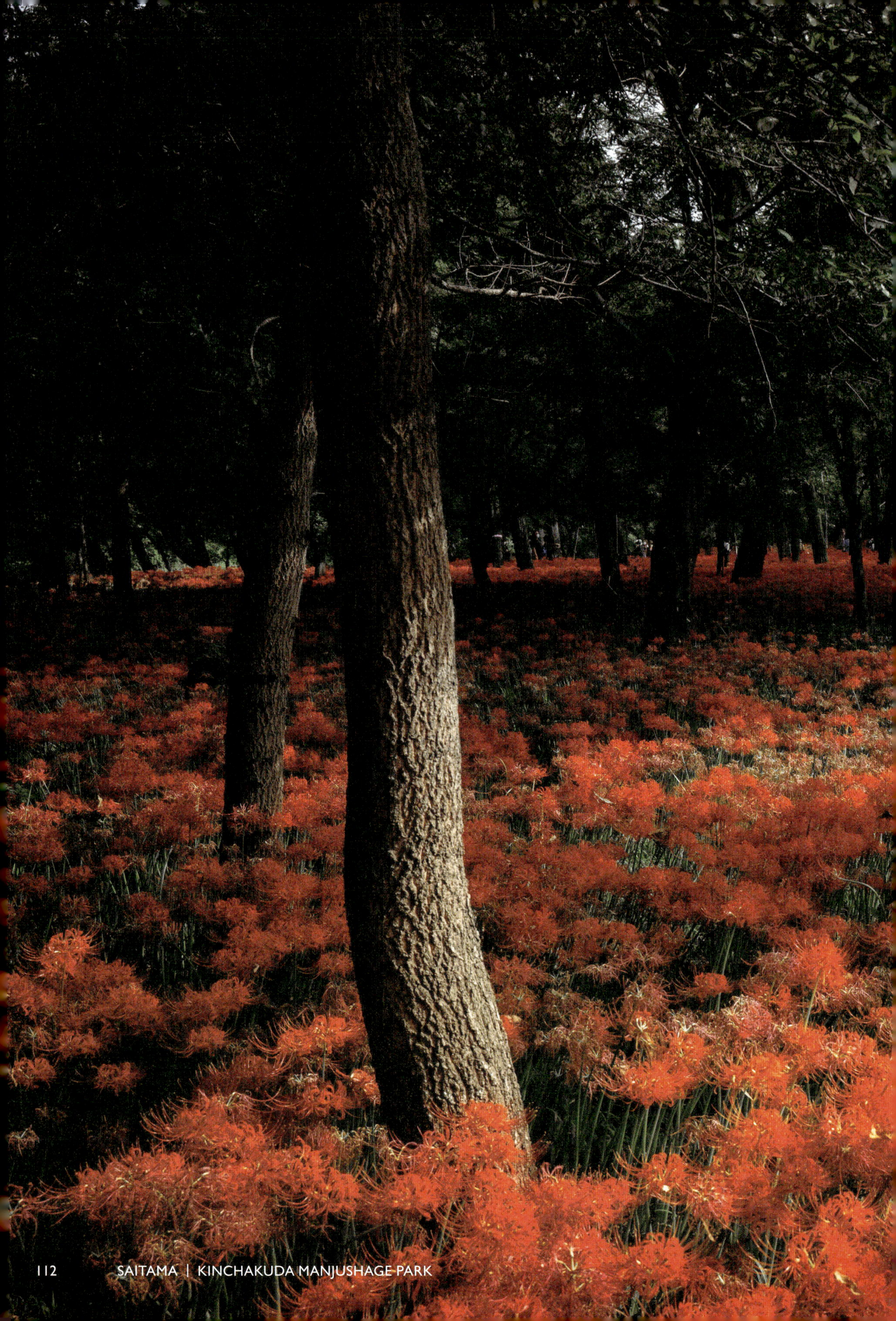

 SAITAMA | KINCHAKUDA MANJUSHAGE PARK

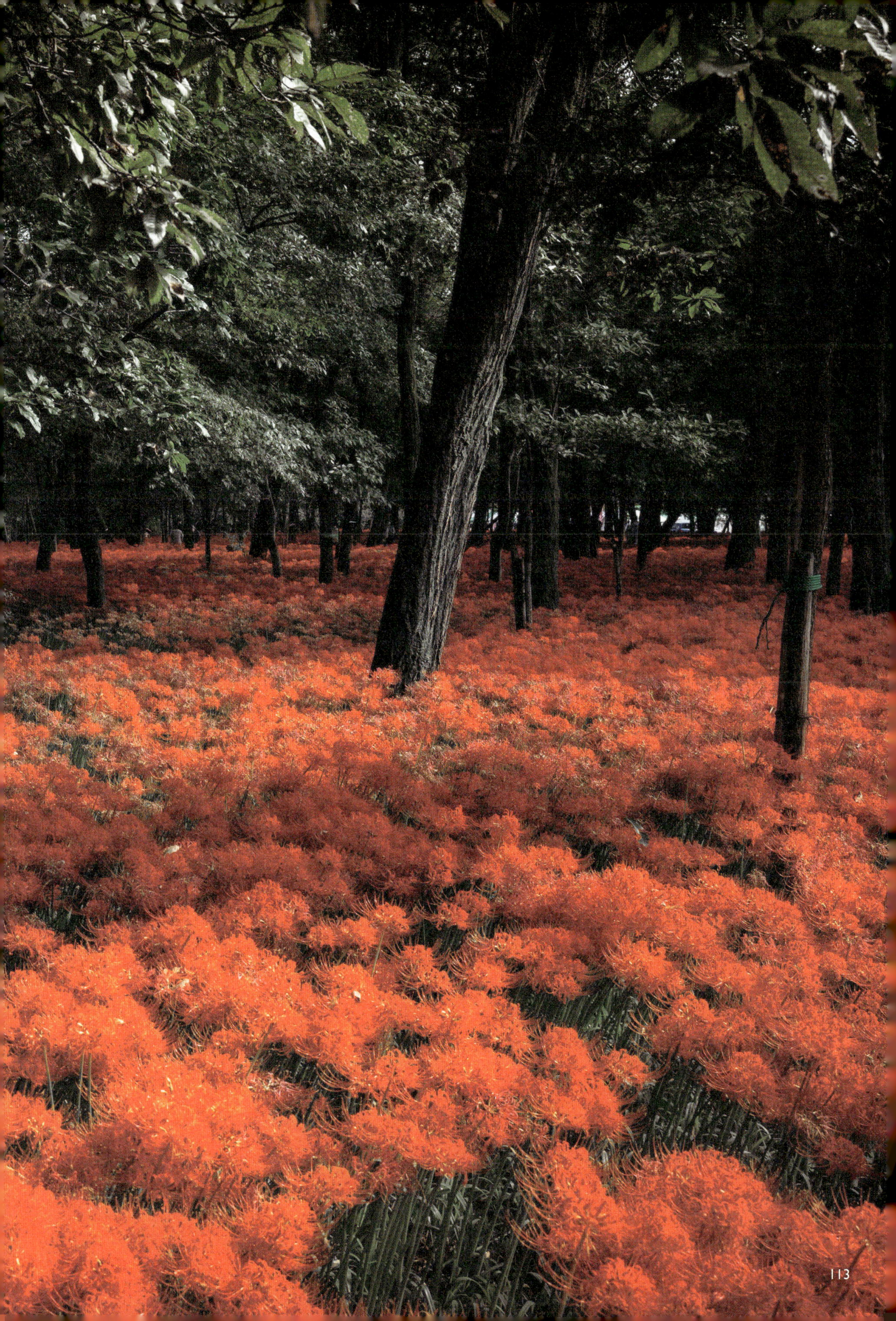

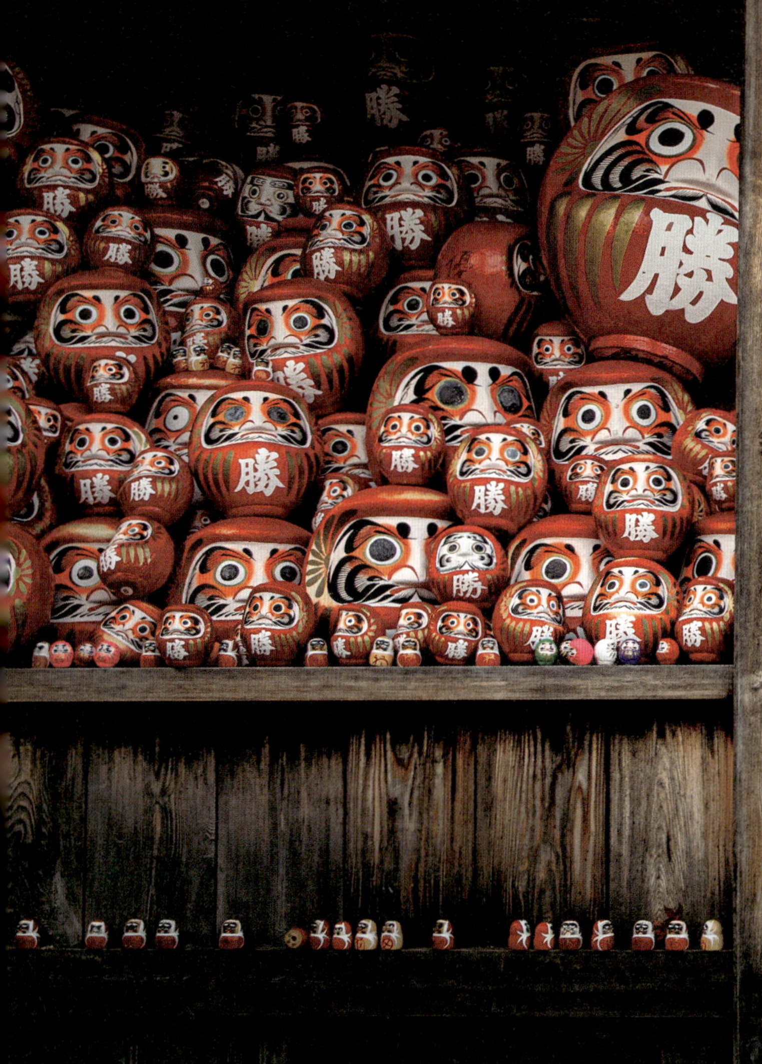
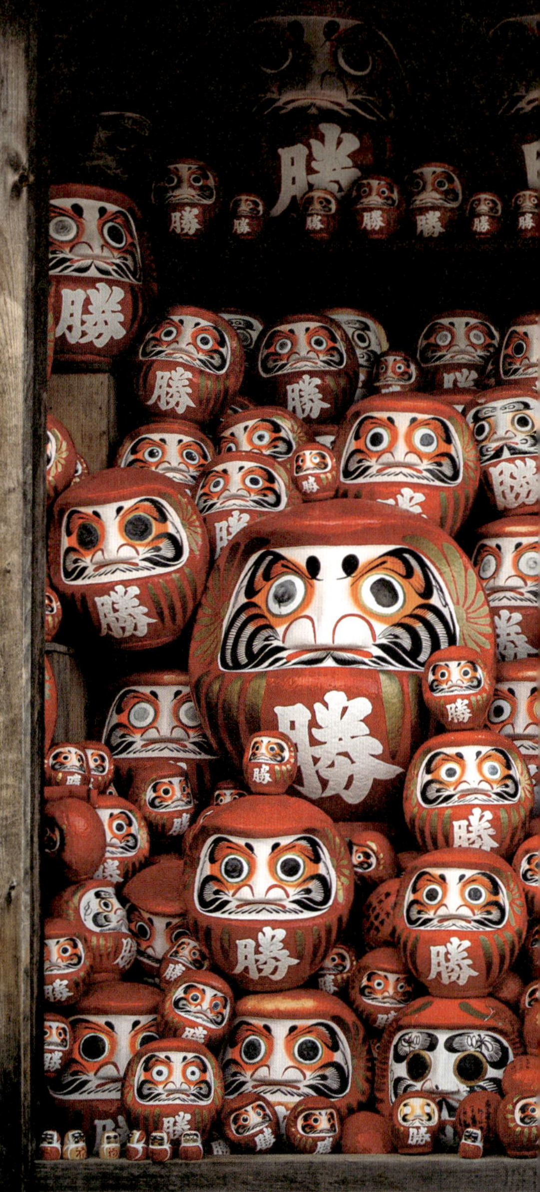

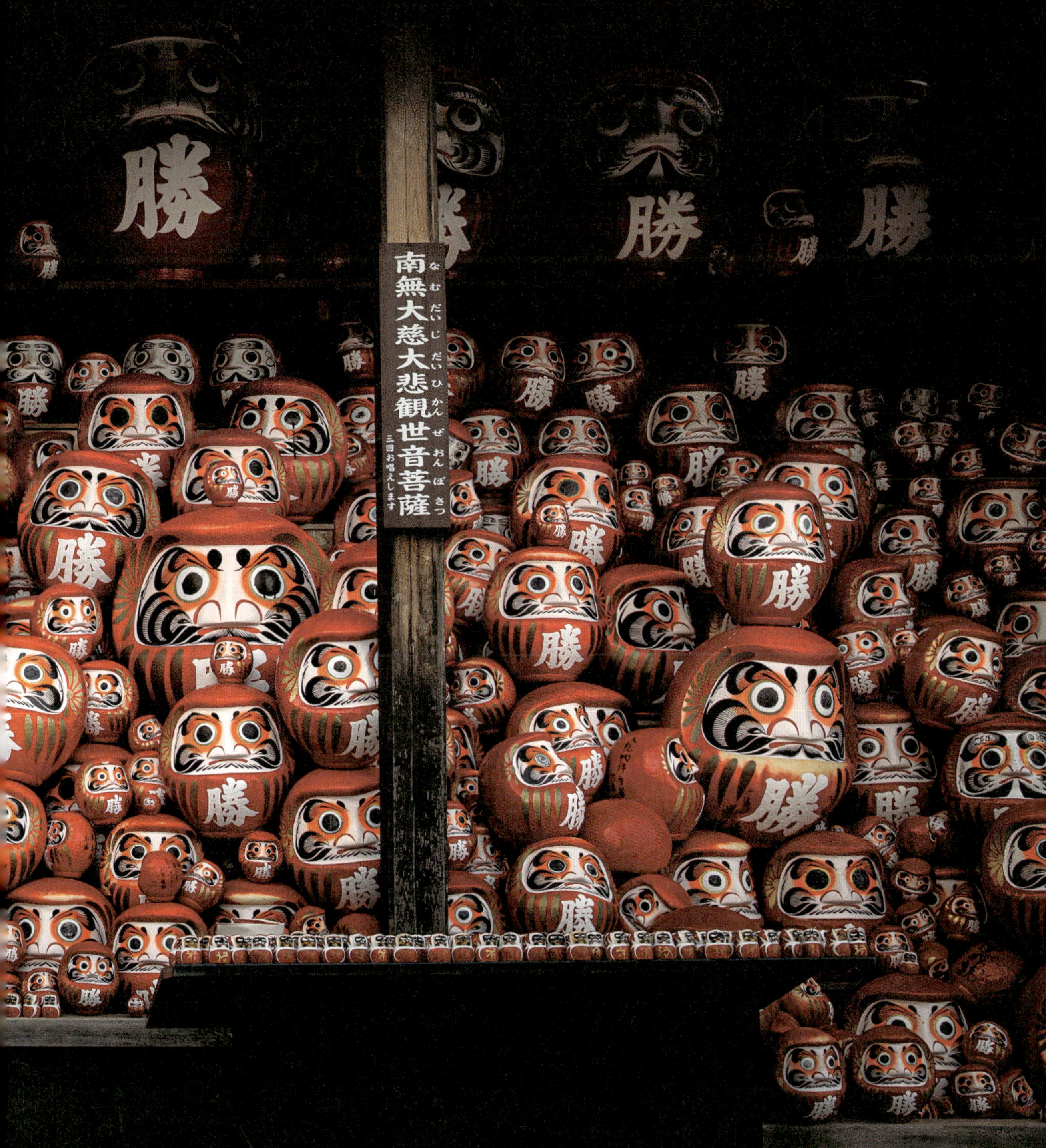
南無大慈大悲観世音菩薩
三回お唱えします

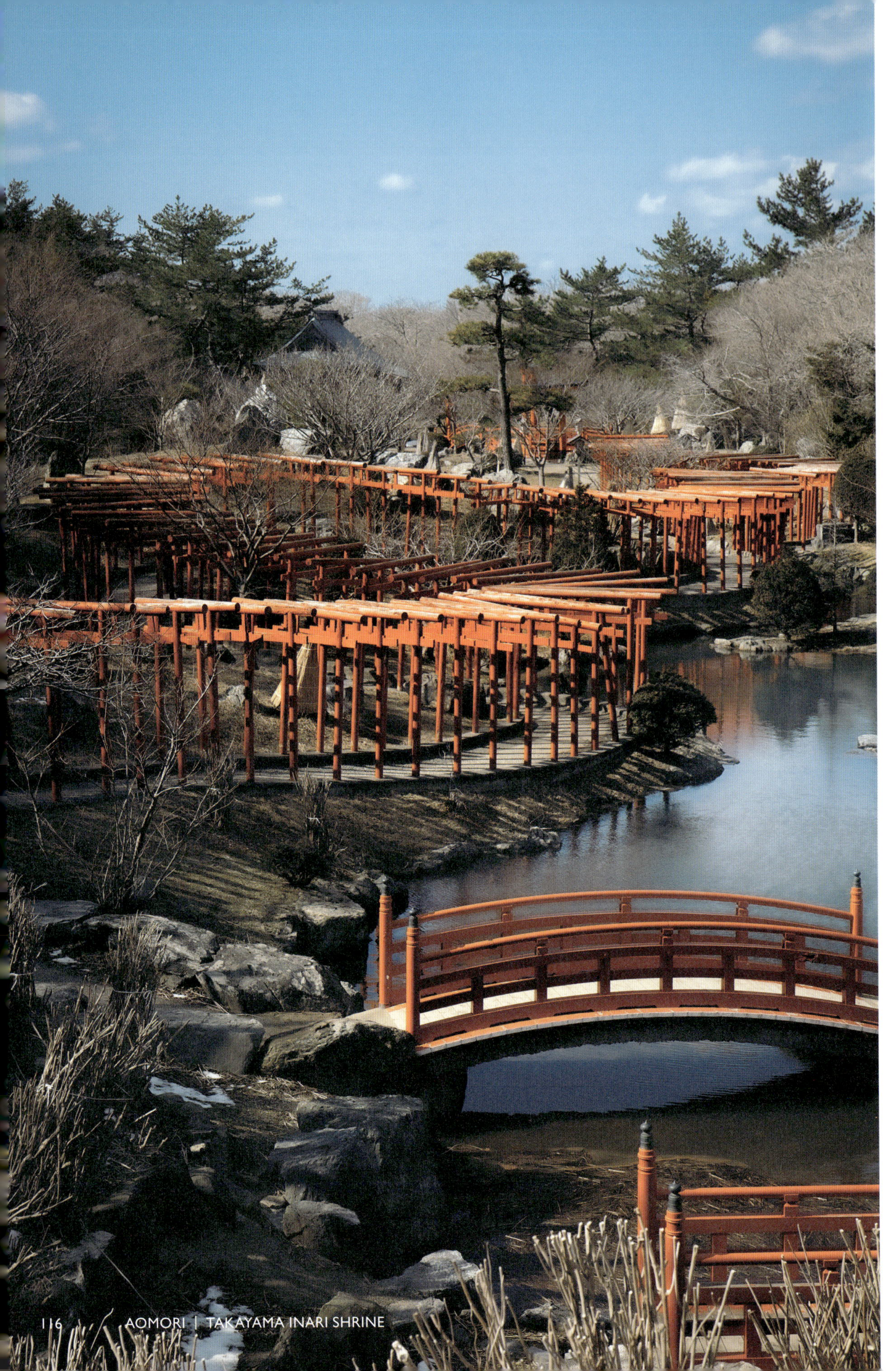

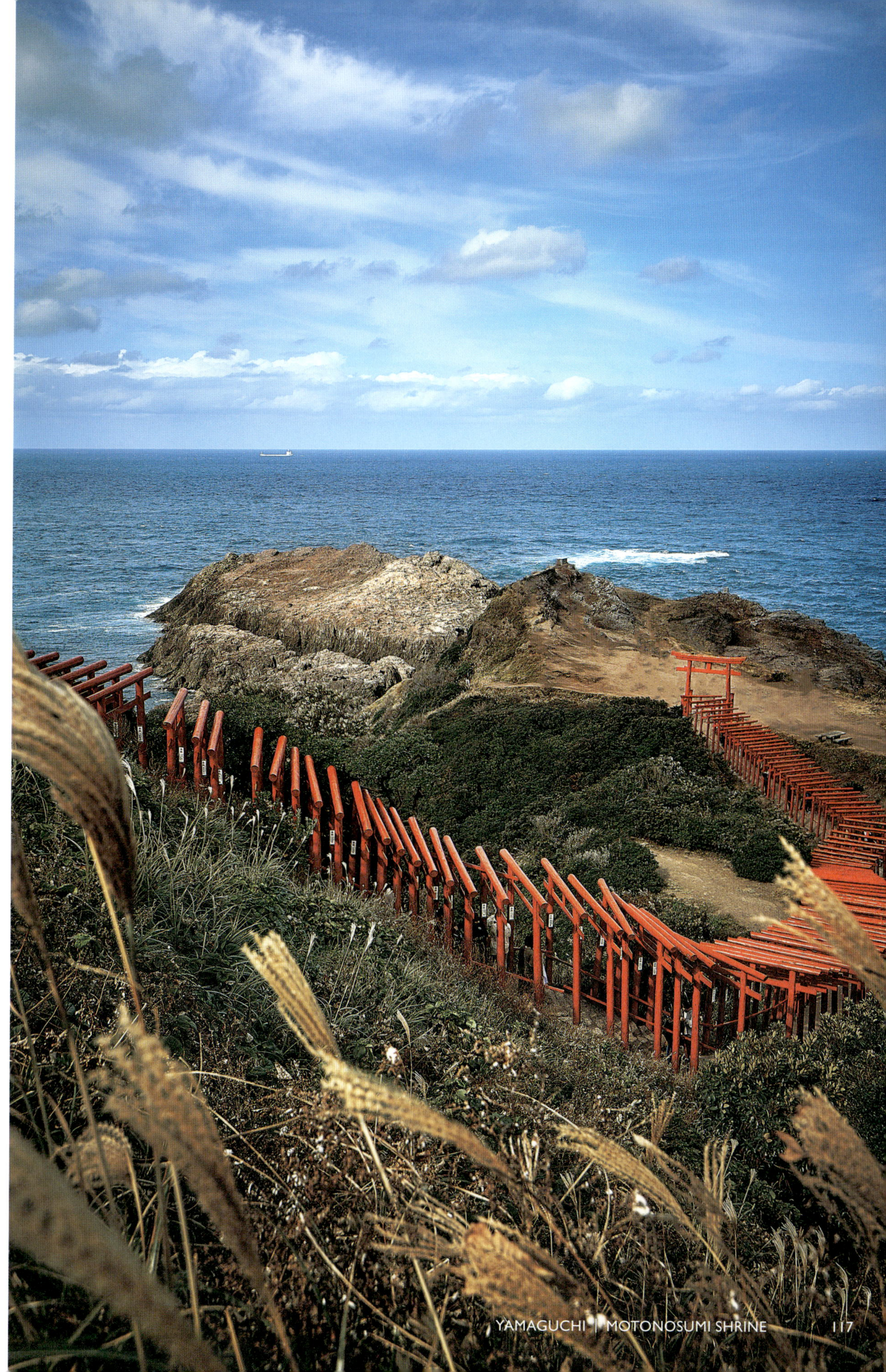

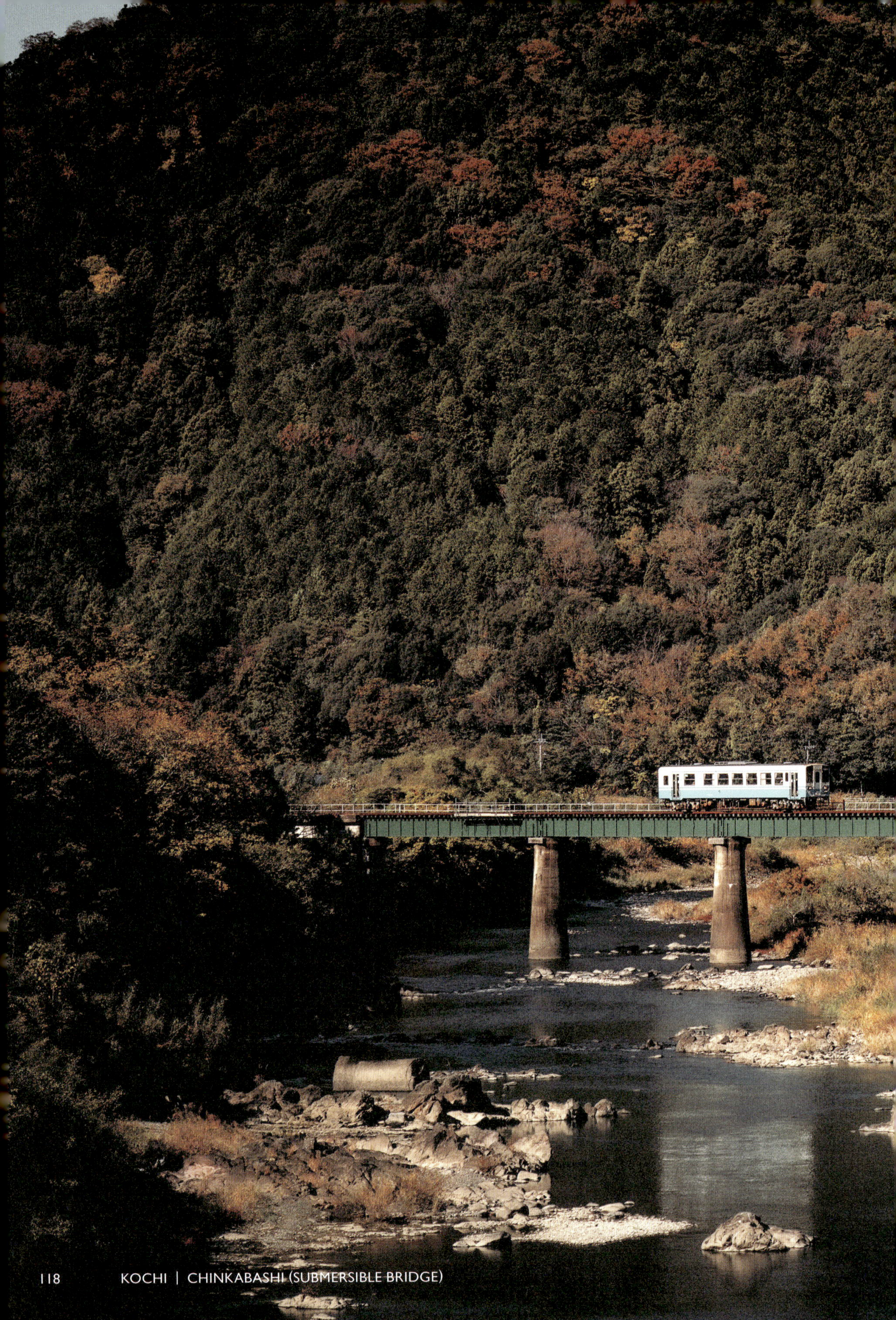

 KOCHI | CHINKABASHI (SUBMERSIBLE BRIDGE)

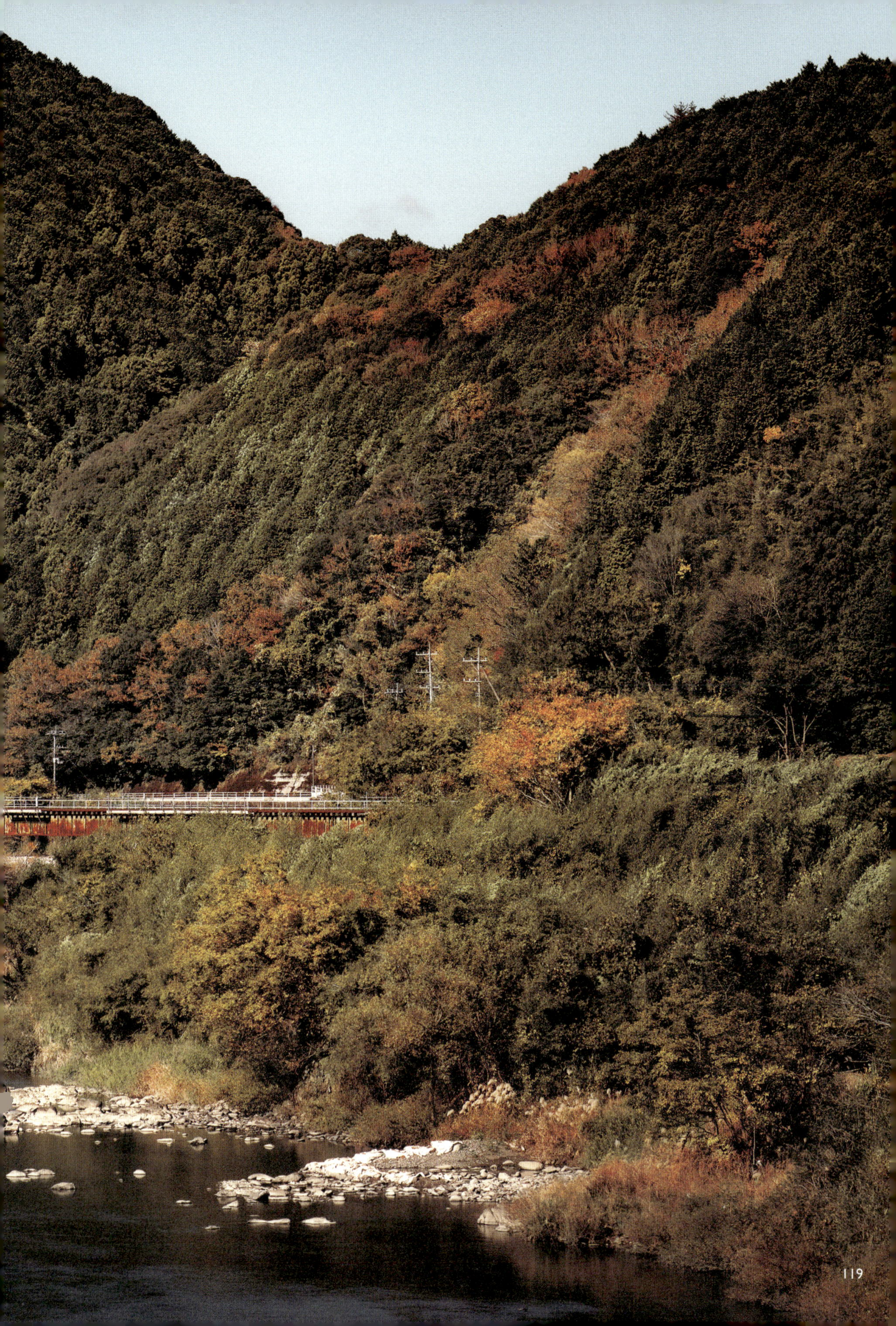

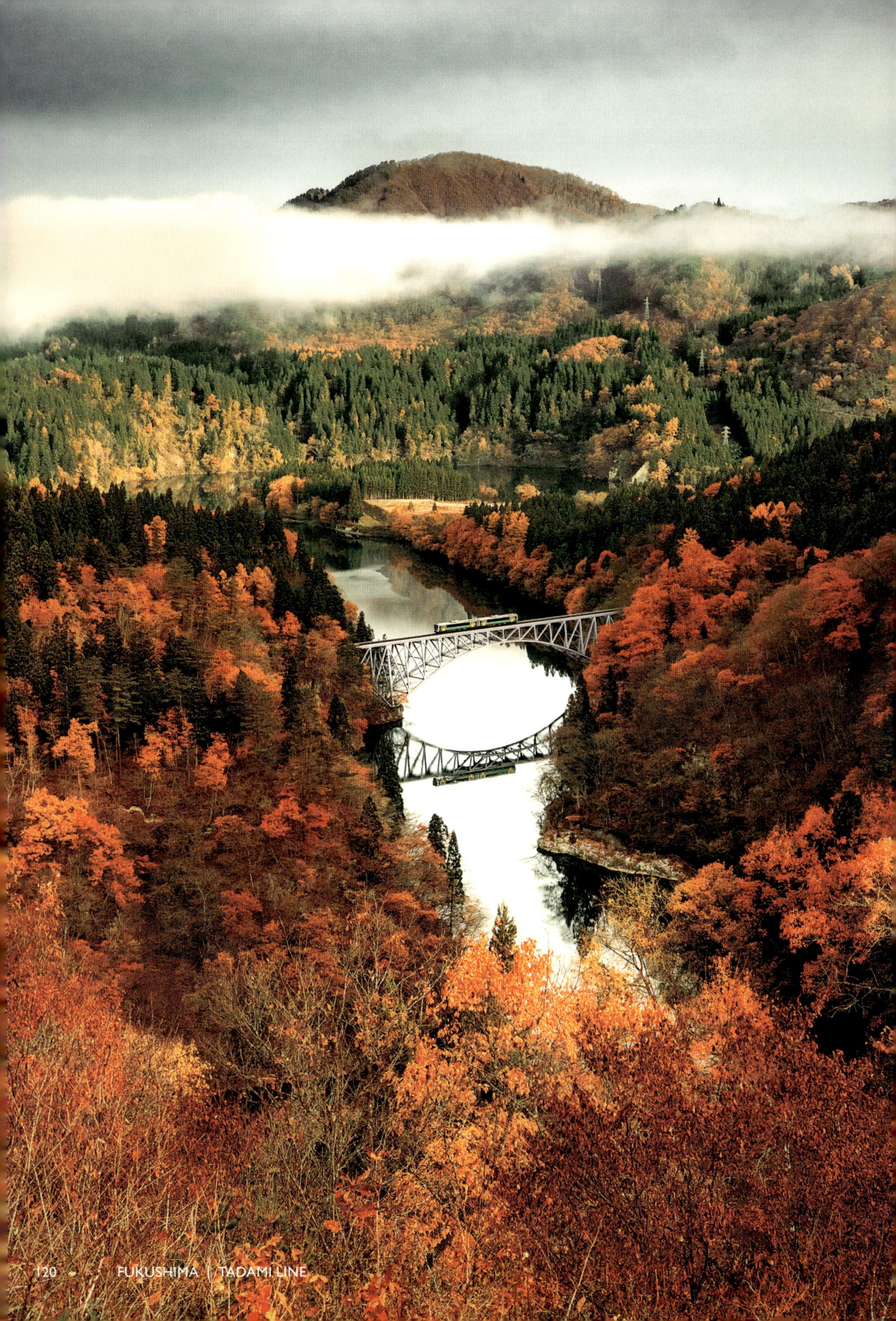

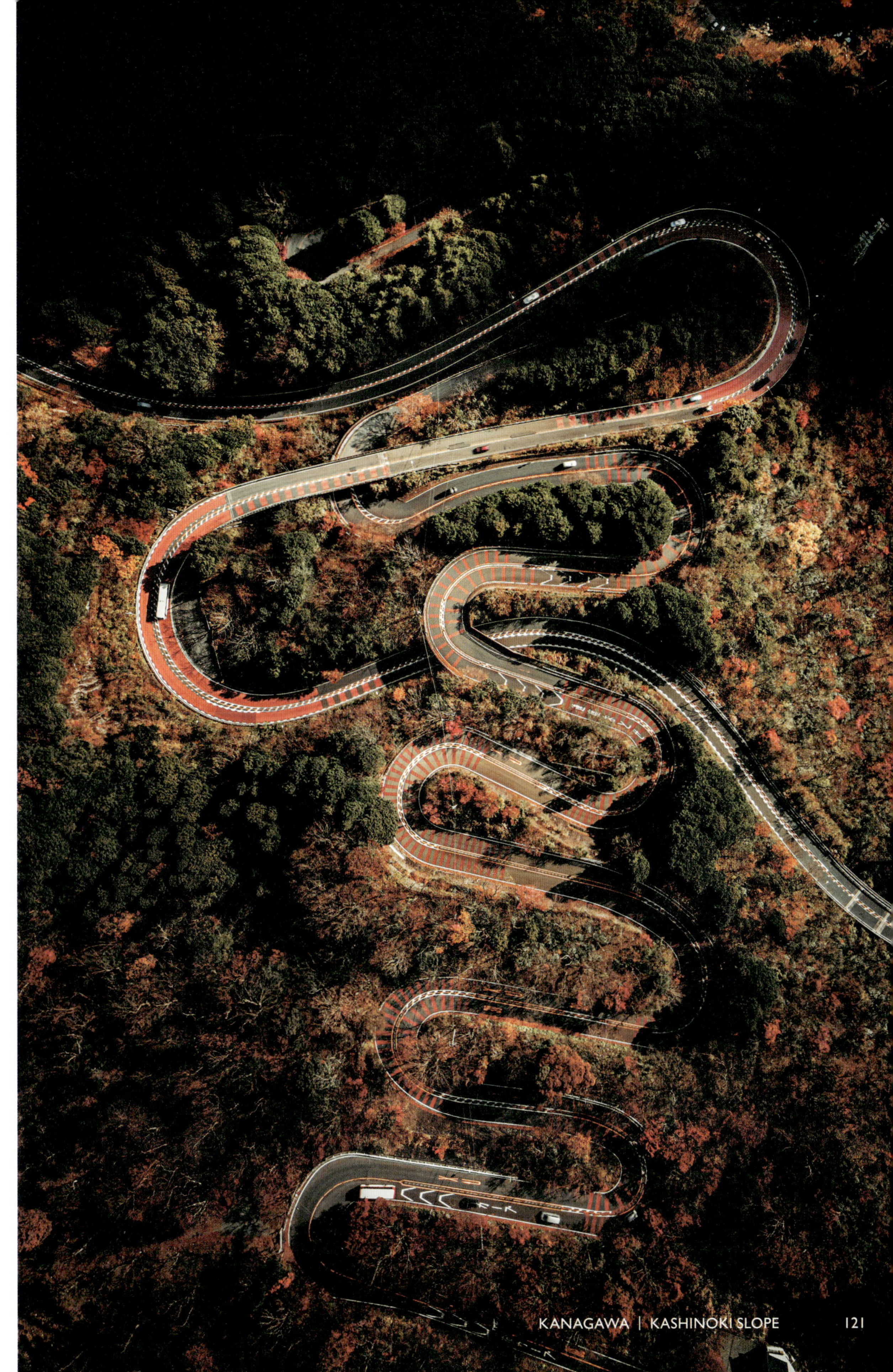

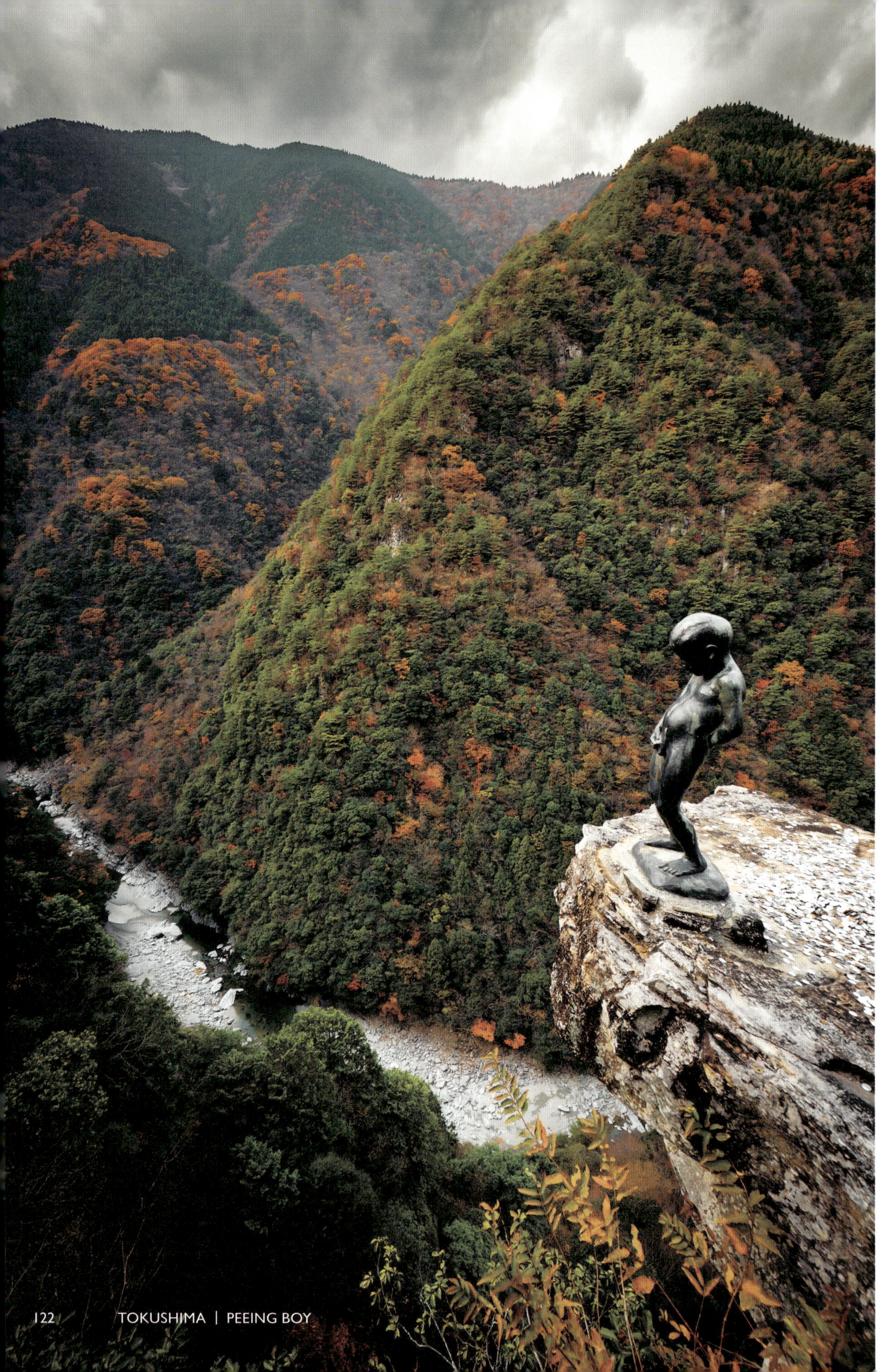

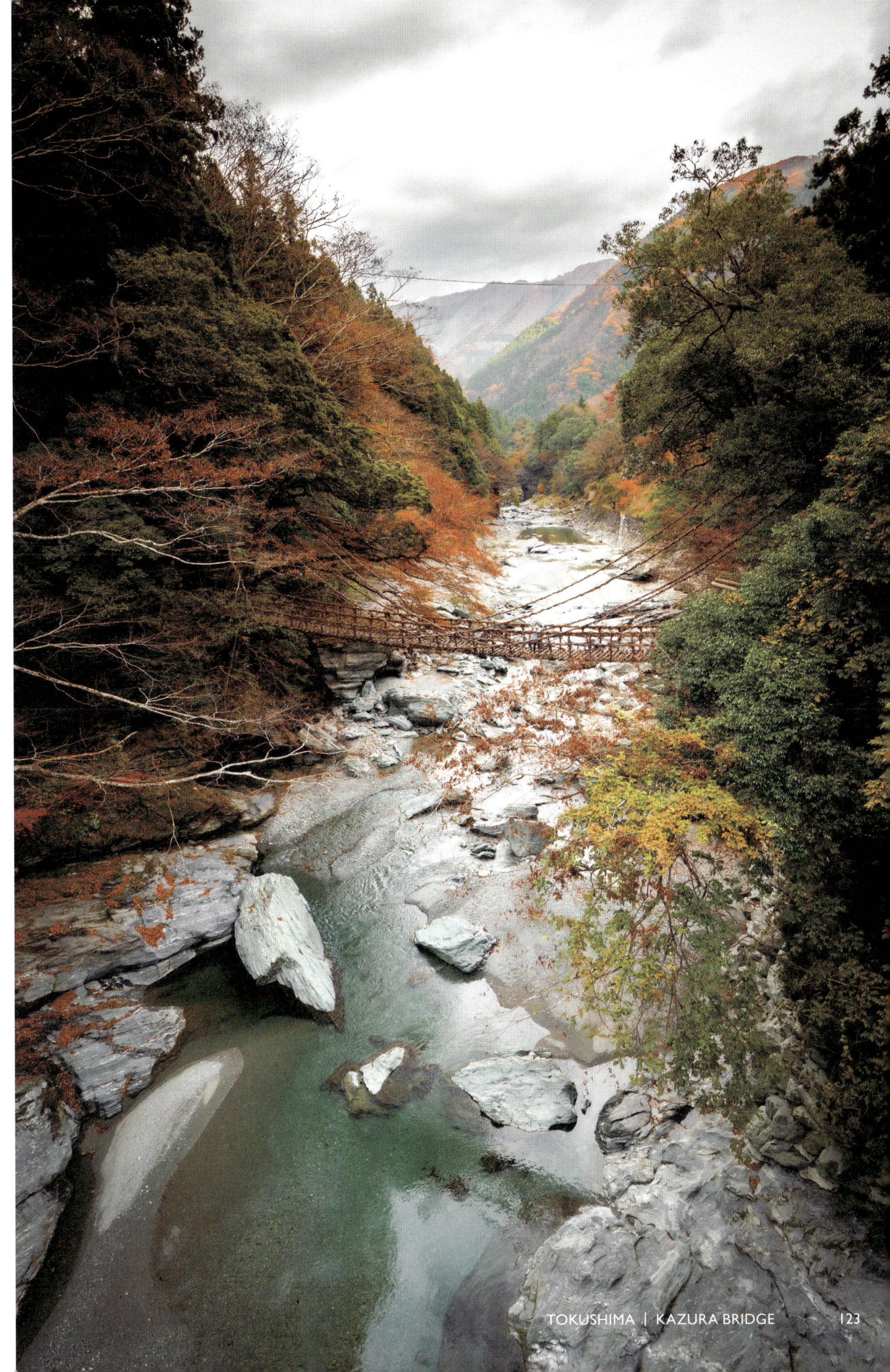

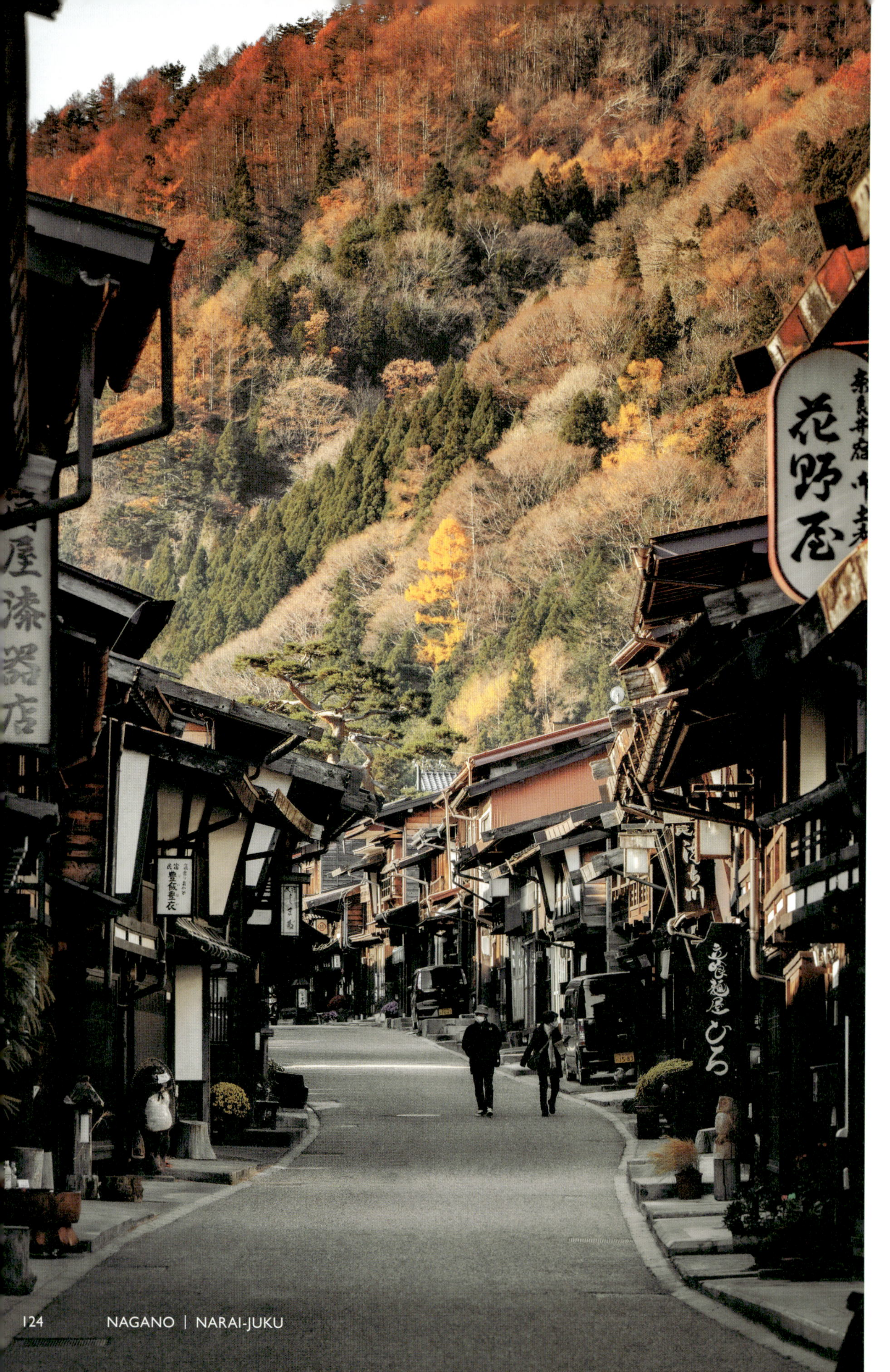

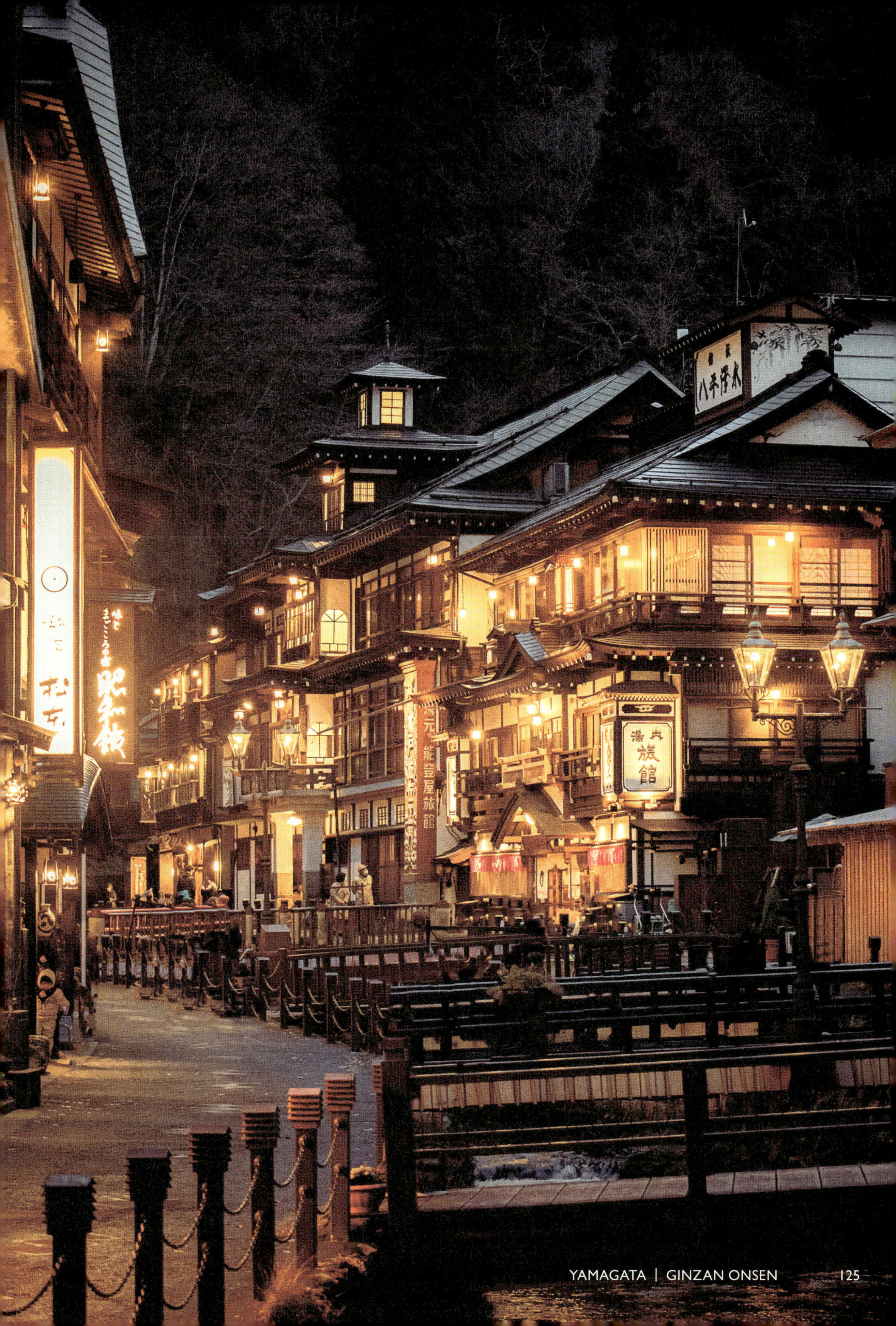

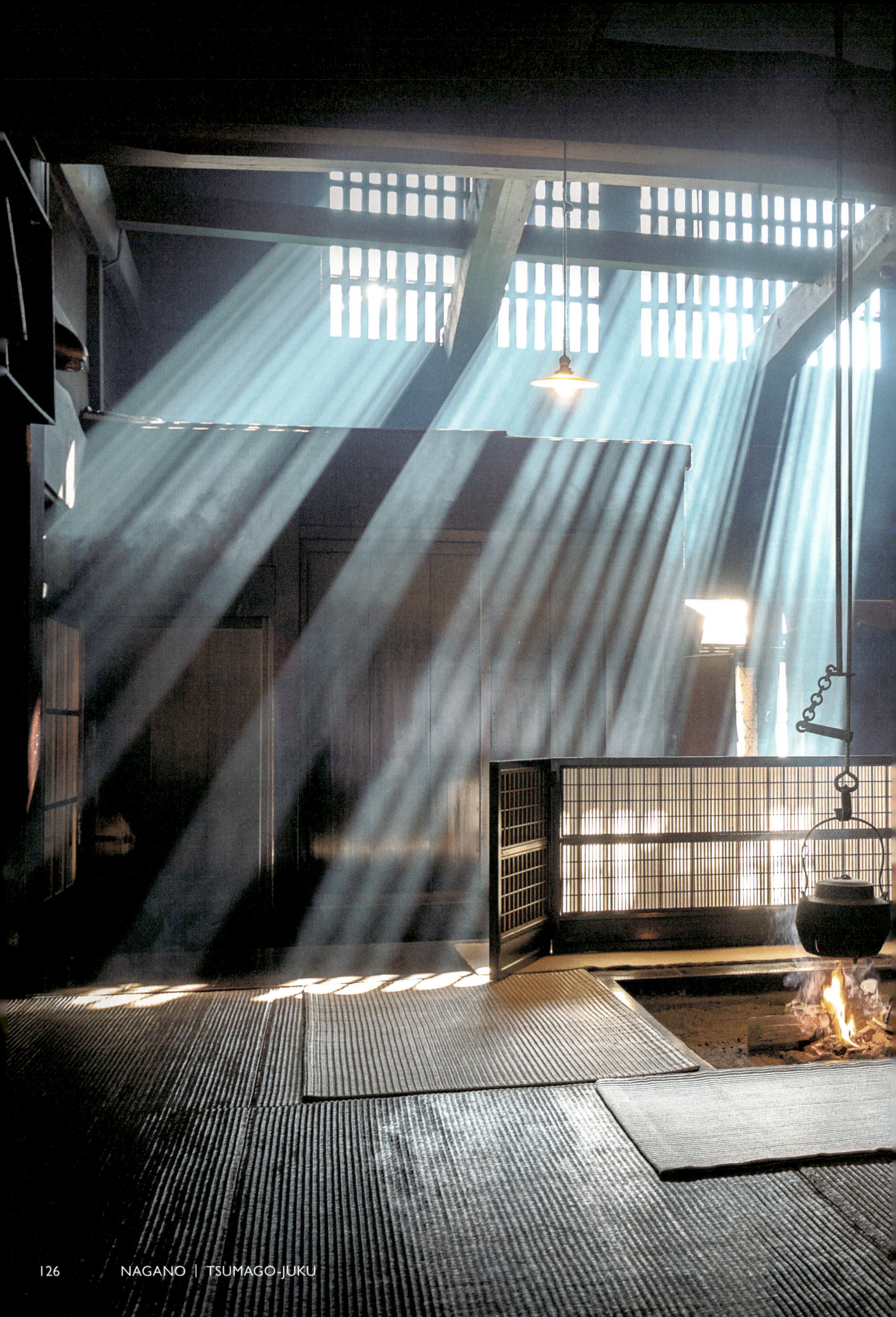

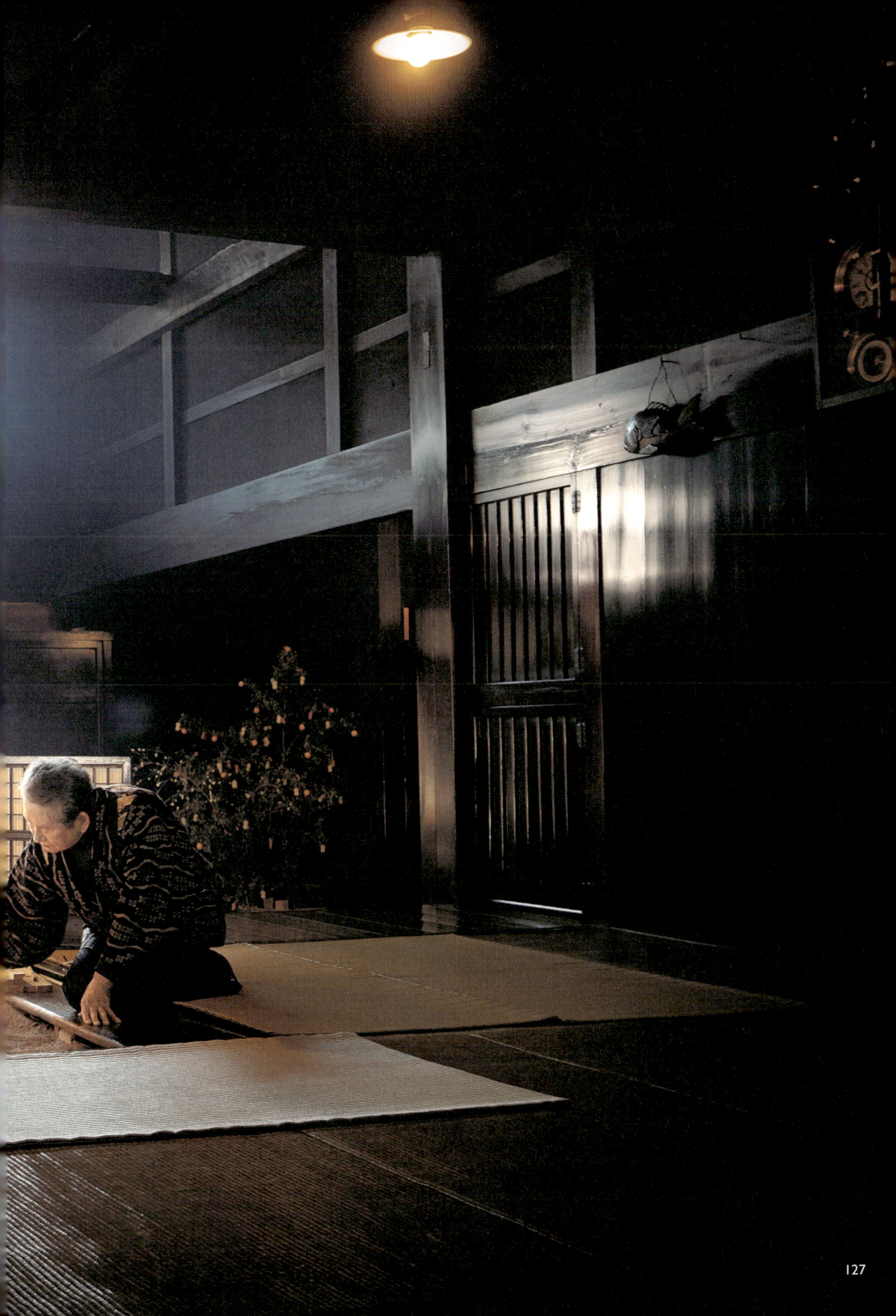

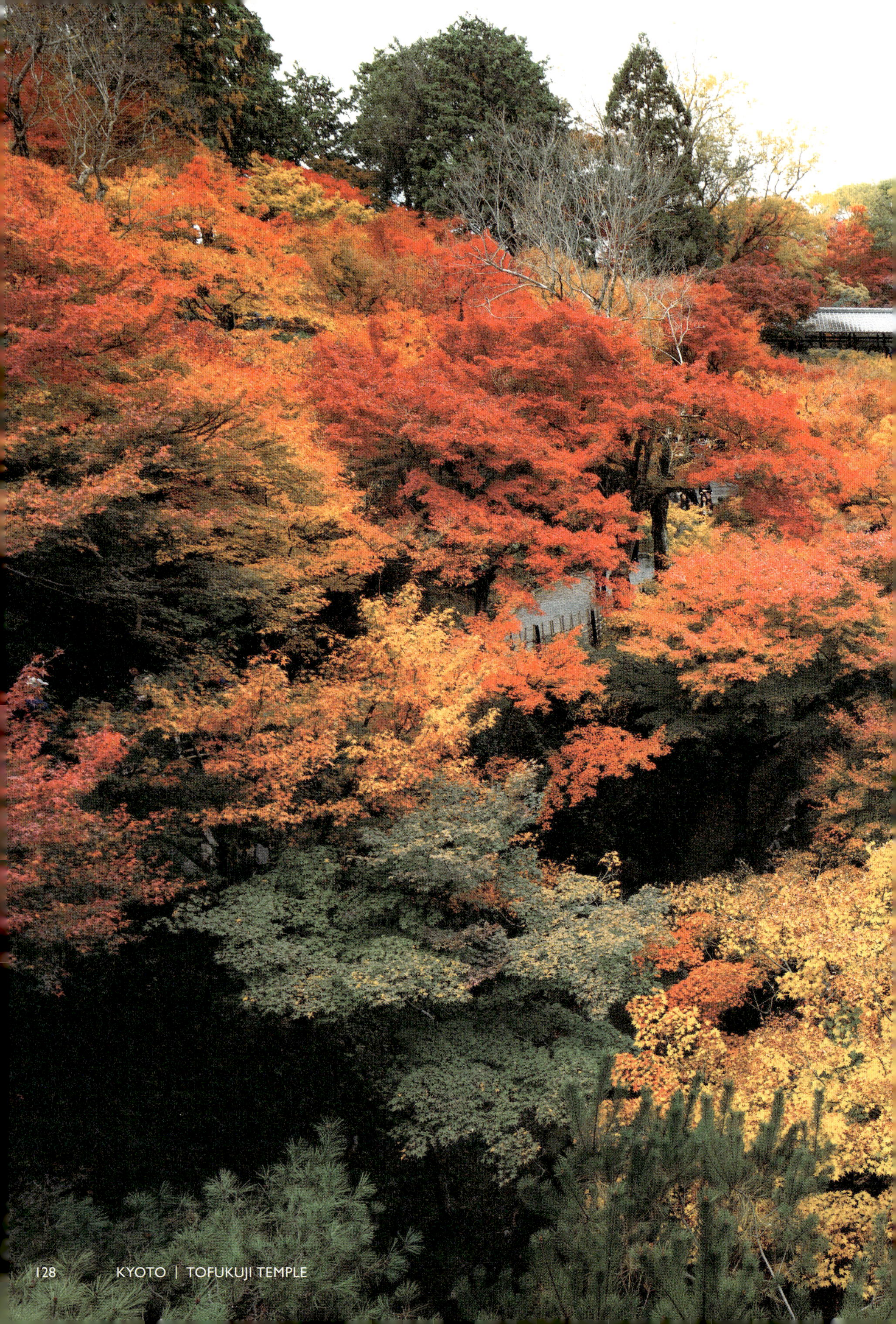

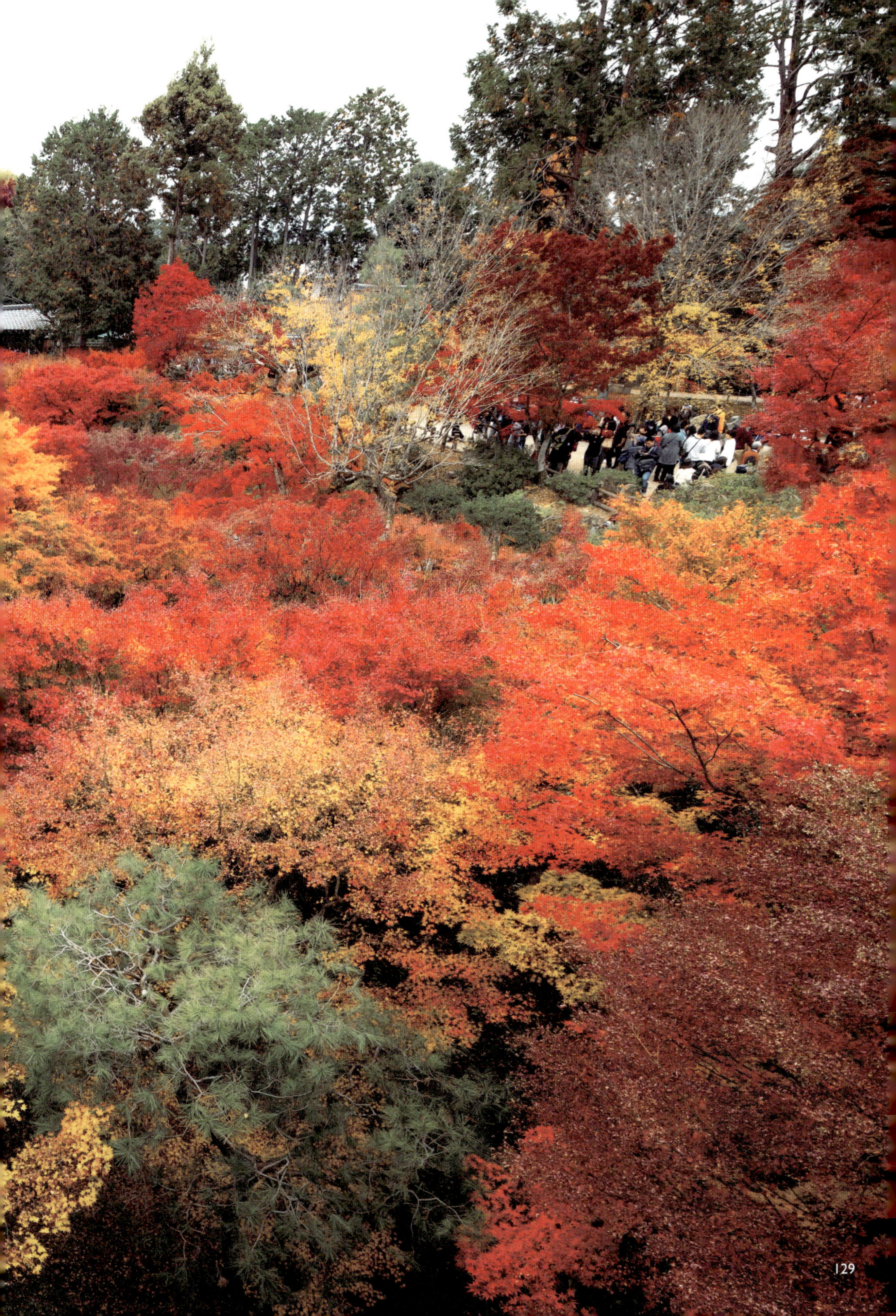

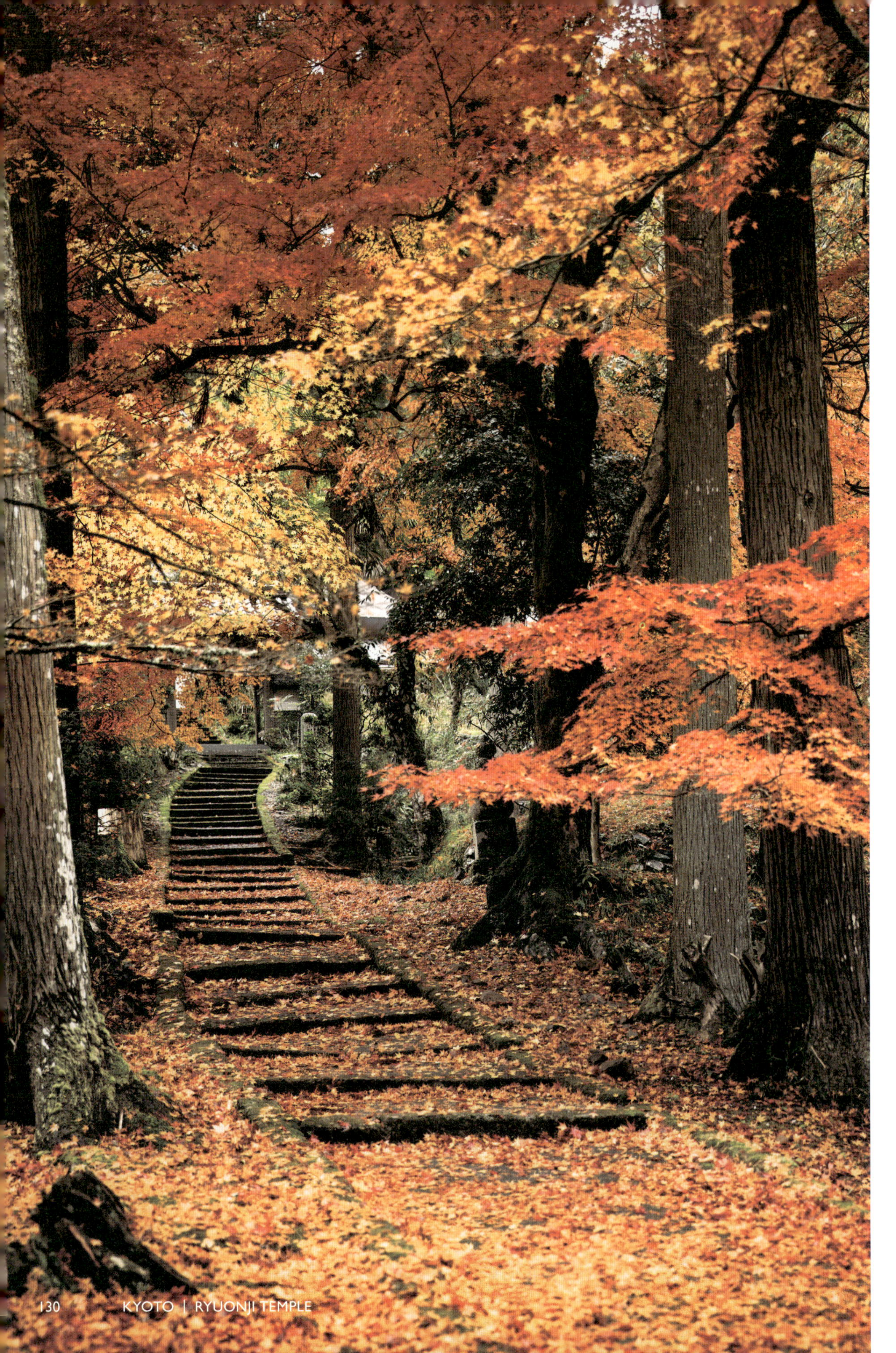

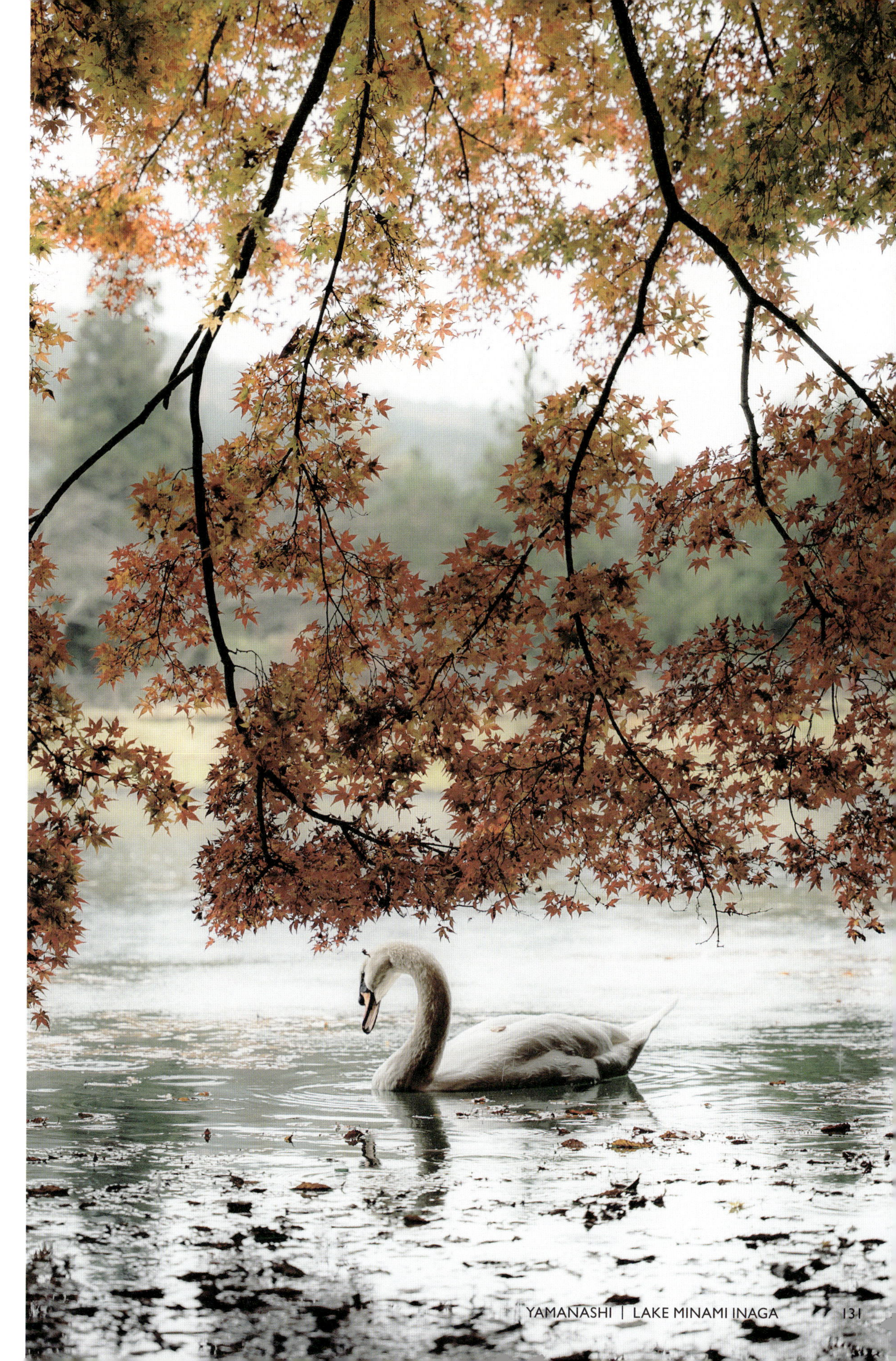

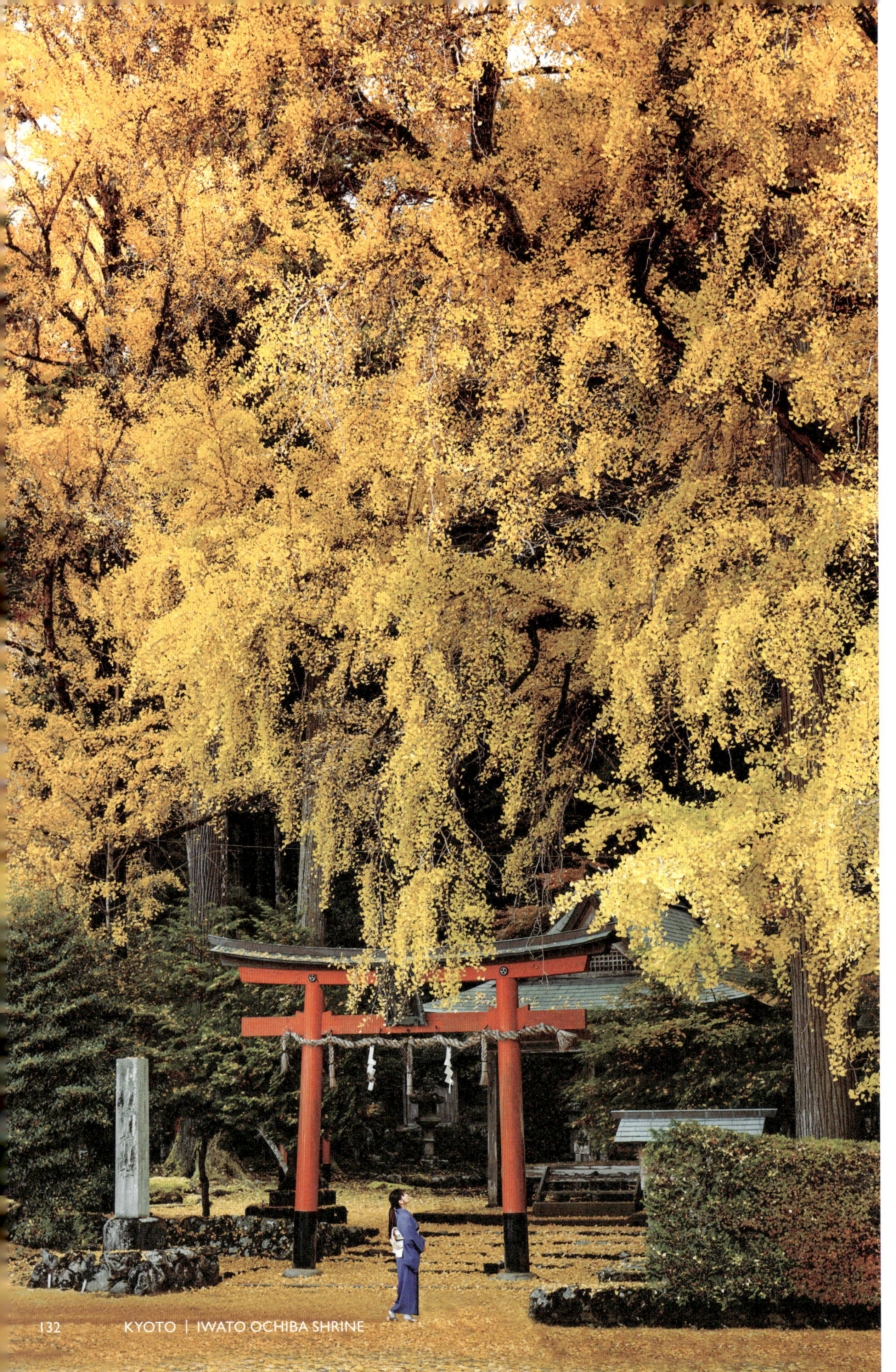

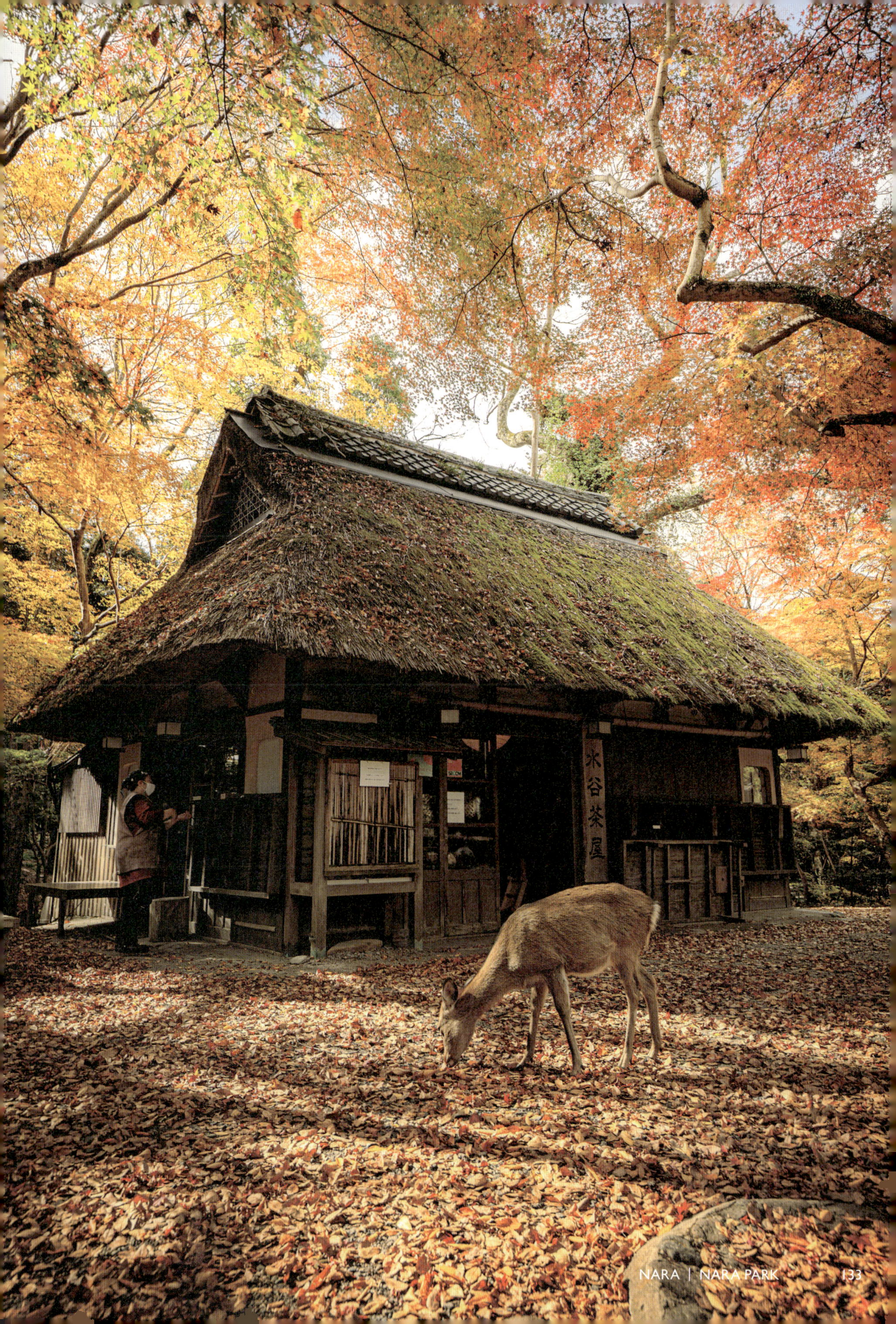
氷谷茶屋

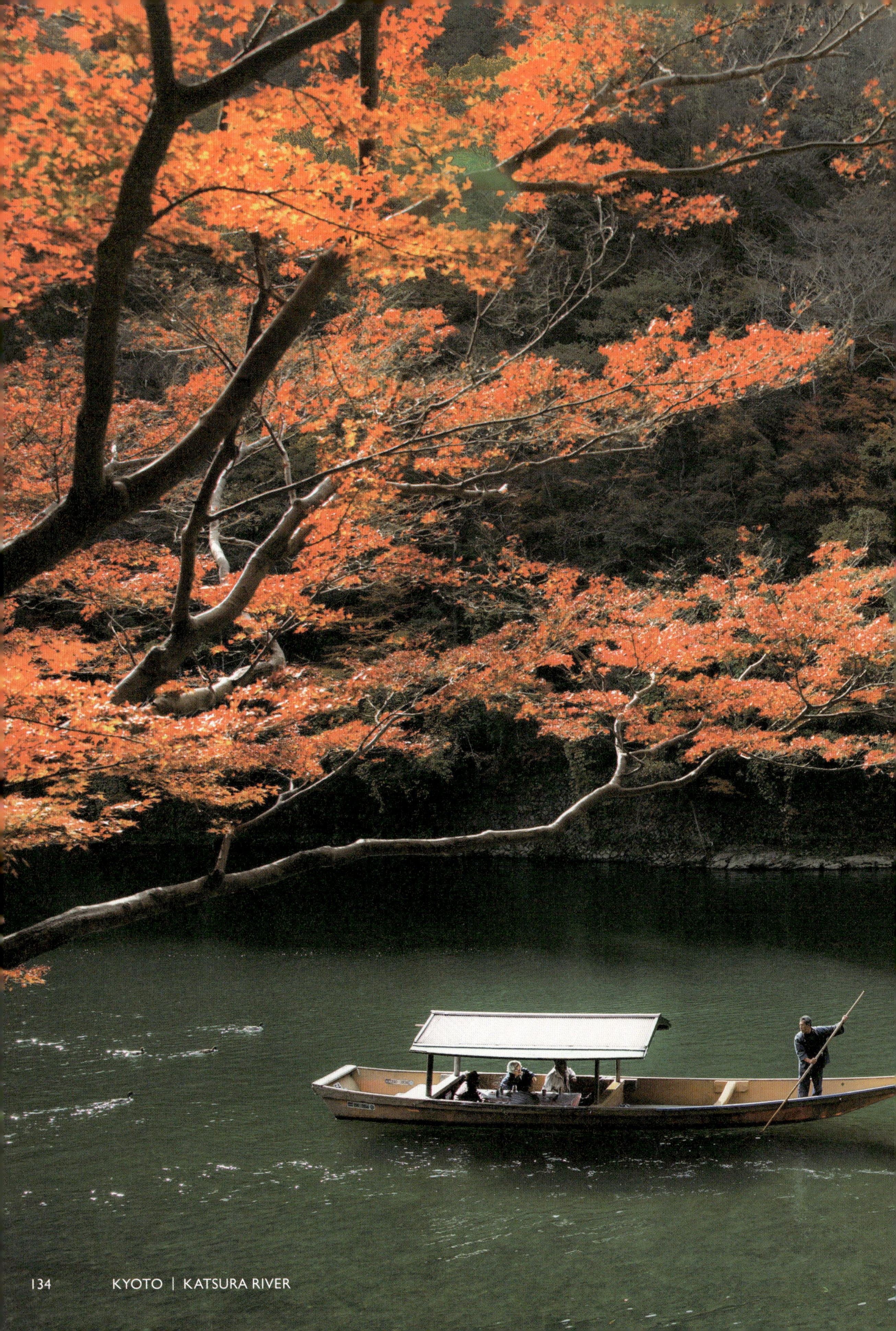

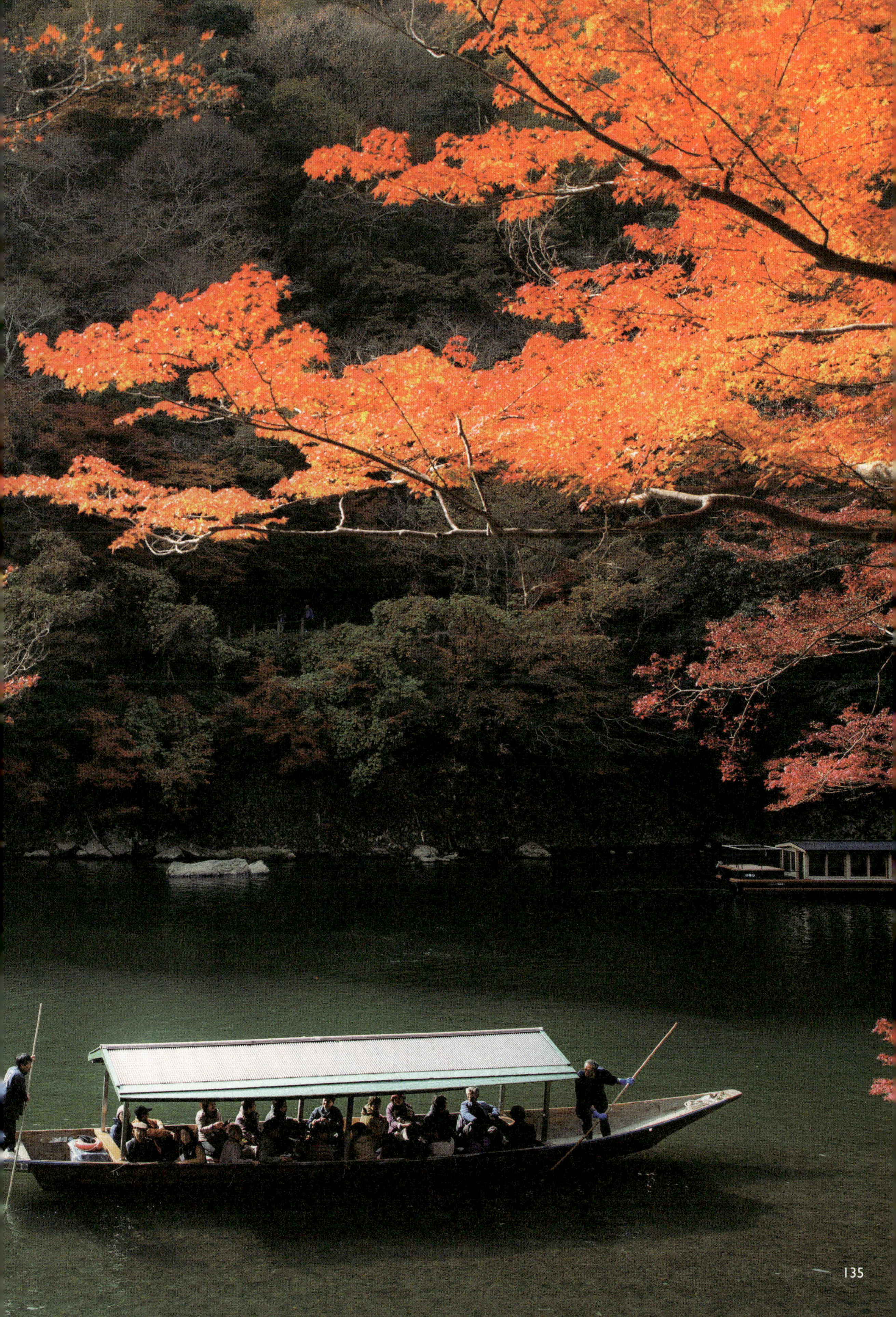

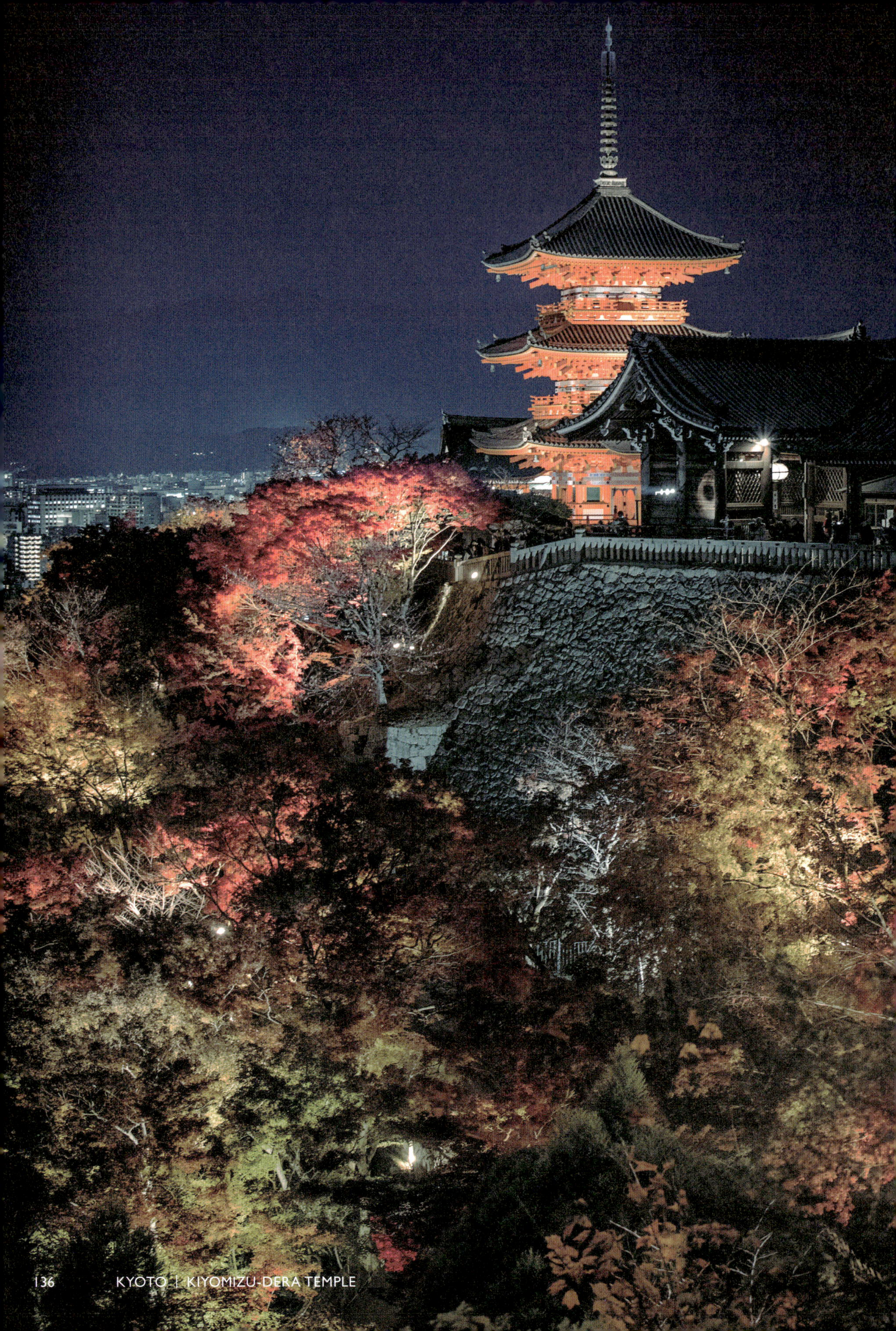

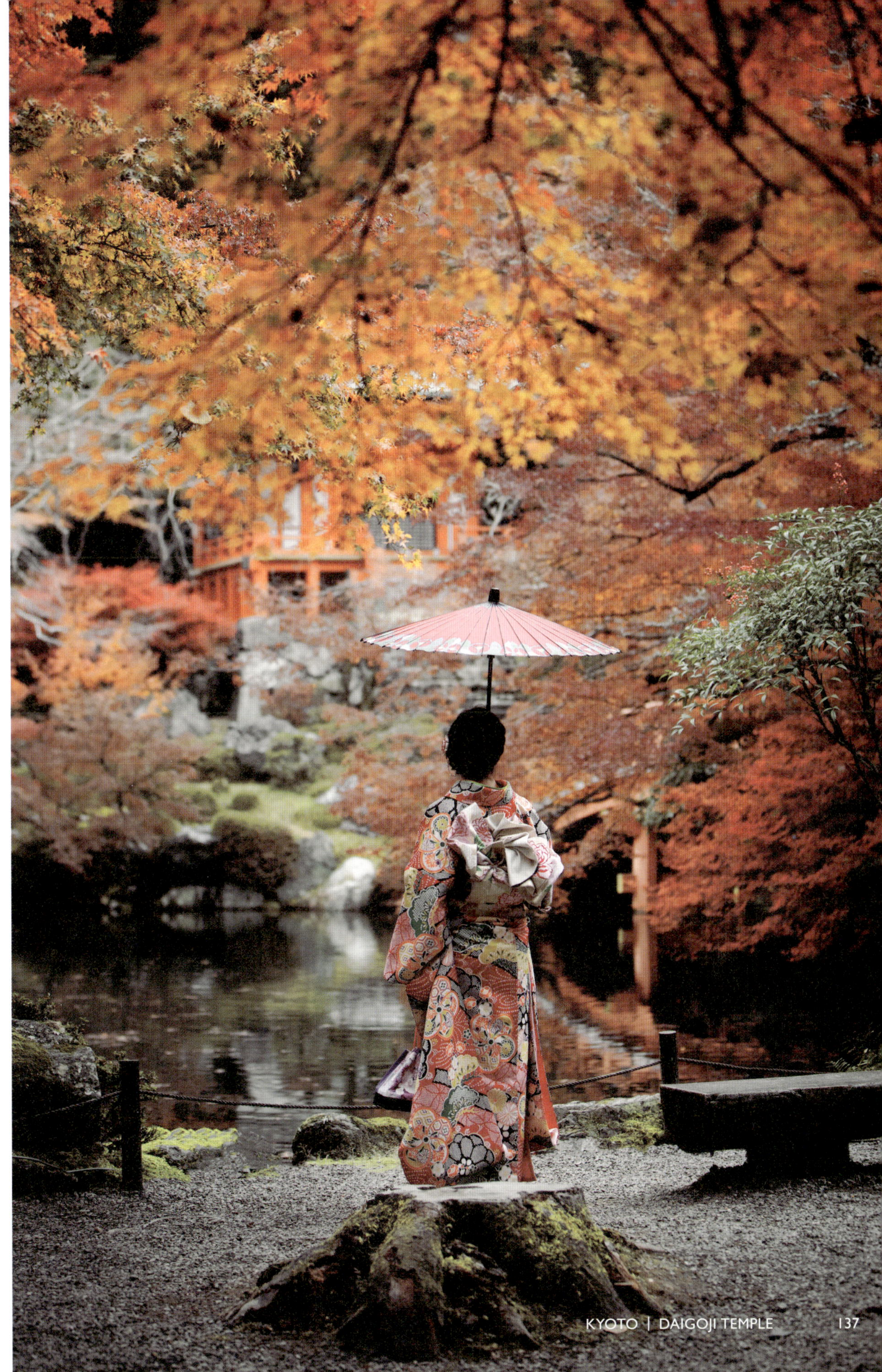

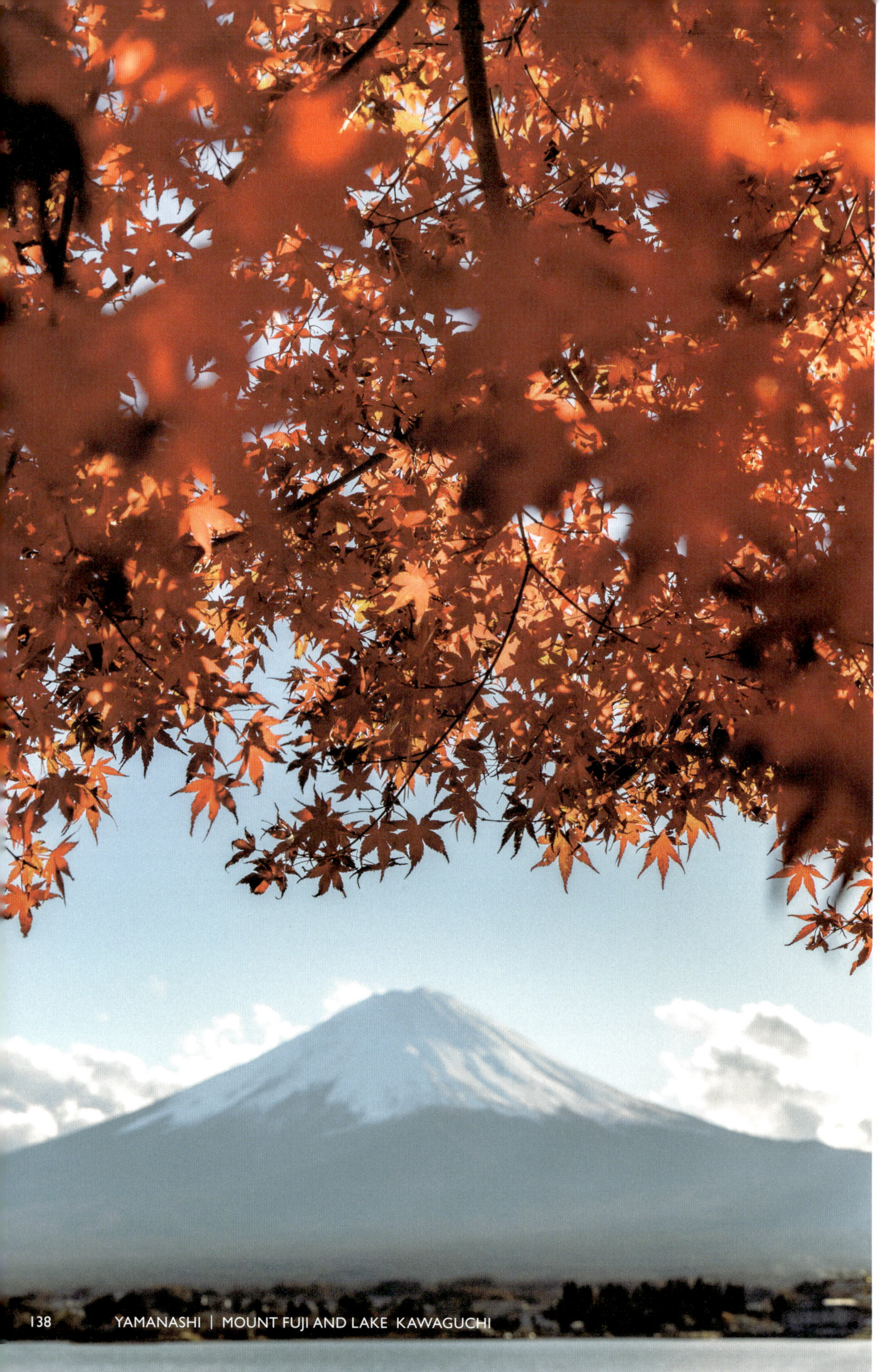

 YAMANASHI | MOUNT FUJI AND LAKE KAWAGUCHI

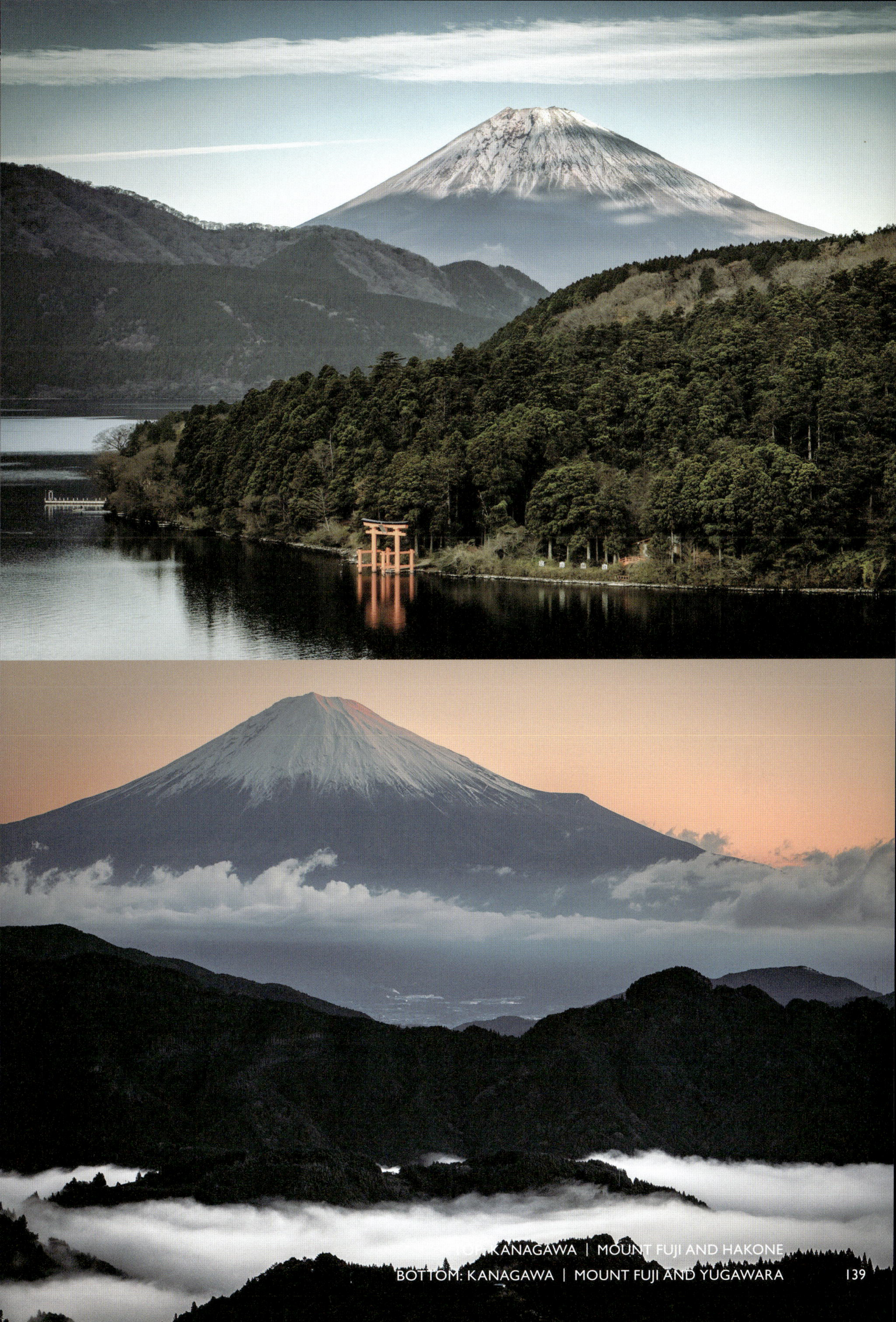

TOP: KANAGAWA | MOUNT FUJI AND HAKONE
BOTTOM: KANAGAWA | MOUNT FUJI AND YUGAWARA

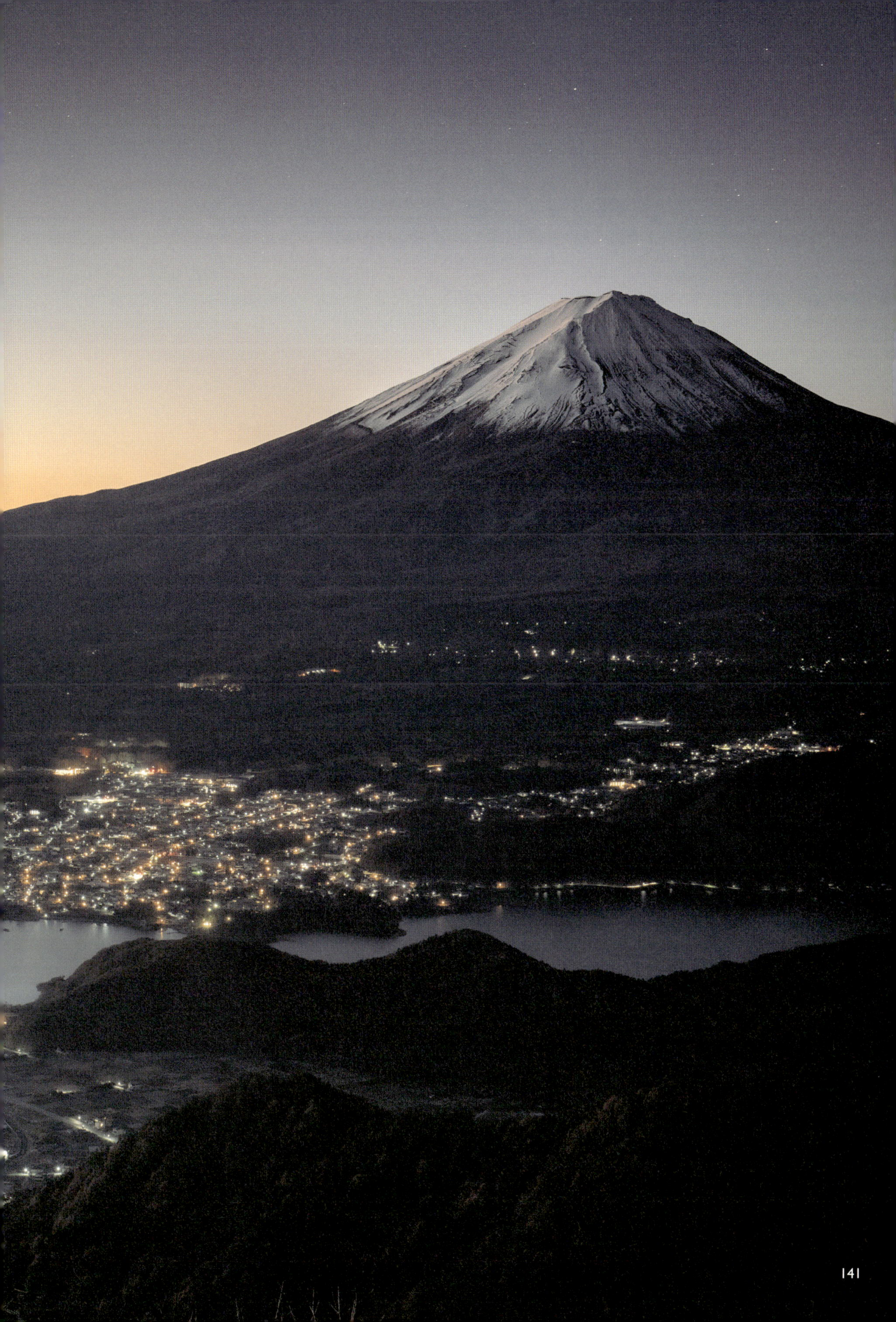

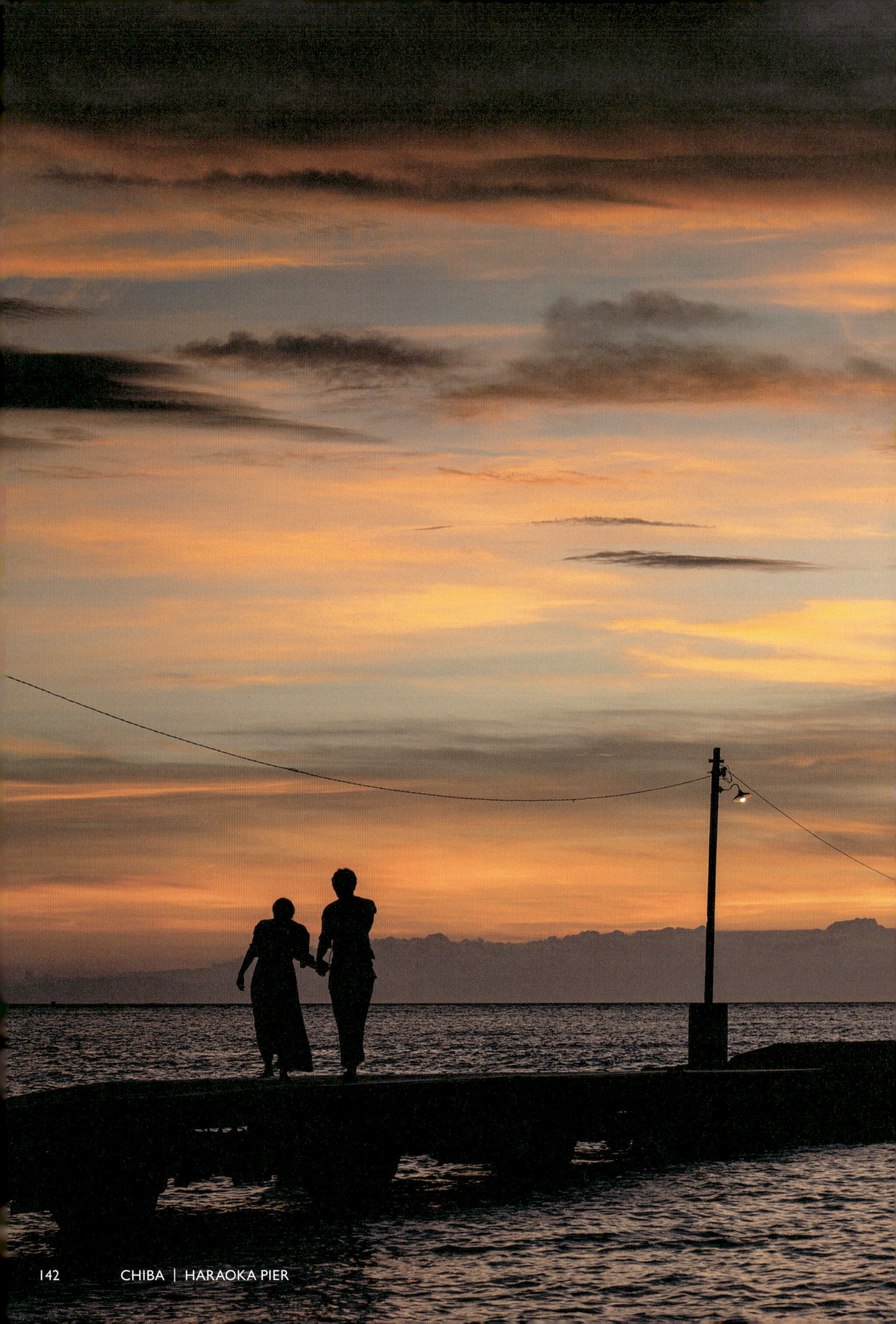

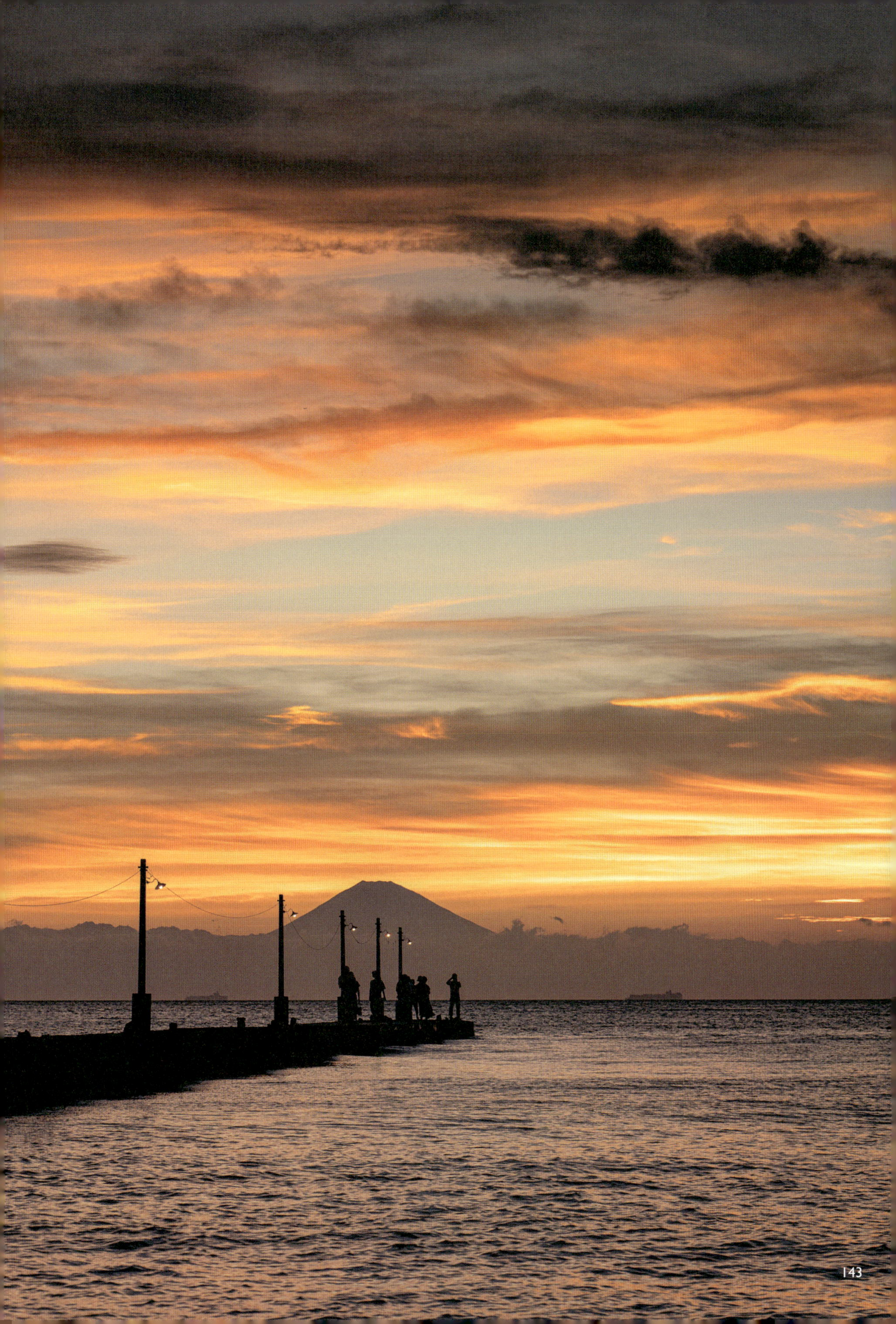

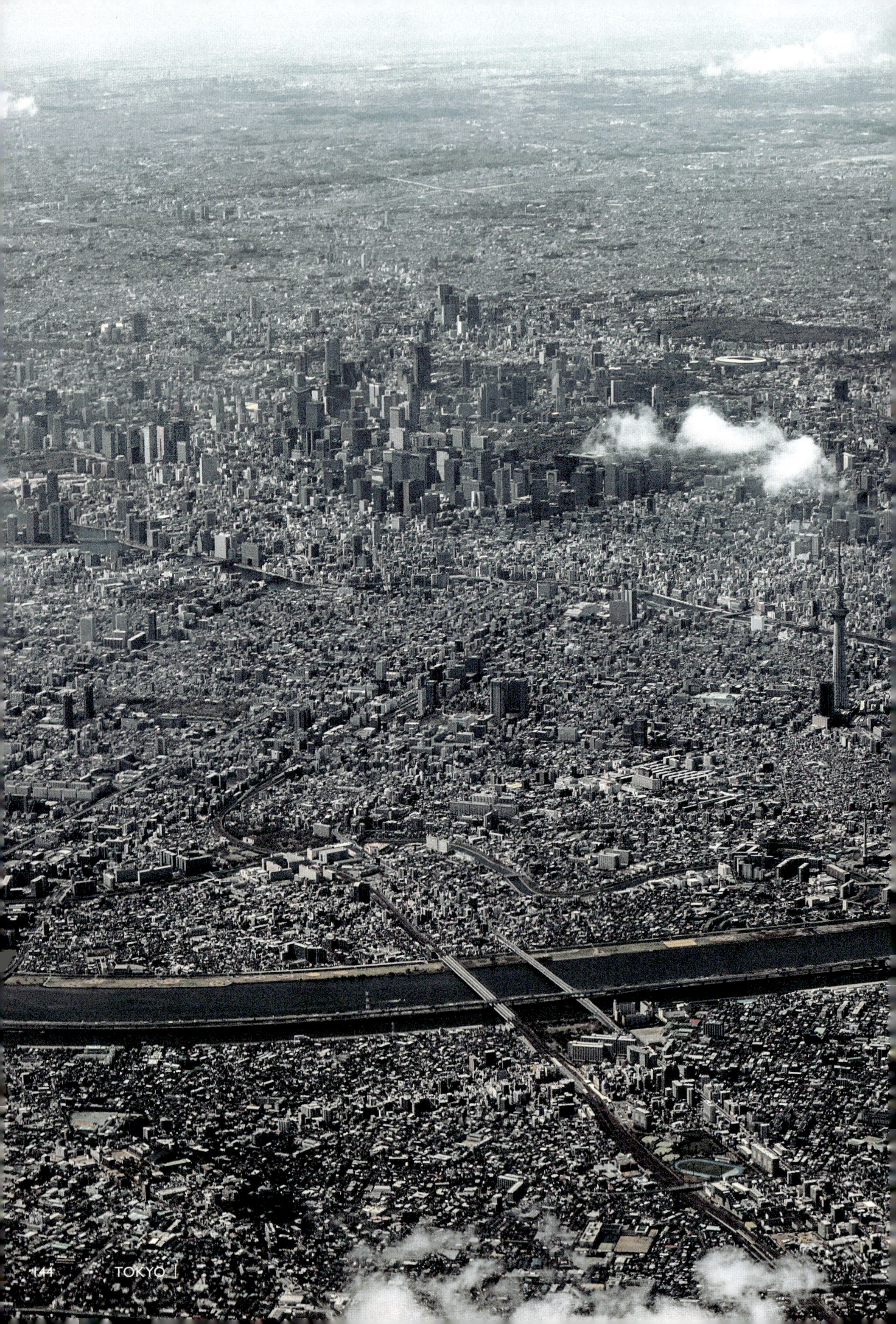

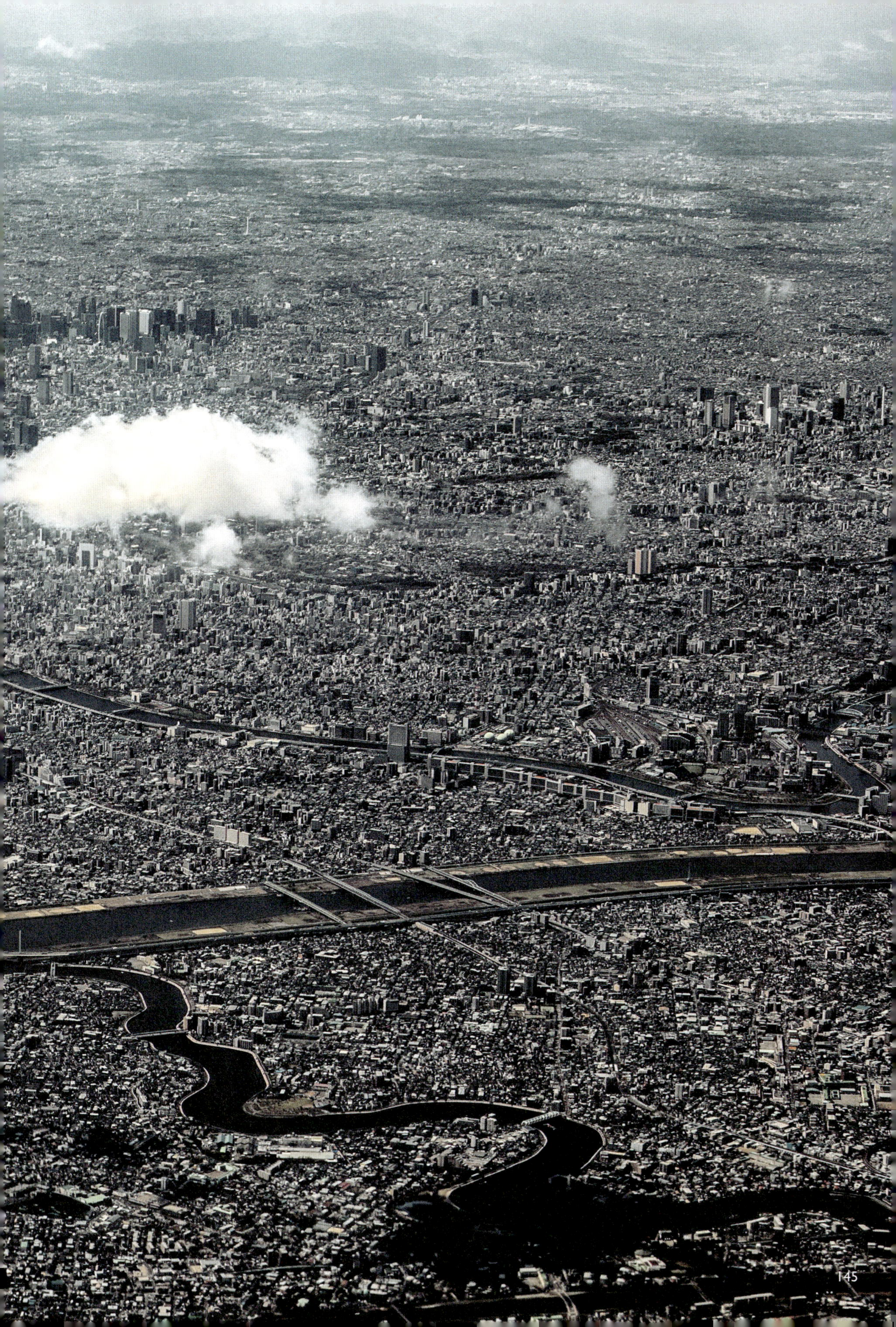

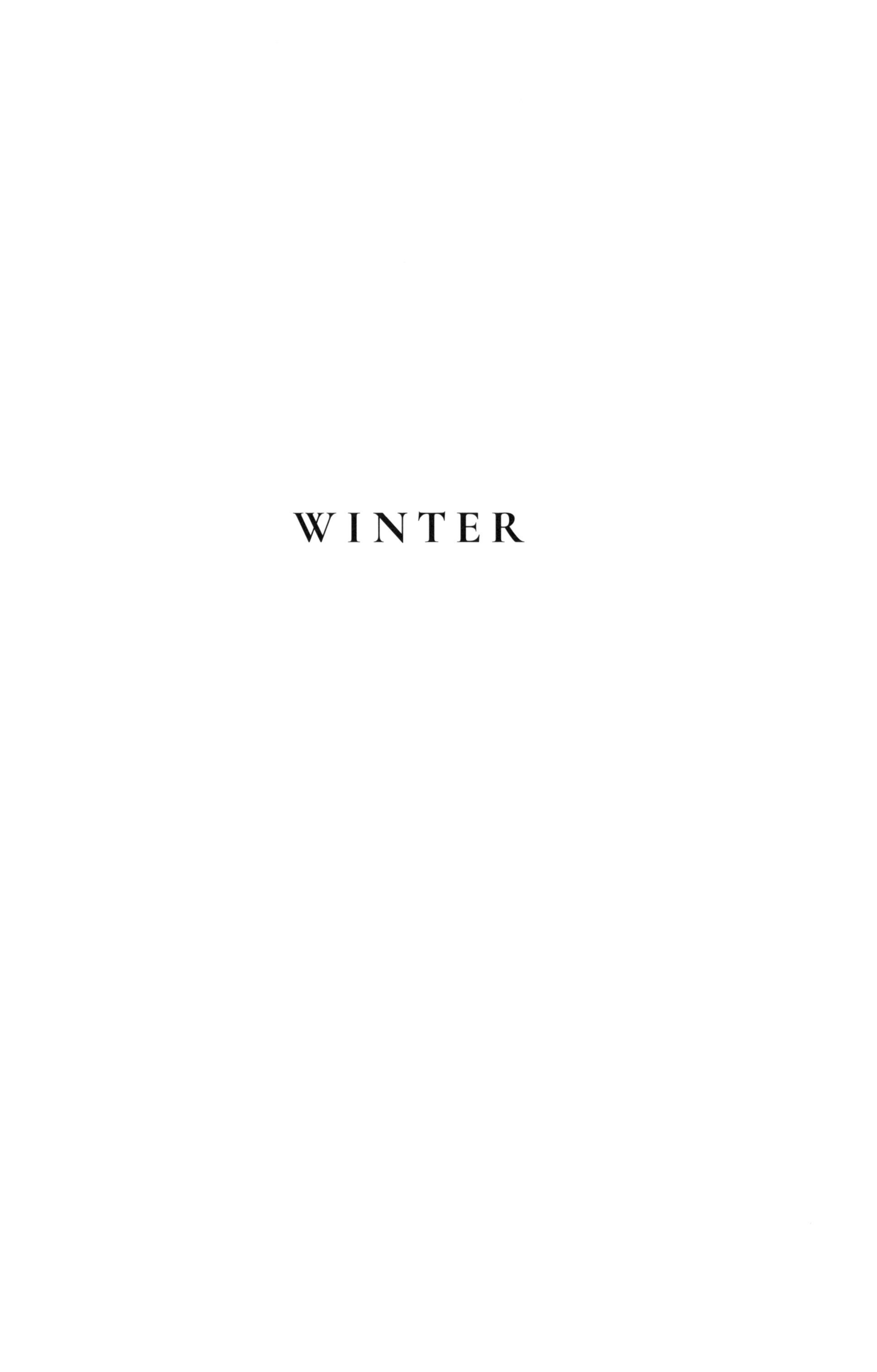

WINTER

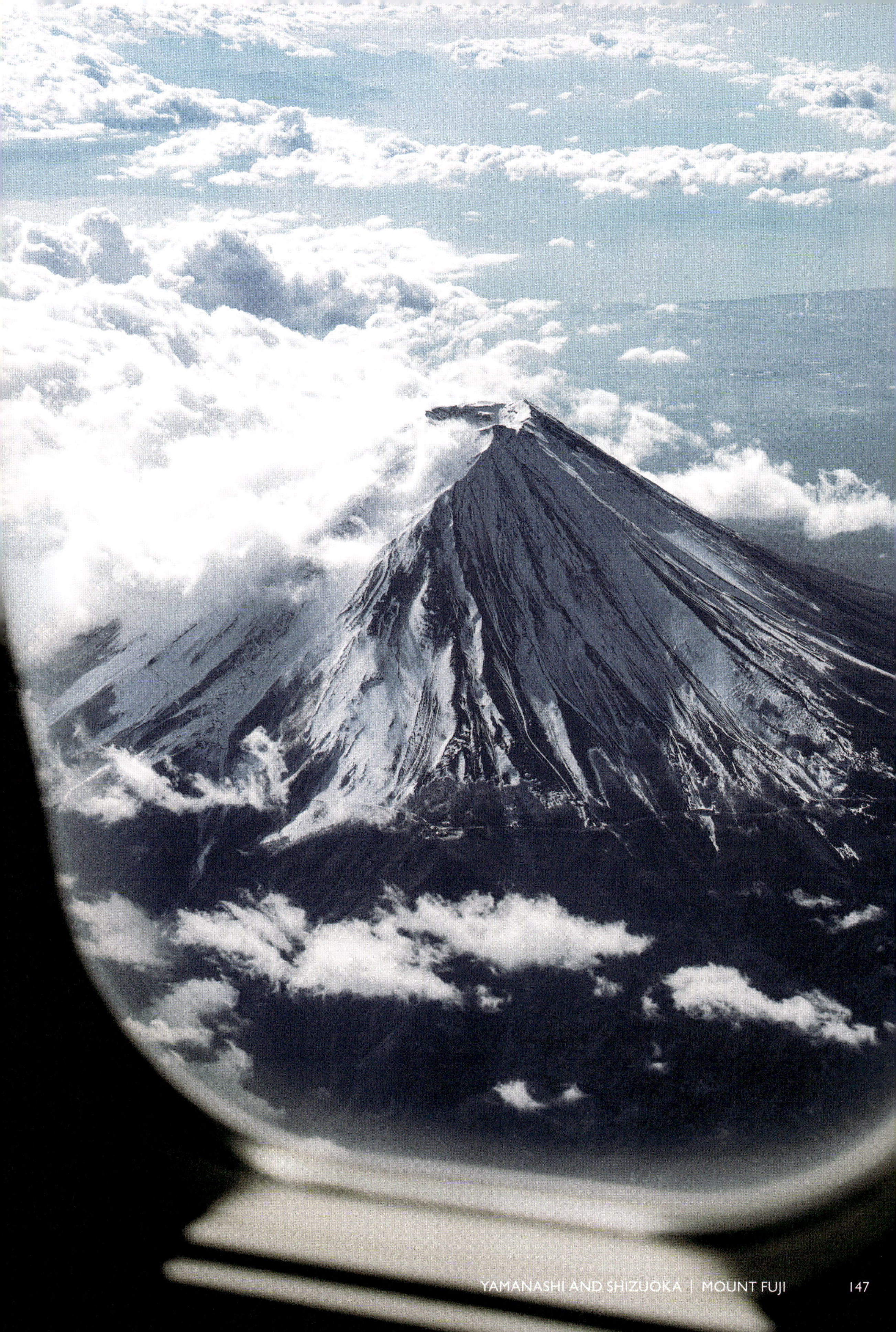

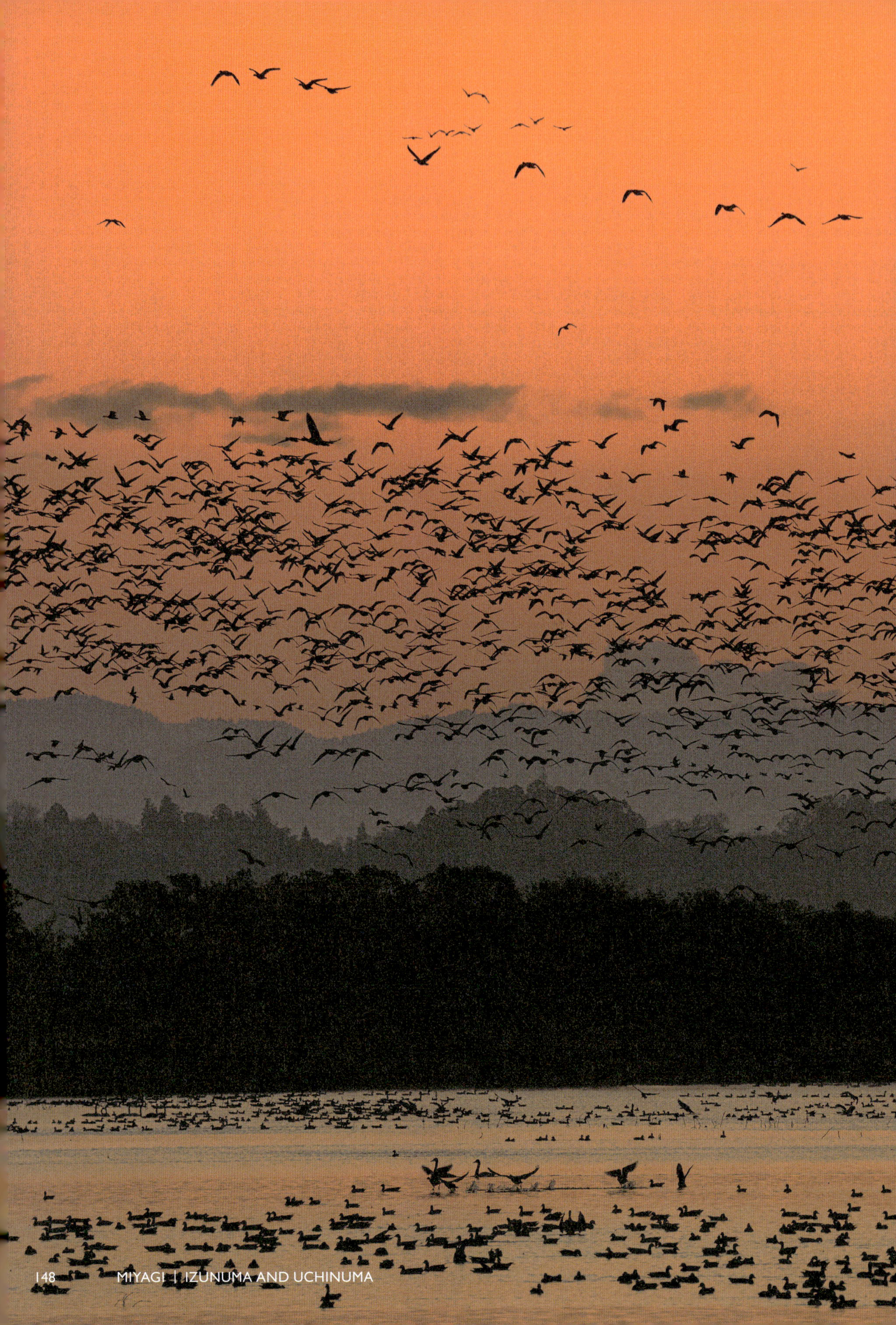

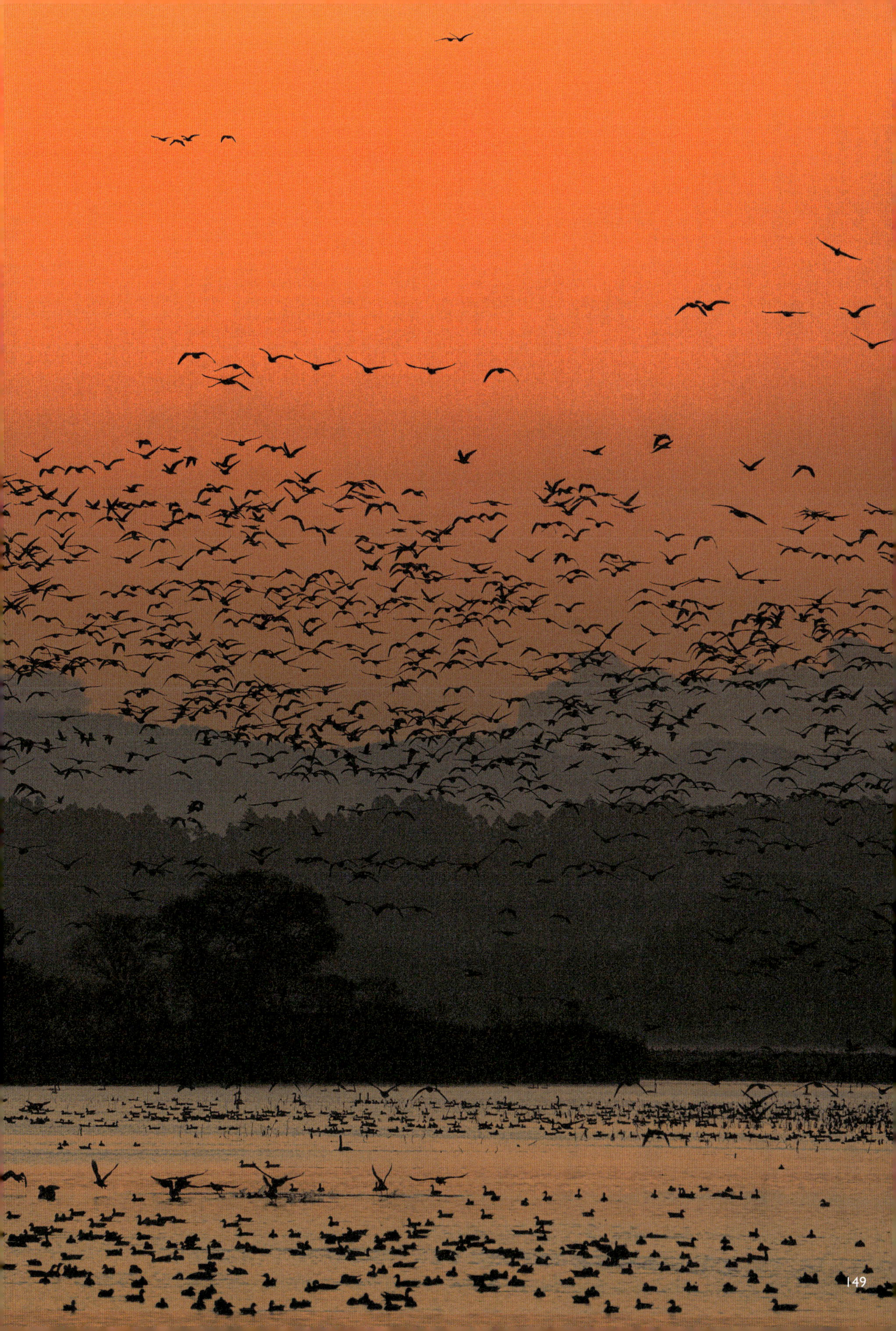

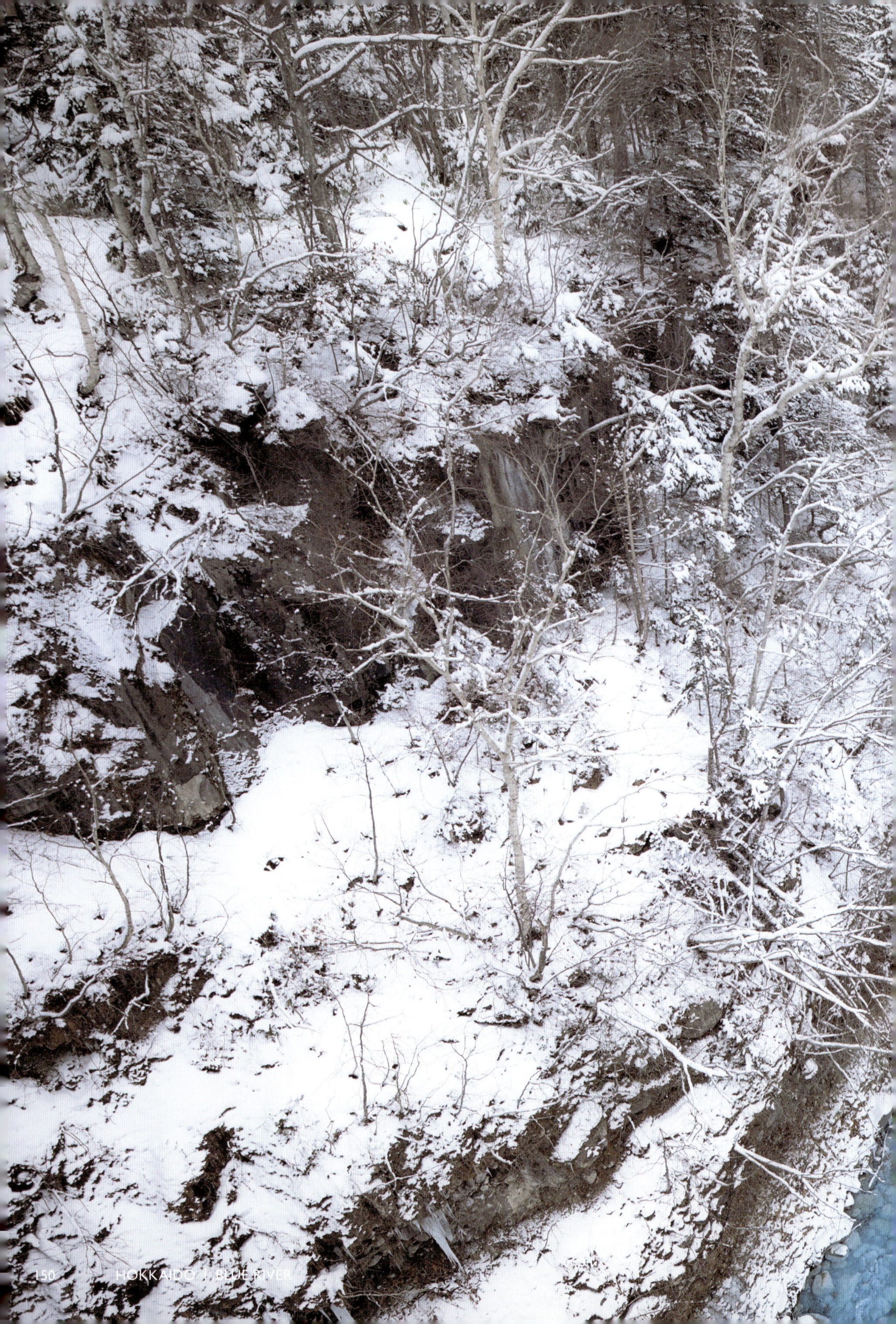

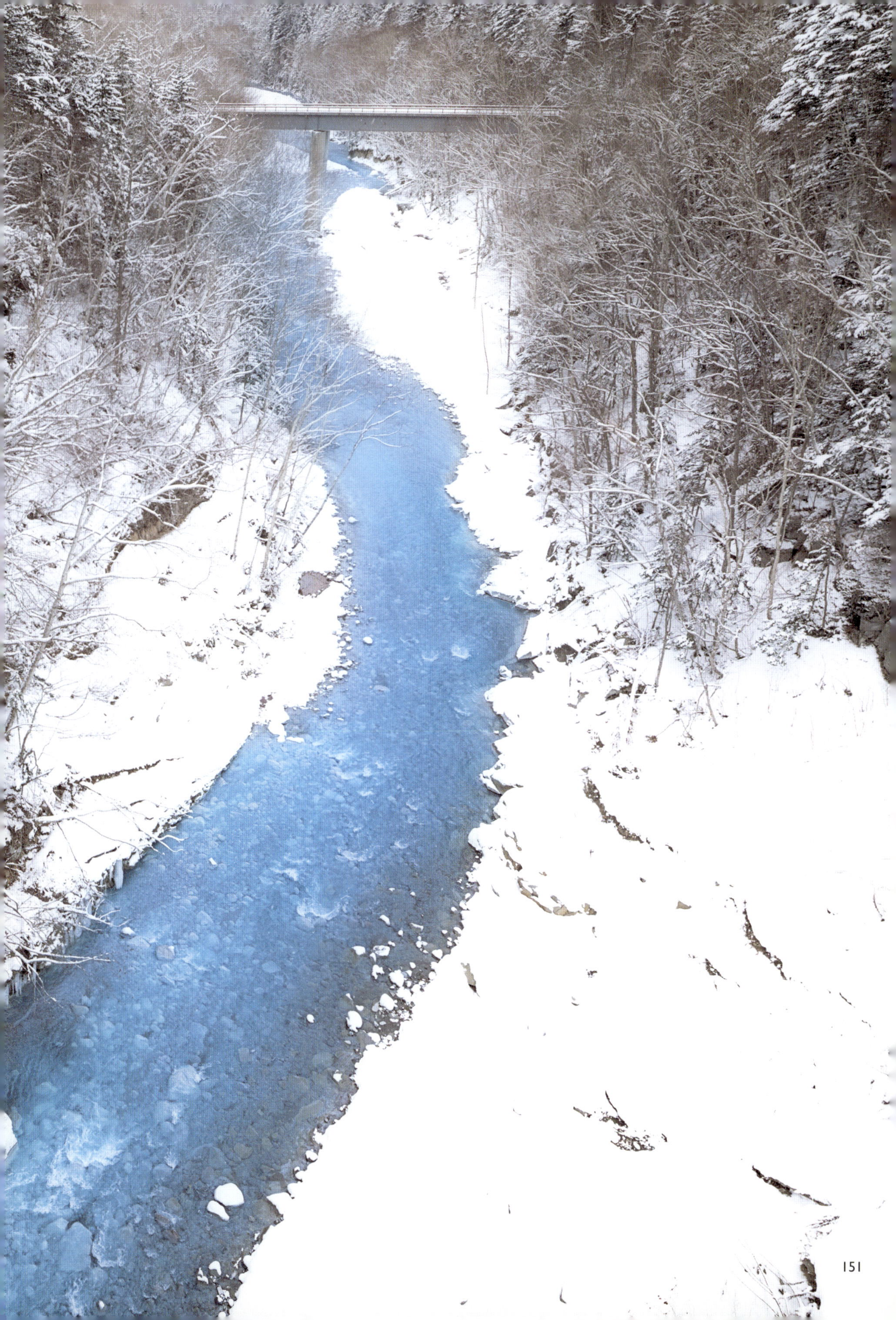

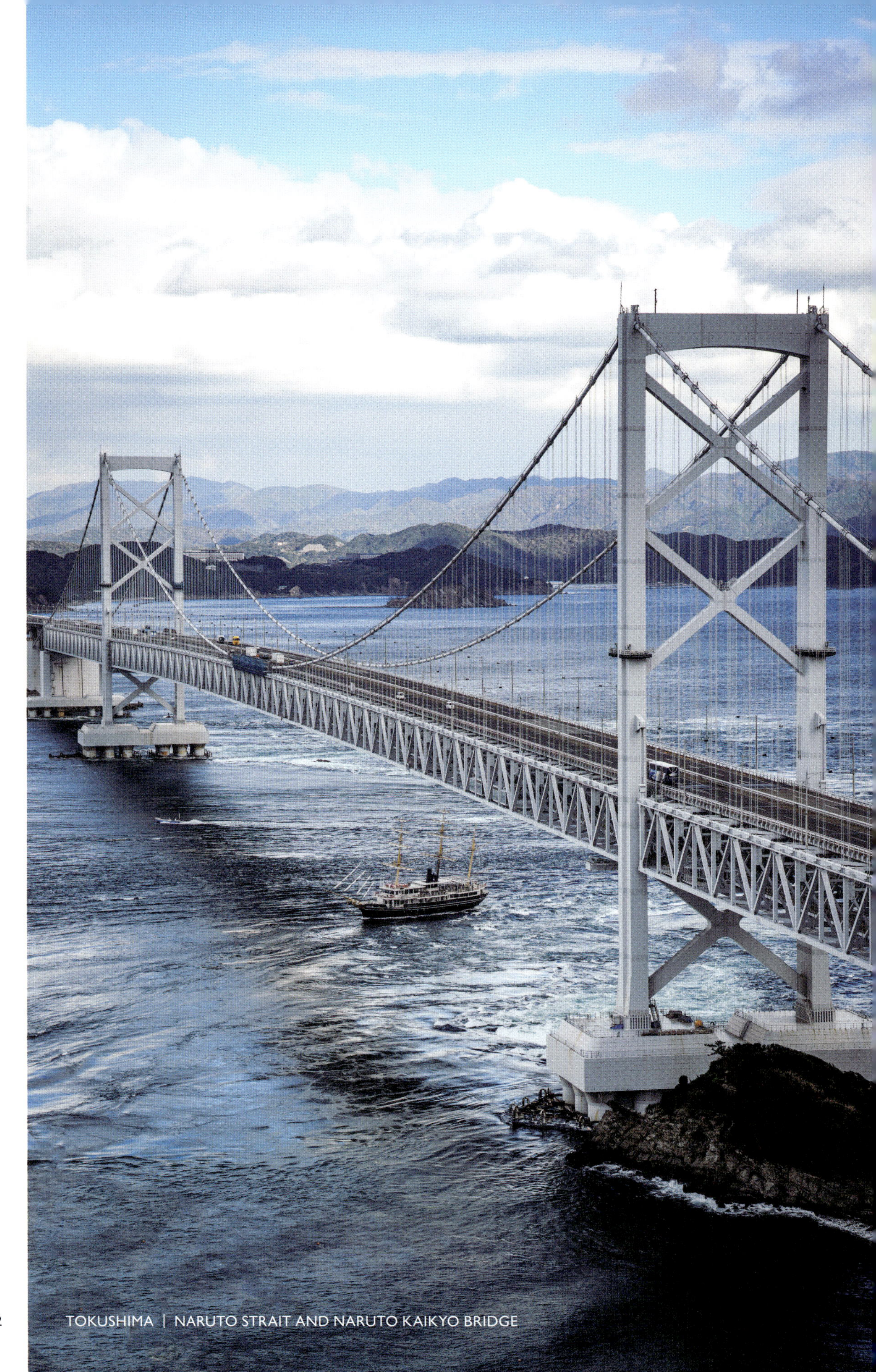

 TOKUSHIMA | NARUTO STRAIT AND NARUTO KAIKYO BRIDGE

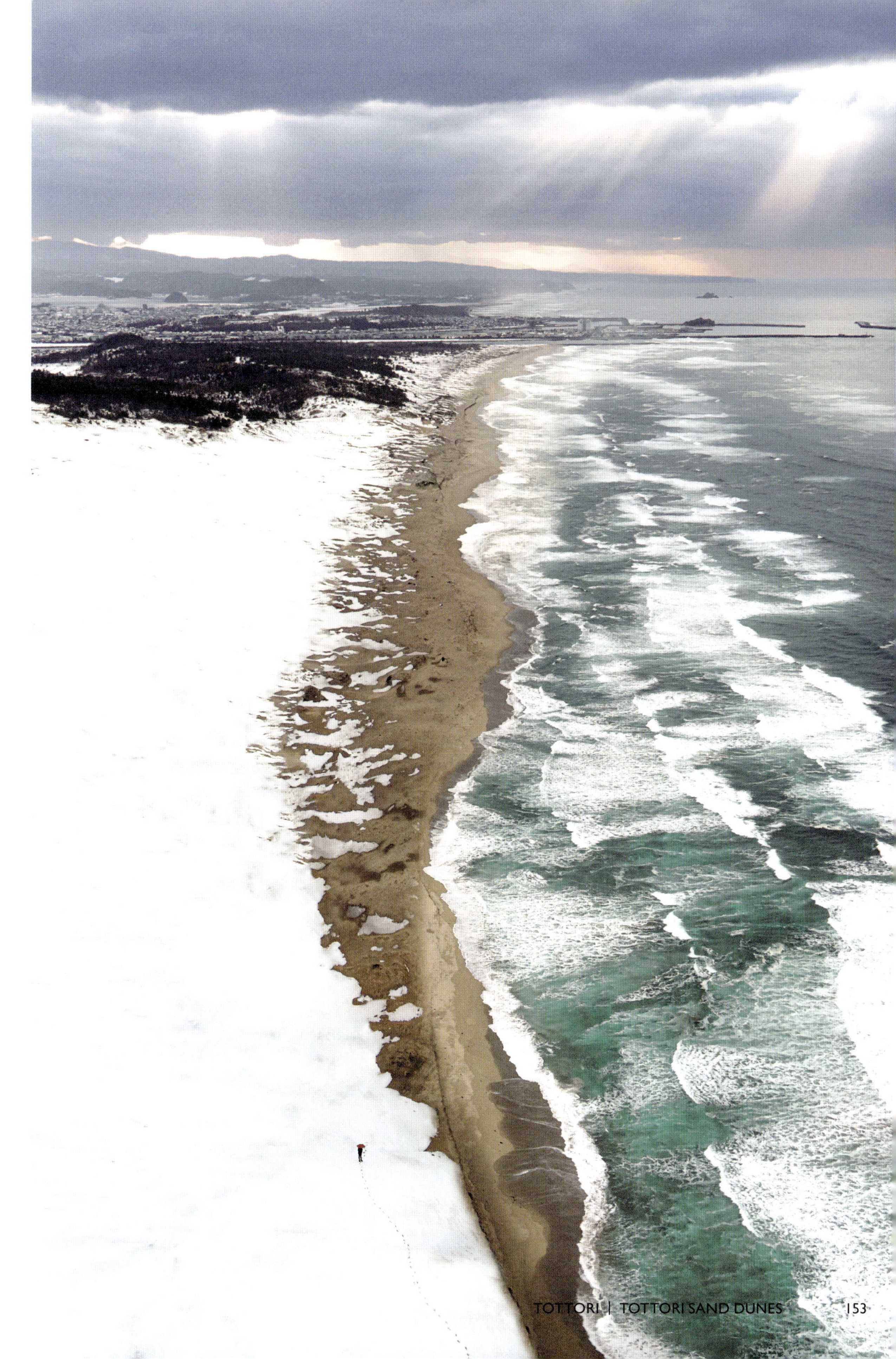

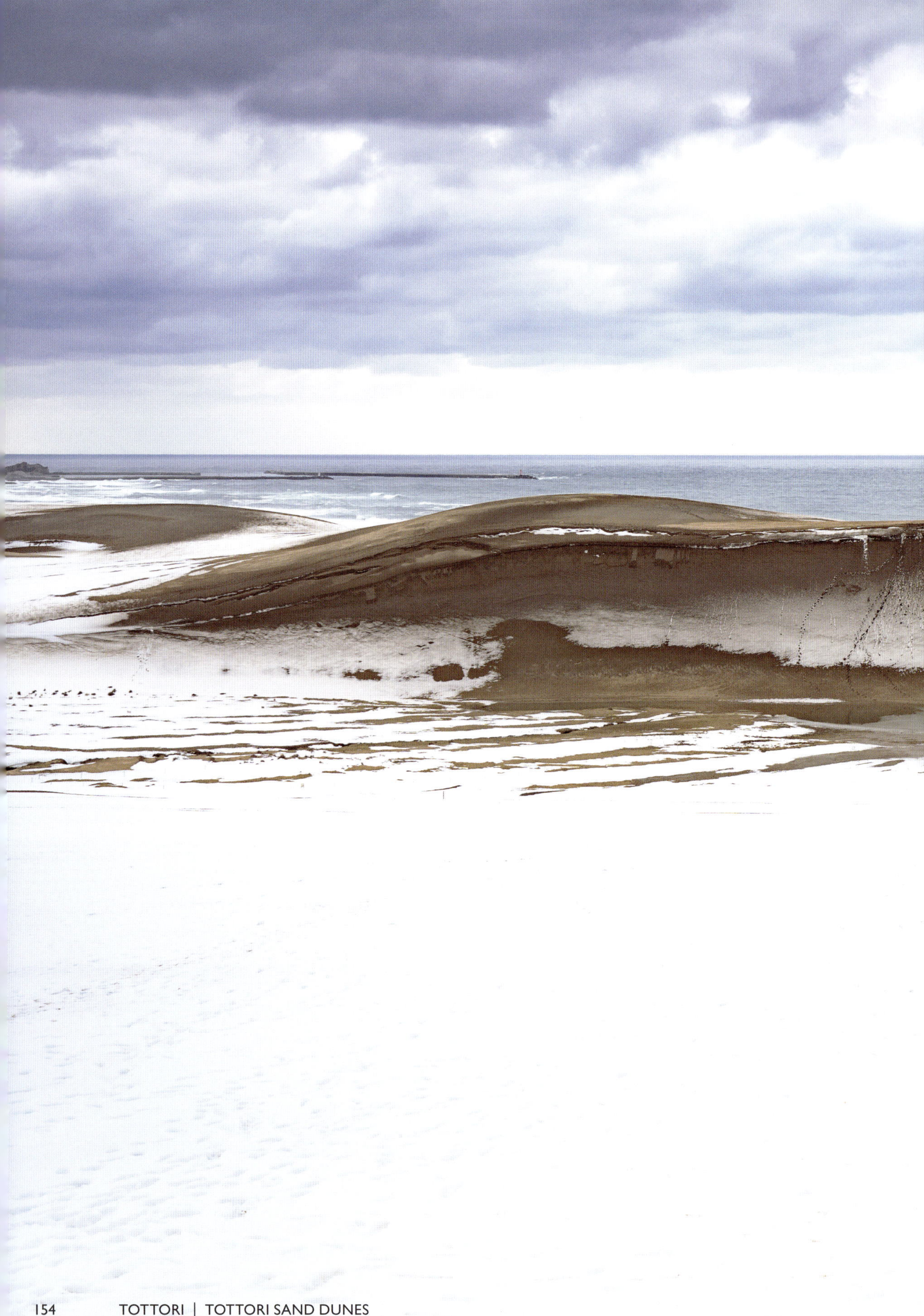

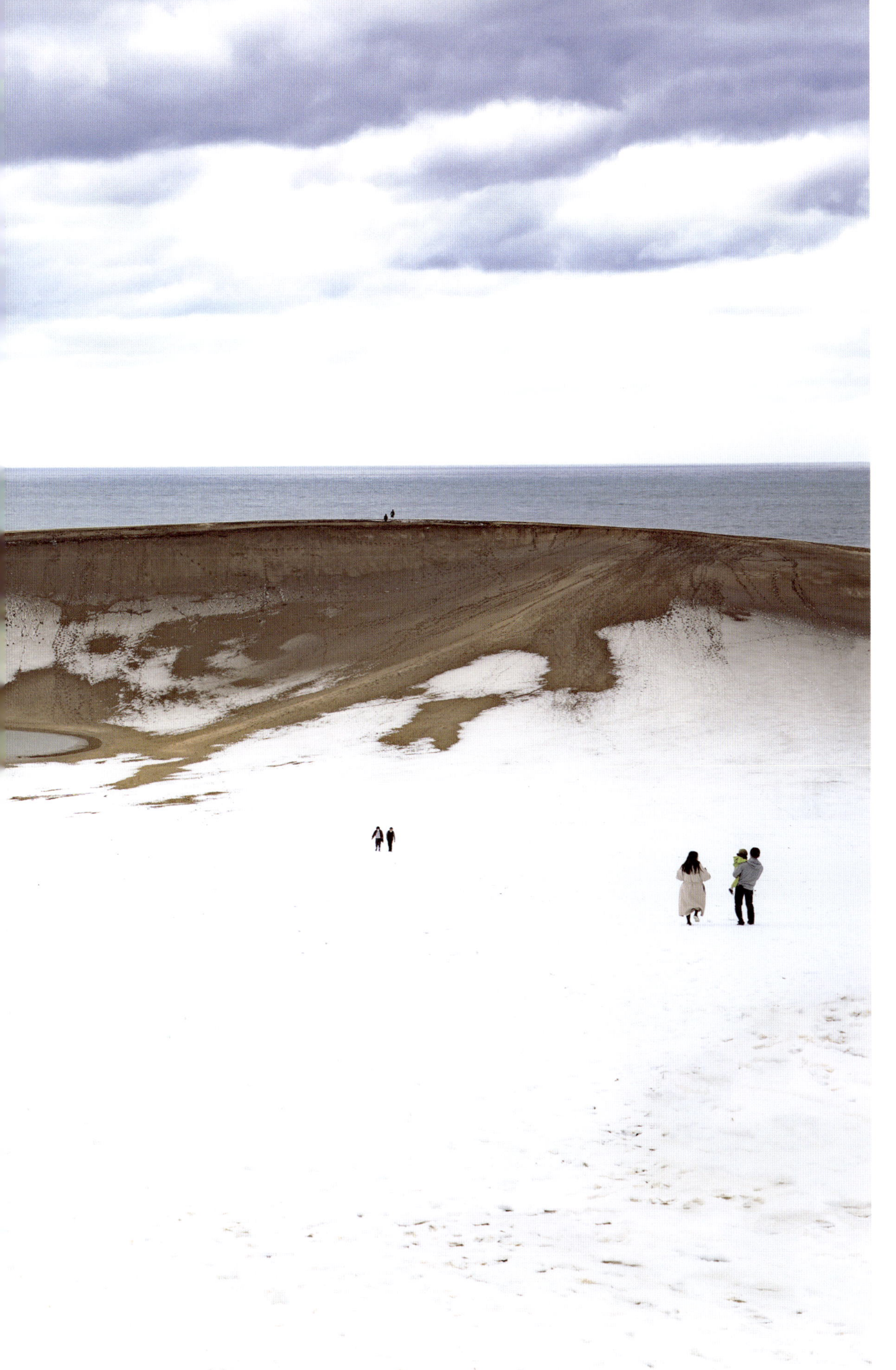

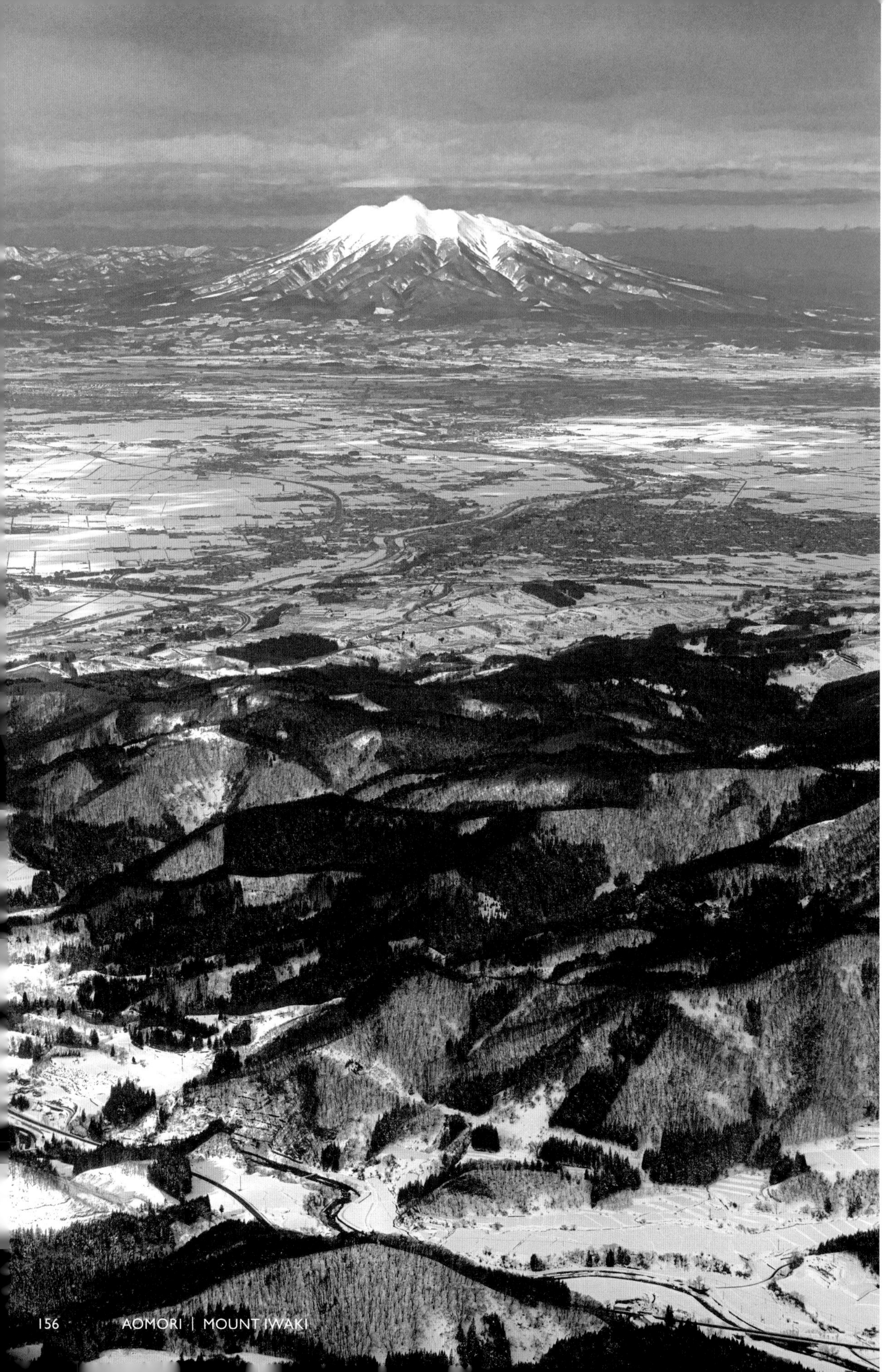

 AOMORI | MOUNT IWAKI

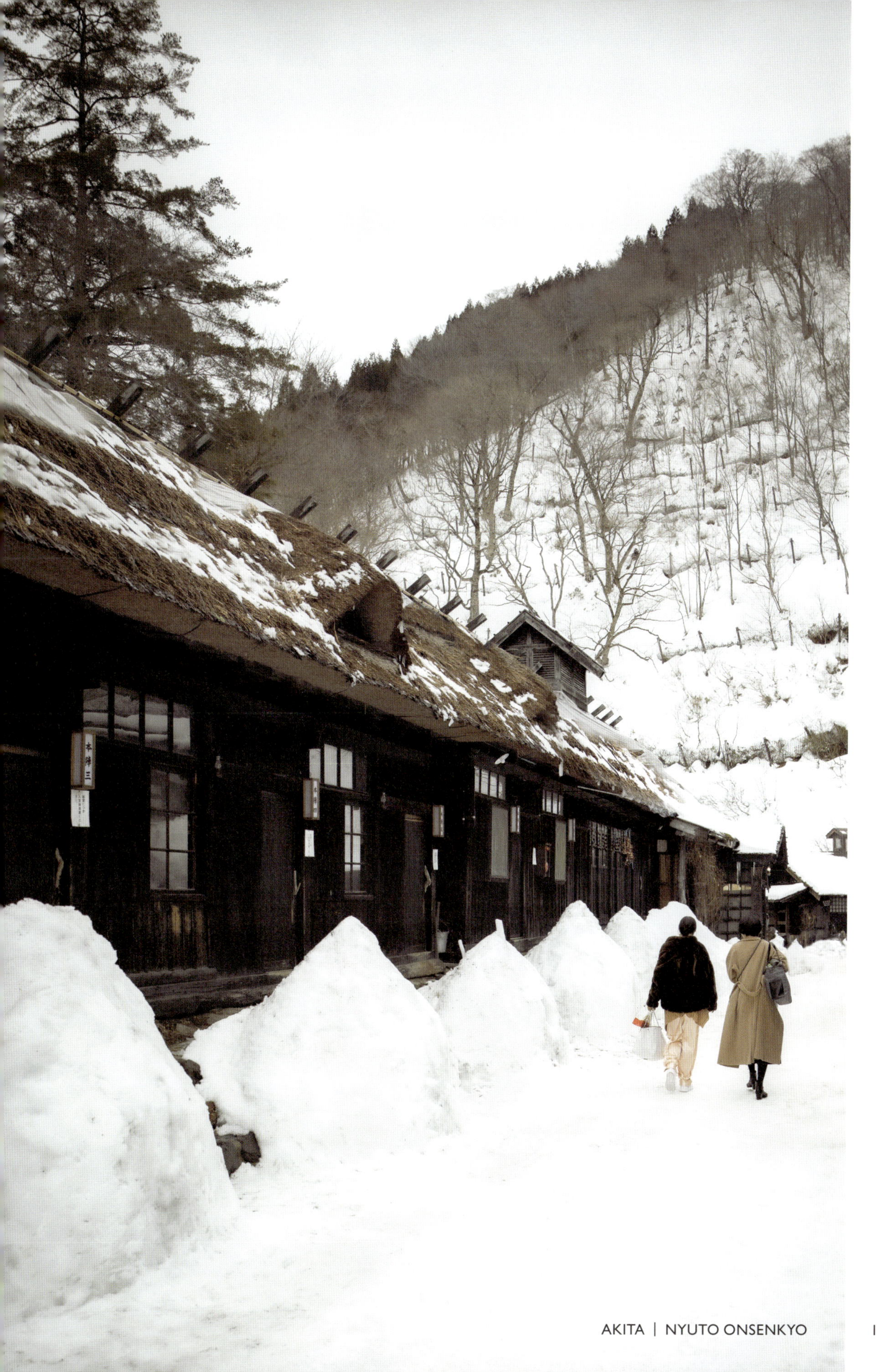

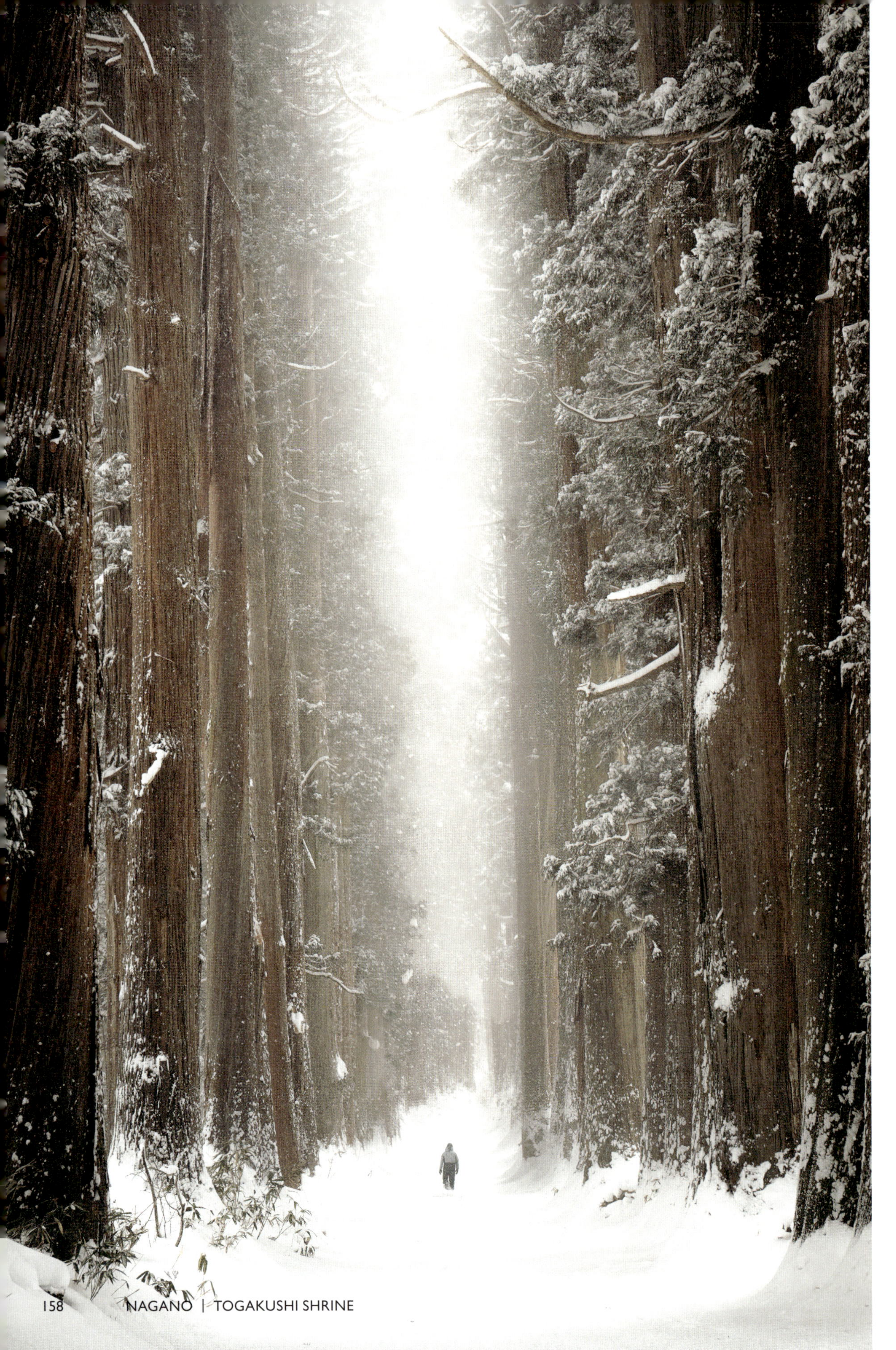

 NAGANO | TOGAKUSHI SHRINE

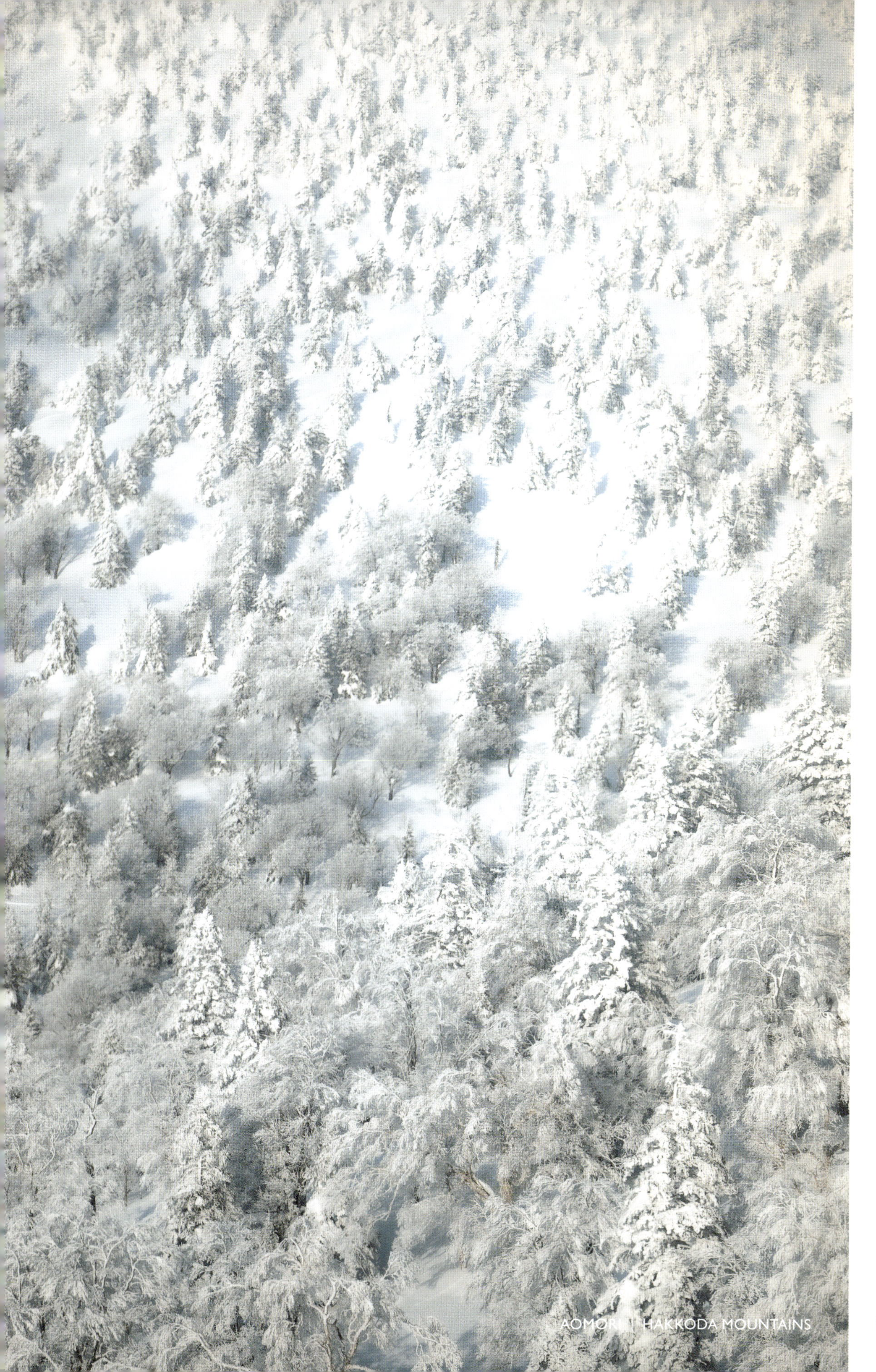

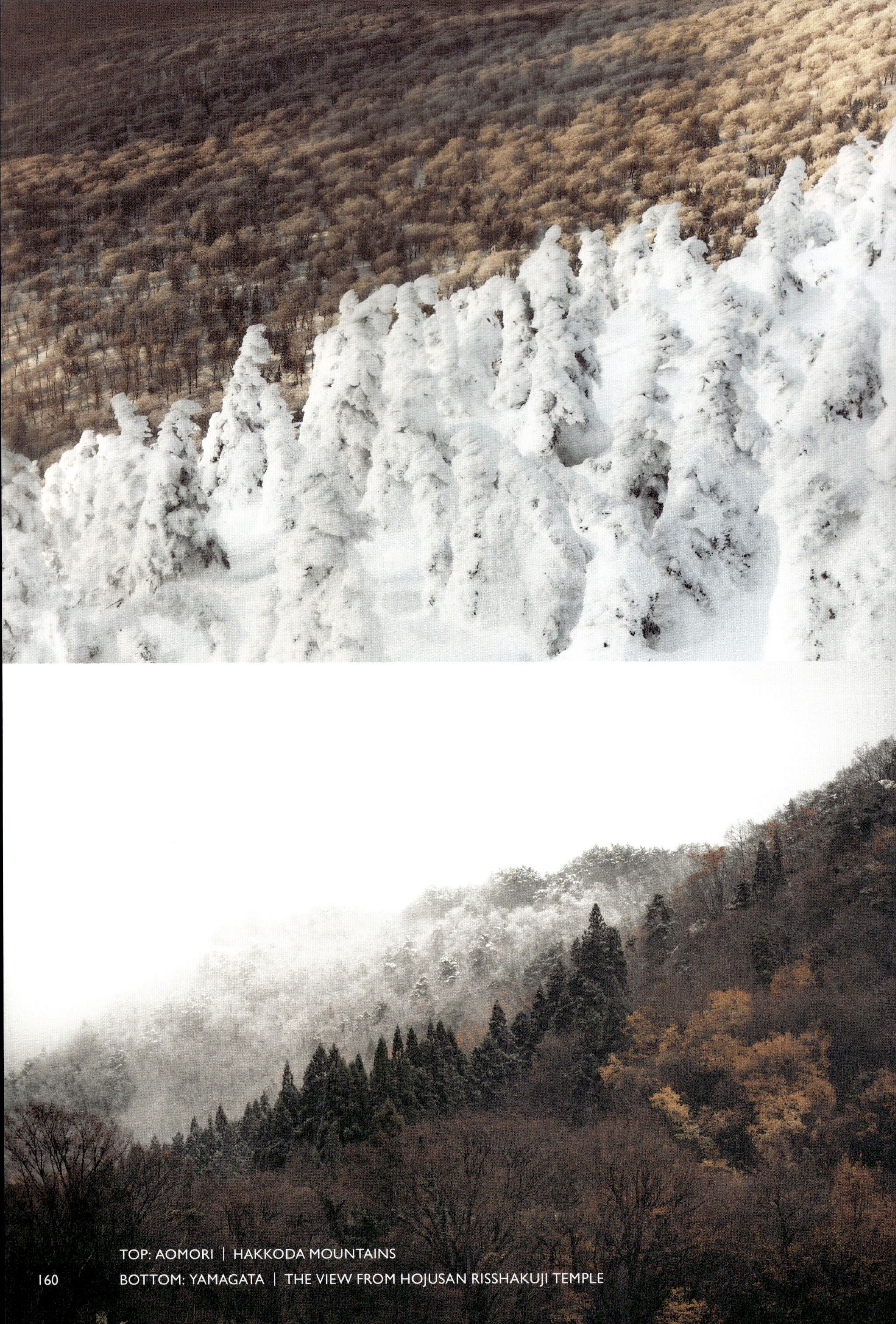

TOP: AOMORI | HAKKODA MOUNTAINS

 BOTTOM: YAMAGATA | THE VIEW FROM HOJUSAN RISSHAKUJI TEMPLE

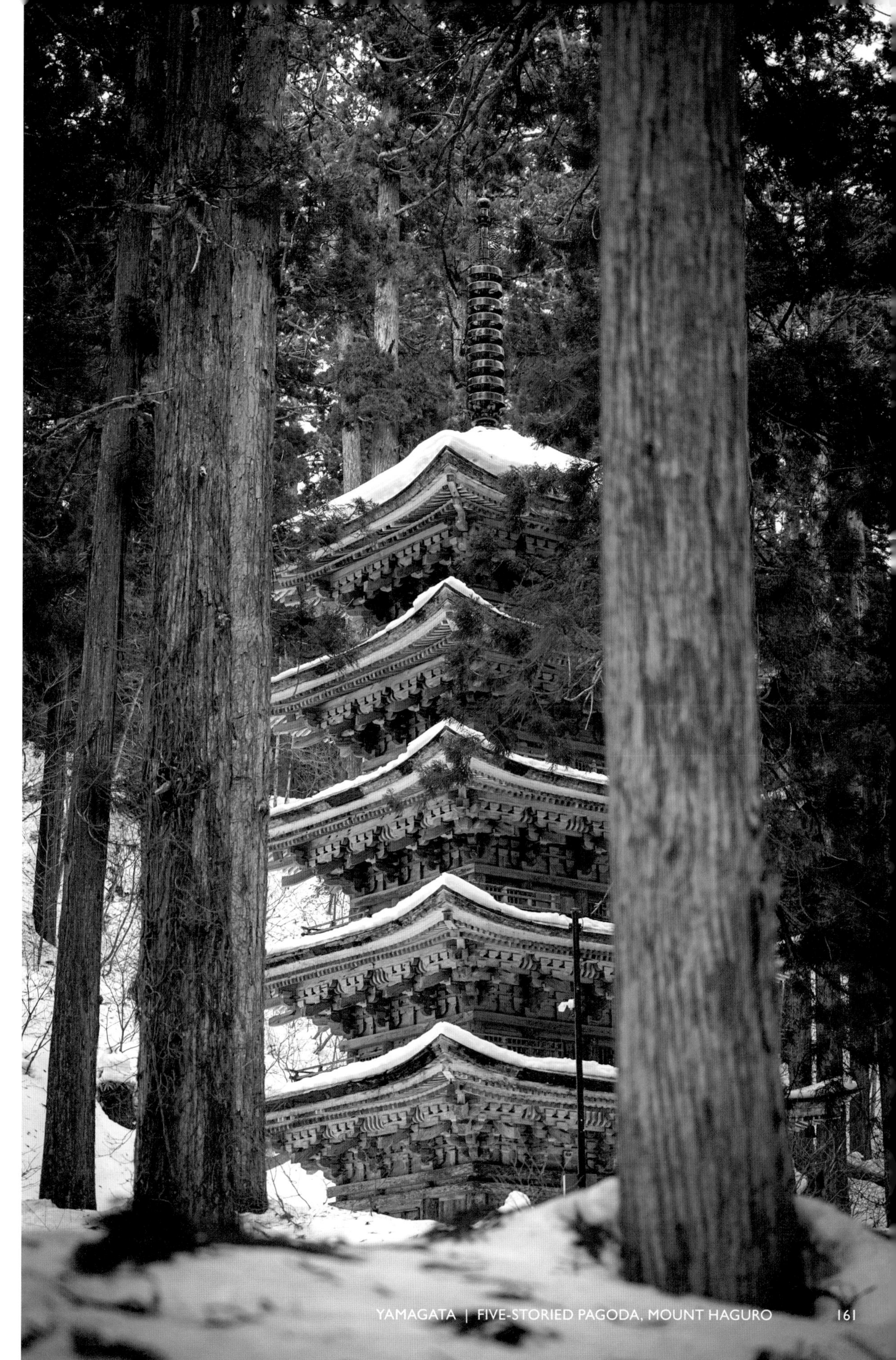

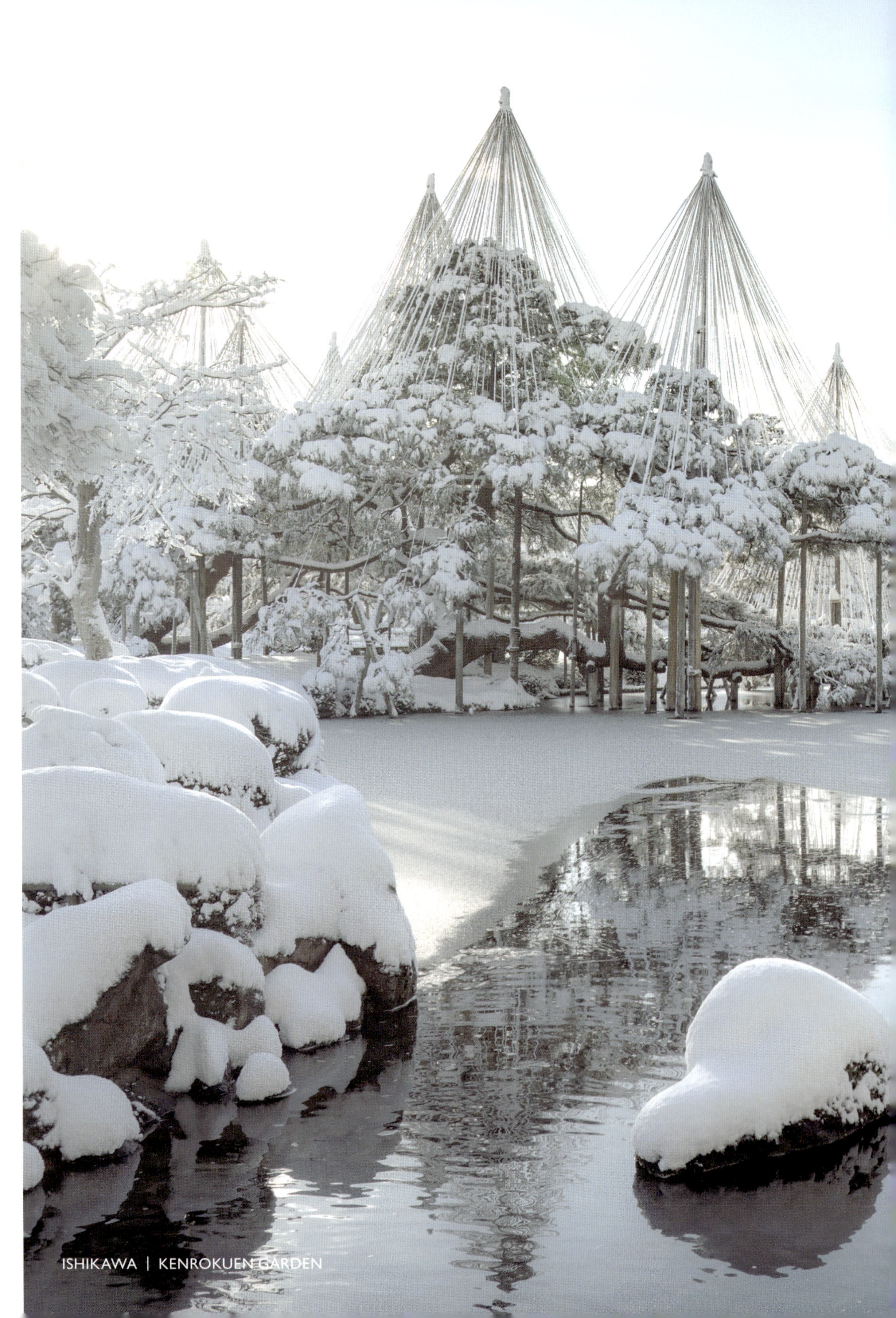

 ISHIKAWA | KENROKUEN GARDEN

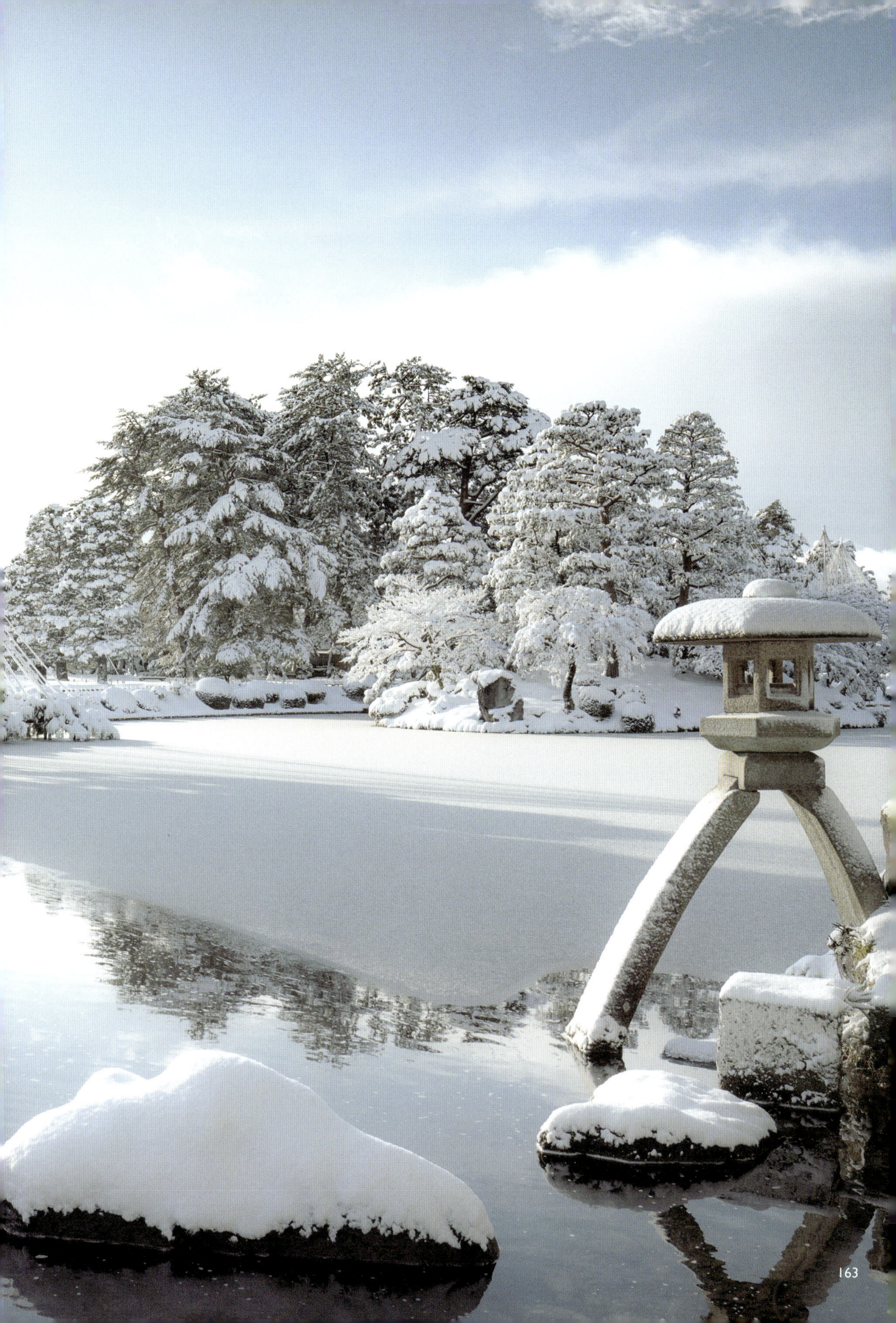

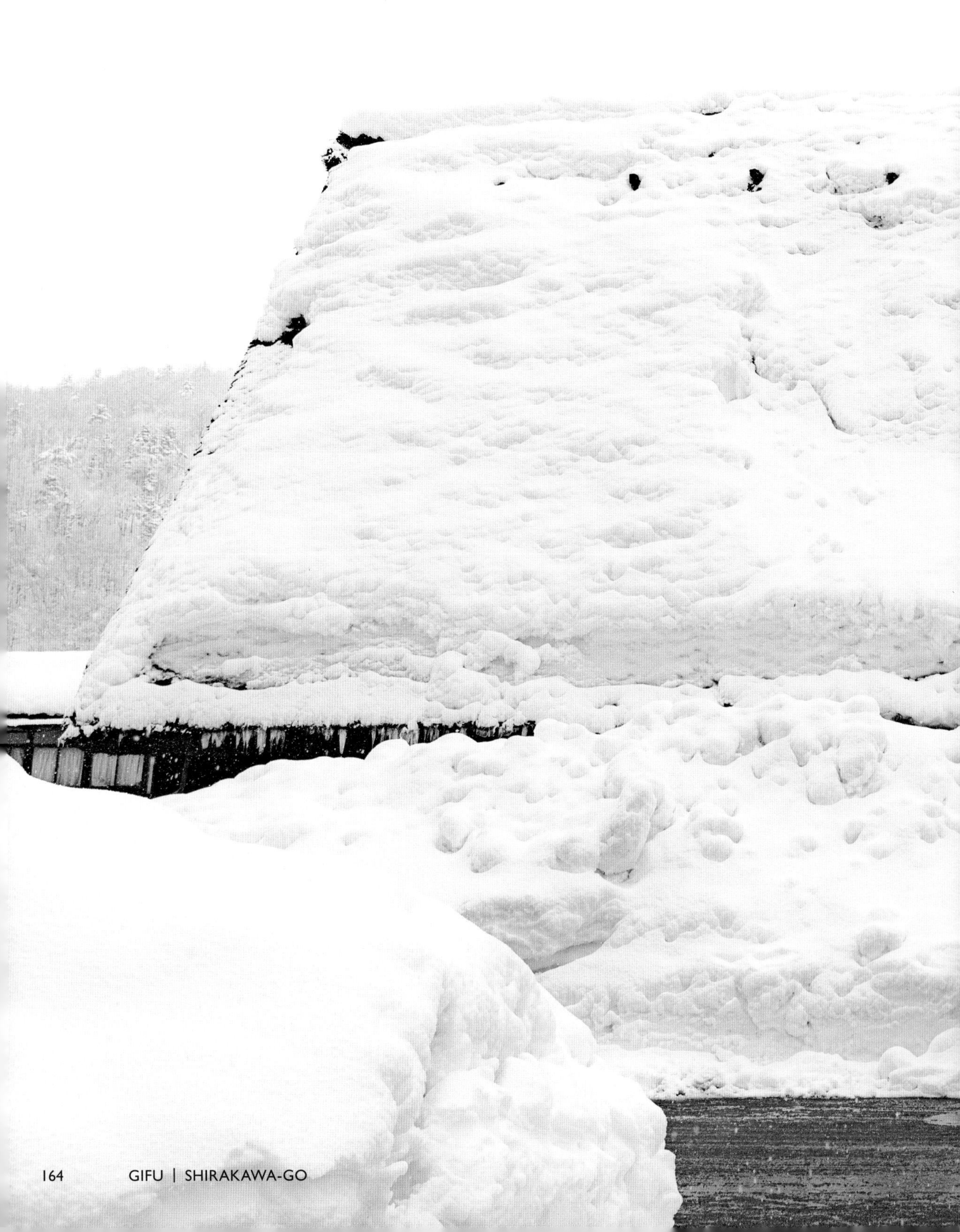

    GIFU | SHIRAKAWA-GO

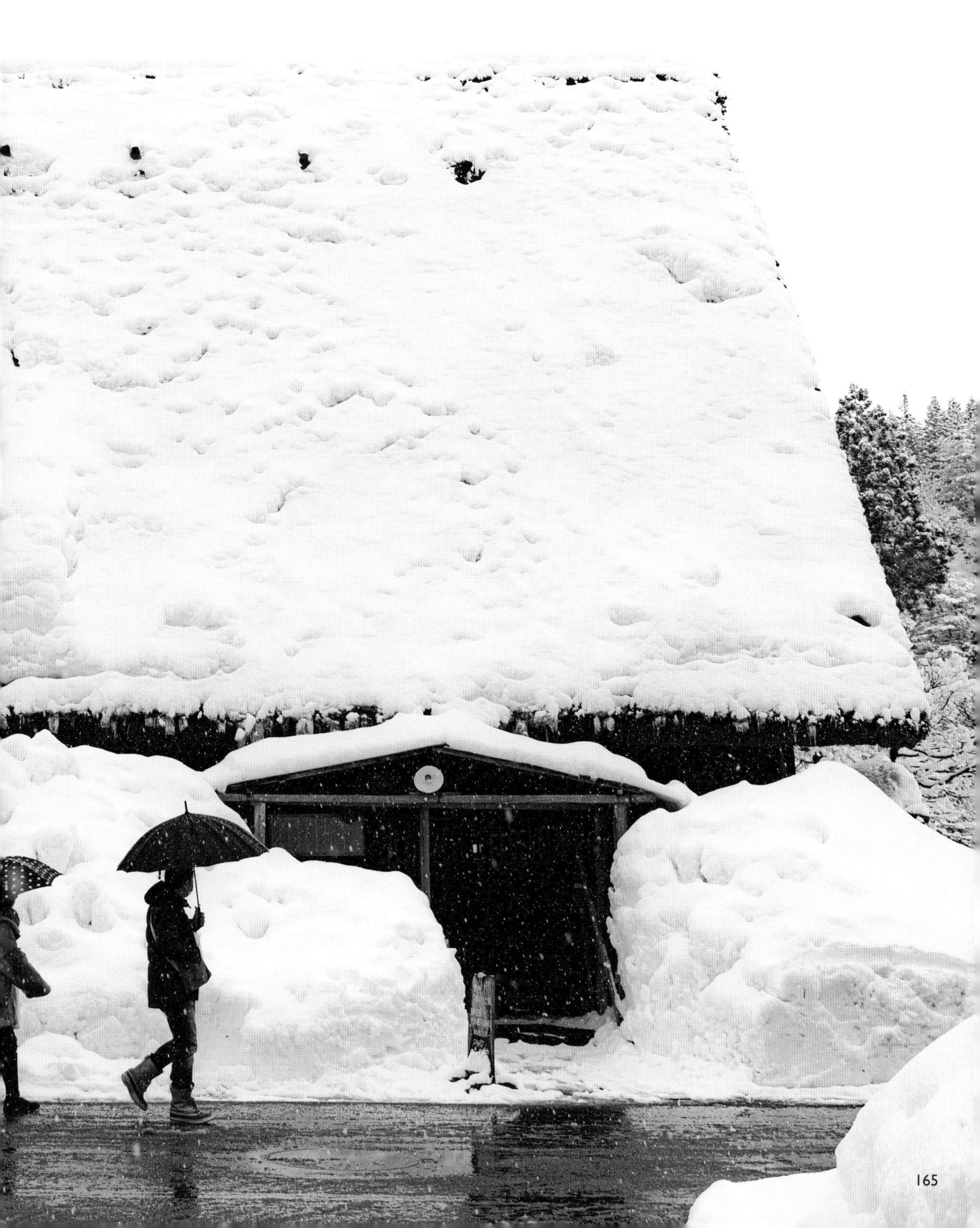

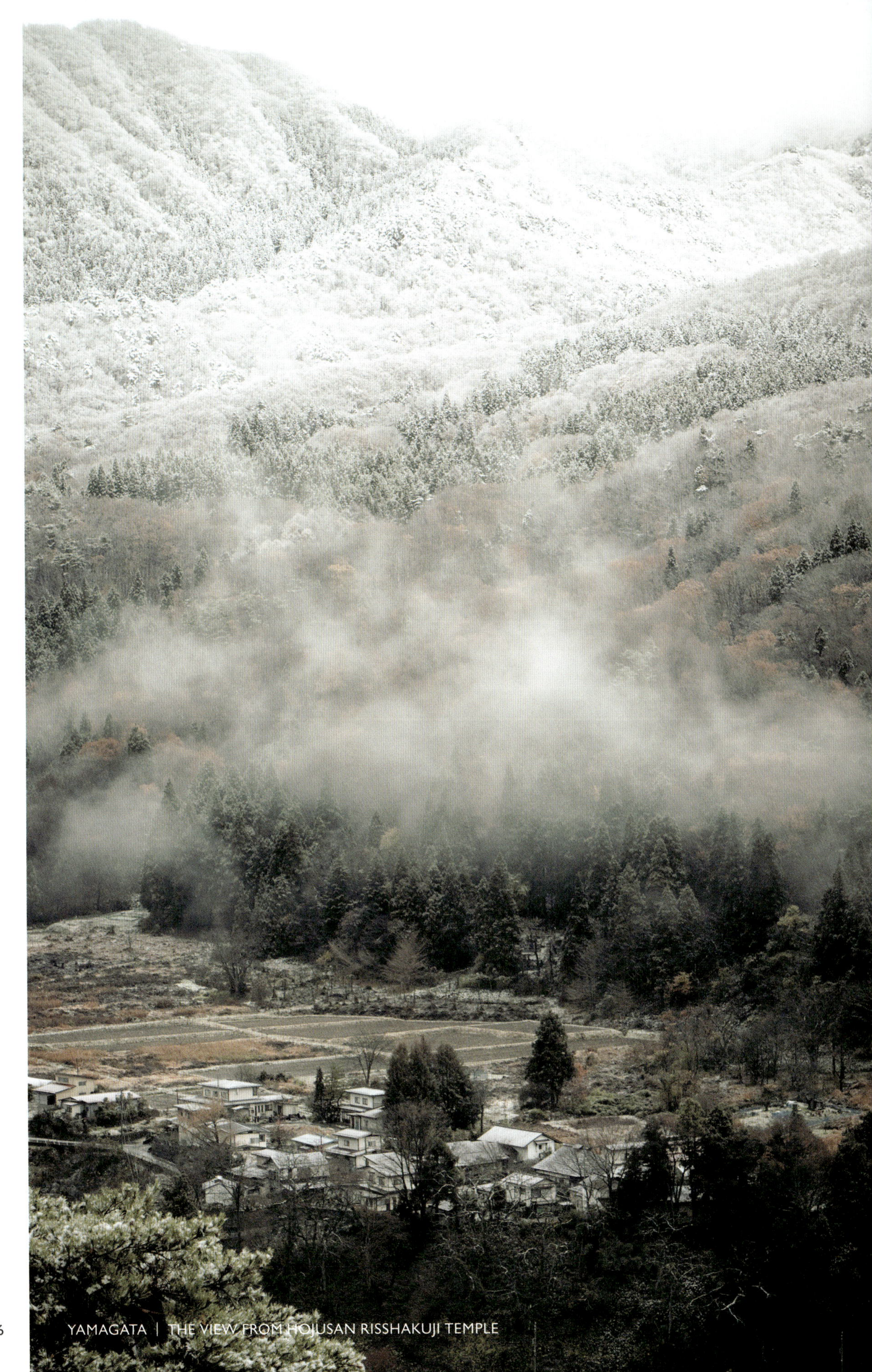

   YAMAGATA | THE VIEW FROM HOJUSAN RISSHAKUJI TEMPLE

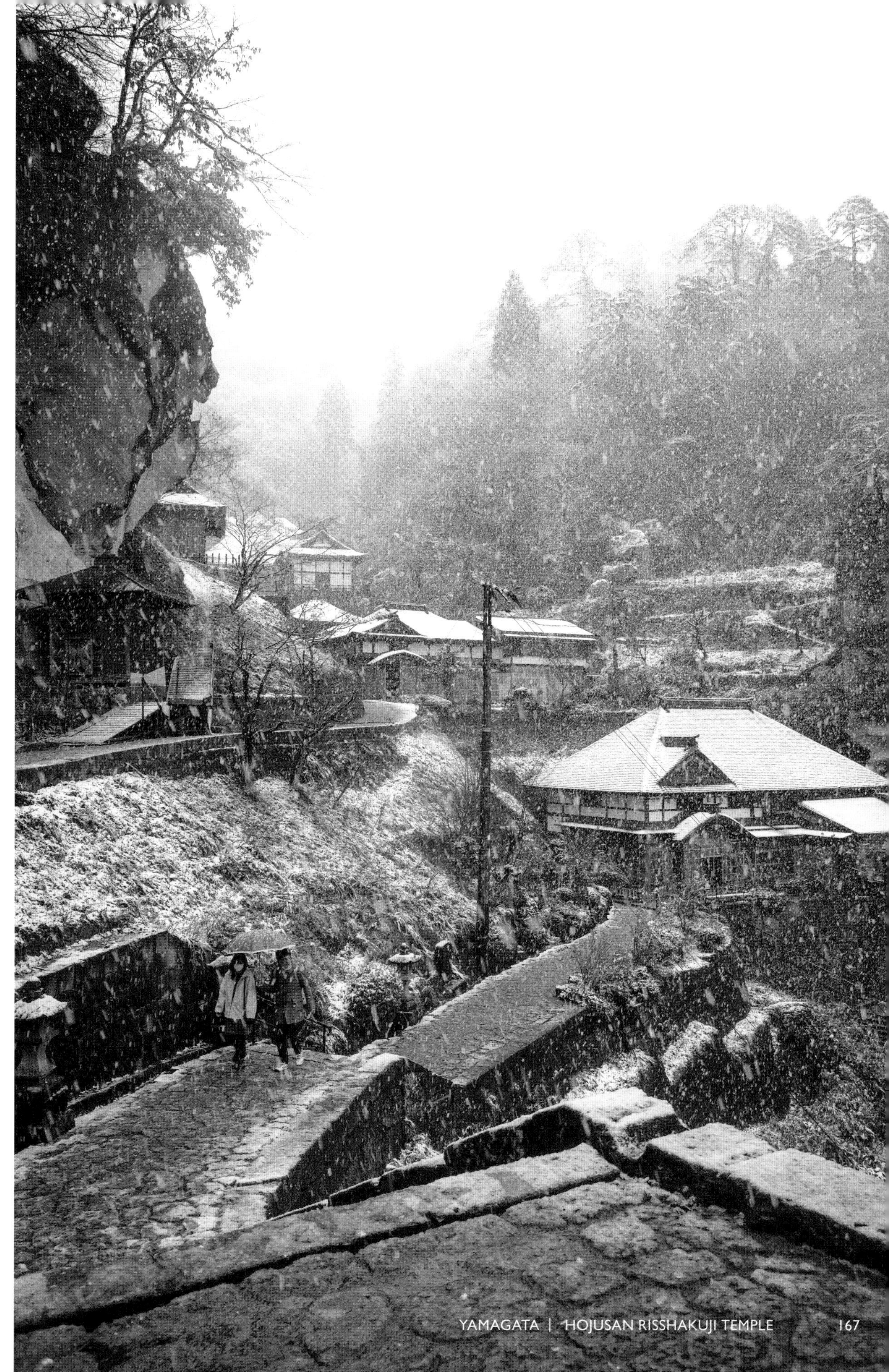

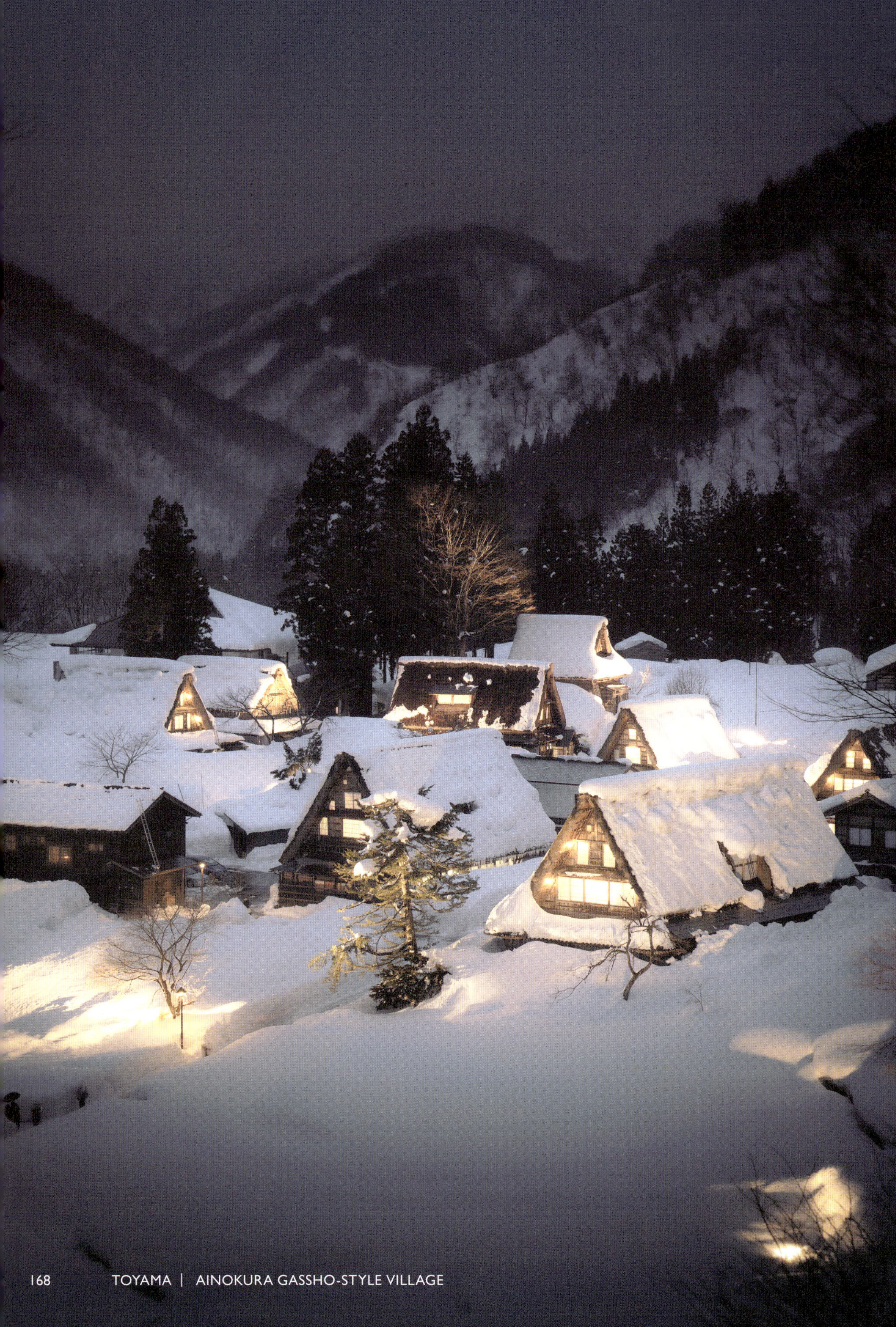

 TOYAMA | AINOKURA GASSHO-STYLE VILLAGE

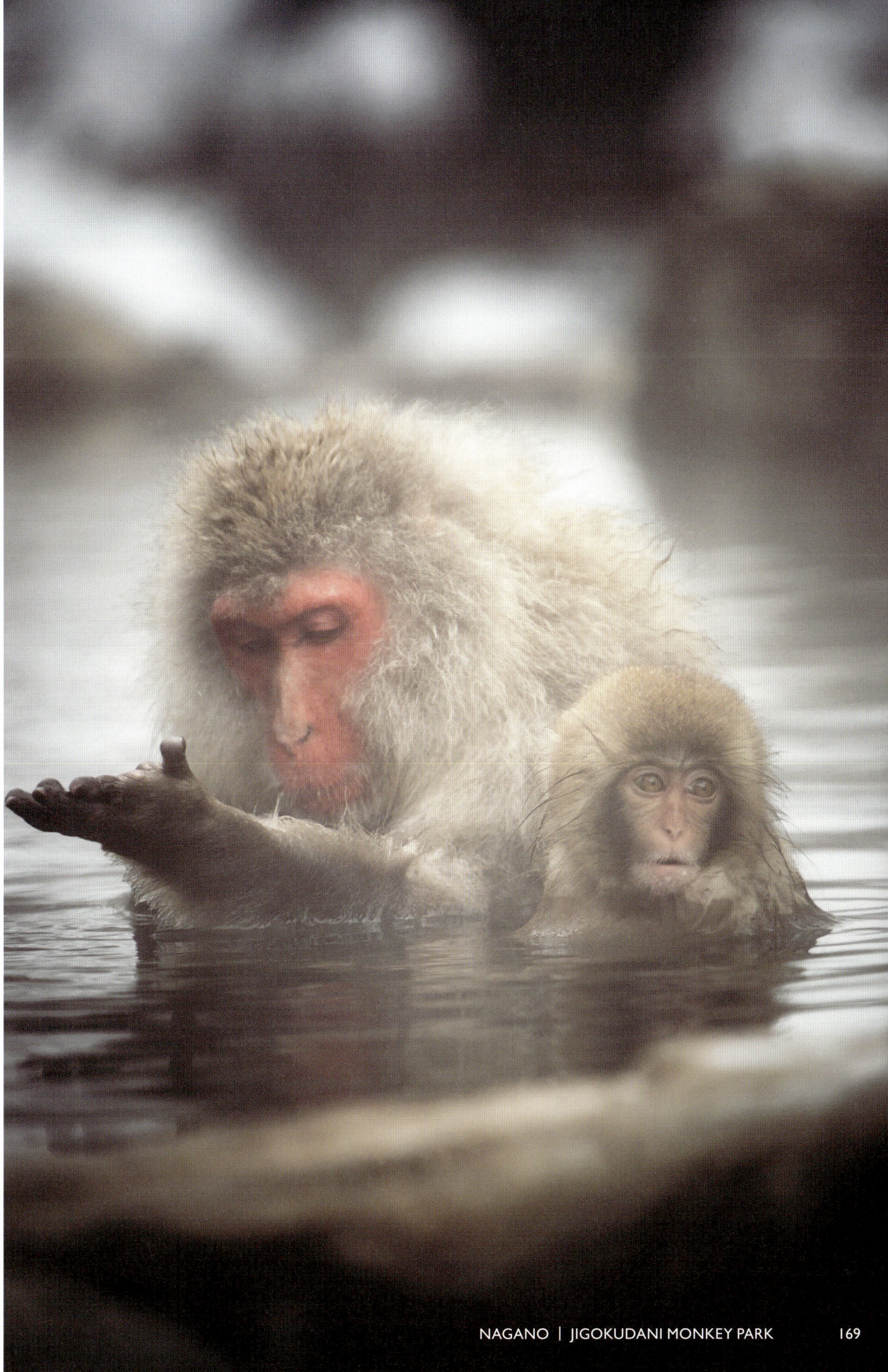

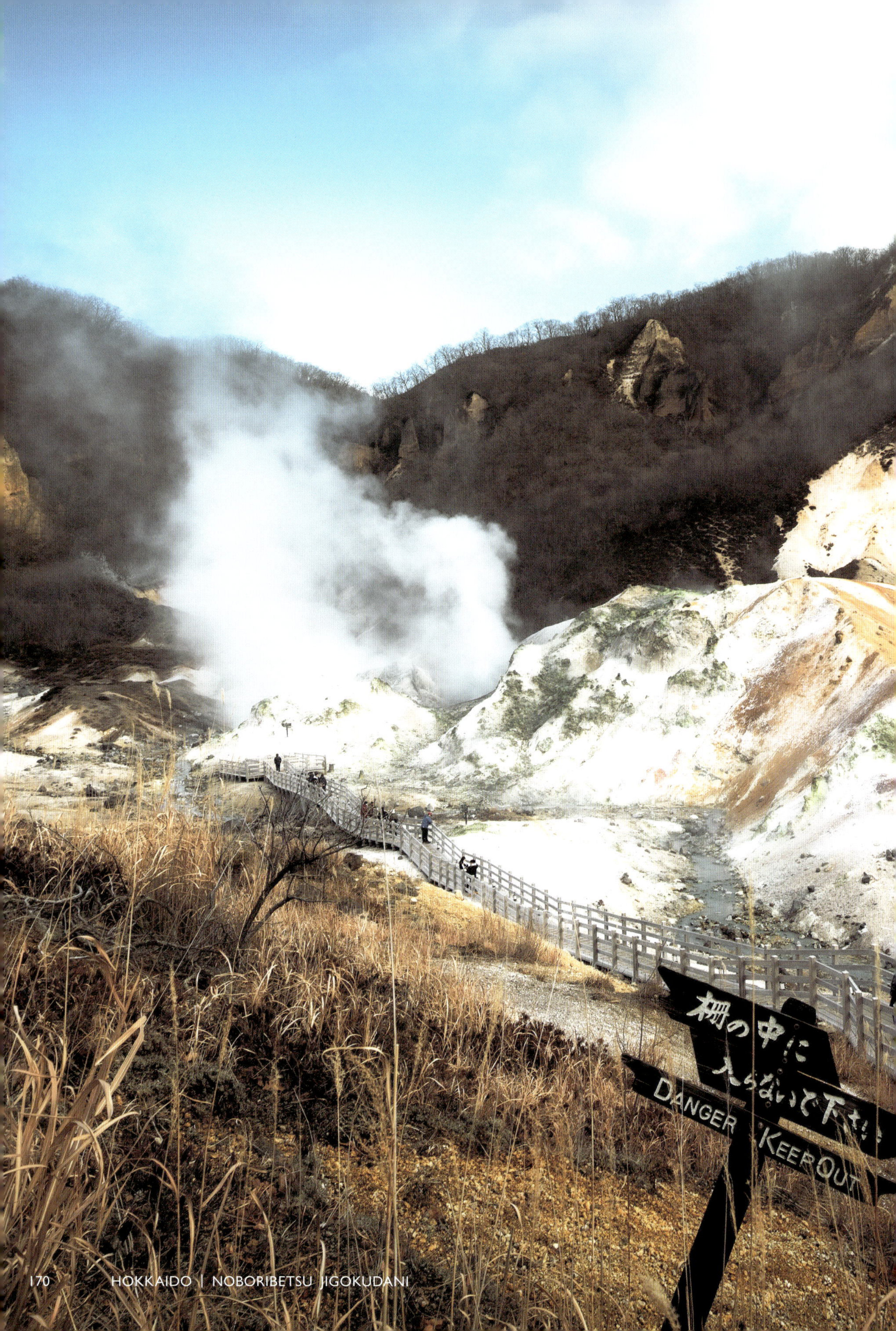

栅の中に
入らないで下さい
DANGER KEEP OUT

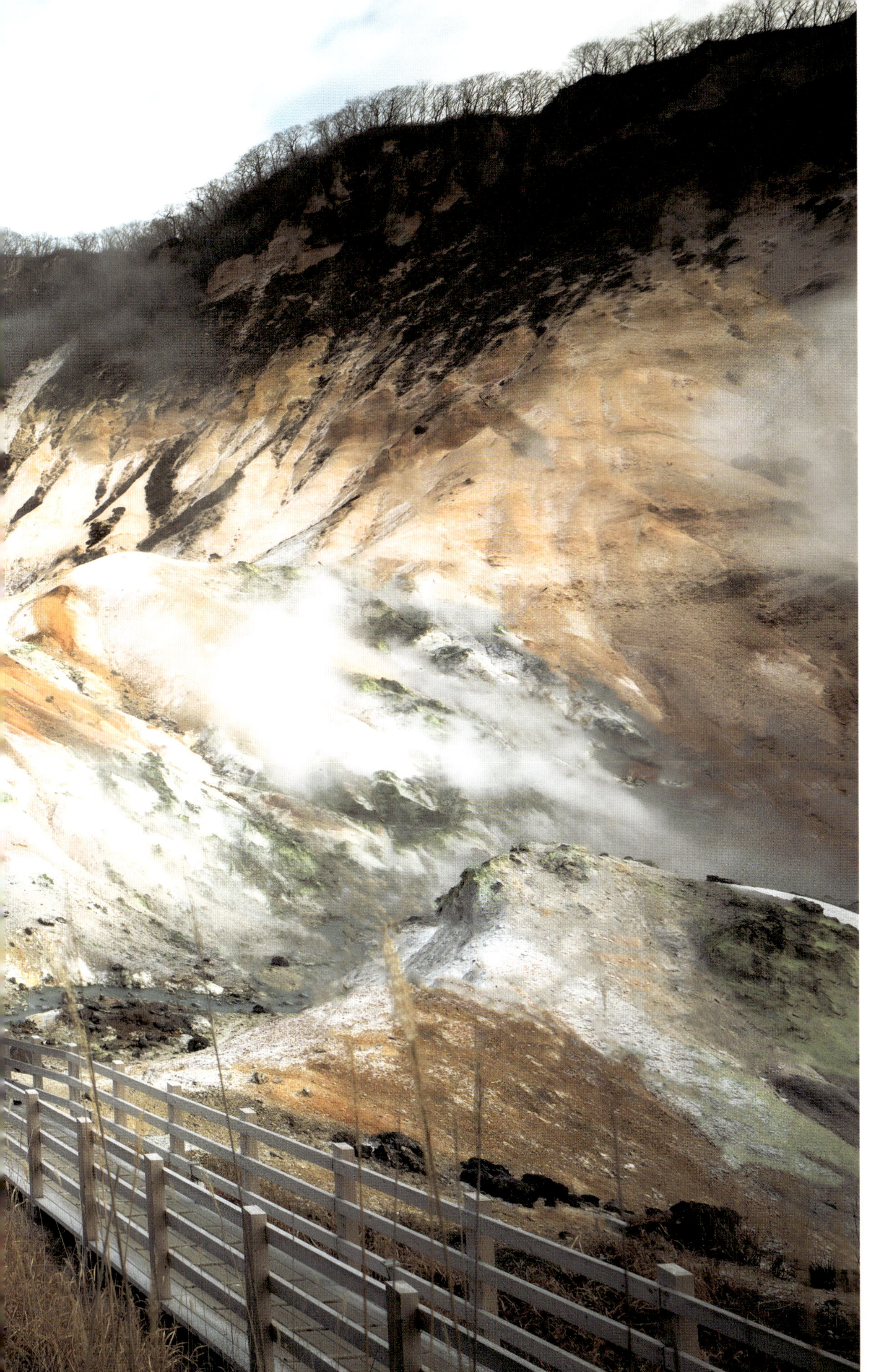

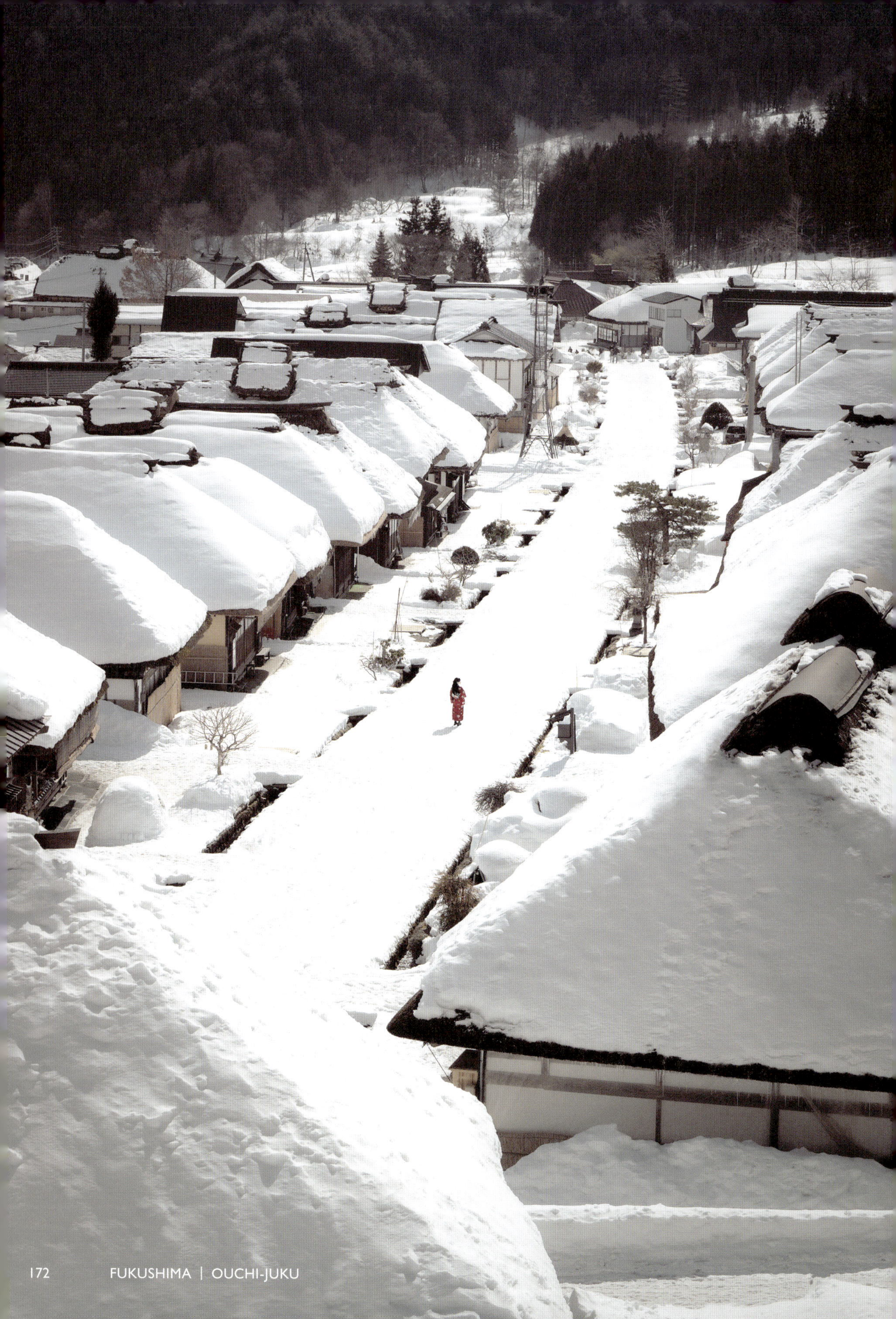

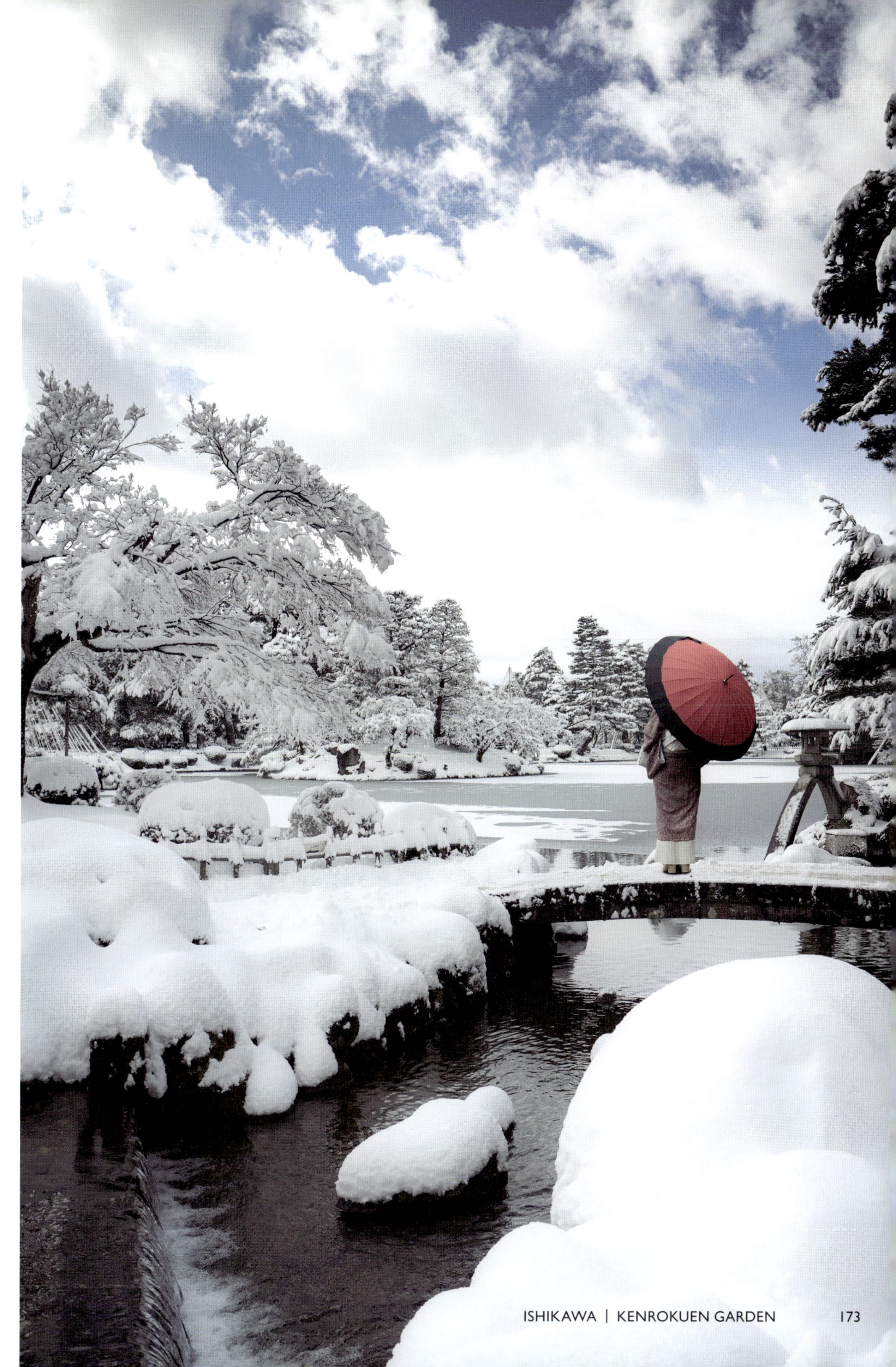

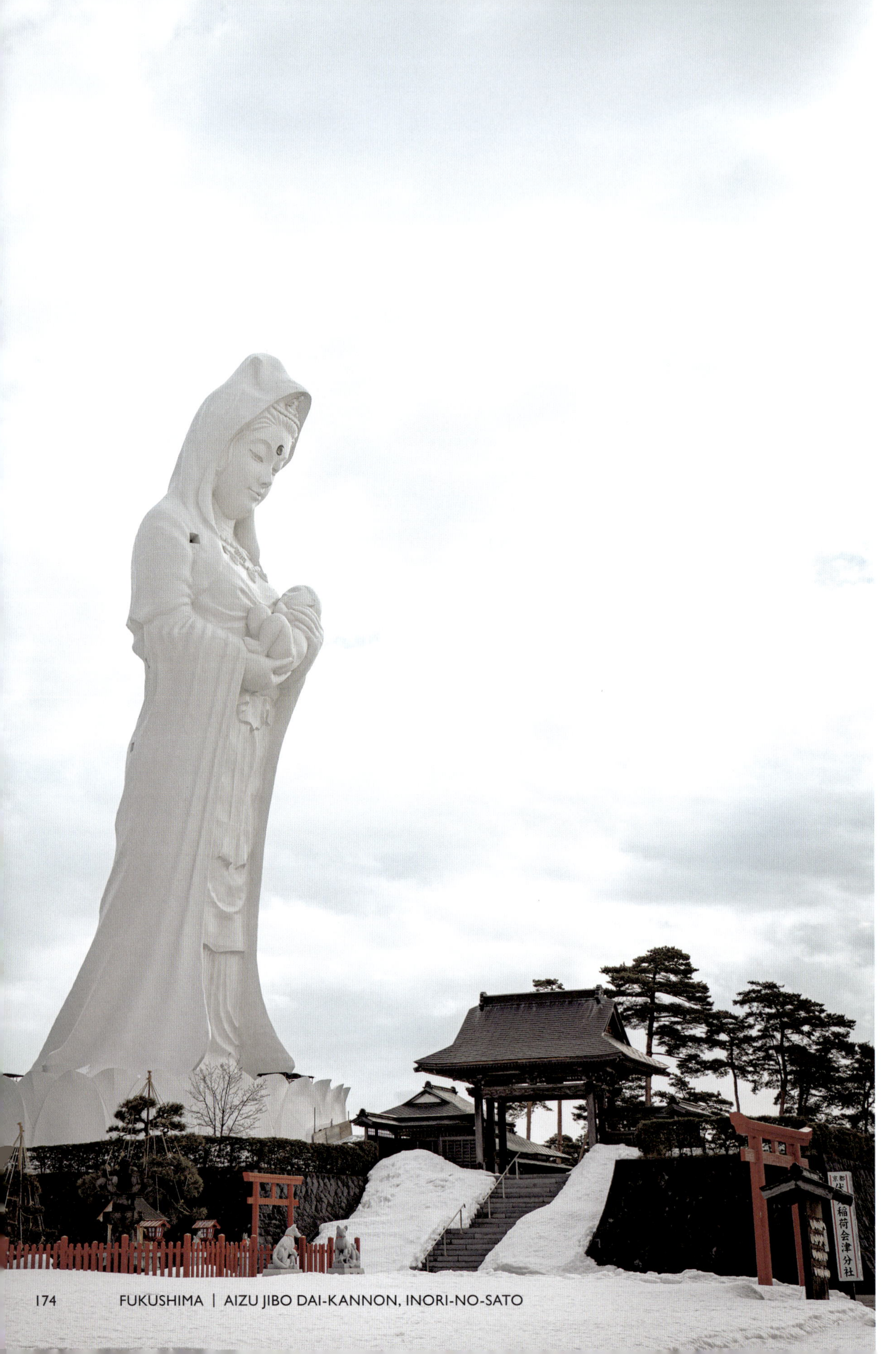

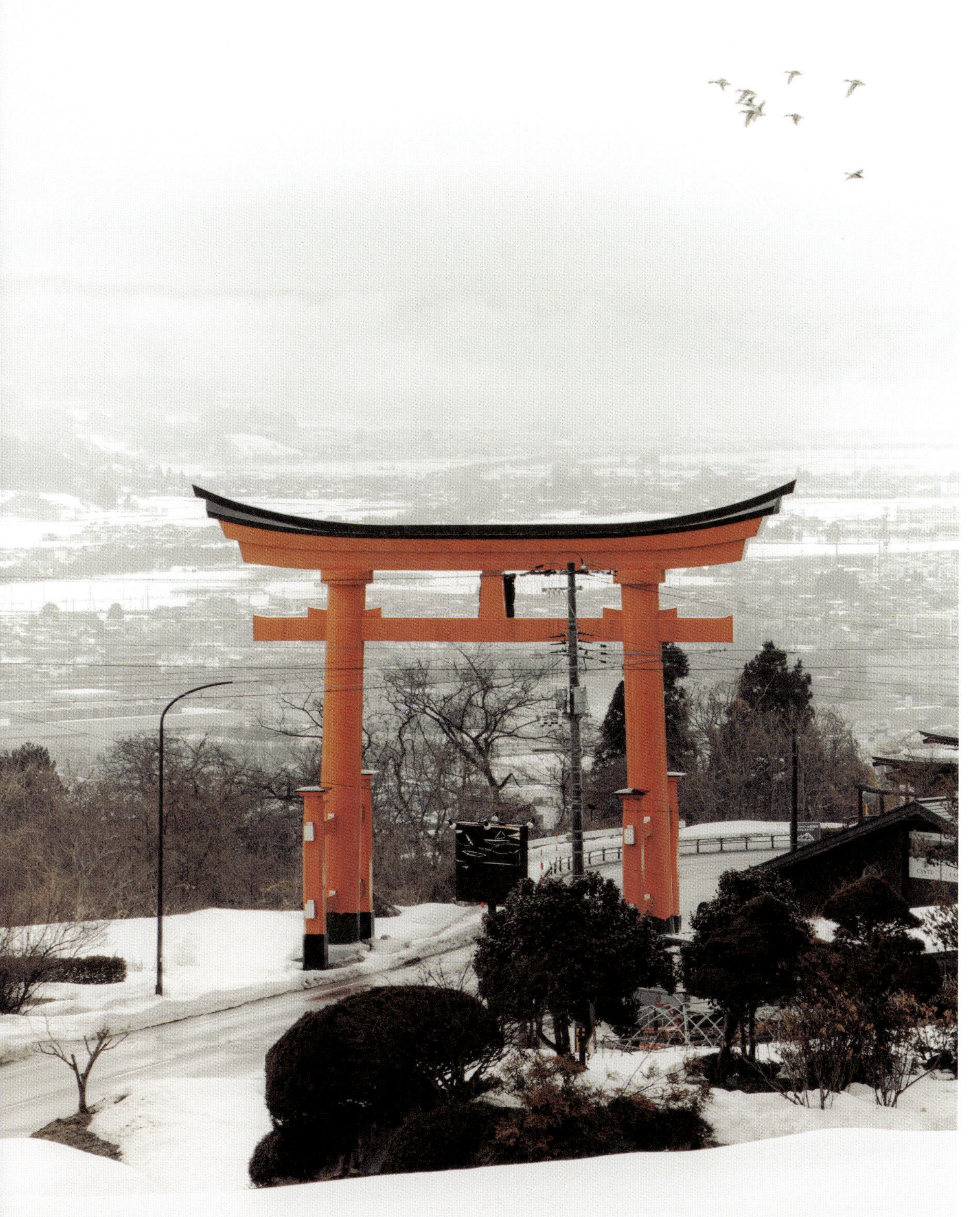

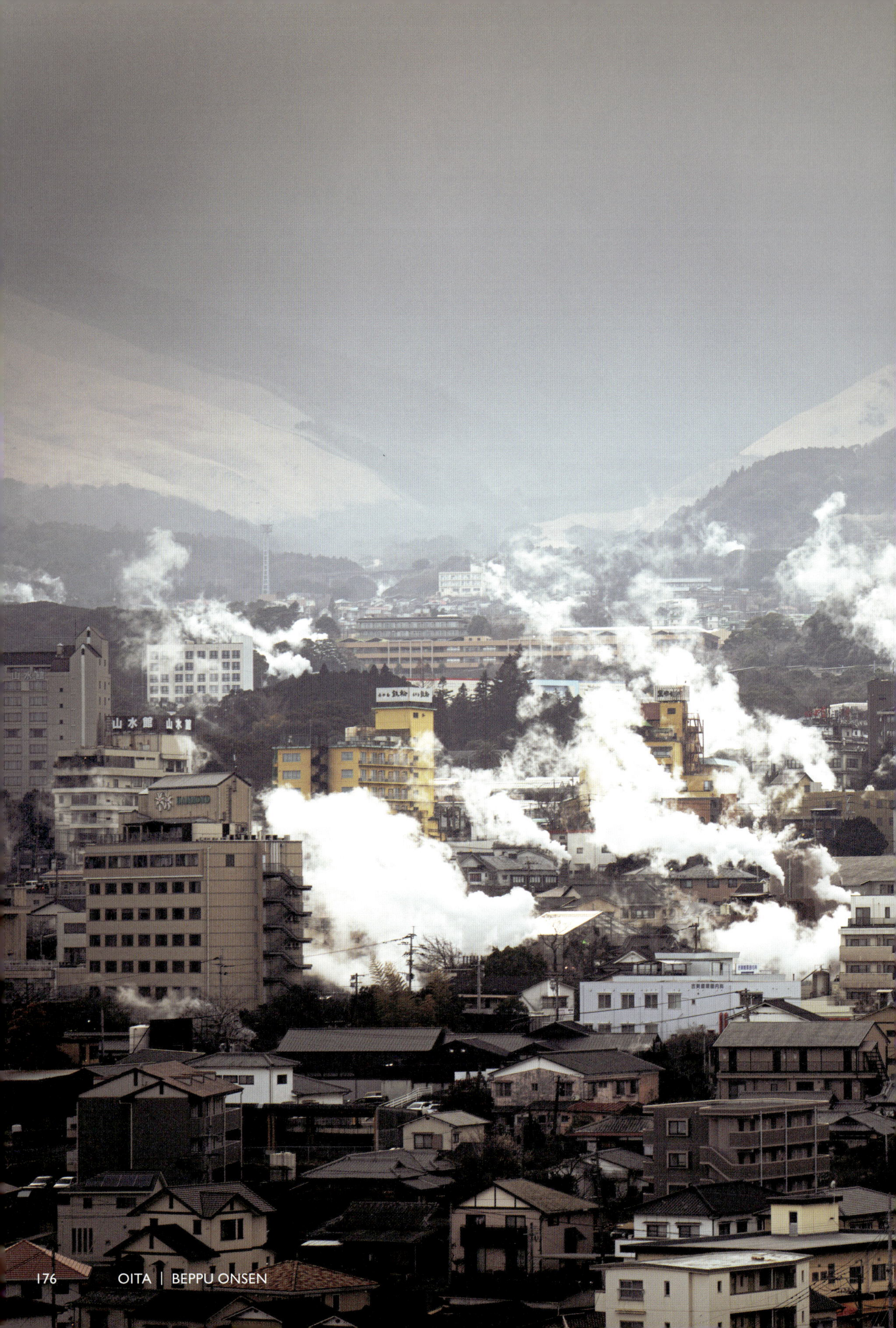

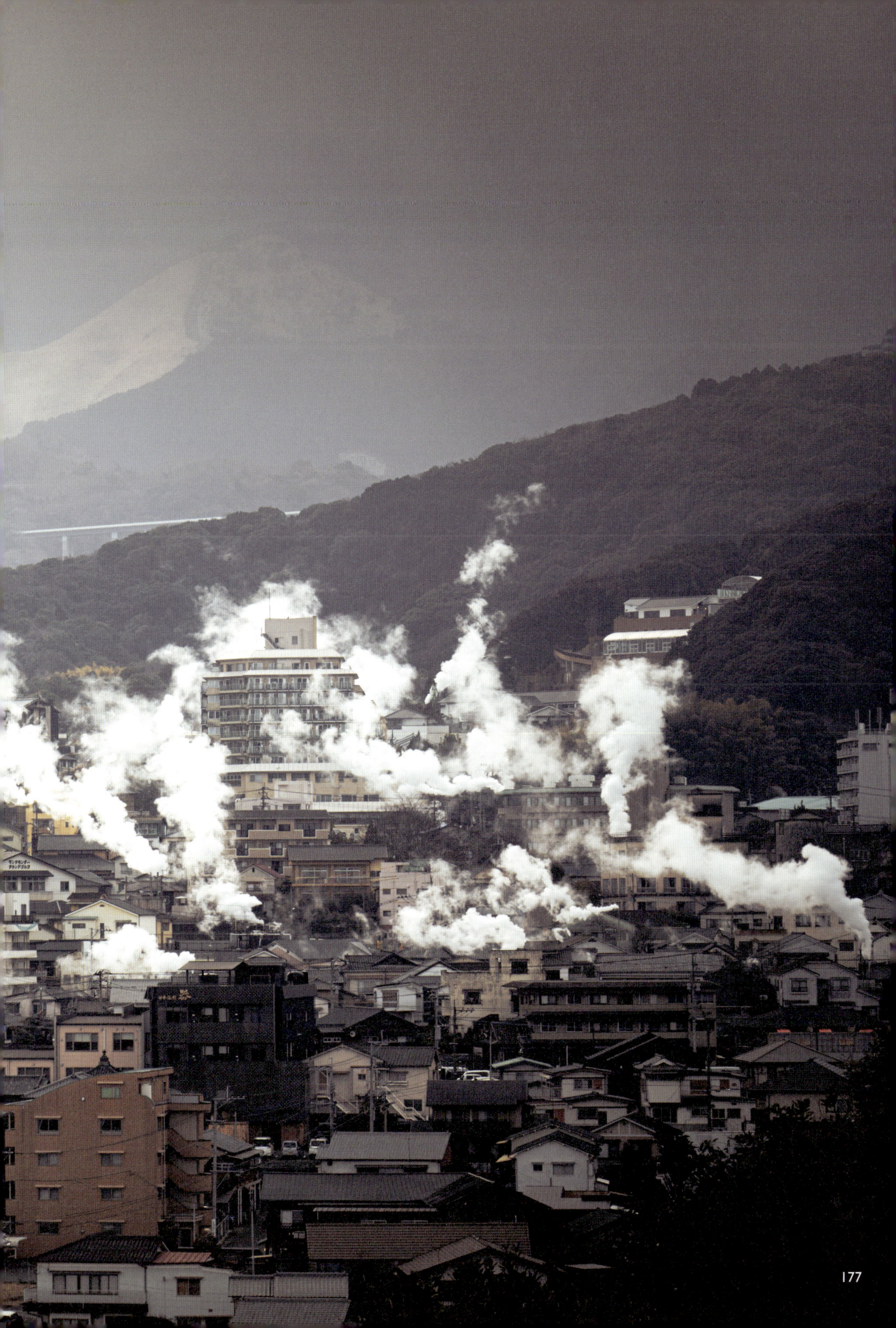

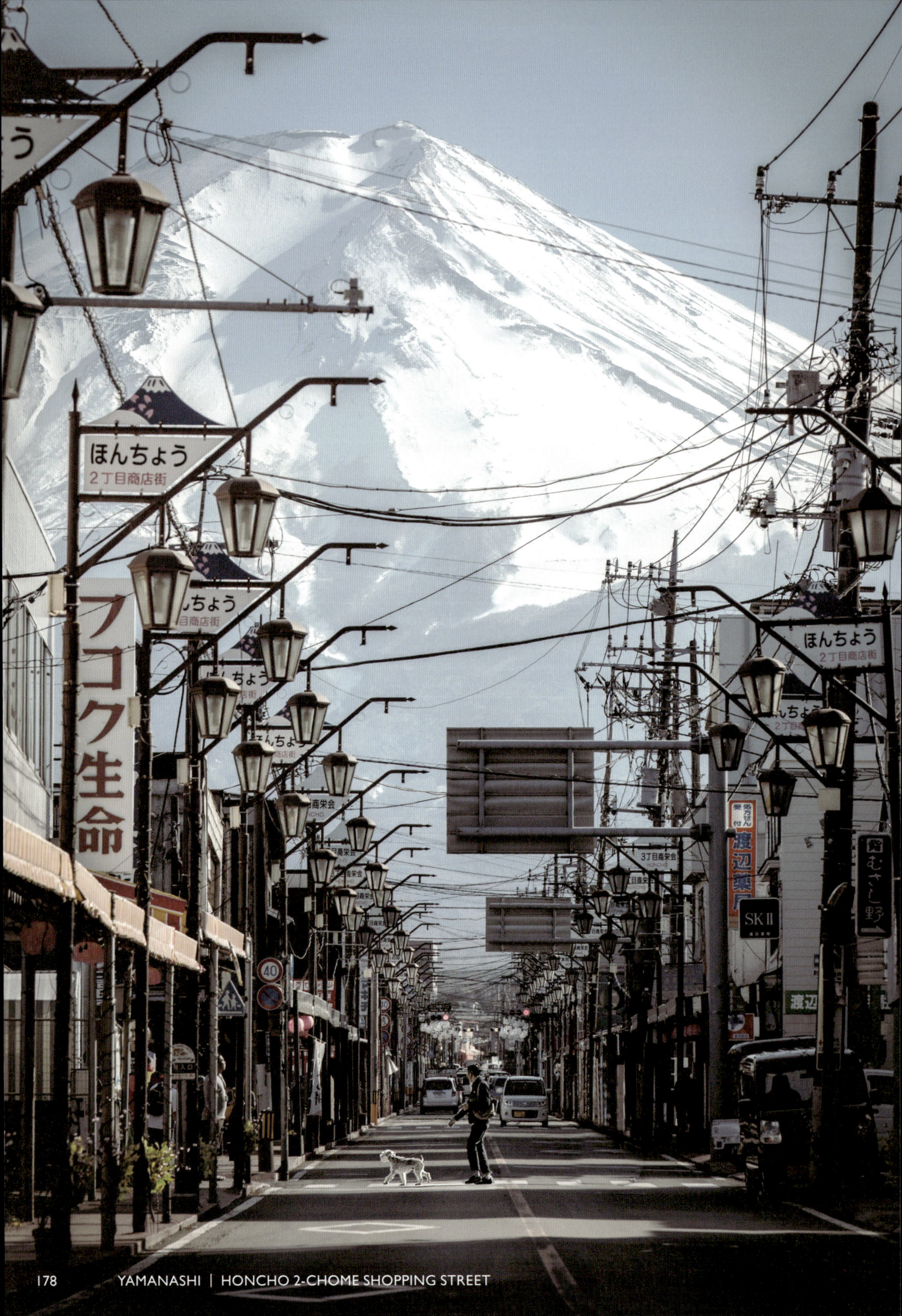

YAMANASHI | HONCHO 2-CHOME SHOPPING STREET

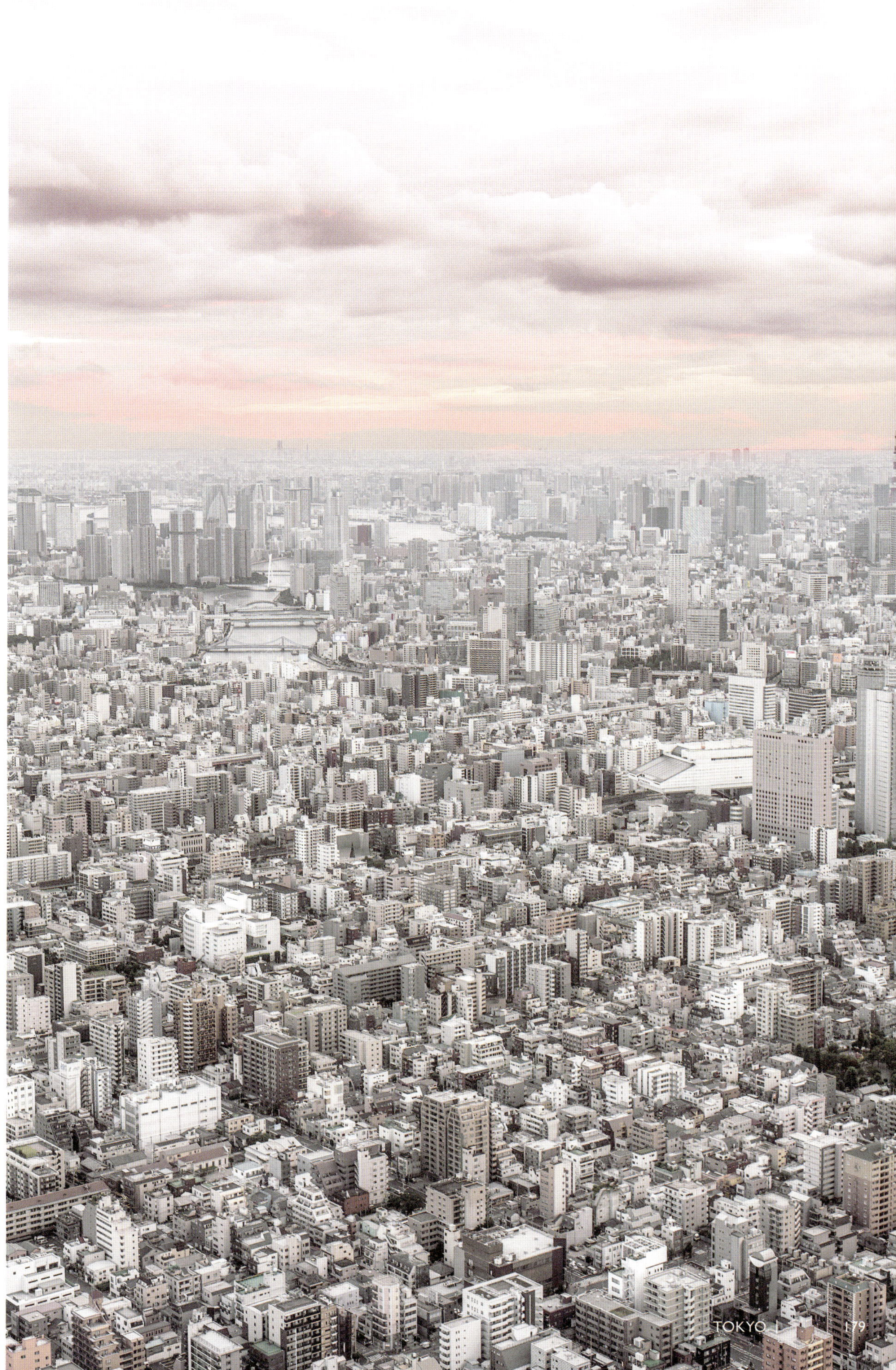

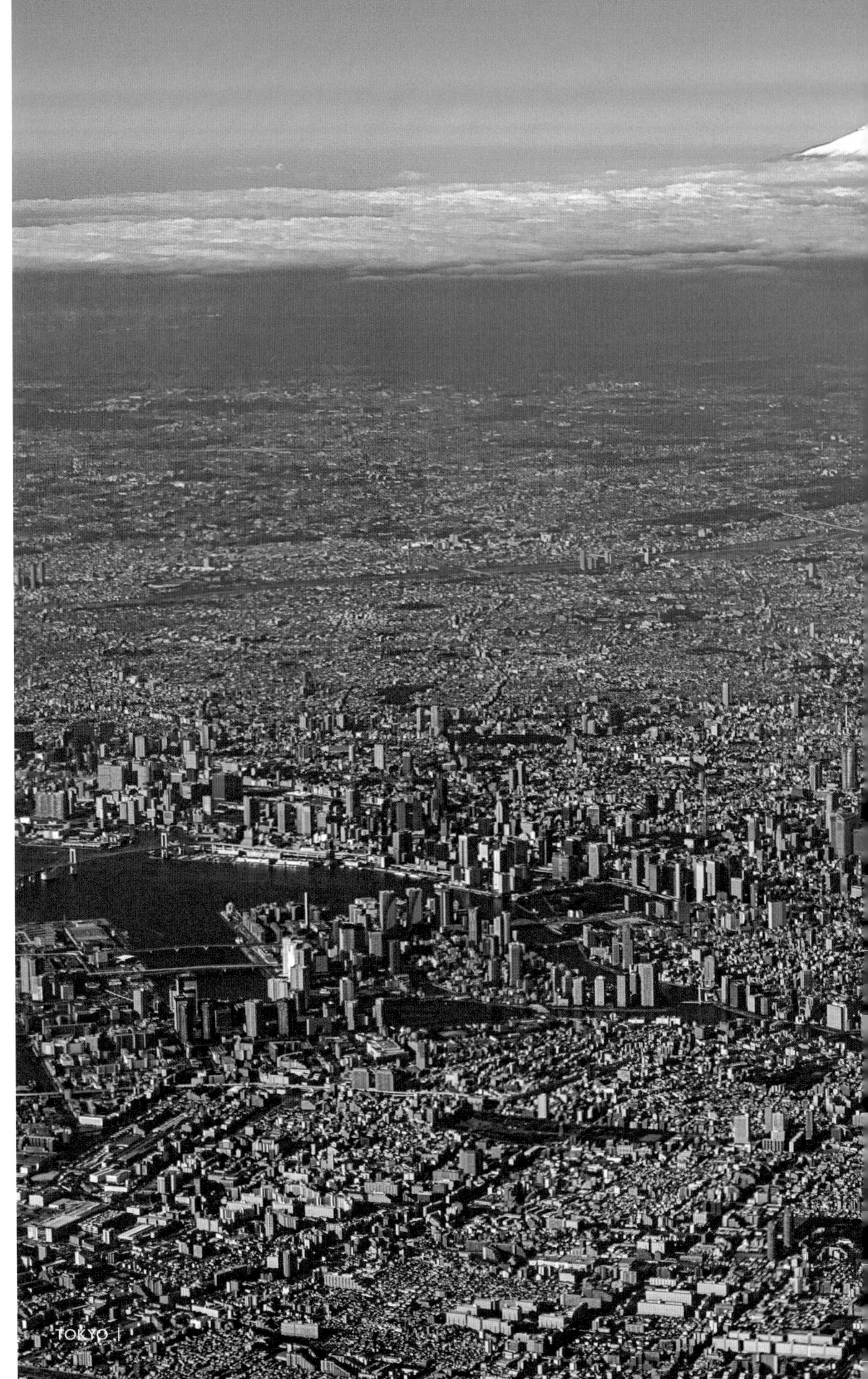

TOKYO

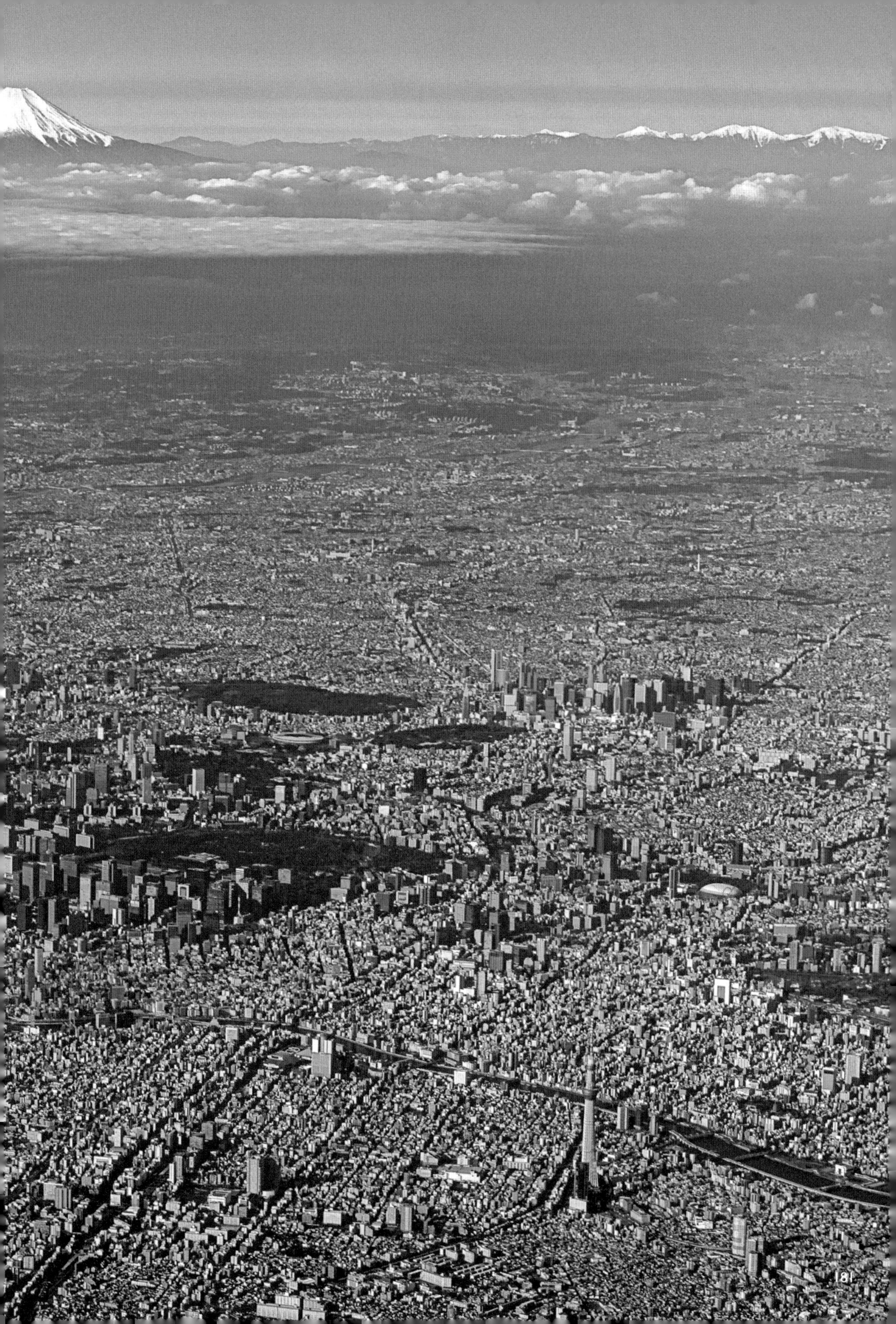

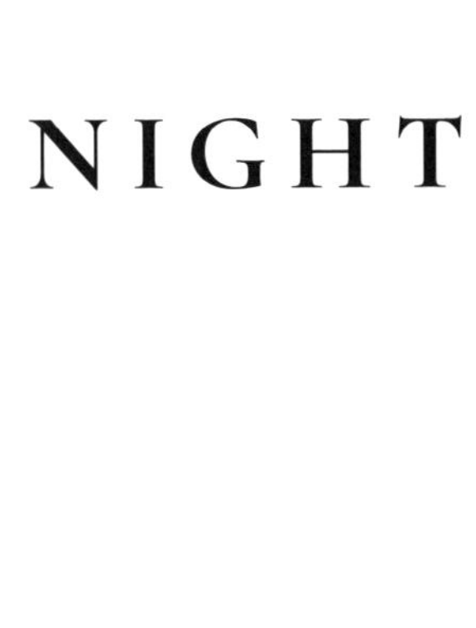

NIGHT

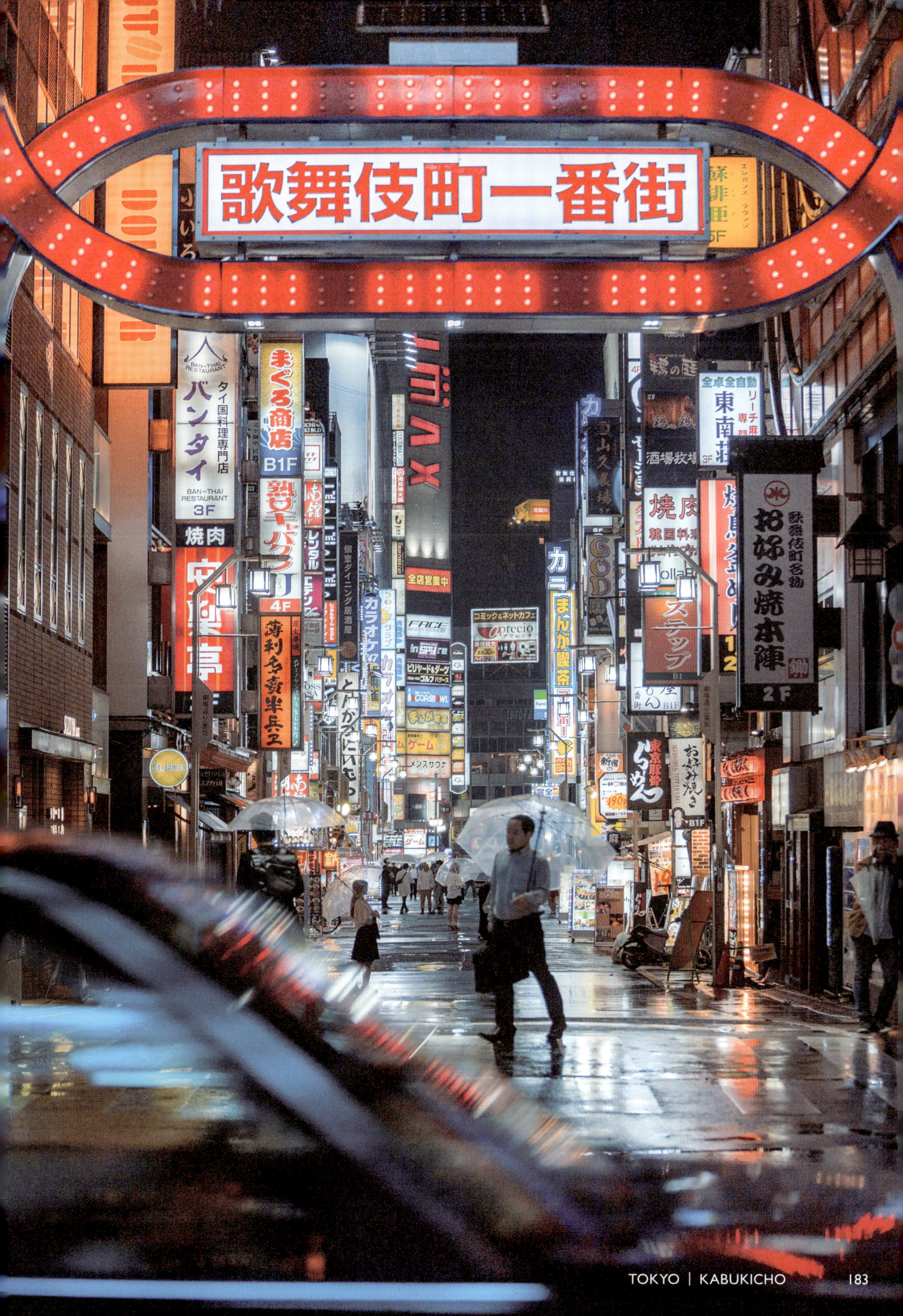

歌舞伎町一番街

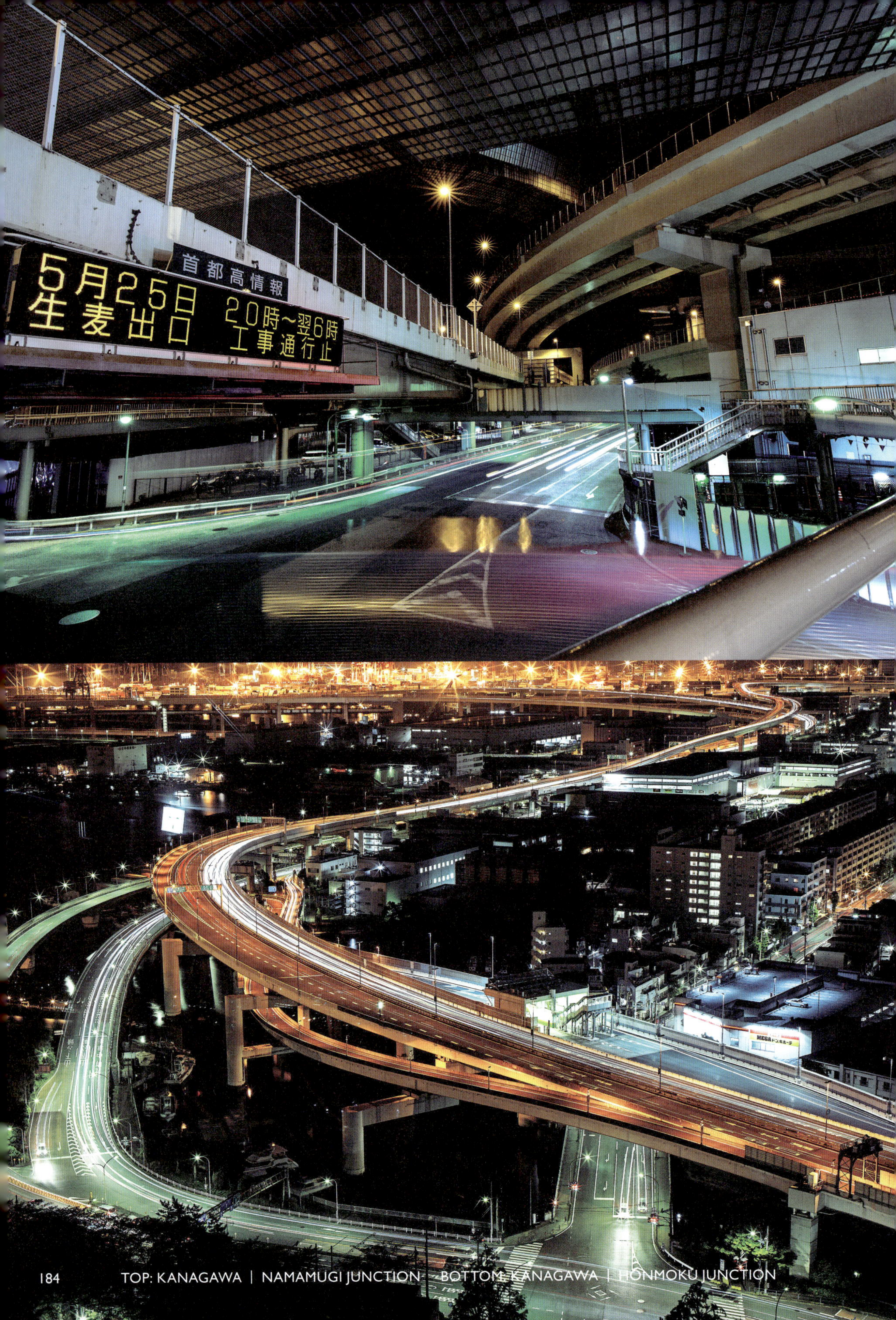首都高情報
5月25日　20時〜翌6時
生麦出口　工事通行止

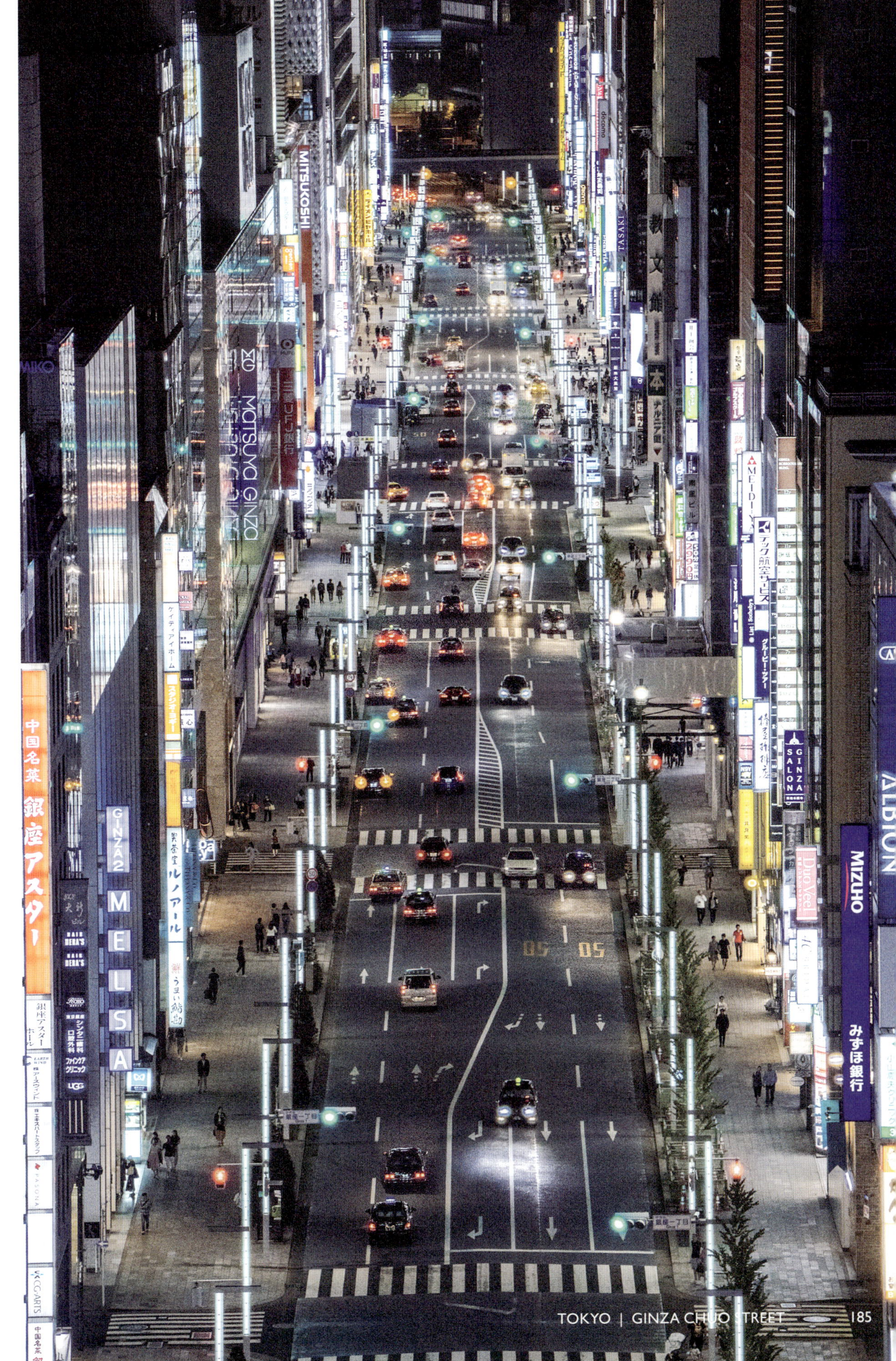

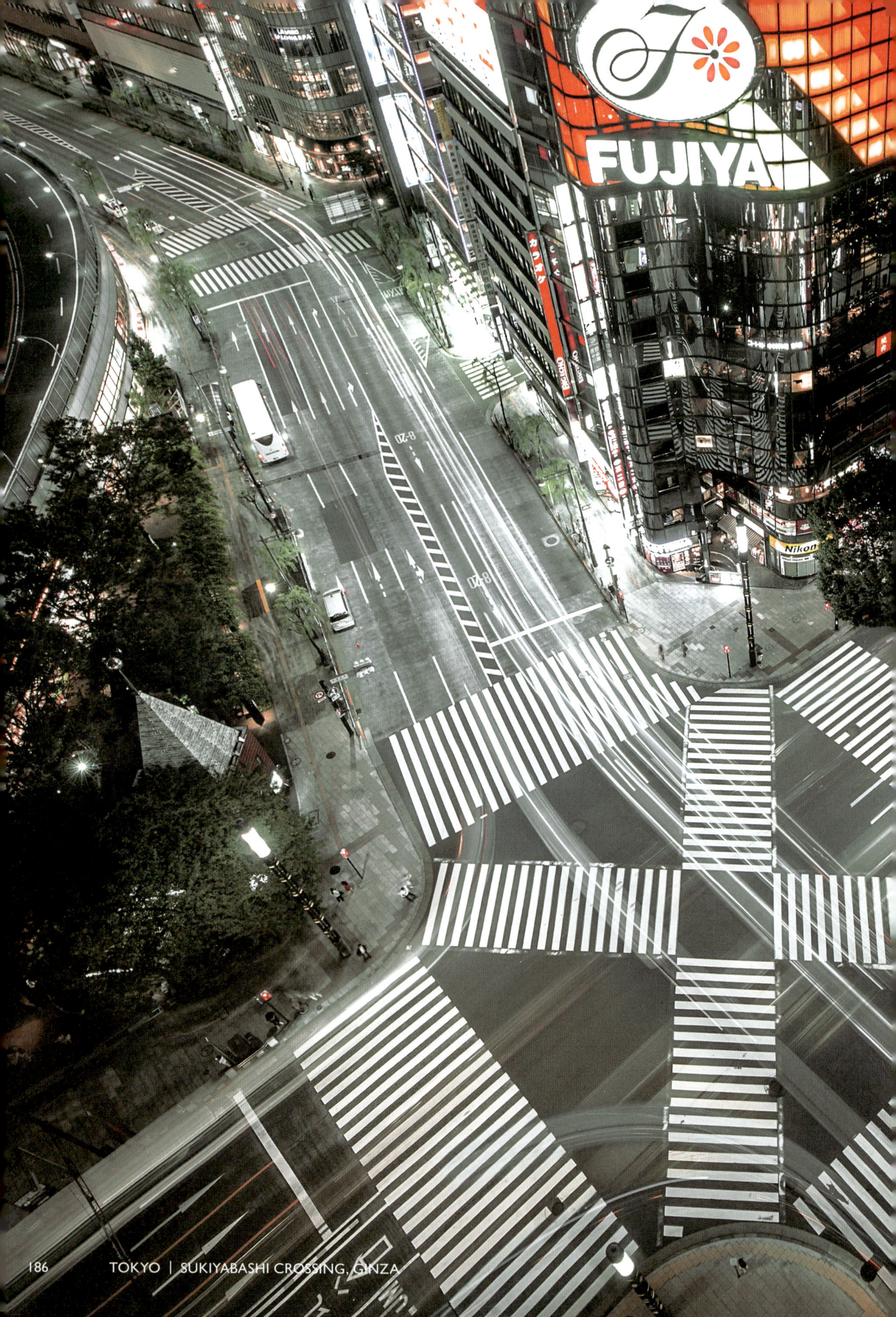

FUJIYA
Nikon

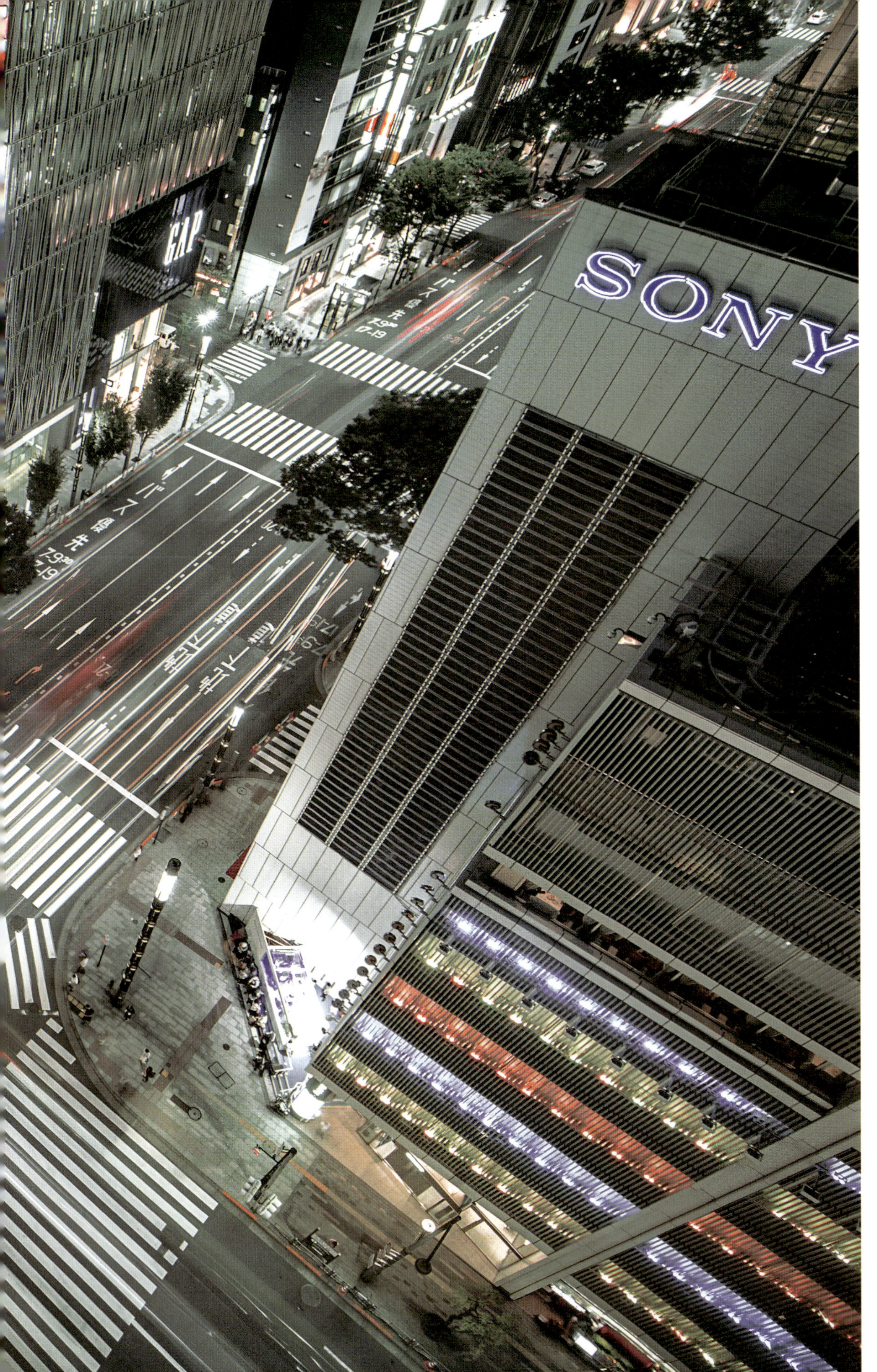

GAP
SONY

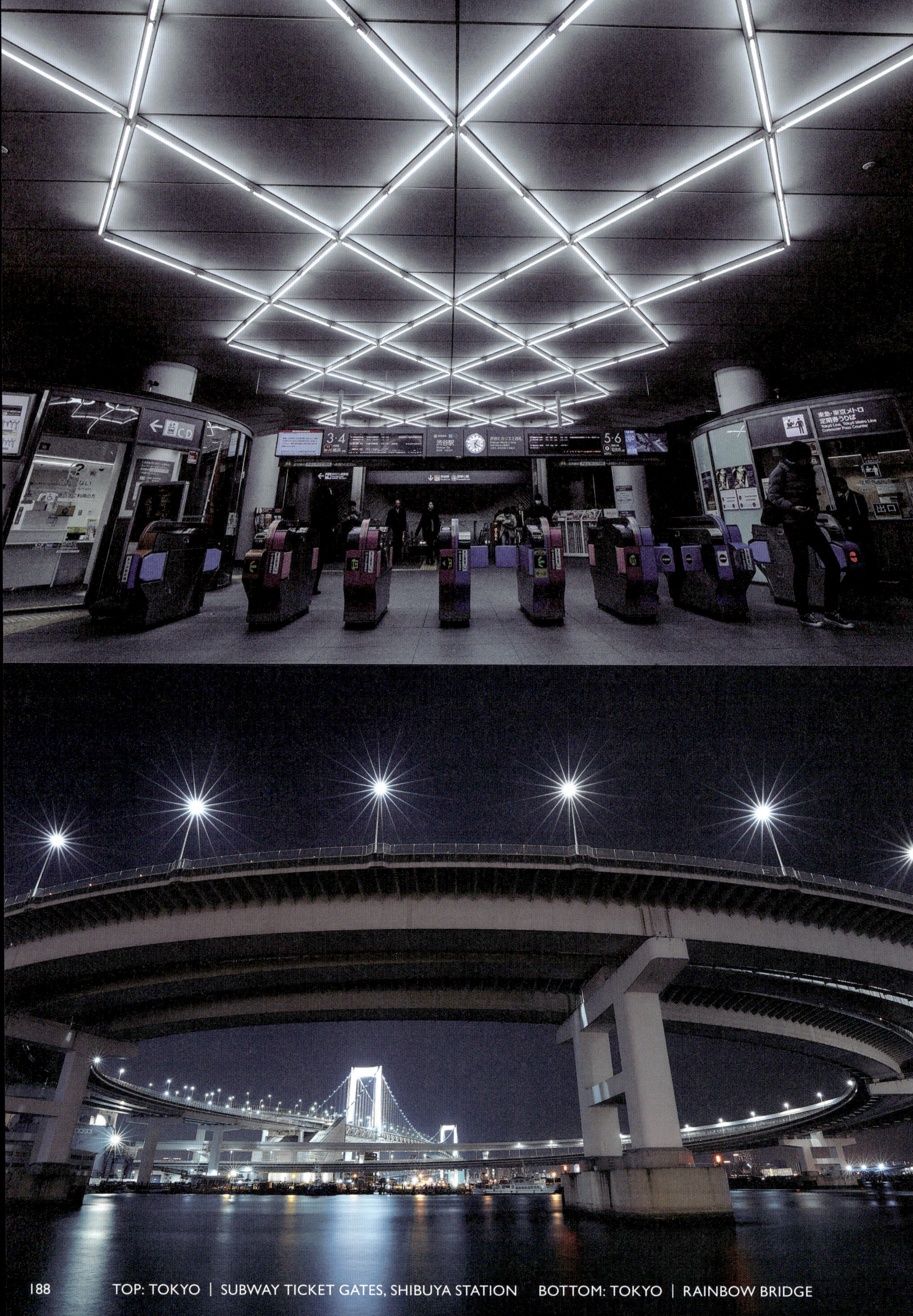

  TOP: TOKYO | SUBWAY TICKET GATES, SHIBUYA STATION   BOTTOM: TOKYO | RAINBOW BRIDGE

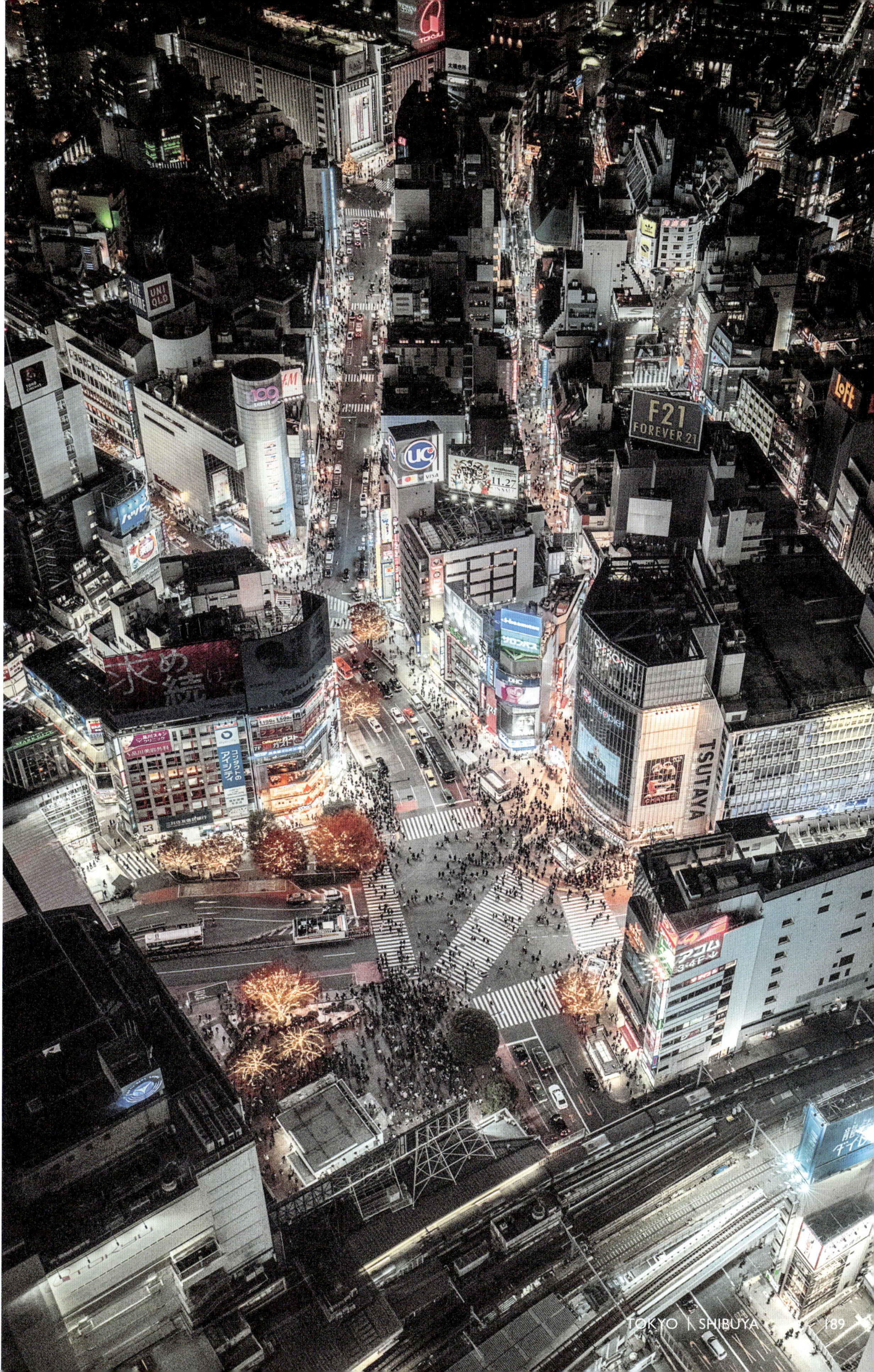

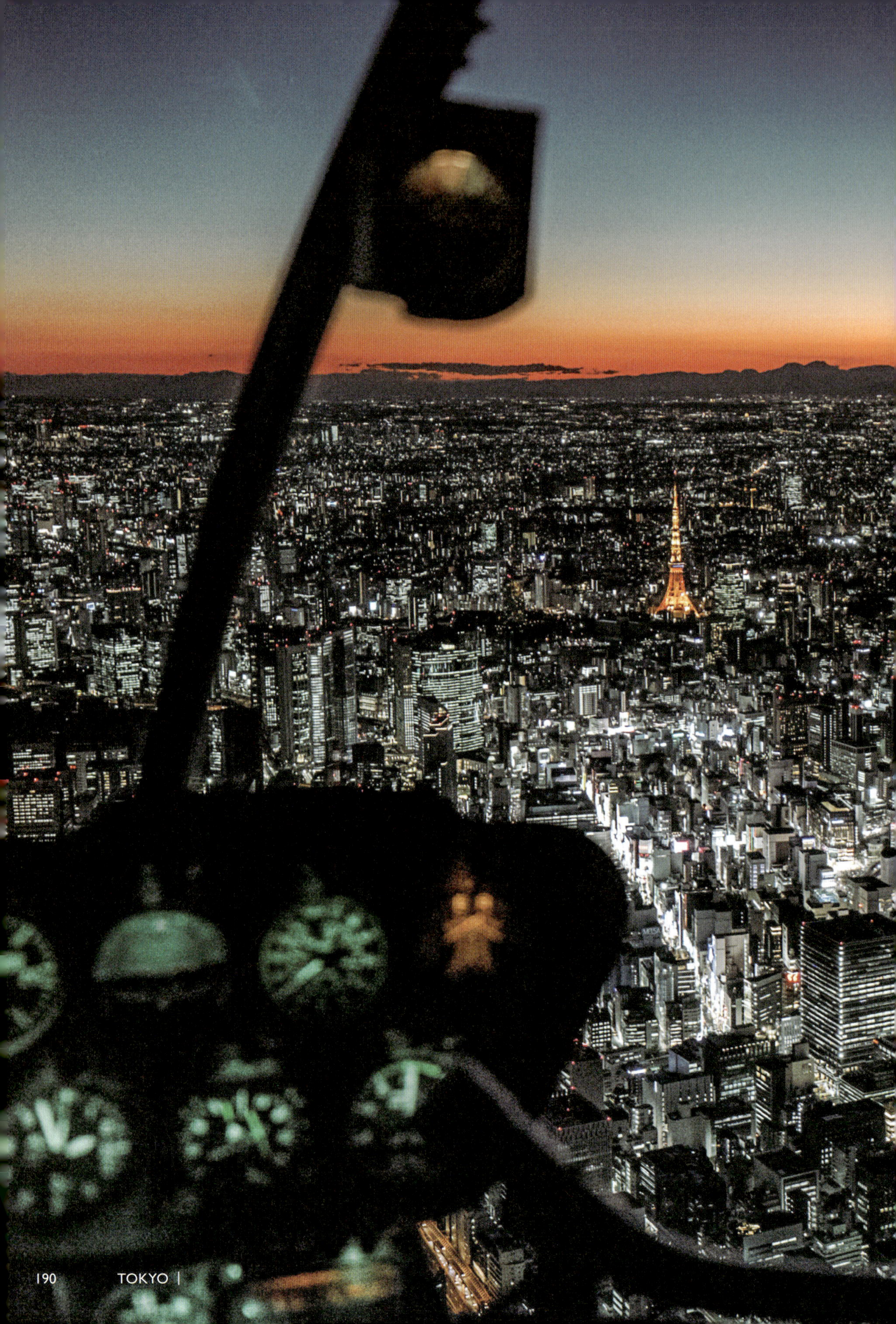

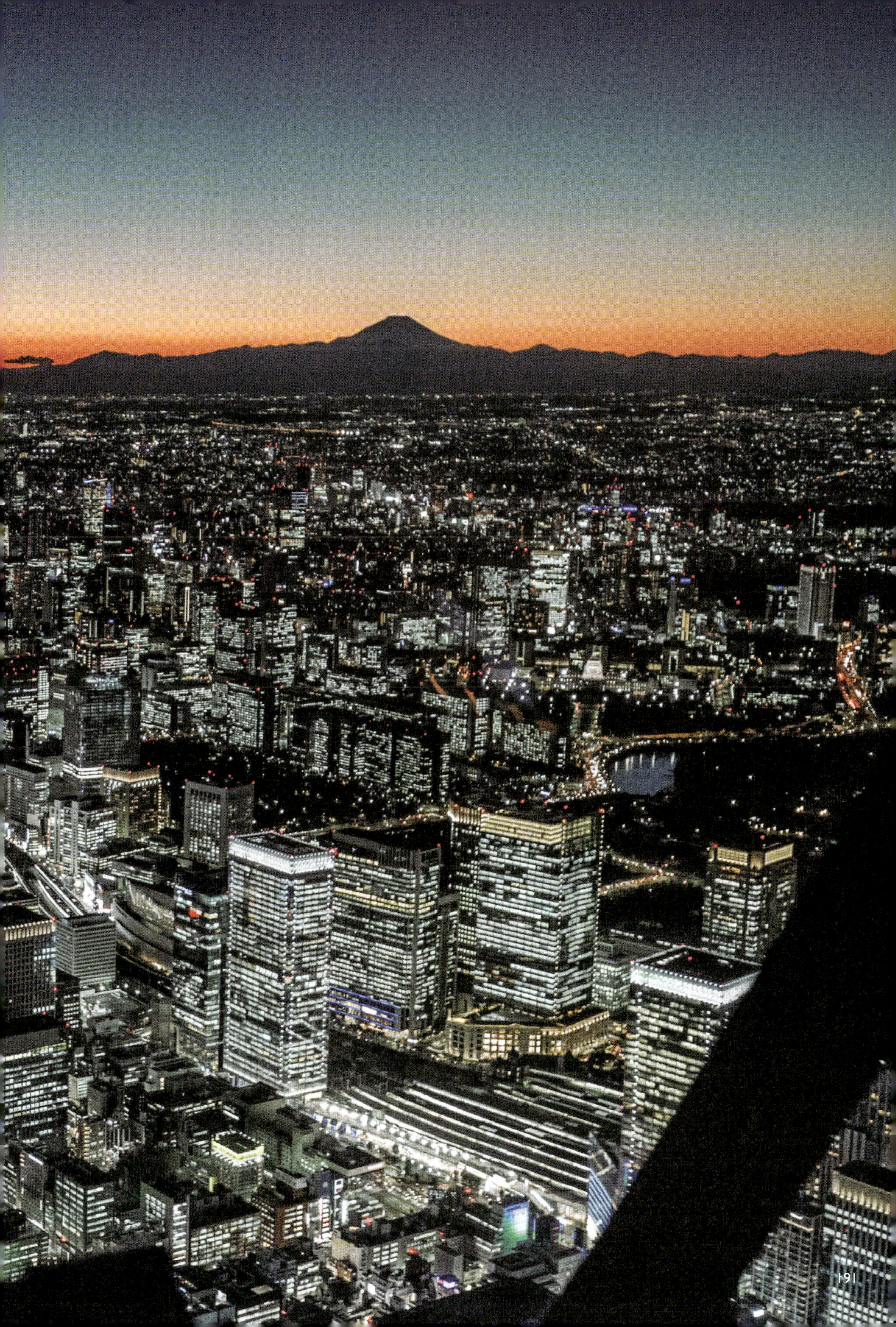

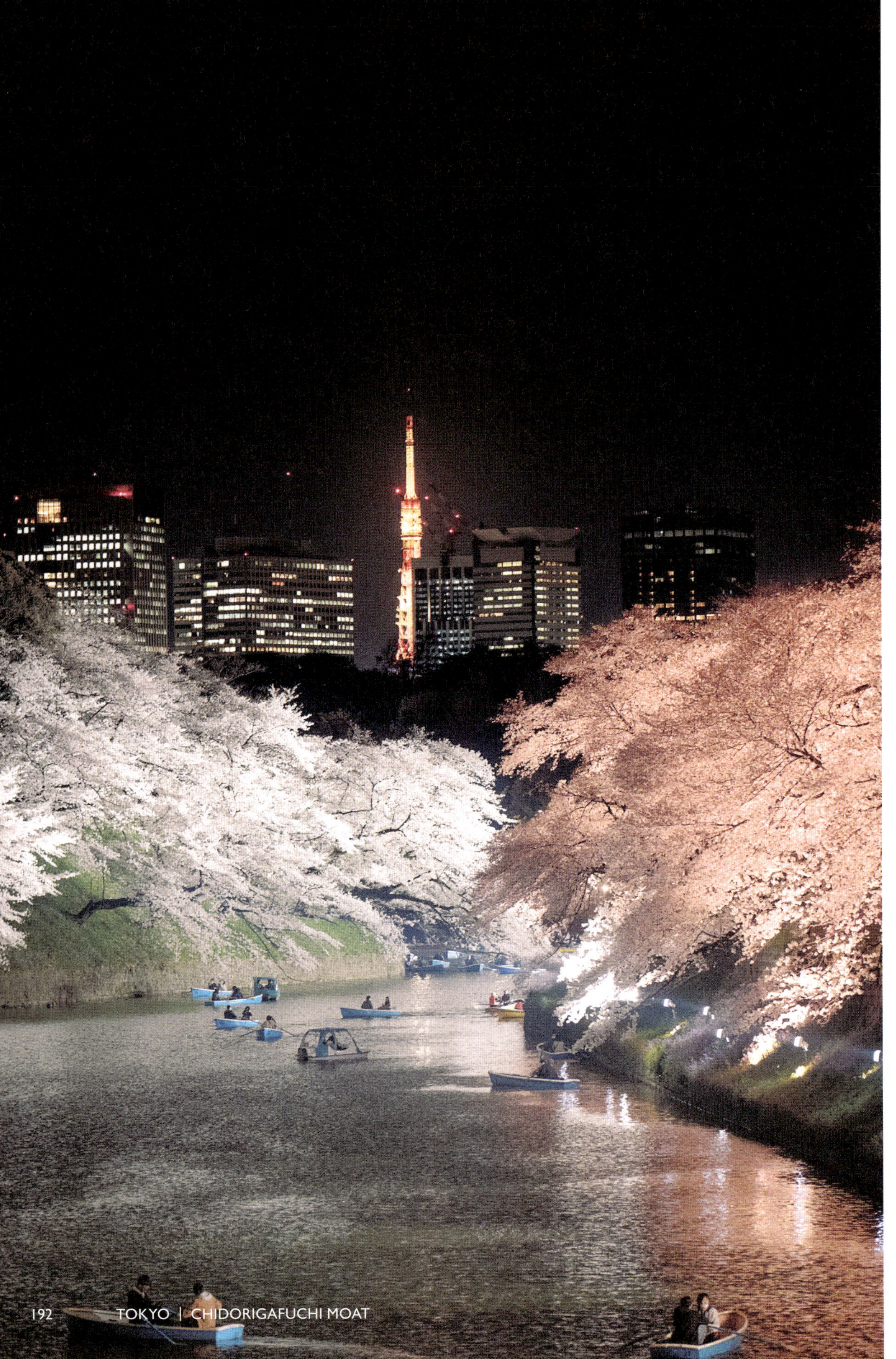

 TOKYO | CHIDORIGAFUCHI MOAT

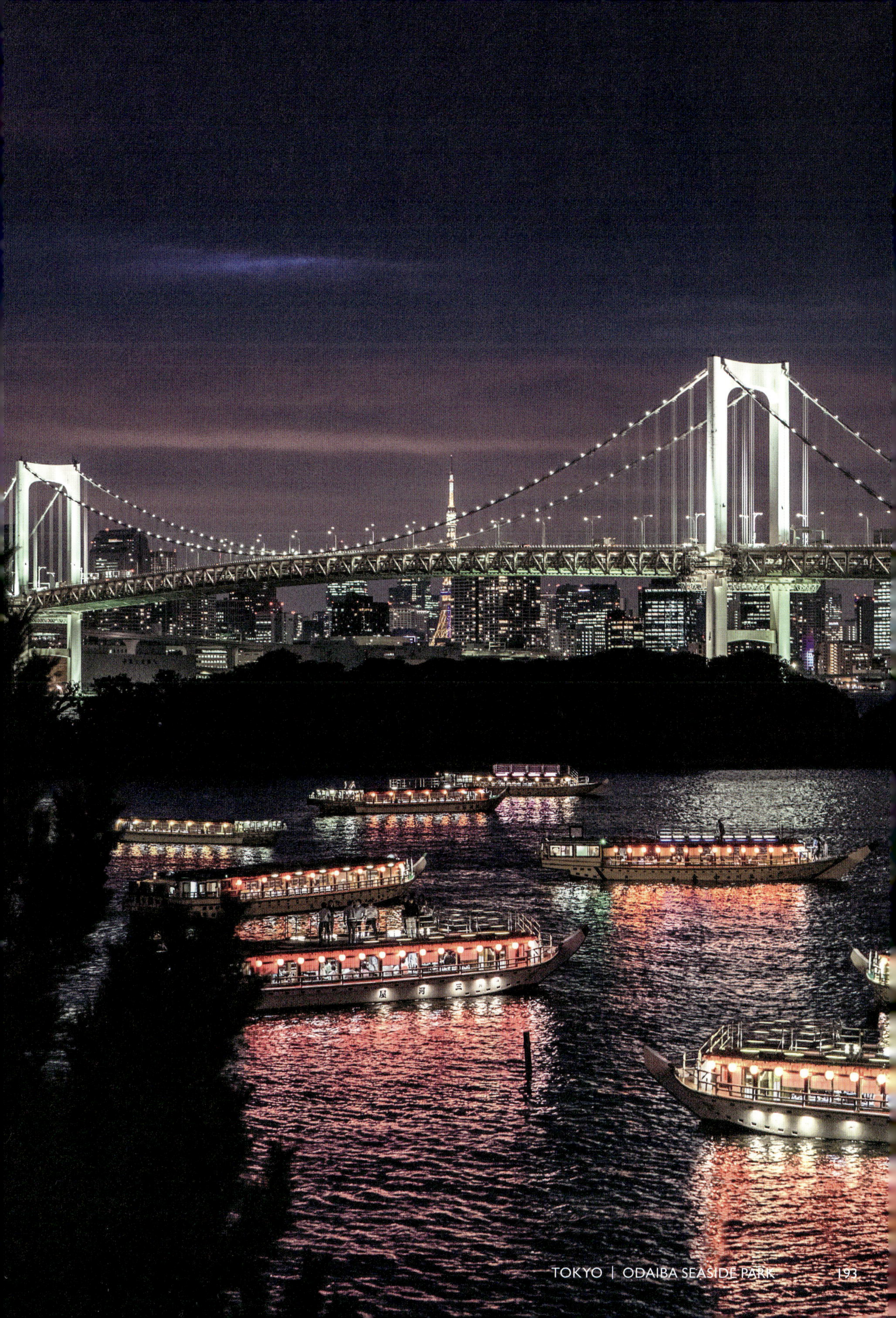

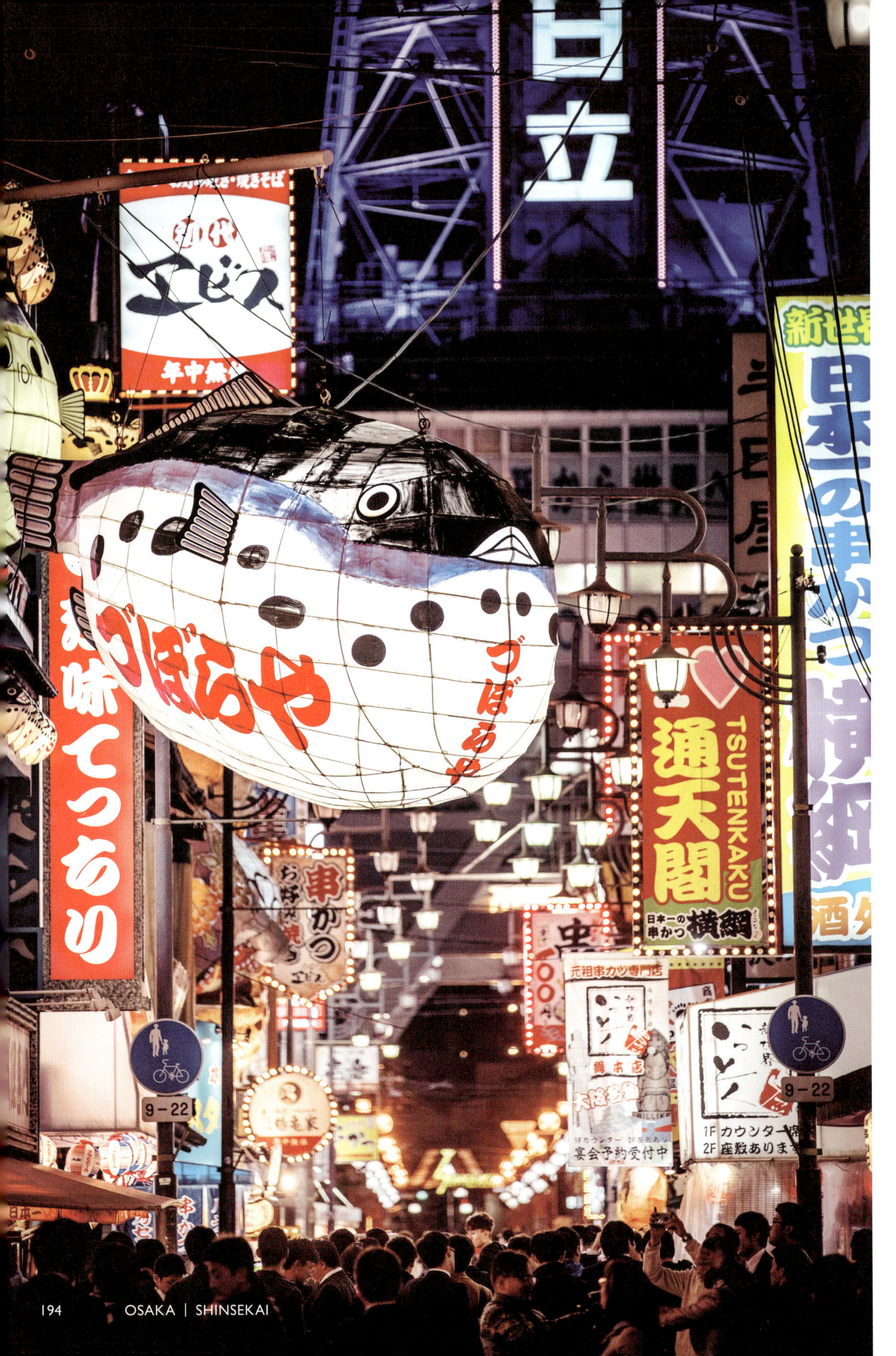
串かつ
づぼらや
づぼらや
珍味てっちり
TSUTENKAKU
通天閣
日本一の串かつ 横綱
元祖串かつ専門店
新世界
日本の串かつ
酒処
9-22
9-22
1F カウンター
2F 座敷あります
宴会予約受付中

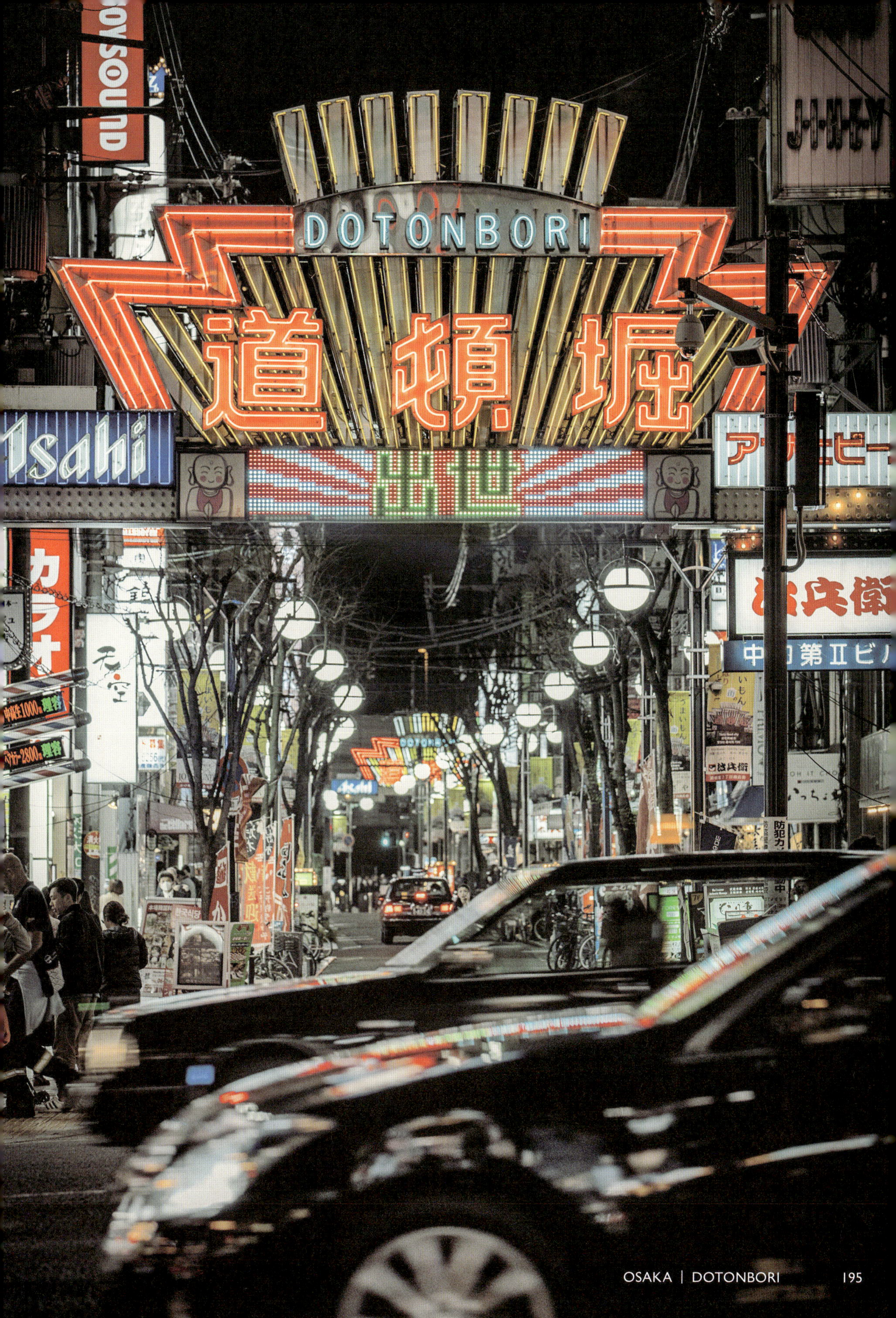

DOTONBORI
道頓堀
出世
Asahi
カラオ

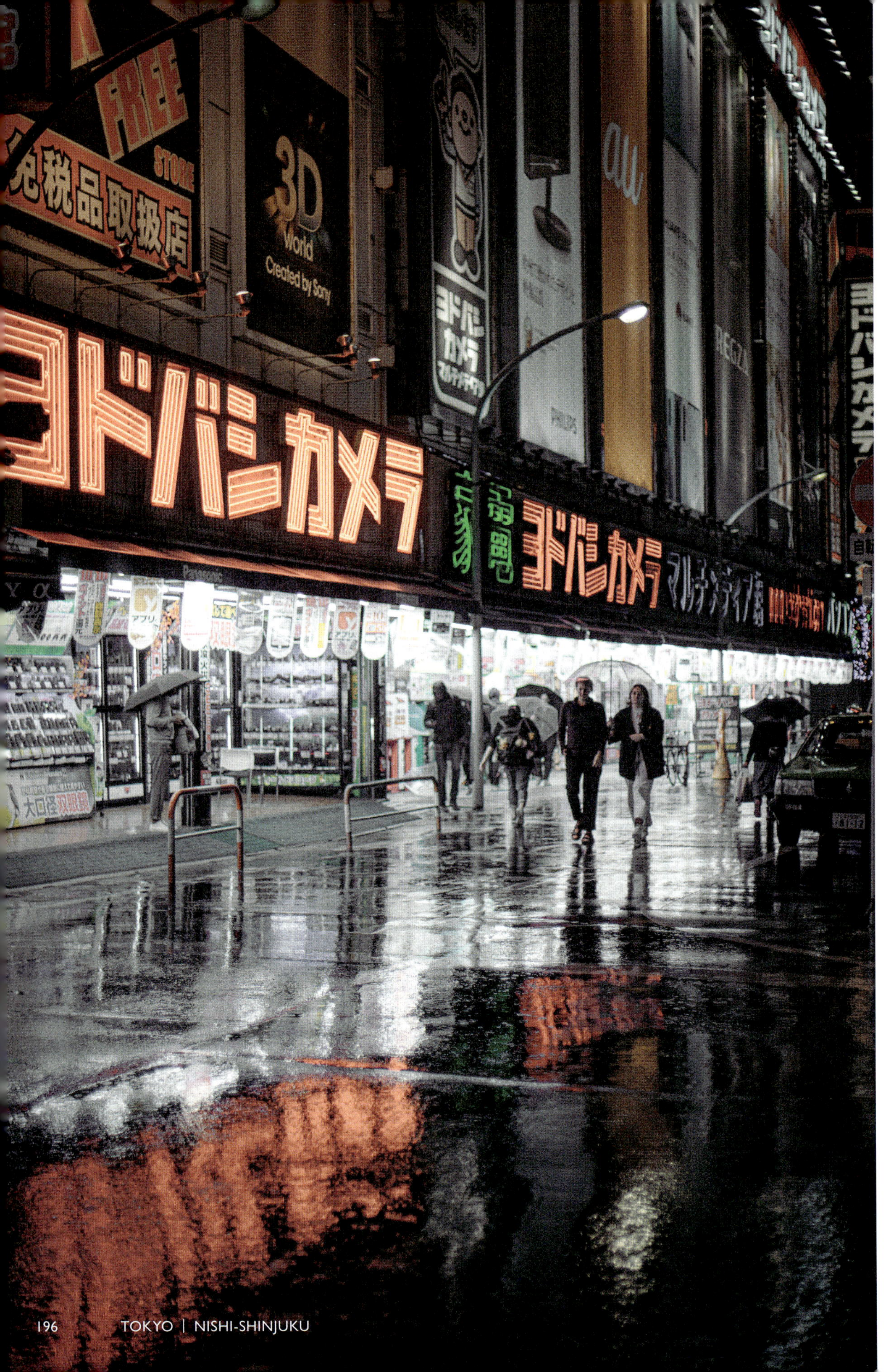

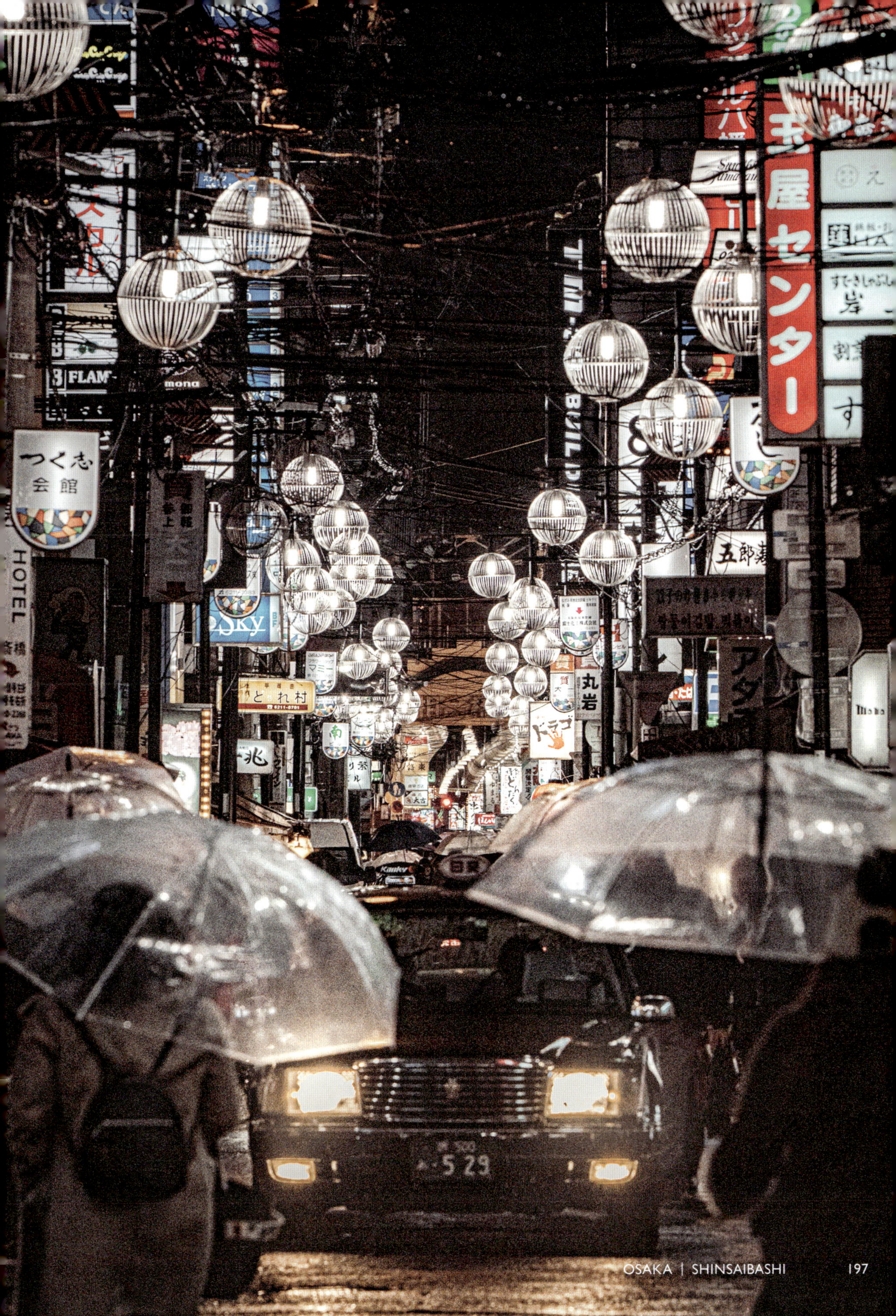

デンター
宝屋
五郎
丸岩
アダ
HOTEL
つく志
会館
FLAM
mono
SKY
と れ村
兆
南

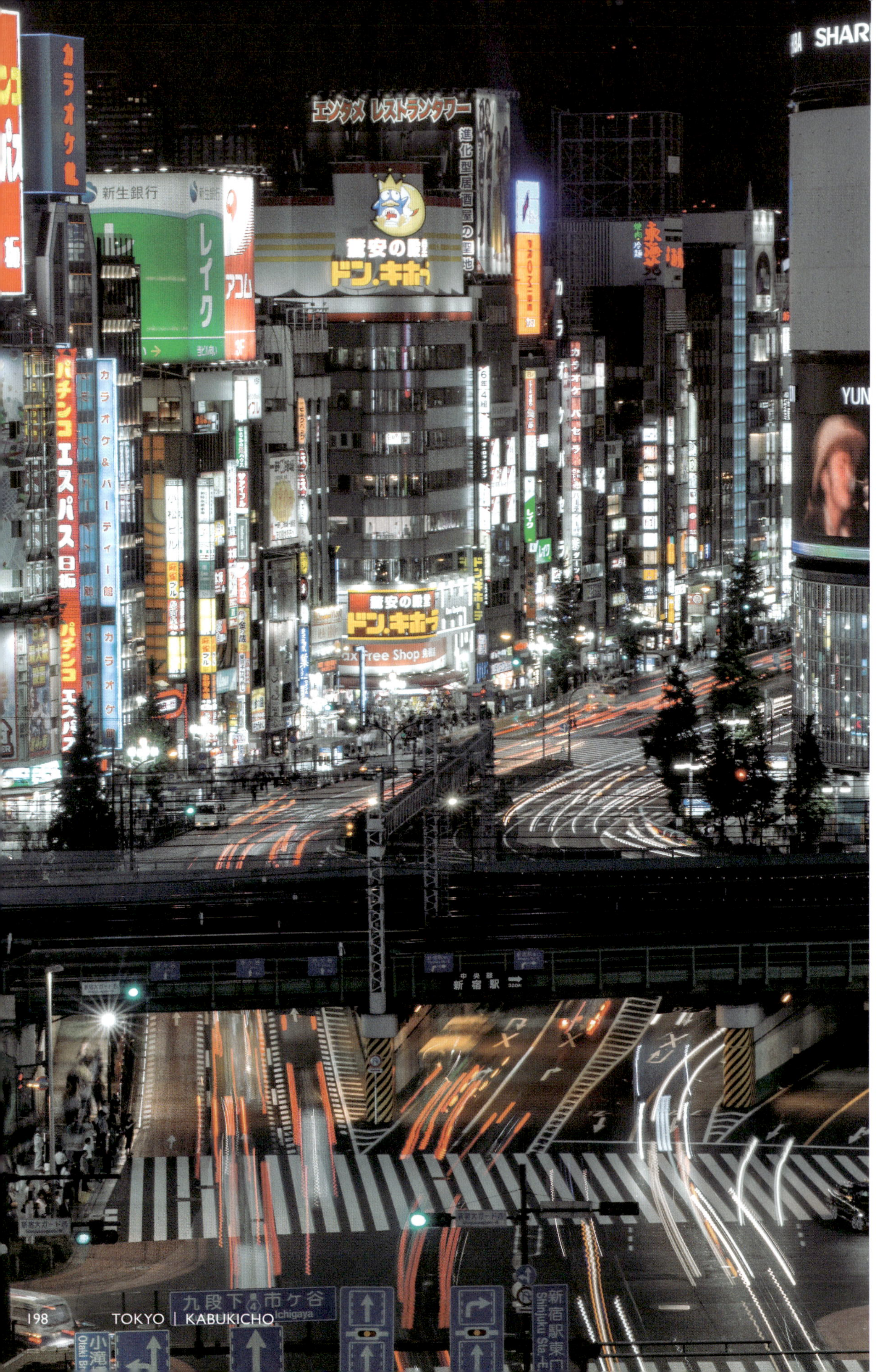

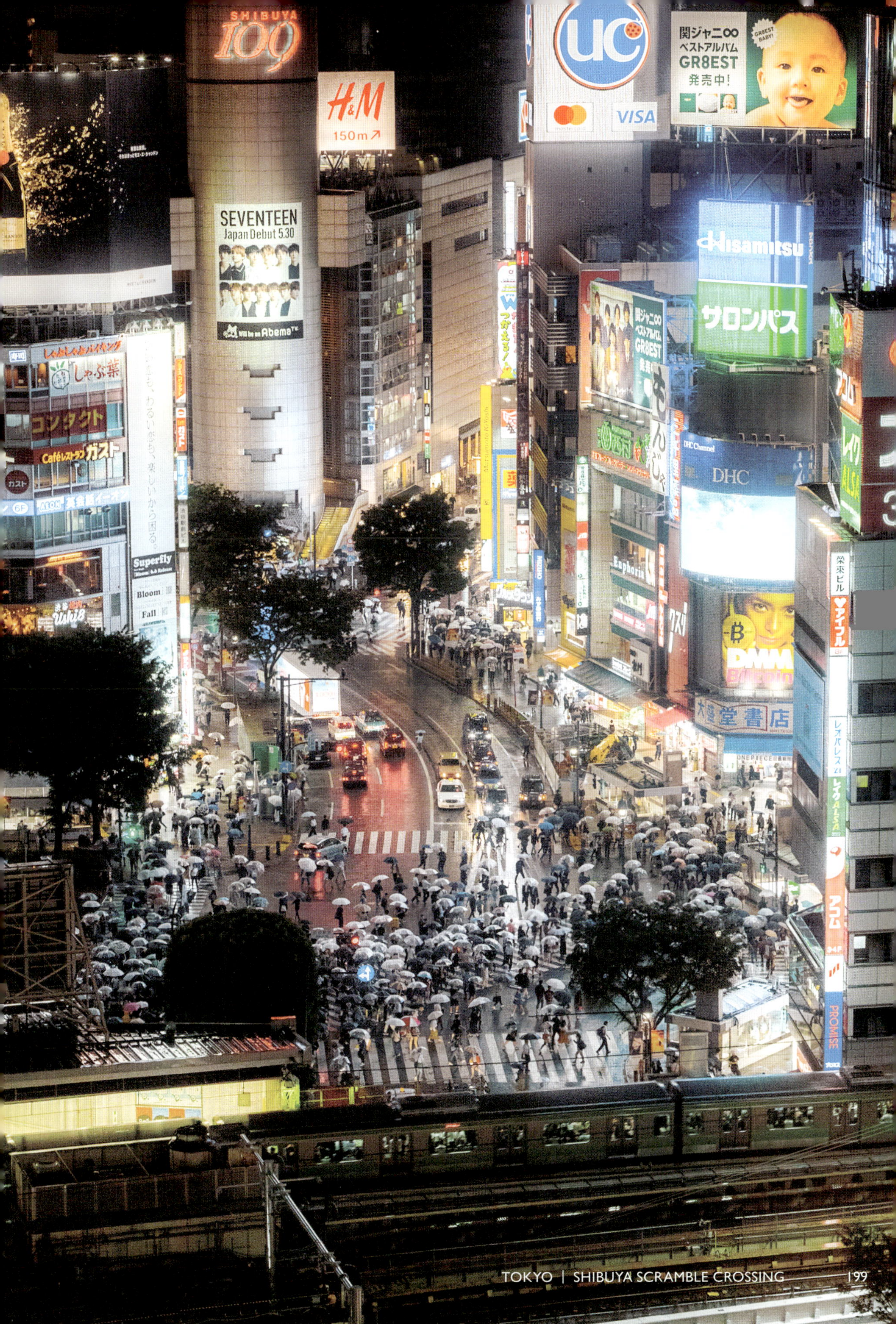

SHIBUYA
109
H&M
150m↗
SEVENTEEN
Japan Debut 5.30
Will be on AbemaTV.
UC
関ジャニ∞
ベストアルバム
GR8EST
発売中!
VISA
Hisamitsu
サロンパス
DHC
Superfly
Bloom
Fall
大盛堂書店
ONE PIECE
PROMISE
しゃぶ葉
コンタクト
Café レストラン ガスト

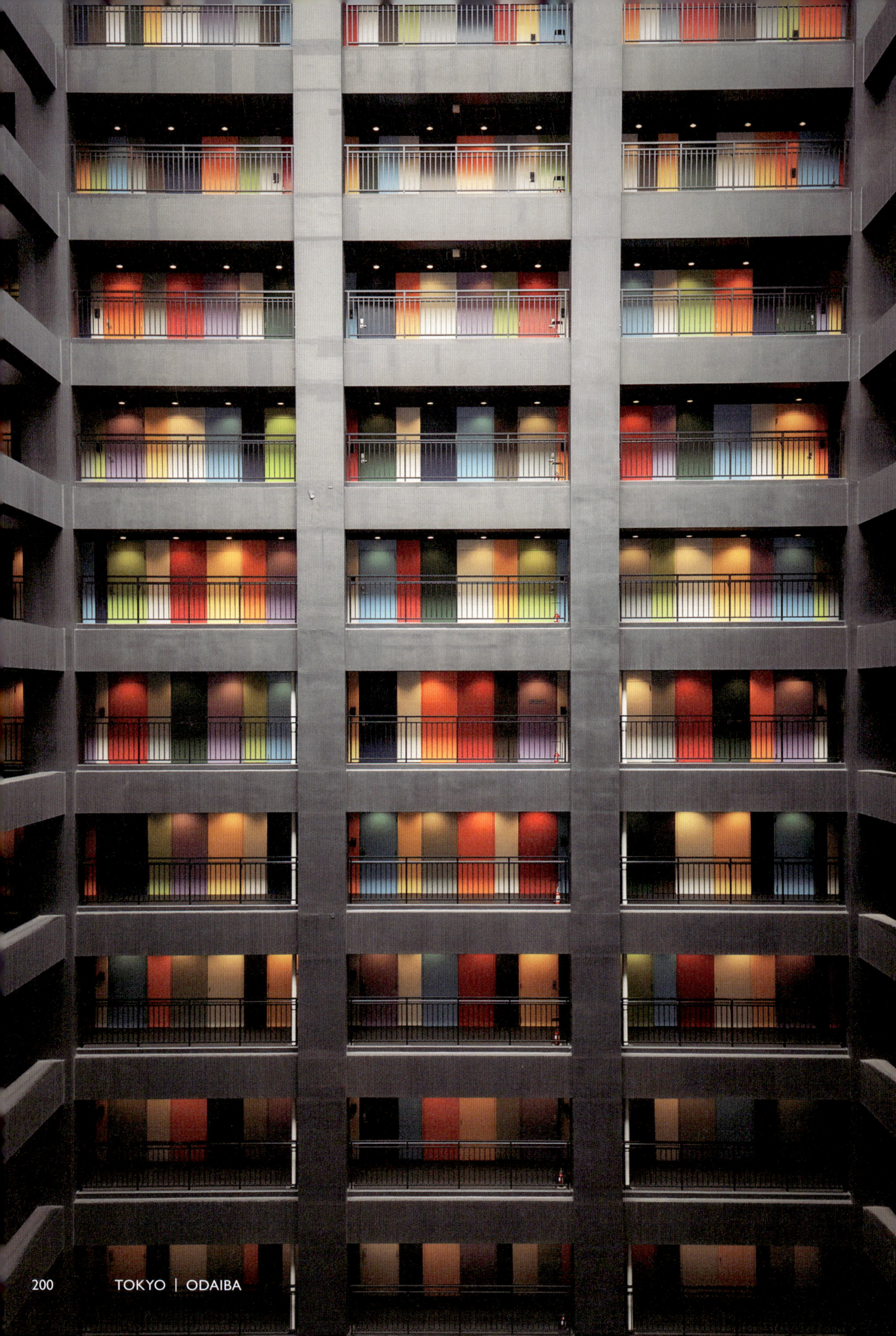

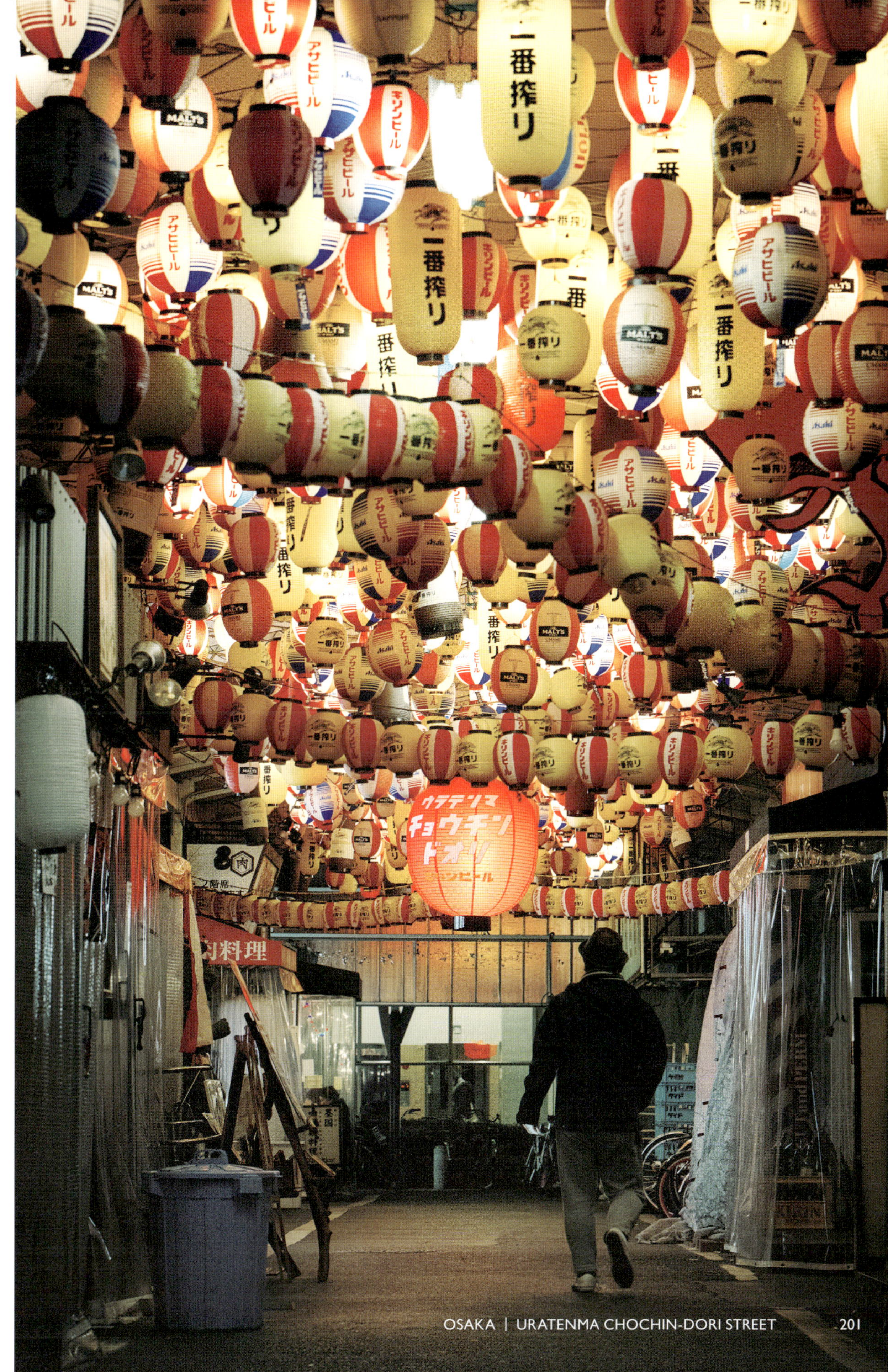

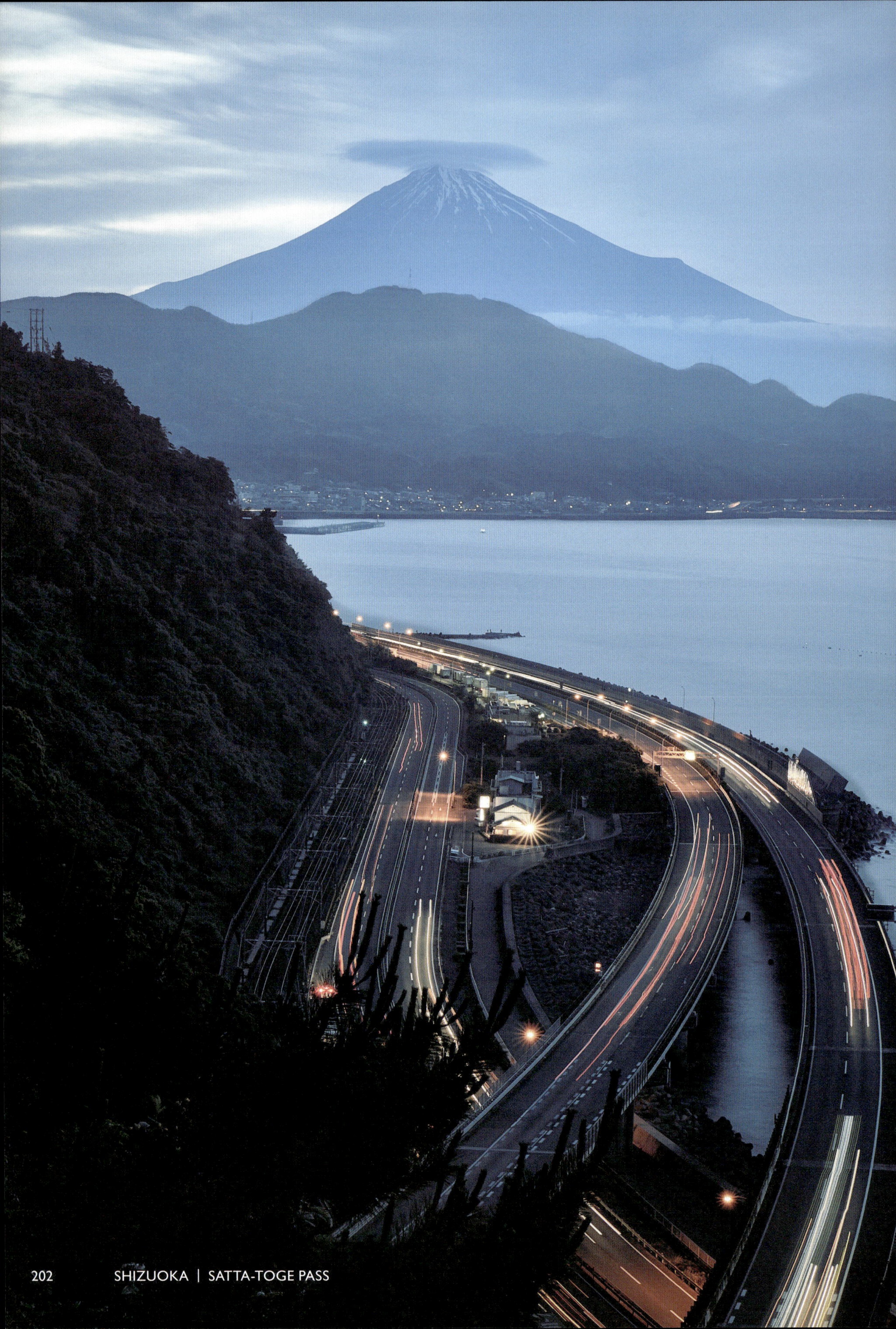

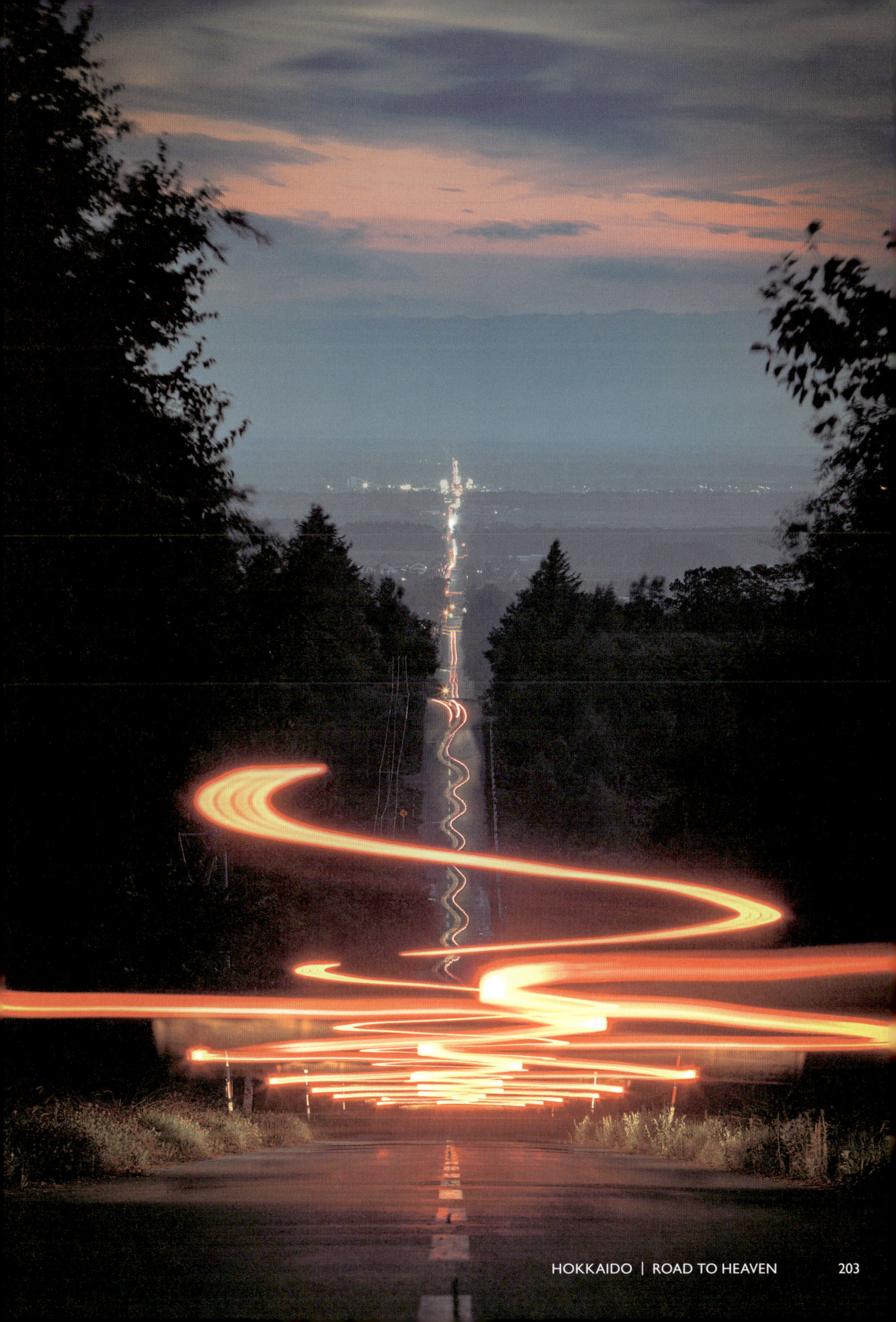

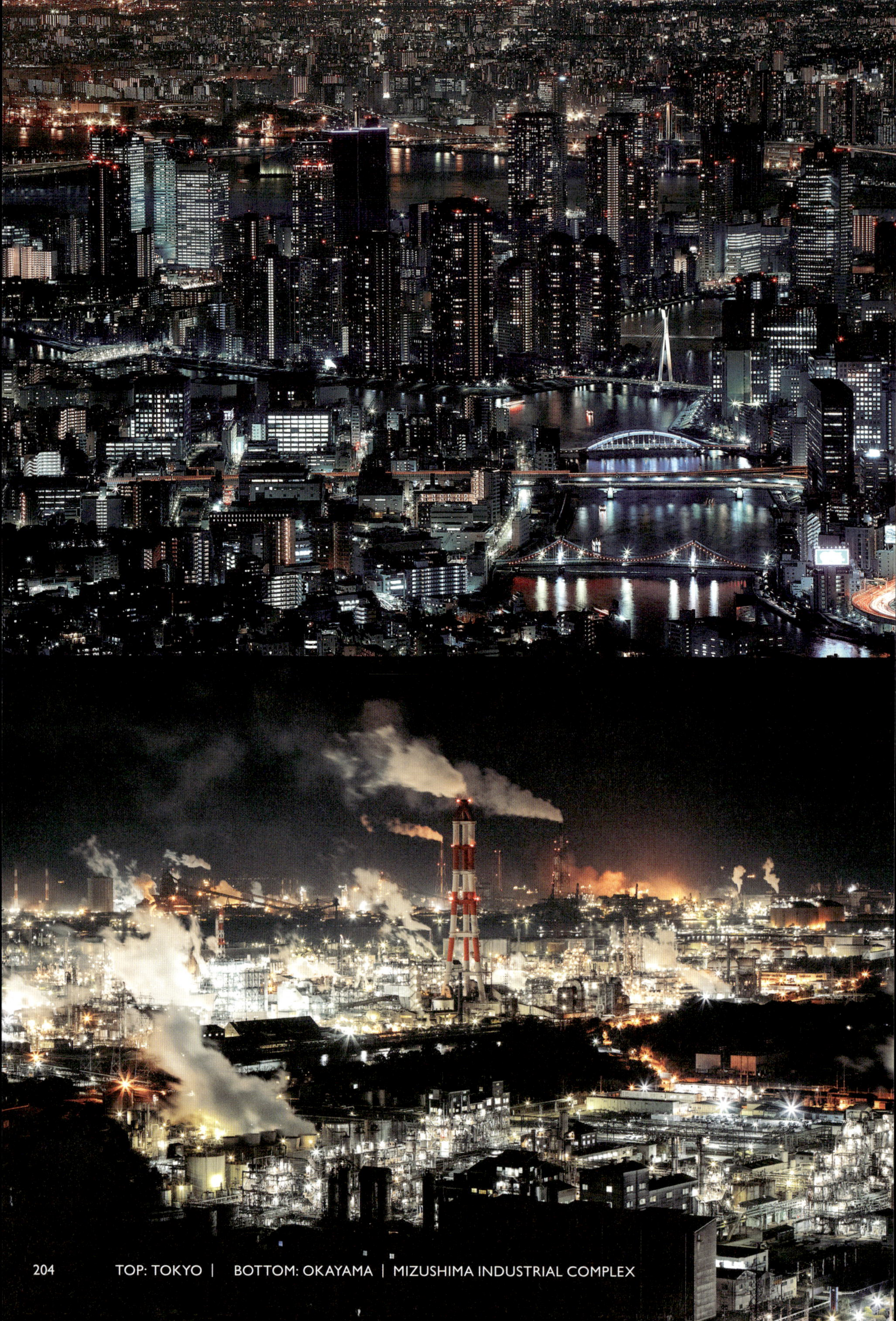

 TOP: TOKYO | BOTTOM: OKAYAMA | MIZUSHIMA INDUSTRIAL COMPLEX

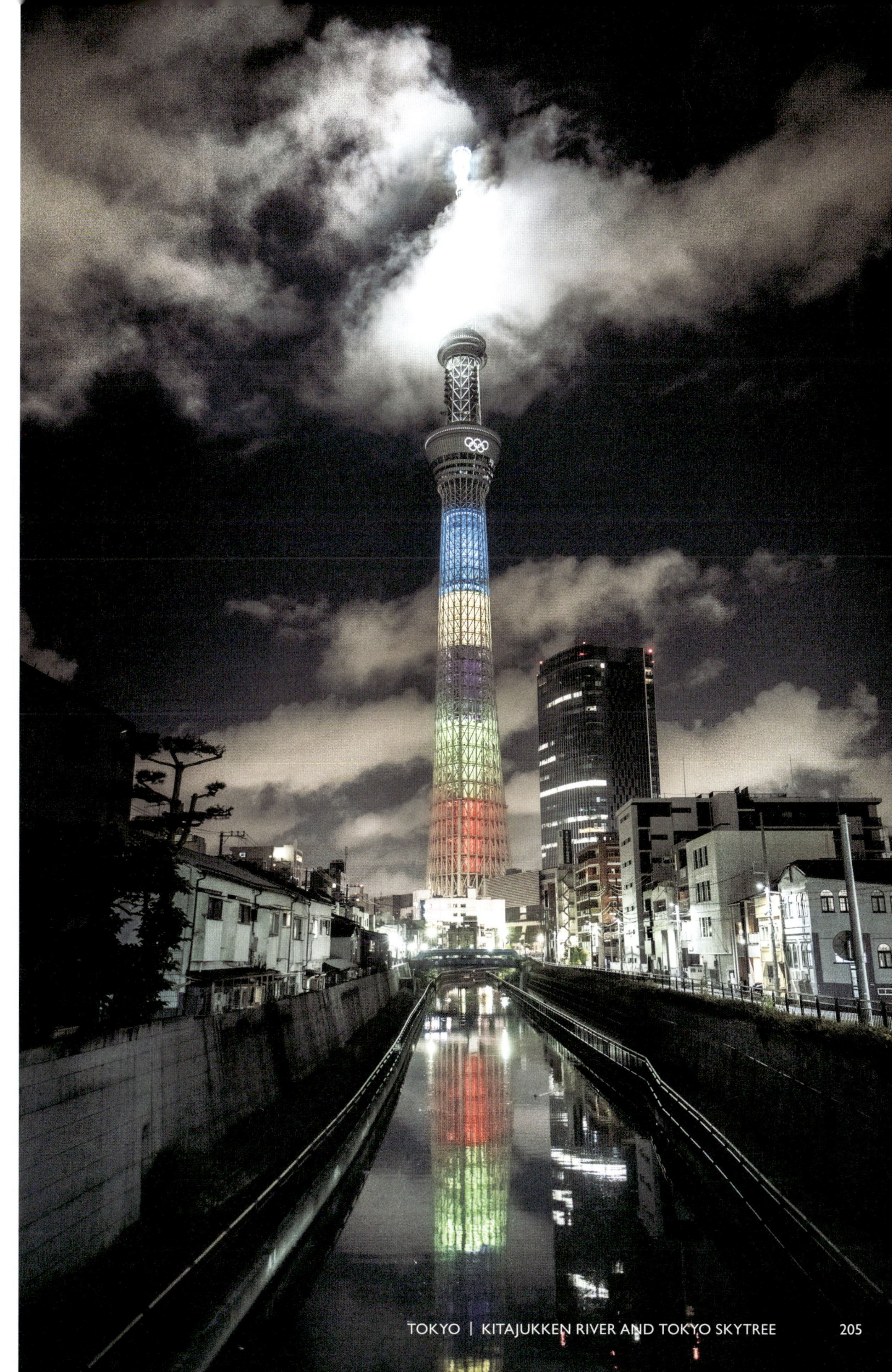

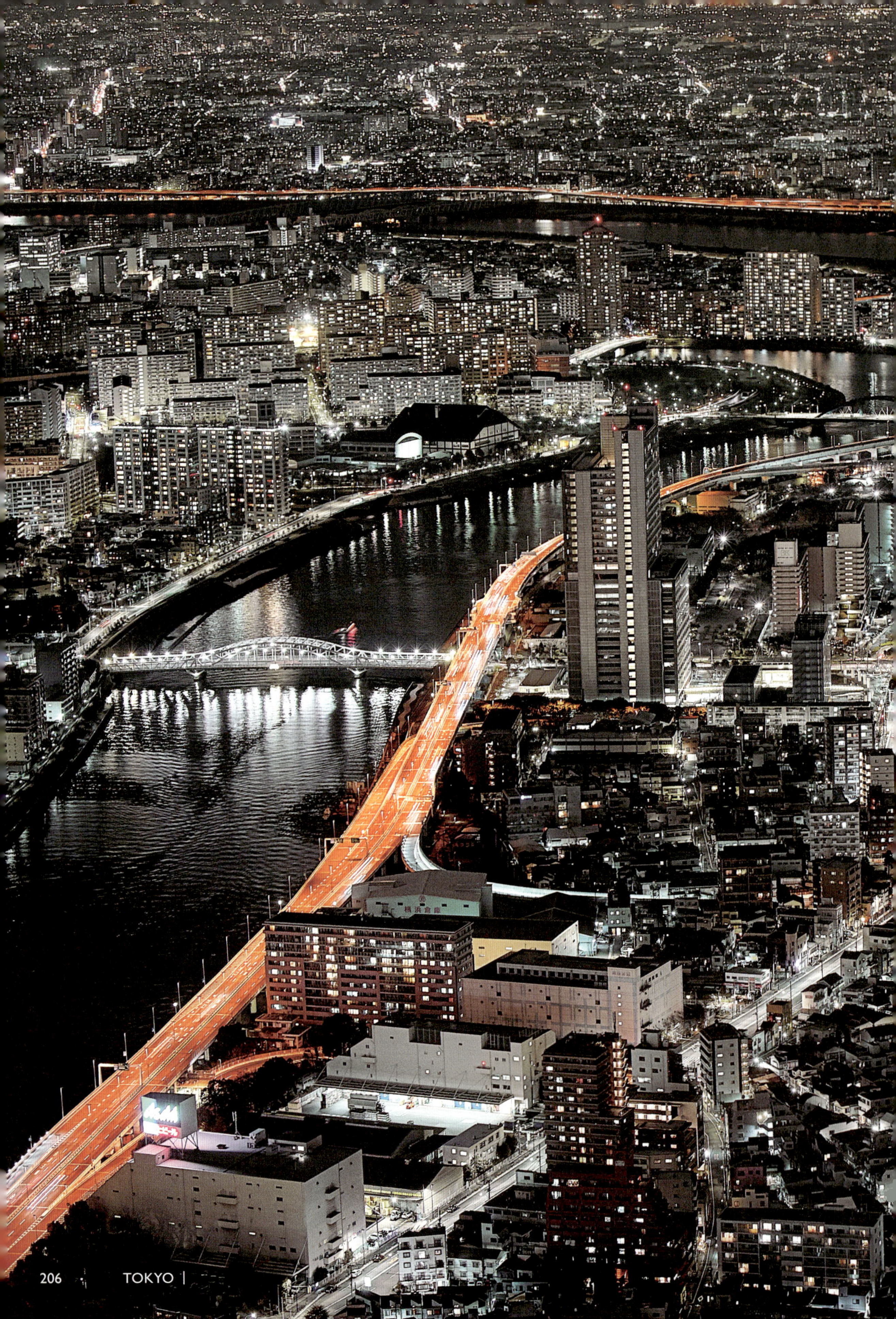

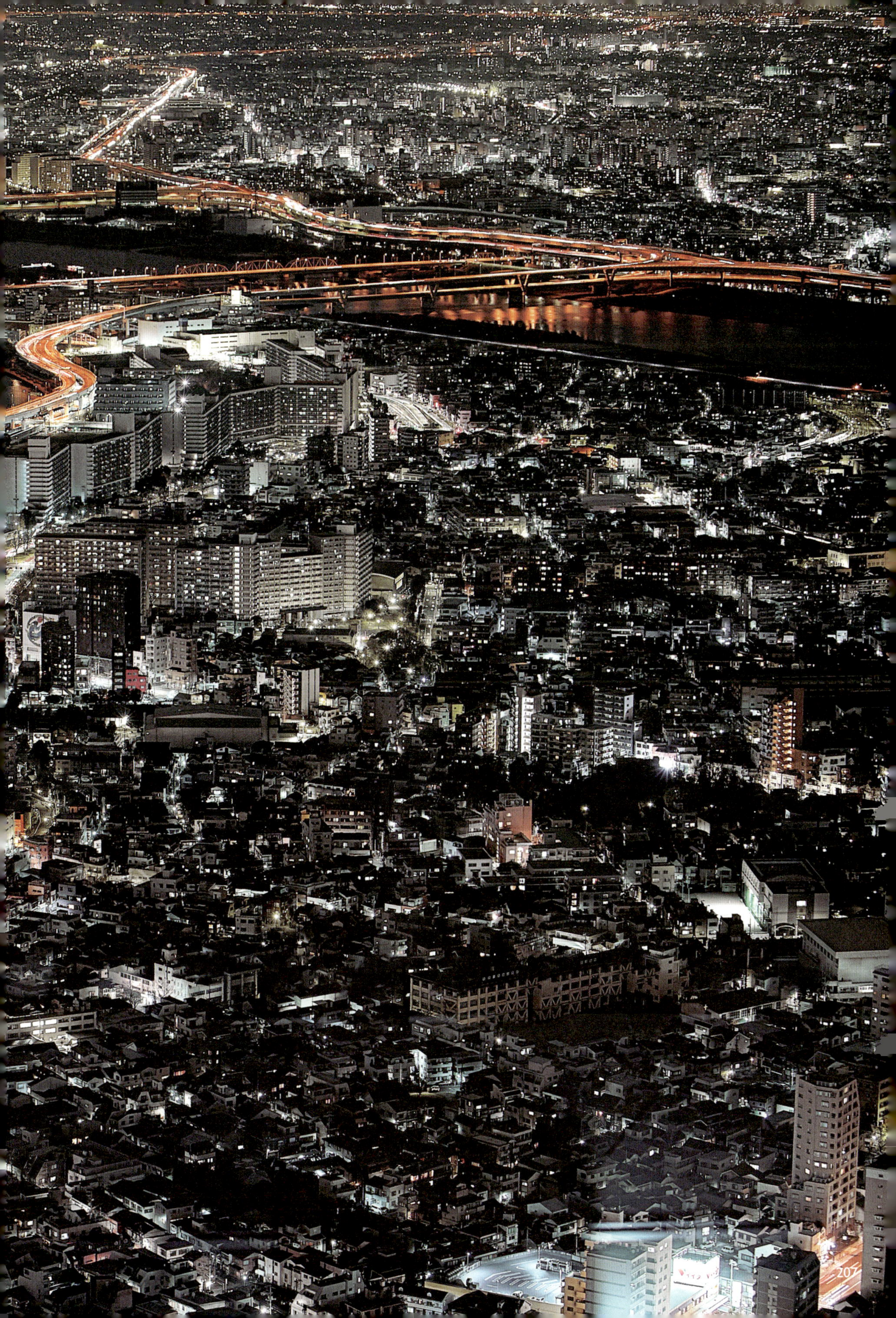

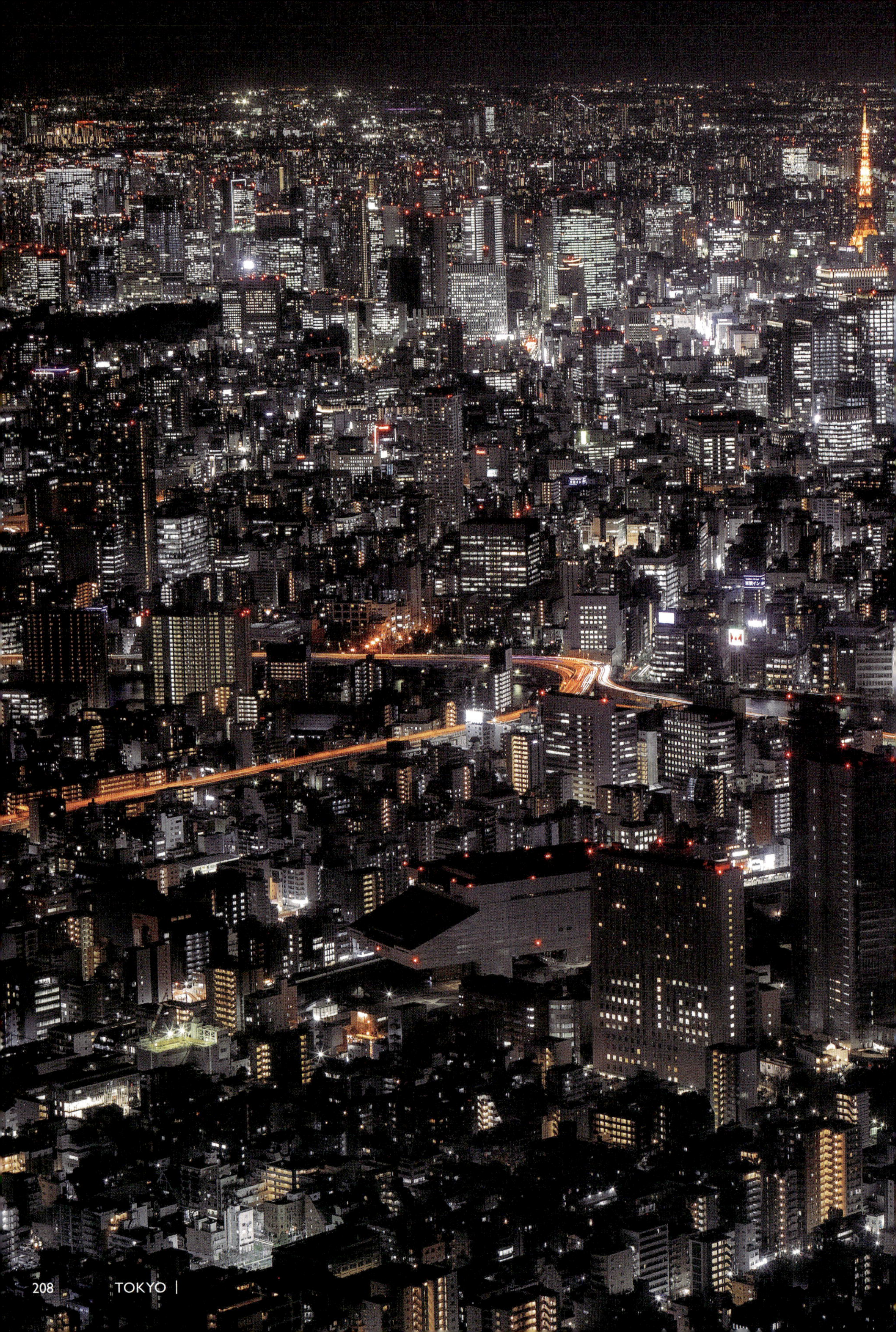

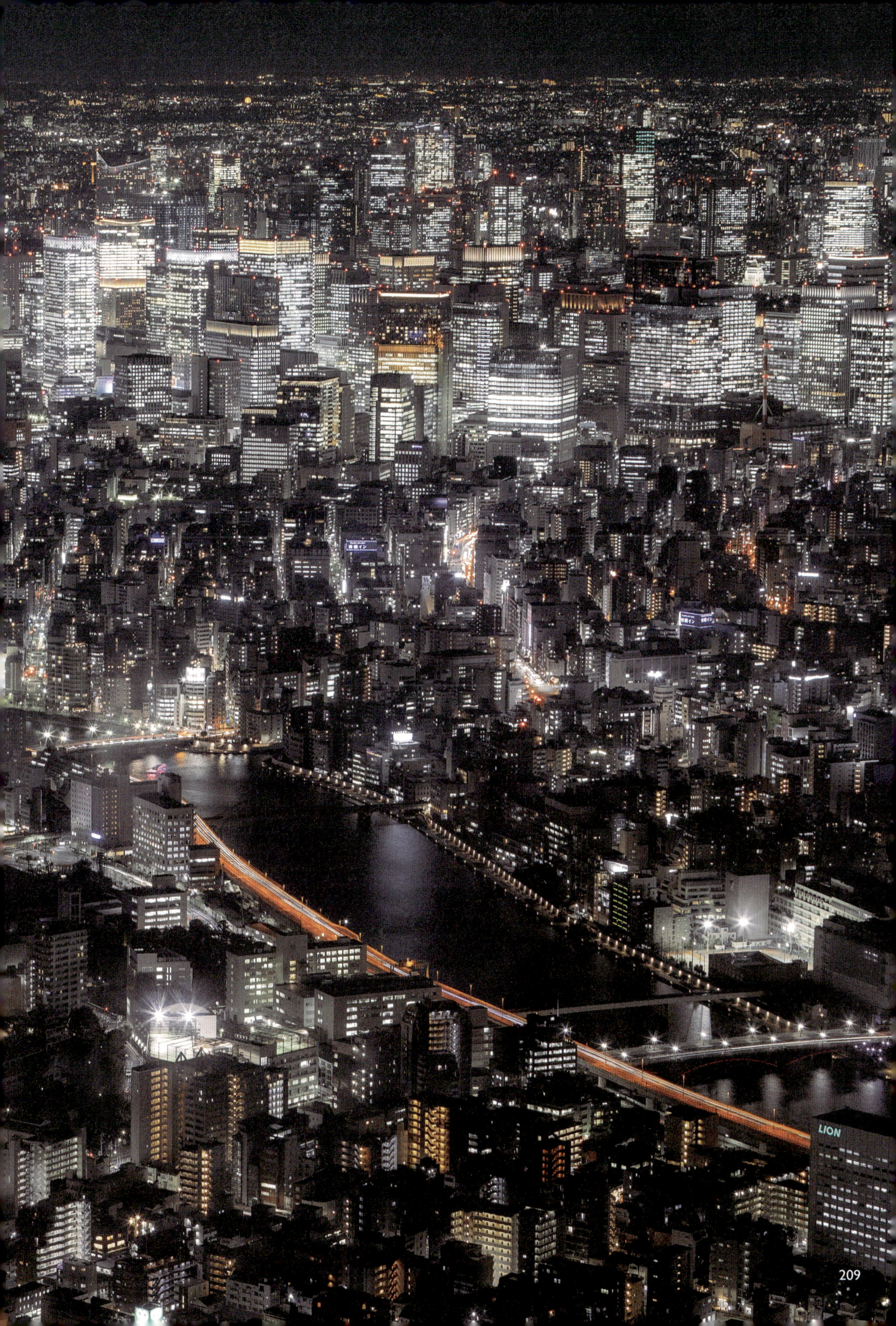
LION

P7

山梨県　富士山と河口湖

河口湖の一角に、桜の花がきれいに咲いている場所があります。その場所に到着したのは夕方少し前でしたが、夕日で雲の色が桜色のようなピンクのグラデーションになり、とてもきれいでした。

P7

Mount Fuji and Lake Kawaguchi - Yamanashi

There is a patch on Lake Kawaguchi where cherry trees are in beautiful bloom. It was a little before dusk when I arrived. The clouds were awash in a cherry-pink gradient, and the view was mesmerizing.

P8-9

青森県弘前市　弘前城の花筏

弘前公園外濠の「花筏（はないかだ）」は、限られた時間のみ、お濠が絨毯のように桜の花びらで埋め尽くされる絶景です。弘前城公園全体の桜、ライトアップされた夜桜もことのほか美しかったです。

P8-9

Flower Raft of Hirosaki Castle - Hirosaki City, Aomori

Hanaikada, or flower raft, of Hirosaki Park is a spectacular phenomenon that occurs for a limited time when the outer moat is filled with a carpet of cherry blossom petals. The views of the cherry blossoms throughout the entire Hirosaki Castle Park as well as the nighttime illuminations were also exceptionally picturesque.

P10

青森県五所川原市　津軽鉄道・芦野公園駅

昭和5年の開通時に建てられた、木造のノスタルジックな当時の駅舎と、桜のトンネルを通り抜ける電車の共演が情緒的です。駅の後ろにある芦野公園の満開の桜も大変きれいでした。

P10

Tsugaru Railway and Ashinokoen Station - Goshogawara City, Aomori

Constructed in 1930, when the railway commenced operation, the wooden station building retains its original and nostalgic charm. The station combined with the train passing through the tunnel of cherry blossoms creates a dramatic scenery. The cherry trees were in full bloom in Ashino Park behind the station, which was also lovely to see.

P11

京都府京都市　伏見十石舟

江戸時代に淀川で酒や米、旅客を運んだ「伏見十石舟」。現在は観光船として、酒蔵に柳が映える運河をゆったりと運航しています。満開の桜と十石舟は、まるで映画のワンシーンのようでした。川にかかる橋上からの撮影も可能です。

P11

Fushimi Jikkoku - bune, Kyoto City, Kyoto

The Fushimi *jikkoku-bune* transported sake, rice, and passengers along the Yodo River during the Edo period. Today, the vessels are used for sightseeing cruises that sail leisurely along the canal, where willow trees complement the sake breweries. The sight of *jikkoku-bune* among the blossoming cherry trees was like a scene from a movie. You can also take pictures from the bridge over the river.

P12

青森県十和田市　桜やぶさめ

駒街道の桜並木がピークを過ぎ、撮影できずにいると、大きなレンズを持った方が「桜やぶさめ」の主催者を紹介してくれました。「桜やぶさめ」は、満開の桜並木の下を女流騎手の乗った馬だけが駆け抜ける、特別なやぶさめです。幸運にもアイドル騎手のななさんを撮影させてもらえ、満開の桜とやぶさめの華麗さに心を打たれました。皆さんに感謝します。

P12

Sakura Yabusame - Towada City, Aomori

The rows of cherry trees along Koma-kaido Street had already passed their peak. and I was unable to take any photos, but a man with a large lens introduced me to the organizer of Sakura Yabusame. The *yabusame* event is a special horseback archery competition of strictly female archers who ride their horses through a row of cherry trees in full bloom. I was lucky to capture the celebrity rider, Ms. Nana, and was deeply impressed by the splendor of the cherry blossoms and *yabusame*. Thank you all.

P13

兵庫県姫路市　姫路城

白鷺が羽を広げたような優美な姿から、「白鷺城」の愛称で親しまれています。子どものときから一番好きなお城で、姫路城と満開の桜との共演を実際に見ることができて感激しました。　機会があれば、また桜の時期に訪れたいです。

P13

Himeji Castle - Himeji City, Hyogo

Himeji Castle is nicknamed the 'White Heron Castle' because of its graceful magnificence resembling a heron spreading its wings. It has been my favorite castle since I was a child, so I was thrilled to see the actual fortress together with the blossoming cherry trees. If given a chance, I'd like to revisit during the sakura season.

P14

東京都目黒区　目黒川の桜並木

ドイツ移住後の6年間、春に帰国したことがなく、日本で桜を見ることが夢でした。撮影当日は空港に到着後、そのまま桜を撮影に行きました。長い間楽しみにし続け、たかぶる想いが伝わったのか、この写真は Instagram でリポストされて150万近いライクがつき、フォロワー数も急増しました。目にした桜は眩いほどに美しく、感無量でした。

P14

Cherry blossom trees along the Meguro River - Meguro Ward, Tokyo

For six years after settling in Germany, I had never returned home in the spring, so I dreamed of seeing the cherry blossoms in Japan. After arriving at the airport, I went directly to the location to shoot. Perhaps the sense of excitement I felt for this much-anticipated opportunity was conveyed through my image and the audience resonated with it—the photo was reposted on Instagram, garnering nearly 1.5 million likes, and the number of followers skyrocketed. The cherry blossoms I saw were breathtaking, and my heart was filled with emotion.

P15

京都府京都市　竹中稲荷神社

赤い鳥居が続く一直線の参道を桜が彩る「竹中稲荷神社」。地元の友人が案内してくれた、隠れた桜の名所です。撮影を開始すると、着物姿の女性が通り過ぎたのでモデルをしていただき、幸運にも神々しい1枚を撮影することができました。

P15

Takenaka Inari Shrine - Kyoto City, Kyoto

Cherry blossoms grace the straight approach lined with red torii gates leading up to Takenaka Inari Shrine. A local friend showed me this little-known cherry-viewing location. When I started shooting, a woman in a kimono passed by, and I requested her to be my model. I was very fortunate to have captured such a divine image.

P16

埼玉県川越市　新河岸川の桜並木

約60年前、戦没者慰霊のために桜の苗が約300本寄贈されたことに始まり、別名「ほまれ桜」と呼ばれています。広大な景色ではありませんが、のんびりとした時間が流れ、川原の緑とのコントラストに魅せられました。

P16

Shingashi Riverbed Cherry Blossoms - Kawagoe City, Saitama

About 60 years ago, approximately 300 cherry seedlings were donated as a memorial to honor the war dead, and today, the trees are also known as Homare-zakura (meaning "cherry blossoms in honor of"). The scenery is by no means expansive, but the time passed leisurely, and I enjoyed the lovely contrast of the cherry blossoms against the greenery of the riverbanks.

P17

京都府嵐山市　桜と日本猿

桜と日本猿の写真が撮りたくて行きましたが、猿たちは人を気にも留めず、地べたで寝そべったりしています。すると、突然喧嘩をし始め、2匹が木の上へ。一瞬の出来事でしたが体が反応してシャッターを切り、イメージしていた写真を撮影することができました。

P17

Cherry blossoms and Japanese monkey - Arashiyama City, Kyoto

I thought it would be wonderful to take pictures of cherry blossoms with Japanese macaques, so I set out to the monkey park. The creatures were lounging around on the ground, paying no attention to humans. Then suddenly, the monkeys started to fight, and two of them climbed up a tree. Everything happened so quickly, but my body responded and pressed the shutter at the exact moment I wanted to capture.

P18-19

山梨県富士吉田市　新倉山浅間公園

富士山と赤い五重塔、そして満開の桜の共演を楽しめる人気スポット「新倉山浅間公園」。初めてこの場所を訪れたときに、公園の裏手にある新倉山の山頂まで登りました。山頂に着いたときには息が切れ、疲れて撮影どころではなくなり、体力作りのために毎朝ジョギングをするきっかけとなった写真です。

P18-19

Arakurayama Sengen Park - Fujiyoshida City, Yamanashi

Arakurayama Sengen Park commands a view of Mount Fuji with the red five-storied pagoda and cherry blossoms in full bloom for visitors to enjoy. On my first visit, I climbed to the summit of Mount Arakura, located at the rear of the park. By the time I reached the peak, I was out of breath and too tired to take pictures. This photo was what inspired me to take up jogging every morning to build up my physical strength.

P20

栃木県日光市　二荒山神社・神橋
世界遺産「日光の社寺」の玄関ともいえる美しい
橋「神橋」。日本三大奇橋のひとつで、現在の橋
は約 120 年前に架けられたものです。朱塗りの
橋と木々の緑のコントラストが美しく幻想的で、過
去にタイムスリップしたような情景が楽しめます。

P20

**Futarasan Shrine and Shinkyo Bridge
- Nikko City, Tochigi**
The stunning Shinkyo Bridge is the gateway to the
Shrines and Temples of Nikko, which is registered
collectively as a World Heritage Site. Constructed
about 120 years ago, the bridge is known as one of
Japan's three most peculiar bridges. The vermilion-
lacquered bridge is juxtaposed with the verdant
green of the trees in a beautiful and enchanting
way. The scenery will make you feel as if you've
traveled back in time.

P21

和歌山県東牟婁郡
熊野那智大社・那智御滝　青岸渡寺・三重塔
三重塔と滝の共演が有名で、長らく行きたかった
場所でした。到着が遅くなり、ゆっくりとはできま
せんでしたが、日本を実感させる明媚な地でした。
滝の下にある「熊野那智大社」の別宮・「飛瀧
神社（ひろうじんじゃ）」にも行きましたが、この
場所全体から、とても良い気を感じました。

P21

**Nachi Falls, Kumano Nachi Taisha Shrine
Three-storied Pagoda, Seiganto-ji Temple
- Higashimuro District, Wakayama**
I had wanted to visit here for a long time because
of its famous three-storied pagoda coexisting with
waterfalls. I arrived late, so I couldn't stay for long,
but the picturesque view was the epitome of
Japanese beauty. I also visited Hiryu Shrine, an
annex of the Kumano Nachi Taisha Shrine, located
at the base of the waterfalls, and I felt very good
energy flowing throughout the entire area.

P22-23

茨城県ひたちなか市　国営ひたち海浜公園
ずっと訪れてみたかった「みはらしの丘」。一年の
うち限られた時期しか見ることができない絶景ス
ポットです。大変混んでいましたが、ネモフィラの
花々、菜の花畑と青空のコントラストが美しかった
です。

P22-23

**Hitachi Seaside Park
- Hitachinaka City, Ibaraki**
I have always wanted to visit the Miharashi Hill
at Hitachi Seaside Park. The magnificent vista can
only be seen during a specific time of the year. It
was very crowded, but the nemophila flowers seen
against the field of rapeseed blossoms and the blue
sky created a fascinating contrast.

P24, 25

山梨県南都留郡　富士山
２枚の写真は 2017 年頃、初めて富士山を撮影
に行ったときの写真です。ビギナーズラックで富士
山の上に傘雲が現れ、初めての撮影にしてはす
ごくいい写真が撮れたので、強く記憶に残ってい
ます。味を占めて、その後再び撮影に行きました
が、雲に隠れて何も見えないことが続きました。

P24, 25

Mount Fuji - Minamitsuru District, Yamanashi
I took the two images around 2017 when I first set
out to Mount Fuji to document it. I was graced by
beginner's luck. An umbrella cloud appeared over
Mount Fuji, and I succeeded in capturing some
phenomenal images on my first shoot. I have a
very vivid memory of this experience. Getting a
taste for it, I went back to take more photos. But
on several occasions, I couldn't get a visual of the
mountain because it was obscured by the clouds.

P26-27

京都府京都市　竹林の小径
美しい竹林が道の両脇に続く、京都を代表する
観光名所です。日中に人がいない幻想的な写真
を撮ることは不可能なため、撮影当日は朝早く起
きて始発で撮影に向かいました。到着すると、幸
運にも着物姿で赤い和傘を持った方が歩いてお
り、見事なまでに完璧な写真を撮影することがで
きました。

P26-27

Bamboo Grove Path - Kyoto City, Kyoto
The splendid bamboo grove stretching along both
sides of the path is one of the most prominent
tourist destinations in Kyoto. It is virtually
impossible to capture the magical charm of the
site during the day without any other human
encounter. So, I set out early in the morning to
catch the first train there. As luck would have it,
there was a person in a kimono walking with a red,
traditional umbrella, and I was able to shoot this
wonderfully perfect image.

P28

愛媛県伊予市　下灘駅
木造の駆体とベンチ、そして瀬戸内海の眺望。
映画やドラマの聖地であり、日本一有名ともいえる
「海が見える駅」です。早朝に到着しましたが、
すでに電車を撮影する方がおり、始発の時間を
教えてもらいました。

P28

Shimonada Station - Iyo City, Ehime
The wooden structure, benches, and a commanding
view of the Seto Inland Sea. It is a favorite location
for movies and TV dramas, and perhaps Japan's
most celebrated station with a view of the ocean.
I arrived early in the morning, but there was a
person already taking pictures of the train who
informed me of the time of the first train.

P29

福岡県北九州市　河内藤園
アメリカのニュース専門放送局・CNN が発表した
「日本の最も美しい場所31選」に選出された「河
内藤園」。しっかりと手入れの行き届いた藤棚と、
藤の花のトンネルが息を呑むほど美しかったです。
日本の伝統と職人さんたちの技術の素晴らしさを
感じました。

P29

Kawachi Wisteria Garden
- Kitakyushu City, Fukuoka
The Kawachi Wisteria Garden has been selected
as one of the 31 Most Beautiful Places in Japan by
the American news channel CNN. The manicured
wisteria trellises and flower tunnels were simply
breathtaking. I was deeply amazed by the traditional
craftsmanship and skills of the artisans.

P30

山梨県南都留郡　西湖いやしの里根場
美しい日本の原風景を前にして、迫力のある富士
山を楽しめる「西湖いやしの里根場」。どことなく
ゆったりとした時間が流れており、茅葺き屋根の
家々と桜、富士山の共演を心ゆくまで楽しむこと
ができます。

P30

**Saiko Iyashi no Sato Nenba
- Minamitsuru District, Yamanashi**
Immerse yourself in the pristine beauty of the
Japanese landscape, where the almighty Mount Fuji
presents itself in the backdrop of the village of
healing. There is something leisurely about the way
time passes in the area, and visitors can enjoy the
harmonious coexistence of thatched-roof houses,
cherry blossoms, and Mount Fuji to their heart's
content.

P31

静岡県島田市　牛代のみずめ桜
山間の茶畑にそびえる、樹齢 300 年の立派な一
本桜。到着時は太陽が出ておらず、いい写真が
撮れるか疑心暗鬼でしたが、後ろの山から朝日が
昇ると、太陽の光がスポットライトのように桜の木
を照らし出し、それまでとは一変して叙情的な光
景が目の前に広がりました。1 粒の種から 300
年の時を経て、こうした立派な桜の木に育った歴
史にロマンを感じます。

P31

**Mizume-zakura of Ushinshiro
- Shimada City, Shizuoka**
A magnificent 300-year-old cherry tree towers over
a tea plantation in the mountains. When I arrived, the
sun wasn't out yet, and I was uncertain if I would
be able to get a good photo. However, when the sun
rose from the mountains behind the tree, its rays
shone on the blossoms like a spotlight, transforming
the landscape before my eyes into a dramatic
spectacle. There is something romantic about the
history of how a single seed matured into such a
majestic cherry tree over the course of 300 years.

P32

京都府京都市　愛宕念仏寺の阿羅漢
一つひとつ表情が異なる「阿羅漢」たちが、苔む
した 1200 体の石像となって並びます。お気に入
りの石像を見つけてはシャッターを切りました。中
には、苔が髪の毛のようになった像、子連れの
像やカメラを持った像もありました。

P32

**Arhat Statues of Otagi Nenbutsuji Temple
- Kyoto City, Kyoto**
There are 1200 moss-covered stone statues of arhats,
each with a different expression, standing in rows.
I found my favorite stone figure and snapped the
shutter. Among them, I also spotted an arhat with a
head of mossy hair, others with children, and one of a
photographer holding a camera.

P33

京都府京都市　伏見桃山陵
伏見区の桃山丘陵にある明治天皇のお墓です。
230 段の急な石の大階段が存在感を放つ、静か
で神秘的な場所で他の京都の観光地とは一線を
画します。神聖な場所で静かに京都を楽しむのも
おすすめです。

P33

**Fushimi Momoyama no Misasagi
- Kyoto City, Kyoto**
The imperial tomb of Emperor Meiji is located on
Momoyama Hill in Fushimi Ward. Steep and imposing,
the 230-step stone staircase evokes a sense of
grandeur. This tranquil and mystical location sets
itself apart from other tourist attractions in Kyoto.
I recommend visiting this sacred site to appreciate
Kyoto in peace and quiet.

P34-35
京都府京都市　竹林の小径
観光客で溢れかえったこの場所も、竹藪に目をやると、そこには静謐な世界が広がっています。

P34-35
Bamboo Grove Path - Kyoto City, Kyoto
Even in this touristy area, where it is crowded with visitors, the bamboo thicket presents a world of peace and tranquility.

P37
東京都小笠原村　小笠原諸島沈没船
父島を訪れた際に、中心地から島一周をスクーターで移動しました。そのとき最初に目に飛び込んできたのがこの沈没船でした。「濱江丸」という貨物船で、第二次大戦中に沈没させられた歴史があります。泳いで中をのぞいたところ、今では魚たちの住処になっていました。

P37
**Sunken ship in Ogasawara
- Ogasawara Village, Tokyo**
When I visited Chichijima Island, I rode a scooter from its central area and toured around the island. The first thing that caught my eye was this shipwreck. The Hinko-maru was a cargo ship that was sunk during World War II. I swam to take a peek inside to discover that it had now become a home for the fish.

P38-39
北海道斜里郡　知床五湖
斜里町にある「知床五湖」は原生林に囲まれ、5つの湖それぞれが幻想的です。遊歩道が整備されてとても歩きやすく、高架木道では立派な角が生えた若い雄鹿に出会えました。広大な大自然を、存分に体感することができます。

P38-39
**Shiretoko Goko Lakes
- Shari District, Hokkaido**
Located within the town of Shari in Hokkaido, the Shiretoko Goko Lakes (Shiretoko Five Lakes) are nestled within primeval forests, and each of the five lakes is enchanting in its own way. The ground pathways are well-maintained and very easy to walk along. I encountered a young stag with magnificent antlers when trekking along the elevated wooden pathway. Visitors can fully immerse themselves in the vast wilderness.

P40
沖縄県八重山郡　竹富島
竹富島は沖縄の原風景に出合える離島で、石垣島からフェリーで10分の距離にあります。写真は「コンドイ浜」と呼ばれる島の南西部にあるビーチで、きれいな青い海と白い砂浜、そして入道雲が夏を演出し、目が醒める美しさでした。

P40
**Taketomi Island
- Yaeyama District, Okinawa**
Taketomi Island is a remote island, just a 10-minute ferry ride from Ishigaki Island, where you can discover the native landscapes of Okinawa. Pictured is Kondoi Beach, located in the southwestern section of the island. The pristine blue sea, the white beach, and the cumulus clouds created the perfect summer scenery that was strikingly beautiful.

P41
東京都八丈町　名古の展望台
八丈島の絶景ポイントをいくつか訪れましたが、中でも「名古の展望台」は左側にきれいな青い海、右側には海外にいるような迫力のある緑豊かな岸が続いています。コントラストが美しく、筆舌に尽くしがたい大自然の姿でした。

P41
Nago Observatory - Hachijo Town, Tokyo
I visited several scenic spots on Hachijojima Island, and Nago Observatory commands a beautiful blue ocean to the left and a lush green shore to the right. The dynamic features of the shoreline made me feel as if I were overseas. The contrast was stunning, and the sight of such bountiful nature was beyond description.

P42
山口県下関市　角島大橋
白い砂浜とコバルトブルーの海が広がる絶景に、真っ直ぐに伸びる角島大橋。文字通り素晴らしい絶景でした。次回訪れるときは、自転車で橋を往復してみたいです。

P42
**Tsunoshima Bridge
- Shimonoseki City, Yamaguchi**
The Tsunoshima Bridge stretches straight into the magnificent panorama of white sandy beaches and the cobalt-blue sea. The view was splendid in every sense of the word. Next time I visit, I'd like to take a round-trip bike ride over the bridge.

P43
沖縄県石垣市　石垣島
石垣島は、大自然に囲まれた日本最南端のとても美しい島です。緑豊かな島を日が昇る前から車で走っていると、明けてゆく空に鳥たちが飛び交い、島自体が目を覚ましているような感じにとらわれます。青い海と木々の緑、そして白い雲と青い空のコントラストが美しく、朝、日没の時間はとくに素晴らしい景色を見ることができました。

P43
Ishigaki Island - Ishigaki City, Okinawa
Ishigaki Island is a very beautiful island surrounded by abundant nature located at the southernmost part of Japan. I drove through the lush greenery before the sun came out, and as the sky brightened, I would see birds flying around, and it felt as if the island itself was waking up from a slumber. The blue sea and the verdant trees, the white clouds and the blue sky—these contrasts were stunning. The views I encountered in the morning and at sunset were particularly breathtaking.

P44-45
長野県茅野市　御射鹿池（みしゃかいけ）
標高1500mの山の中にあって、鏡のように水面に木々が逆さに映り込み、幻想的な風景を創り出しています。到着した際、車から鹿の姿が見えたので急いで駐車場から池まで走り、鹿の家族が見えなくなるまでの数分間、無事に撮影することができました。あと少し到着が遅れていたら、鹿の家族と出会えなかったと思うと、とてもラッキーでした。

P44-45
Mishaka Pond - Chino City, Nagano
Nestled in the mountains at an elevation of 1,500 meters, the scenic Mishaka Pond offers a magical landscape created by the mirror-like surface of the water capturing upside-down reflections of the trees. When I arrived, I spotted a deer from the car, so I hurried and ran to the pond from the parking lot. I succeeded in photographing the family of deer for a few minutes until they were out of sight. If I had arrived a few moments later, I would have missed been able to encounter the deer, so I was extremely lucky.

P46-47
鹿児島県鹿児島市　桜島
日頃、運がいいことが多く、当然のように桜島から煙が出ている写真を撮れると思っていましたがそのようなことはなく……。親切にも、屋久島に行くフェリーのウェイターさんが、桜島が噴火していることをメール連絡してくださいました。そのおかげで想像していた写真を撮影できました。

P46-47
Sakurajima - Kagoshima City, Kagoshima
I'm usually lucky, so I was hoping to catch some pictures of volcanic smoke coming out of Mount Sakurajima, but with no such luck... A waiter working on the ferry to Yakushima was kind enough to email me to let me know that there was activity on Sakurajima. Thanks to that, I was able to take the photographs I had envisioned.

P48-49
京都府京都市　瑠璃光院
黒塗りの机の天板に、カエデが映り込む光景で知られる「瑠璃光院」。手入れの行き届いた日本庭園の造形美に魅せられます。通常は非公開ですが、春と秋に公開されます。春の新緑も秋の紅葉も、どちらもとても美しく、日本の伝統が色濃く残る素晴らしいところです。

P48-49
Rurikoin Temple - Kyoto City, Kyoto
Rurikoin Temple is known for the view of maple trees reflected off the black lacquered table tops. The aesthetic beauty of the well-kept Japanese garden is mesmerizing. Normally closed to the public, the garden opens for public viewing in spring and fall. The fresh greenery in spring and the colorful leaves in autumn are both exceptionally picturesque. It is a wonderful location where Japanese traditions are richly preserved.

P50
宮崎県西臼杵郡　高千穂峡
国の天然記念物に指定されている「高千穂峡」。高千穂峡の代名詞ともいえ、「日本の滝百選」に選ばれている「真名井の滝」の下を、ボートが通る瞬間に撮影しました。この場所も夏と秋の季節が秀麗です。

P50
Takachiho Gorge - Nishiusuki District, Miyazaki
Takachiho Gorge is designated as a National Natural Monument. This photo was taken at the moment a boat passed under the Minainotaki Waterfall, which is synonymous with Takachiho Gorge and also selected as one of the Best 100 Waterfalls in Japan. The views are also spectacular in summer and autumn.

P51
北海道斜里郡　知床連山
霧がかかり、中国の水墨画のようなこの写真は、知床の観光船から撮影した知床の山々。「シレトコ」とは、アイヌ語で「地の涯（ちのはて）」という意味です。ユネスコ世界自然遺産に選ばれた深い森と山々は、日本に残された原始郷のひとつです。

P51
**Shiretoko Mountain Range
- Shari Town, Hokkaido**
This misty landscape reminded me of a Chinese ink painting. I took this image of the surrounding

mountains from a sightseeing boat in Shiretoko. Shiretoko means "the ends of the earth" in the native Ainu language. Selected as a UNESCO World Natural Heritage Site, the deep forests and mountains are one of Japan's remaining primitive landscapes.

P52-53
新潟県十日町市　清津峡渓谷トンネル
日本三大渓谷の「清津峡」。Instagram などで有名なスポットのため、多くの観光客がいました。夏の暑い時期に行きましたがトンネル内は涼しく、汗が引いたのを覚えています。

P52-53
**Kiyotsu Gorge Tunnel
- Tokamachi City, Niigata**
Kiyotsu Gorge is one of the three great gorges of Japan. The location has gone viral on Instagram and other social media, so there were a lot of visitors. I went during the hot summer season, but it was cool inside the tunnel, and I could feel my sweat drying off.

P54-55
長崎県長崎市　軍艦島
廃墟好きの間では、人気観光スポットになっています。「端島」という、長崎の沖合にあり廃墟となった炭鉱施設です。夕日に照らされ、ゆったりとした時間が流れているように見えましたが、一度海が荒れると容赦ない波風に晒されると聞き、当時の暮らしに想いを馳せました。

P54-55
Gunkanjima - Nagasaki City, Nagasaki
Gunkanjima is a famous sightseeing destination among urban explorers. It is an abandoned coal-mining facility located on Hashima Island off the coast of Nagasaki Prefecture. Illuminated by the setting sun, the ruins appeared as though time moved slowly and peacefully, but I was told that you would be exposed to unforgiving winds and waves once the sea turned violent. My thoughts turned to the lives of the people in those days.

P56-57
愛媛県今治市　来島海峡
日本三大急潮流のひとつ「来島海峡」と、世界初の三連吊橋「来島海峡大橋」の後ろに夕日が沈む景色です。写真では伝わりませんが、この写真を撮影した日はものすごい強風で髪の毛や着衣が強風でぐちゃぐちゃになり、無事に撮影を終えられてホッとしたのを覚えています。

P56-57
Kurushima Strait - Imabari City, Ehime
Pictured in the landscape is the sun setting behind the Kurushima Strait, one of Japan's three greatest rapids, and the Kurushima Kaikyo Bridge, the world's first three-span suspension bridge. What the photograph doesn't convey is that, on the day I shot this image, the winds were so extremely strong that my hair and clothes became a complete mess. I remember being relieved to finish the shoot.

P58-59
鹿児島県屋久島町　屋久島
屋久島は、年間降水量が日本一といわれますが、行った 2 日目に雨が降り、想像通りの幻想的な屋久島を撮影することができました。国内最大級の巨木である縄文杉や、中に入って見上げるとハートの形が見える屋久杉の切り株、ウィルソン株、トロッコ鉄道の線路など、霧の中で見る屋久島の景色は非現実的で SF 映画のシーンに紛れ込んだようでした。

P58-59
Yakushima - Yakushima Town, Kagoshima
Yakushima is said to have the highest annual rainfall in Japan. It rained on the second day I was there, so I was lucky to capture the ethereal images I had envisioned. The giant Jomon Sugi (Cryptomeria tree) is one of the largest conifers in Japan. The Wilson's Stump reveals a heart-shaped opening when you look up from the inside. These features of Yakushima combined with the trolley tracks created a surreal landscape under the foggy mist, and it was like being in a science fiction movie.

P60
北海道斜里郡　知床連山

P60
**Shiretoko Mountain Range
- Shari Town, Hokkaido**

P61, 62, 63
鹿児島県屋久島町　屋久島
屋久島の旅で何か大きな力（写真の神様のような力）が働いて、良い写真を撮らせてもらっているような気持ちになりました。普段はドイツに住み、日本で撮影する日数は限られることから、常に下見なしのぶっつけ本番。しかし高確率で天候に恵まれ、撮影をサポートしてくれる方々に出会い、思い描いた通りに撮れたことが多かったからです。

P61, 62, 63
Yakushima - Yakushima Town, Kagoshima
On this trip to Yakushima Island, I experienced a feeling as if some great power (like the god of photography) was working to grant me good photo opportunities. I mostly live in Germany, so the days I can be in Japan to shoot are numbered, and I always take my photographs spontaneously without prior scouting. However, I was blessed with good weather more often than not, and I met people who provided me with information and support for my shoot. Thanks to that, I was often able to capture the exact images I had in mind.

P64
東京都大島町　三原山・中央火口
島全体が活火山の伊豆大島において、そのシンボルでもある三原山。日本全国回った中で一番地球外感が強い場所で、目の前に広がる月や火星を思わせる景色に圧倒されました。

P64
**Central Cone, Mount Mihara
- Oshima Town, Tokyo**
Mount Mihara is the symbol of Izu Oshima where the entire island is an active volcano. It had the most intense extraterrestrial feel of any place I had visited in Japan, and I was awestruck by the landscape that stretched before me, which made me think of the moon and Mars.

P64
新潟県十日町市　星峠の棚田
新潟の棚田のなかでも、特に有名な「星峠の棚田」。緑が一面に広がる夏に訪れ、撮影をしました。眼前に広がる無数の水田はまさに絶景です。手の行き届いた水田が作り出す日本の原風景を、絶対に後世に残してほしいです。

P64
**Hoshitoge Rice Terraces
- Tokamachi Town, Niigata**
Among the terraced rice paddies in Niigata, the Hoshitoge Rice Terraces are particularly well-known. I visited and photographed the scenery in the summer when the paddies were covered in green. The countless rice paddies stretching out

in front of my eyes were truly a marvelous sight. Witnessing the nostalgic Japanese landscape of well-tended rice paddies, I strongly wished for this spectacular view to be preserved for future generations.

P65
北海道斜里郡　知床連山

P65
**Shiretoko Mountain Range
- Shari Town, Hokkaido**

P66-67
三重県志摩市　横山展望台
伊勢志摩地域の特徴ともいえる、日本有数のリアス海岸美を誇る英虞湾（あごわん）。それを一望できる「横山展望台」からの風景です。雨が降っていたこともあり、どこかアマゾンを彷彿とさせる雰囲気でした。（行ったことはありませんが）

P66-67
**Yokoyama Observatory Deck
- Shima City, Mie**
Ago Bay boasts one of the most beautiful ria shorelines in the nation, and the coastal formations are a distinctive feature of the Ise-Shima region. This is the vista from the Yokoyama Observatory Deck overlooking the bay. The rainy weather made the atmosphere somewhat reminiscent of the Amazon (though I have never been there).

P68
沖縄県石垣市　石垣島

P68
Ishigaki Island - Ishigaki City, Okinawa

P69
佐賀県東松浦郡　浜野浦の棚田
玄海町にある、海に面した棚田「浜野浦の棚田」。一年の限られた時期にのみ田植えの水を張った棚田が、夕焼けを映し出して光り輝き、至極の美景に我を忘れます。

P69
**Hamanoura Rice Terraces
- Matsuura District, Saga**
Situated in the town of Genkai-cho, Hamanoura Rice Terraces is the location of a series of *tanada* (terraced rice fields) overlooking the ocean. It is only for a limited period of the year when the rice paddies are filled with water that the sunset is reflected on their mirrored surfaces to illuminate the area in a gleaming glow. The view was absolutely spectacular.

P70-71
沖縄県石垣市　平久保遠見台
石垣島の最北端の岬にあり、日本ロマンチスト協会と日本財団が実施する「恋する灯台プロジェクト」の認定灯台です。珊瑚礁の美しい海に沈む夕日はとてもきれいで、ロマンチック。まさにロマンスの聖地でした。

P70-71
**Hirakubo Lighthouse
- Ishigaki City, Okinawa**
Located at the northernmost cape of Ishigaki Island, the tower is listed as one of the certified lighthouses of the "Lovers Lighthouse Project" organized by the Nippon Romantist Association and the Nippon Foundation. The view of the sun

setting over the stunning coral reefs is quite lovely and romantic. It was indeed a sacred place for lovers.

P72

神奈川県足柄下郡　箱根神社・平和の鳥居
人気スポットでたくさんの人々でにぎわっていました。スワンボートに乗って湖側からも撮影しましたが、「平和」と書かれた額が湖に面して掲げられていました。「平和の鳥居」とも呼ばれており、杉の木に囲まれたとても気の良い場所です。

P72

Torii Gate in the Water of Hakone Shrine - Ashigarashimo District, Kanagawa
The popular spot on Lake Ashinoko was bustling with many tourists. I also took photos from the lake on a swan boat and noticed a plaque on the torii gate facing the lake with the word " 平和 (*Heiwa*, or Peace)" written on it. Surrounded by cedar trees, the area had a very pleasant atmosphere.

P73

三重県伊勢市　伊勢神宮
すべての神社の上に立つ神社であり、「日本国民の総氏神」とされている「伊勢神宮」。川の音と風を感じながら宇治橋を渡って内宮に入ると、静寂な空気が流れ、神聖な世界に入ったことを感じられます。日本最大級のパワースポットともいわれ、時間をかけてゆっくり参拝し、御祈祷をさせていただきました。毎年訪れたい場所のひとつです。

P73

Ise Grand Shrine - Ise City, Mie
The Ise Grand Shrine stands above all shrines and is considered the "general guardian deity of the Japanese people." You'll need to walk across the Uji Bridge to enter the Inner Shrine (Naiku), enjoying the breeze and the sounds of the river as you do so. Once inside, the air is tranquil and you will sense that you have entered a sacred world. The shrine is said to be one of the largest locations that possesses spiritual power in Japan, and I took my time to pay my respects and receive prayers. It is one of the places I hope to visit every year.

P74-75

広島県廿日市市　厳島神社
島自体が「神」として信仰されていたという厳島。その島を傷つけないようにと、海上に建てられた「厳島神社」。世界遺産に登録されたその姿はとても神秘的で、神社と鳥居の朱赤と海の色のコントラストがとても美しく、時間を忘れてしまいます。

P74-75

Itsukushima Shrine - Hatsukaichi City, Hiroshima
The island of Itsukushima itself had been worshipped as a deity, and Itsukushima Shrine was built on the sea to protect the sacred island from harm. Registered as a World Heritage site, the architecture exudes an ethereal ambiance. The vermillion-red shrine and torii gate set against the color of the sea is so enchanting that you can easily lose track of time.

P76

島根県出雲市　出雲大社
縁結びの神様として名高く、日本神話のふるさと出雲にある「出雲大社」。個人的にずっと行ってみたい場所でしたが、東京から距離があるので訪れる機会がありませんでした。撮影当日は悪天候ながら、山々に霧がかかり、雨に濡れた神社と石畳が厳かで幻想的かつ神秘的な情景でした。

P76

Izumo Taisha Grand Shrine - Izumo City, Shimane
Izumo Taisha is located in Izumo, the home of Japanese mythology. The shrine is famous for its deity of romance and marriage. I had always been personally interested in visiting this place but had never had a chance to do so because of its distance from Tokyo. Despite the bad weather on the day of the shoot, the fog-covered mountains and the rain-soaked shrine and cobblestone pavement made for a majestic scenery that was both mystical and heavenly.

P77

岩手県西磐井郡　中尊寺・弁慶堂
1000 年以上の歴史をもち、世界遺産に登録されている「中尊寺」。大きな杉の木の参道、そして月見坂を登って入口を入ると、荘厳な雰囲気に包まれます。金色堂など、数多くの国宝や重要文化財を拝観することができ、丹精な日本美術工芸品を堪能できます。

P77

Benkeido Hall, Chusonji Temple - Nishiiwai District, Iwate
Chusonji Temple is a registered World Heritage Site boasting a history of over 1,000 years. The approach to the temple is lined with large cryptomeria trees, and as you climb Tsukimizaka (moon-viewing slope) and enter the grounds, you will be embraced by the majestic grandeur of the compounds. Visitors can view numerous national treasures and important cultural properties, such as Konjikido Hall, and admire the elaborate arts and craftsmanship of Japan.

P78

福井県吉田郡　永平寺
道元禅師によって開かれた坐禅修行の道場で、約 160 名の僧が修行生活を送る「永平寺」。参道に入ると苔むした岩群と緑に囲まれ、心が落ち着きます。歩み進むと樹齢 500 年という、岩をも飲み込む大杉の先に唐門が見えてきます。突然天気雨が降り出したのですが、とても雰囲気のある写真が撮影でき、神秘的な体験をしました。

P78

Eiheiji Temple - Yoshida District, Fukui
Eiheiji Temple is a monastery for *zazen* training founded by Zen master Dogen, where about 160 monks lead a life of ascetic practice. The approach to the temple is surrounded by moss-covered rocks and greenery, which was calming and relaxing. As I continued, I saw the Karamon Gate ahead of 500-year-old giant cedars that can engulf even rocks. Then suddenly, it began to rain, but I was able to take some very atmospheric pictures, and it was a magical experience.

P79

山形県鶴岡市　羽黒山・五重塔
羽黒山は東北仏教文化の中心であり、国宝の五重塔は 600 年前に再建されたもので、東北地方における最古の塔といわれています。五重塔の近くには樹齢 1000 年の巨杉があり、杉並木の中に塔があり、過去にタイムスリップしたかのような錯覚に陥る、とても厳かな場所です。

P79

Five-storied Pagoda of Mount Haguro - Tsuruoka City, Yamagata
Hagurosan (Mount Haguro) is the center of the Buddhist faith in the Tohoku region. Its five-storied pagoda, a National Treasure, was reconstructed some 600 years ago and is said to be the oldest pagoda in the Tohoku region. Near this five-storied pagoda is a 1,000-year-old giant cedar tree. The pagoda stands amidst a cedar forest, creating the illusion that you have stepped back in time. The location possesses an air of majestic solemnity.

P80

千葉県安房郡
日本寺・薬師瑠璃光如来大仏
東京から車で1時間ほどの場所に日本最大の磨崖仏（まがいぶつ）があります。石切場として栄えた鋸山には、大仏の他にも山の岩肌に彫られた「百尺観音」、断崖絶壁の「地獄覗き」などもあって楽しめます。登山道や山頂から望む景観が素晴らしく、富士山も堪能できます。

P80

Yakushi Ruriko Nyorai Daibutsu of Nihonji Temple - Awa District, Chiba
Japan's largest stone cliff statue of Buddha is only an hour's drive from Tokyo! Nokogiriyama (Mount Nokogiri) prospered as a stone quarry and features other points of interest besides the Giant Buddha, such as the Hyakushaku Kannon image carved into the rock face of the mountain as well as the Jigoku-nozoki (Peep into Hell) on the precipitous overhang. The sights from the mountain trails and summit are splendid, and you can also enjoy a view of Mount Fuji.

P81, 82-83

福岡県糟屋郡　南蔵院・寝大仏
一番の見どころは、世界一大きいとされるブロンズ製の「釈迦涅槃像」です。その大きさは全長41 メートル、高さ 11 メートル、重さ約 300 トン。頭の上のイボイボの「螺髪（らほつ）」も近くで見ることができ、686 個もあるそうです。大仏の他にも、「出世大黒天」や「不動明王像」など、見どころがたくさんあります。

P81, 82-83

The Reclining Buddha of Nanzoin Temple - Kasuya District, Fukuoka
Nanzoin Temple boasts the world's largest statue of the Reclining Buddha, which is 41 meters long, 11 meters high, and weighs approximately 300 tons. The ringlets on the top of the Buddha's head are called *rahotsu*, and visitors can get a clear view of these features up close. It is said that there are a total of 686 spirals. In addition to the Great Buddha, there are also many other attractions, such as the statues of Shusse Daikokuten (the god of wealth) and Fudo Myoo (the immovable protector and god of fire).

P84-85

北海道札幌市　真駒内滝野霊園・頭大仏
真駒内滝野霊園にある「頭大仏」、建築家の安藤忠雄さんが設計した大仏殿に鎮座しており、ドーム状の建物のてっぺんに空いた穴から、大仏の頭がつき出して見えます。また、大仏までへの道もトンネルのようになっており、非日常的な空間を体感できます。

P84-85

Atama Daibutsu - Sapporo City, Hokkaido
The Atama Daibutsu (Great Buddha Head) in Makomanai Takino Cemetery is located in the Daibutsuden Hall, designed by architect Tadao Ando. The head of the Great Buddha can be seen protruding through a hole in the center of the domed roof. The path to the Daibutsuden Hall is designed like a tunnel to create a surrealistic environment for visitors to experience.

P86-87

愛知県豊川市　豊川閣妙厳寺

日本三大稲荷のひとつとされる、別名「豊川稲荷」。
「霊狐塚」は、1000体以上の狐の石像が辺り一
面を埋め尽くし、このような光景はここでしか見る
ことができません。この日は雨が降っており、濡れ
た狐たちが立ち並ぶ風景は、少し怖い感じもしま
したが幻想的でした。

P86-87
**Toyokawa Kaku Myogonji Temple
- Toyokawa City, Aichi**
Toyokawa Inari is regarded as one of the three
great Inari (fox god) shrines in Japan. The Reiko-
zuka (Fox Spirit Mound) is covered with more than
1,000 stone statues of foxes, a spectacle that can
only be seen here. It was raining that day, and the
sight of the soaked foxes lined up was a bit eerie
but magical nonetheless.

P88
山口県美祢市　秋芳洞の入り口
秋吉台国定公園の地下 100m にあり、日本最大
規模といわれる大鍾乳洞です。夏に行きましたが、
中はとても涼しく快適でした。長い歳月をかけて
作られた鍾乳洞道は巨大で想像した以上に長く、
とても驚きます。

P88
**Akiyoshido Cave Entrance
– Mine City, Yamaguchi**
Located 100 meters underground in Akiyoshidai
Quasi-National Park, this limestone cave is said to be
one of the largest of its kind in Japan. I visited in
summer, and it was very cool and comfortable inside.
The underground cavities, which took countless years
to develop, was surprisingly vast and much longer
than I had imagined.

P89
熊本県阿蘇郡　上色見熊野座神社
苔むした神殿が風情を醸し出す「上色見熊野座
神社」。参道沿いには 97 基の石灯籠が並び、美
しい神社と深い自然のコントラストを楽しむことが
できます。鳥居は「神聖な世界への入り口」とい
われますが、この場所の幻想的な雰囲気は本当
にそう思わせるのです。

P89
**Kamishikimi Kumanoimasu Shrine
- Aso District, Kumamoto**
Kamishikimi Kumanoimasu Shrine is home to a
temple whose mossy greenery gives it a quaint
appeal. There are 97 stone lanterns lining the
approach to the shrine, providing a stunning contrast
between the beautiful shrine and the rich natural
surroundings. The torii gate is said to be the
entrance to the sacred world, and the fantastical
atmosphere of this site truly makes you believe so.

P90
三重県伊勢市　二見興玉神社・夫婦岩
大注連縄（おおしめなわ）で太く堅く結ばれた、
男岩と女岩。夫婦円満、カップルの恋愛の象徴で
あり、縁結び信仰としても有名な夫婦岩です。一
年に数回、夫婦岩の間から昇る朝日と満月を見る
ことができるそうなので、機会があれば再訪した
いです。

P90
**Wedded Rocks,
Futami Okitama Shrine - Ise City, Mie**
Two boulders, Otoko-iwa (Male Rock) and the
Onna-iwa (Female Rock), are joined firmly together
by a sacred heavy rope called *oshimenawa*. The
pair of rocks symbolize marital bliss and romantic
relationships and are famous objects of faith for
those seeking happy marriages. Several times a

year, the sunrise and full moon can be seen rising
from between the rocks, so I'd like to revisit when
I have the chance.

P91
滋賀県高島市　白鬚神社・大鳥居
日本一の大きさを誇る琵琶湖のほとりにある「白
鬚神社」。大鳥居はその神社前に、琵琶湖畔に
浮かぶようにして建てられています。早朝の白々と
した雰囲気と、ひっそりと静寂な湖に朱塗りの大
鳥居が浮かぶ景色は神秘的で佳麗でした。

P91
**Otorii, Shirahige Shrine,
- Takashima City, Shiga**
Shirahige Shrine can be found on the shore of Lake
Biwa, the largest lake in Japan. In front of it, the
Otorii (Grand Gate) stands erect like a floating
gateway on the banks of the lake. The serenity of
the hazy morning and the tranquil appearance of
the vermilion-lacquered Otorii gate floating on the
lake were both mystical and magnificent.

P92
東京都　新宿高層ビル群と富士山
到着時は曇りで、年配の方がいたので話しかける
とビル建設時から展望台で撮影を続け、展望台
のパンフレットに写真が使用されている写真家の
方でした。日が沈むのを待つと雲が流れて富士山
が姿を現し、太陽が空を赤く焼き、見たこともな
い夕焼けを背景に撮影ができたのです。「こんな
夕日見たことない、あなたツイてるね」と嬉しいお
言葉を頂戴しました。

P92
Shinjuku Skyscrapers and Mount Fuji, Tokyo
When I arrived, Mount Fuji was hidden behind the
clouds. I spoke to an elderly photographer there
who had been taking pictures from the building
since it was constructed, and whose pictures are
used in the observatory pamphlet. As I waited for
the sun to set, the clouds drifted to reveal the
mountain, and the sunset set the sky ablaze. I
captured an image of the most beautiful sunset I
had ever seen. I received a pleasant comment from
the elderly photographer, "I've never seen a sunset
like this. You must be very lucky."

P93
大分県杵築市　八幡奈多宮・海中鳥居
奈多海岸のほぼ中央に位置し、海岸の沖合にあ
る岩礁の上に鳥居が建てられています。1年のう
ち、数回だけ鳥居の後ろに朝日が昇ります。撮影
前日は天気が悪かったのですが、当日は運良く天
気に恵まれて、思い描いた通りの美しい写真が撮
れました。とても素晴らしい印象的な朝でした。

P93
**Torii Gate Above the Sea,
Hachiman Nada Shrine - Kitsuki City, Oita**
Roughly located at the center of Nada Beach,
the torii gate is built on a reef off the coast. The
sun rises behind the gate only on a few occasions
during the year. The weather was unfavorable the
day before the shoot, but I was fortunate to have
good weather on the day of, and was able to take
the stunning photos I had in mind. It was a glorious
and memorable morning.

P94
岐阜県岐阜市　岐阜城
金華山の山頂に位置し、巨大な満月と城のコラボ
が撮影できるのは、日本でここだけかもしれませ
ん。撮影当日は、140 年に一度のスーパームーン

皆既月食。月が地球にもっとも接近し、さらに地
球の影に月が隠れるということで、望遠レンズを
購入して臨みました。目星をつけた撮影ポイント
が正解で、赤銅色に輝く月と岐阜城を撮影できた
のです。

P94
Gifu Castle - Gifu City, Gifu
Built on top of Mount Kinka, Gifu Castle may be
the only place in Japan that can be photographed
together with a colossal full moon. This was on the
day of the total supermoon lunar eclipse, which
occurs only once every 140 years. Since the moon
would be closest to Earth and hidden in Earth's
shadow, I purchased a telephoto lens required to
capture this phenomenon. The location I had set
my sights on turned out to be perfect, and I was
able to photograph the moon and Gifu Castle
ablaze in the copper-reddish glow of the eclipse.

P95
群馬県館林市　館林手筒花火大会
三河地方に伝わるもので、手に持った花火から
約 10m もの火柱が吹き上がる様子は迫力満点で
した。撮影当日、到着すると最前列はすべて席が
埋まっていました。前の方に最前列で撮影をさせ
てもらえないかと伝えると、奇遇にもその方は手
筒花火師の後輩で花火師の方をご紹介くださいま
した。臨場感のある写真が撮れたのは、最前列
で撮影させてもらえたおかげです。

P95
**Tatebayashi Arm-Held Fireworks Festival
- Tatebayashi City, Gunma**
A traditional event of the Mikawa region, the hand-
held fireworks shoot up pillars of fire about 10
meters into the air. The power and energy of the
spectacle were extravagant. On the day of the
event, when I arrived at the venue, all the front-
row seats were occupied. I asked the person in
front of me if I could shoot from the front row.
As luck would have it, the gentleman happened to
be a junior member of the fireworks crew, and he
introduced me to the pyrotechnicians. This dynamic
capture of the performers in action was possible
thanks to the generous people who granted me
front-row access.

P97
長野県塩尻市　高ボッチ高原
塩尻市と岡谷市にまたがる、標高 1665 メートル
の「高ボッチ山」。富士山の前に雲海が広がる写
真を撮影したいと思って数回訪れてはいるのです
が、まだ撮影できていません。雲海を撮影できる
までチャレンジし続けることになりそうです。

P97
Takabocchi Plateau - Shiojiri City, Nagano
Mount Takabocchi straddles the cities of Shiojiri
and Okaya in Nagano Prefecture at an elevation of
1,665 meters. I have visited several times with the
hope of capturing the sea of clouds spreading out
in front of Mt. Fuji, but with no luck so far. It looks
like I will be continuing the challenge until I've
succeeded.

P98-99
京都府東山区　東福寺
京都屈指の紅葉の名所である東福寺。赤、オレ
ンジ、黄色に染まった 2000 本のカエデが境内
を埋め尽くし、本堂と開山堂を結ぶ渡り廊下から
見える「紅葉の雲海」は、まさに絶景です。

P98-99
**Tofukuji Temple
- Higashiyama Ward, Kyoto**

Tofukuji Temple is one of the most well-renowned locations in Kyoto for autumn foliage. The view from the corridor connecting the Main Hall and the Kaisando-Hall offers a truly spectacular sight where the clustered maple leaves appear like a sea of autumn-colored clouds.

P100

京都府京都市　清水寺・三重塔

三重塔としては日本最大級で、高さは約 31 メートル。現在の三重塔は、1632 年に再建された重要文化財です。清水寺周辺を歩くと、遠くからも目にすることができます。この写真を撮影した日はライトアップされ、まるで SF 映画のようで格好良かったです。

P100

Three-storied Pagoda, Kiyomizu -dera Temple - Kyoto City, Kyoto
Standing approximately 31 meters tall, it is one of the tallest three-storied pagodas in Japan. The current tower was reconstructed in 1632 and is a designated Important Cultural Property. The pagoda can be seen from a distance when walking in the vicinity of the temple. On the day I took this photo, the way the tower was lit up made it look like something out of a sci-fi movie, which I thought was cool.

P101

京都府京都市　錦鯉と紅葉

日本の「泳ぐ宝石」ともいわれる錦鯉と、紅葉の美しい共演。水面に浮かぶ、紅葉して色とりどりに染まった葉と、その下を泳ぐ美しい鯉たちの姿に、時を忘れてシャッターを何度も切りました。

P101

Nishikigoi and Autumn Leaves - Kyoto City, Kyoto
Nishikigoi (multicolored koi fish) are considered "swimming treasures" in Japan. I captured the beautiful harmony of these koi fish with the autumn leaves. The colorful array of leaves floating on the surface of the water and the graceful koi swimming beneath them made me forget the time, and I shot countless photos.

P102

京都府京都市　法観寺・八坂の塔

八坂神社と清水寺の中間に位置し、1440 年に再興された「法観寺五重塔」は、通称「八坂の塔」と呼ばれます。五重塔と石畳と周りの建物との共演は、過去にタイムスリップしたような美しい情景です。夕日の時間が美麗ですが観光客が多いことから、人が少ない夜の時間がおすすめです。

P102

Yasaka Pagoda, Hokanji Temple - Kyoto City, Kyoto
Located between Yasaka Shrine and Kiyomizu-dera Temple, the five-storied pagoda of Hokanji Temple was rebuilt in 1440 and is commonly called Yasaka-no-To (Tower of Yasaka). The five-storied pagoda, the cobblestone pavement, and the surrounding buildings create a wonderful scenery as if you were transported back in time. It is beautiful at sunset, but there are many tourists, so I recommend visiting at night when there are fewer people.

P103

京都府京都市　舞妓さん

舞踊などの芸で宴席に興を添える舞妓さん。京都の街を歩いていると、華があり美しい舞妓さんたちを目にする機会があります。日本の伝統文化を継承している姿に、とても嬉しくなり気持ちがたかぶります。

P103

Maiko - Kyoto City, Kyoto
Maiko provides entertainment at banquets with their dance and arts. When walking through the streets of Kyoto, you are likely to witness glamorous and gorgeous maiko. It makes me very happy to see them continuing the traditional culture of Japan.

P104-105

奈良県吉野郡　吉野山

日本一の桜の名所として知られる吉野山。紅く染まった山々が夕日に照らされてさらに赤みを増し、美しく素晴らしかったです。山頂までタクシーで行きましたが、運転手さんは「新緑の季節が一番きれいだ」と話していました。春、夏、冬にも再訪したいです。

P104-105

Mount Yoshino - Yoshino District, Nara
Mount Yoshino is famed for being the best destination to view cherry blossoms in Japan. The mountains, tinted in autumn, turned even redder when illuminated by the setting sun, and it was absolutely gorgeous. We took a taxi to the top of the mountain, and the driver told us that the view is most beautiful during the season of fresh green leaves. I'd like to visit again in spring, summer, and winter.

P106

長野県松本市　松本城

松本城は、全国に 5 つしかない国宝 5 城のうちのひとつです。現存天守としては珍しい五重六階の構造で、430 年以上の歴史があります。北アルプスの山々を背景にそびえる姿は威風堂々とし、黒と白のコントラストが際立ちます。

106

National Treasure Matsumoto Castle – Matsumoto City, Nagano
Matsumoto Castle is one of only five castles designated as National Treasures in Japan.Dating back more than 430 years, the five-tiered, six-floor structure is rare among castles still existing today. The majestic grandeur of the architecture towering against the backdrop of the Northern Alps is accentuated by the black and white contrast.

P107

香川県高松市　栗林公園

百年余りの歳月をかけて完成させた大名庭園で、国の特別名勝に指定されている庭園の中で最大の広さを誇ります。紅葉した紫雲山を背景に、綺麗に整備された庭園は、日本の伝統と美を凝縮させた絶景です。

P107

Ritsurin Garden - Takamatsu City, Kagawa
It took more than 100 years to complete the Ritsurin Garden, originally constructed for the *daimyo* (feudal lord). It is now the most extensive of the gardens designated as a Special Place of Scenic Beauty of Japan. The beautifully landscaped garden, set against the backdrop of the autumn leaves of Mount Shiun, is a remarkable display of Japanese tradition and beauty.

P108-109, 111

福井県勝山市　大師山清大寺・越前大仏

像高が 17 ｍあり、奈良の大仏様より 2 ｍあまりも大きく、建物内に鎮座している日本最大の座像の仏様。　大仏殿位には壁一面に何百もの座像が並んでいて圧巻です。大仏本殿は非現実的な空間なので、写真を撮る方にはおすすめの場所です。

P108-109, 111

Echizen Great Buddha, Daishizan Seidaiji Temple - Katsuyama City, Fukui
The Great Buddha is 17 meters tall, more than two meters taller than the Daibutsu statue in Nara, and is the largest Buddha in Japan seated inside a building. The Daibutsuden Hall is a sight to behold, with hundreds of seated statues lined up on the walls. The atmosphere inside the Main Hall is very surreal, making it the perfect location for photographers.

P110

島根県出雲市　出雲大社

P110

Izumo Taisha Grand Shrine - Izumo City, Shimane

P112-113

埼玉県日高市　巾着田曼珠沙華公園

約 500 万本もの曼珠沙華の群生地で、赤いじゅうたんを敷き詰めたように一面が真紅に染まる光景は、まさに圧巻でした。限られた観賞期間ですが、文字通りの絶景でおすすめの場所です。

P112-113

Kinchakuda Manjushage Park - Hidaka City, Saitama
With roughly 5 million *manjushage* (red spider lilies) growing in clusters, the entire landscape is awash in crimson, as if covered with a red carpet, and the sight is awe-inspiring. Although the viewing period is limited, the scenery is truly spectacular and highly recommended.

P114-115

大阪府箕面市　勝尾寺

箕面国定公園の中心にあり、1300 年前から「勝運の寺」として信仰されています。無数の「勝ダルマ」と、境内のいたるところに並べられている「ダルマみくじ」が目を引きます。境内は広く、紅葉がとても美しい幻想的な空間です。

P114-115

Katsuoji Temple - Minoo City, Osaka
Located at the center of Mino Quasi-National Park, Katsuoji Temple has been worshipped as the temple of victory for over 1,300 years. The numerous *kachi-daruma* (daruma dolls of victory) and *daruma-mikuji* (daruma doll fortunes) placed around various parts of the temple precincts are sure to catch your attention. The grounds of the temple are spacious, and the autumn foliage is very beautiful. *Daruma is a doll modeled after Bodhidharma, a Buddhist monk.

P116

青森県つがる市　高山稲荷神社

牛潟町鷲野沢にある「高山稲荷神社」。朱色の千本鳥居と「龍神池」と呼ばれる湧水の池が美しい異世界を創出しています。高台から見下ろすと、まるで赤い大蛇が海に向かっていくような光景です。

P116

Takayama Inari Shrine - Tsugaru City, Aomori
Takayama Inari Shrine is located in Washinosawa of Ushigata Town. The vermilion Senbon Torii (One Thousand Gateways) and a spring-fed pond called Ryujin-ike (Dragon God Pond) complete this other-

worldly landscape. Looking down from above, the succession of torii gates appears like a red serpent heading toward the sea.

P117
山口県長門市　元乃隅神社
アメリカ CNN が発表した「日本の最も美しい場所 31 選」に選出されています。123 基の鳥居が 100m 以上にわたって並ぶ景色は荘厳で、海と空の青色とのコントラストの眩さに目が奪われました。

P117
Motonosumi Shrine - Nagato City, Yamaguchi
The shrine has been selected as one of the 31 Most Beautiful Places in Japan by CNN. The 123 torii gates lined up over a length of more than 100 meters were impressive. The blue colors of the ocean and sky created a dazzling contrast against the gates.

P118-119
高知県四万十市　沈下橋
先に撮影をしていた方がいたので話をしたところ、1日数本のローカル線が通るというので一緒に撮影をしました。とてものどかで、四万十川に沿って電車が走っているので、電車の旅も魅力的だろうと思いました。

P118-119
Chinkabashi (Submersible Bridge)
- Shimanto City, Kochi
I spoke with the photographer who was shooting before me, and I was told that a local train, which only runs several times a day, was about to pass, so I joined in the photo shoot. The location was very idyllic, and the train tracks run along the Shimanto River, so I imagine a rail trip would be fascinating as well.

P120
福島県下郷町　只見線
福島・奥会津地域の只見川にかかる橋梁を走る只見線と、大自然のコラボレーションの景観が楽しめます。紅葉以外にも新緑の春、川霧が立ち込める夏、そして雪景色と 1 年を通じて絶景列車が撮影できる、おすすめのスポットです。

P120
Tadami Line - Shimogo Town, Fukushima
This is a splendid vantage point in the Oku-Aizu region of Fukushima Prefecture, where you can enjoy the picturesque view of the Tadami Line crossing over the Tadami River Bridge in harmony with the natural beauty of the area. In addition to autumn foliage, you can observe fresh greenery in spring, river mists in the summer, and snowy wonderlands in winter. The location is highly recommended for taking scenic photos of the train year-round.

P121
神奈川県足柄下郡　橿の木坂
江戸時代の書物に、「東海道一番の難所」と書かれた箱根旧街道。七曲りの坂があり、当時は石畳の道。草鞋で歩いて転べば、千仞（せんじん）の谷へ落ちたともいわれています。山を染める紅葉の美しさが見事です。

P121
Kashinoki Slope
- Ashigarashimo District, Kanagawa
According to an account written in the Edo period, this section of the Hakone Kyu-kaido Road was the most challenging and dangerous point along the Tokaido Road. The Nanamagari-zaka, which literally translates to 'a slope of seven turns', was paved

with cobblestones at the time. It was said that if you stumbled while wearing Japanese zori sandals, you would plunge into a bottomless valley. The mountain tinged with autumn colors is absolutely stunning.

P122
徳島県三好市　しょんべん小僧
「小便岩」と呼ばれる、谷底まで 200m の高さがある大断崖に小便小僧が立っています。柵はありますが、高所恐怖症なので結構怖かったです。

P122
Peeing Boy - Miyoshi City, Tokushima
On a massive cliff—known as the Pissing Rock—overlooking a 200-meter precipice to the bottom of the valley, stands the statue of the Pissing Boy. The area is fenced, but I am afraid of heights, so it was quite intimidating.

P123
徳島県三好市　かずら橋
日本三奇橋のひとつとして知られている「祖谷のかずら橋」。重さ約 5 トンのシラクチカズラという植物で作られており、実際に橋を渡ることができます。紅葉と川の水の青さがきれいなコントラストを演出していました。

P123
Kazura Bridge - Miyoshi City, Tokushima
Known as one of the three most peculiar bridges in Japan, Iya-no-Kazurabashi (Kazura Bridge of Iya) is made of vines from *shirakuchi-kazura* (hardy kiwi), which weighs about five tons and allows visitors to actually cross the bridge. The autumn-colored leaves and the blue of the river water created a striking contrast.

P124
長野県塩尻市　奈良井宿
江戸時代にあった中山道の宿場で、江戸時代に当時の町並みが現在までほぼ完全に保存され、「伝統的建造物群保存地区」の指定を受けています。2018 年の大晦日、日本を撮影し始めた最初の撮影場所で、江戸時代にタイムスリップしたような錯覚に陥ったのを覚えています。その後、撮影した写真が Instagram で過去一番のライクをいただきました。

P124
Narai-juku - Shiojiri City, Nagano
A former post station along the Nakasendo Highway during the Edo period, the townscape has been almost completely preserved to this day. It is a designated National Architectural Preservation Site for Groups of Historic Buildings. The photo was taken on 2018 on New Year's Eve, and I started my photographic journey of Japan at this location. I remember feeling as if I had time-traveled back to the Edo period. Later, this photo received the most likes ever on Instagram.

P125
山形県尾花沢市　銀山温泉
奥州街道より山間部に向かって 12km ほどの場所にある、世間とは遮断された仙境。大正ロマン漂う光景は絶景で、特に陽が落ちて街灯と建物の灯りが夕闇を照らす時間の情景は、ノスタルジックで幻想的です。

P125
Ginzan Onsen - Obanazawa Town, Yamagata
Approximately 12 km into the mountains from the Oshu Highway and tucked away from the rest of the world is this heavenly hot spring retreat. The place is drenched in Taisho-era ambiance and

evokes a feeling of nostalgia and enchantment, especially at dusk when the streets are bathed in the glow of the street lamps and buildings.

P126-127
長野県木曽郡　妻籠宿
江戸時代において中山道 42 番目の宿場で、木曽路を代表する観光名所です。「脇本陣奥谷」という写真の建物は 1877 年の建築で、木曽ヒノキを豊富に使った重厚な構造。大変な維持管理のおかげで、日本の古き良き伝統を後世に伝え続けることができています。

P126-127
Tsumago-juku - Kiso District, Nagano
As the 42nd post station along the Nakasendo Highway in the Edo Period, Tsumago-juku is one of the most notable landmarks along the Kisoji road. The building is called Wakihonjin Okuya, built in 1877, and the Kiso-hinoki cypress was used extensively to construct this magnificent architecture. Thanks to the arduous maintenance of the building, it continues to pass on the classic traditions of Japan to future generations.

P128-129
京都府東山区　東福寺

P128-129
Tofukuji Temple - Higashiyama Ward, Kyoto

P130
京都府南丹市　龍穏寺
境内へ続く紅葉のトンネルと石の階段のコントラストが美しい「龍穏寺」。撮影時はちょうど雨が止んで、しっとりと濡れた紅葉が色の濃さを増し、とてもきれいでした。京都市内からは少し遠いですが、紅葉撮影におすすめです。

P130
Ryuonji Temple - Nantan City, Kyoto
The stone steps of Ryuonji Temple offer a beautiful contrast to the tunnel of autumn leaves that leads to the temple grounds. When I took this photo, it had just stopped raining, and the wet autumn leaves grew more intense in color from the moisture, and it was quite lovely. Although the location is distant from Kyoto City, it is a wonderful place to photograph autumn foliage.

P131
山梨県南アルプス市　南伊奈ヶ湖
紅葉と白鳥の幻想的な写真を撮影できる「南伊奈ヶ湖」。白鳥は近寄ってきてくれましたが、この日は天気が悪く、雨が降っていて足元がぬかるみ、思い通りの構図で撮影するのが大変でした。なんとかムードのある写真を撮影することができ、安堵しました。

P131
Lake Minami Inaga
- Minami-Alps City, Yamanashi
Lake Minami Inaga offers opportunities to take magical photos of autumn foliage and swans. The swan came up to me, but the weather was bad that day—it was raining and muddy underfoot—so I had a hard time composing the shot the way I wanted, but I was able to create a moody photograph.

P132
京都府京都市　岩戸落葉神社
京都の外れにあり、境内には樹齢 400 年といわ

れる大銀杏の巨樹４本が林立しています。銀杏
の樹々と落ち葉で黄色く染め上げられた境内に、
赤い鳥居のコントラストが見事に映えます。

P132
**Iwato Ochiba Shrine
- Kyoto City, Kyoto**
The shrine is in a remote area of Kyoto, and within
its precincts stands a forest of four enormous
ginkgo trees said to be 400 years old. The ginkgo
trees and their fallen leaves paint the temple
grounds in golden yellow, contrasting brilliantly
with the vermillion torii gate.

P133
奈良県奈良市　奈良公園
茅葺き屋根の趣のあるお茶屋さんと紅葉、そして
奈良名物である鹿のコラボレーションの撮影に成
功。撮影場所に到着すると、タイミング良くきれい
な牝鹿が現れ、いい写真が撮れるまでしっかりと
モデルを務めてくれました。

P133
Nara Park - Nara City, Nara
I was successful in capturing the charming,
thatched-roof teahouse together with the autumn
leaves and Nara's celebrity, a deer. When I arrived
at the site, a gorgeous doe appeared at just the
right moment and modeled for me patiently until I
was able to get a good shot.

P134-135
京都府亀岡市　桂川
京都嵐山の保津川下り。大自然に囲まれた桂川
を、船頭さんが昔ながらの竹の棒を使って優雅に
進んで行く姿はとても美しいものです。特に、紅
葉の季節は、紅葉と光り輝く川面のカラーコント
ラストが絶妙です。

P134-135
Katsura River - Kameoka City, Kyoto
Hozugawa River cruise in Arashiyama, Kyoto. It
was lovely to watch the boatmen moving gracefully
along the natural setting of the Katsura River using
old-fashioned bamboo poles. In particular, the
complementing colors of the bright leaves and the
shiny surface of the river are exquisite during the
autumn foliage season.

P136
京都府京都市　清水寺
「秋の夜間特別拝観」での風趣に富んだ情景。ラ
イトアップで朱色の三重塔がオレンジ色に照らさ
れ、紅葉とグラデーションを織り成します。この時
期にしか目にできない幻想夜です。

P136
**Kiyomizu-dera Temple
- Kyoto City, Kyoto Prefecture**
The image is a picturesque autumn scene from
the special night viewing event. The three-storied
vermilion pagoda is awash in an orange glow,
forming a gradation of colors with the autumn
leaves. It is a nighttime wonder that can only be
witnessed at this time of year.

P137
京都府京都市　醍醐寺
広く自然豊かな境内に並ぶ立派なお堂や五重塔
と、紅葉のコラボレーションは必見です。その美
しさに惹かれて夜の紅葉ライトアップにも訪れまし
たが、夜もまた昼とは違った美しさがありました。

P137
Daigoji Temple - Kyoto City, Kyoto
Must-sees are the beautifully kept gardens and
ponds located within the expansive temple grounds
as well as the collaborative spectacle of autumn
maple leaves set amongst the majestic temples
and five-storied pagoda. I was enthralled by the
splendor and visited the temple in the evening
to view the illuminated maple leaves. The night
views offered another facet of beauty that was not
apparent in the daytime.

P138
山梨県南都留郡　富士山・河口湖
秋の昼下がり、太陽に照らされて美しく輝く紅葉
と富士山の共演。撮影日は紅葉も終わりかけて
いましたが、イメージ通りの写真が撮れてホッとし
たのを覚えています。富士山は春夏秋冬、時間、
場所によってまったく違う写真が撮れるので一番
好きな被写体です。

P138
**Mount Fuji and Lake Kawaguchi
- Minamitsuru District, Yamanashi**
The harmonious composition of Mount Fuji and the
crimson leaves glittering brightly in the sun on an
autumn afternoon. Autumn foliage had passed its
peak, and I recall feeling relieved that I was able to
capture the image I had in mind. Mount Fuji is my
favorite subject because I can photograph it in so
many different ways depending on the time, place,
and season.

P139
神奈川県足柄下郡　富士山・箱根
富士山と箱根、芦ノ湖の共演。箱根神社の「平
和の鳥居」の裏手に広がる豊かな自然と、富士
山を望む素晴らしい眺望。秋の終わりの明け方に
撮影し、早朝で観光客がまだ訪れない箱根の空
気は格別でした。

P139
**Mount Fuji and Hakone
- Ashigarashimo District, Kanagawa**
A symphony of Mount Fuji and Lake Ashinoko
in Hakone. The picturesque panorama features
Mount Fuji together with the abundant natural
surroundings behind the Heiwa no Torii (Gate of
Peace) at Hakone Shrine. Taken at dawn at the
end of autumn with no spectators yet, the early
morning air in Hakone felt very special.

P139
神奈川県足柄下郡　富士山・湯河原
富士山と霧の写真を撮りたいとチャレンジをし続け
てきて、初めて撮影できたのがこの写真です。山
道を車で登り、暗がりに霧が出ているのが見えた
ときには、嬉しくて撮影ポイント到着まで待ちきれ
ない想いでした。背後に昇る太陽のまばゆい光
によって、幻想的で美麗な写真を撮影できて幸せ
でした。

P139
**Mount Fuji and Yugawara
- Ashigarashimo District, Kanagawa**
I have been trying to capture Mount Fuji in the mist
for a long time, and this was my first successful
photo. When I drove up the mountain road and
noticed the fog in the dark, I was so excited that I
couldn't wait to reach the location. I was ecstatic to
be able to take this phenomenal and breathtaking
photo with the glory of the sunlight rising in the
background.

P140-141
山梨県笛吹市　富士山・新道峠

夜明け前の河口湖と富士山の大パノラマを「新道
峠」から撮影した写真です。この展望台は夜間
車の通行ができないため、機材を背負って山道を
登らなければなりません。空気の澄んだ冬に撮影
するのでとても寒いですが、この景色のためなら
と頑張れるほどの美景です。

P140-141
**Mount Fuji and Shindo Pass
- Fuefuki City, Yamanashi**
I captured this sweeping panorama of Mount
Fuji and Lake Kawaguchi before dawn from the
Shindo Pass. Cars were not allowed to access
this observatory at night, so I had to carry my
equipment on my back up the mountain road. I
had been aiming to shoot in the winter when the
air was crisp and clear, so it was extremely cold.
But the view was so splendid that I would have
made any effort to make the shoot possible.

P142-143
千葉県南房総市　原岡桟橋
原岡海岸にあり、東京湾越しに見える富士山を撮
影に訪れました。到着までは予想もしていなかっ
た、とても美しいサンセットが目の前に広がり、フォ
トジェニックな桟橋と美しい夕日、そして富士山の
大共演を撮影でき、多幸感に包まれました。

P142-143
Haraoka Pier - Minamiboso City, Chiba
I visited the pier at Haraoka Beach to photograph
the view of Mount Fuji seen over Tokyo Bay.
Upon arrival, and to my great surprise, a very
beautiful sunset unfolded before me. The pier was
photogenic in the glorious sunset, and accompanied
by Mount Fuji, created the perfect picture. I was
completely overcome with joy.

P144-145
東京都
ドイツへの帰途、飛行機から撮影した東京の写真
です。飛行機では常に窓際に座り、シャッターチャ
ンスを狙っています。以前からトライしていたので
すがこの日は天気も良く、あまり雲もなかったので
思い描いていた写真を撮影することに成功し、歓
喜しました。

P144-145
Tokyo
I took this photo of Tokyo from the airplane
on my way back to Germany. I always take the
window seat when flying so I'll never miss a photo
opportunity. I had been trying this shot for a long
time, and on this particular day, the weather was
good and the sky was fairly cloudless, so I was
delighted when I succeeded in capturing the image I
had envisioned.

P147
山梨県・静岡県　富士山
日本の撮影を始めた最初の旅の始まりにこの写真
が撮れたことで、かなり気持ちが楽になったのを
覚えています。撮影後、夜寝る前にこの写真を
Instagram に投稿したところ、翌朝、過去一番
のライクとコメントがあり、興奮したのを思い出し
ます。

P147
Mount Fuji - Yamanashi And Shizuoka
The fact that I was able to capture this image at the
start of my first trip to document Japanese landscapes
gave me a great sense of relief. After taking the photo,
I posted it on Instagram before I went to bed at night.
The next morning, I woke up to see my account
flooded with the most likes and comments I ever had,
and I remember being very excited.

P148-149
宮城県登米市　伊豆沼・内沼
自身の力強さをアピールする鳥たちの、今までに
聴いたことがない大音量の鳴き声に圧倒されまし
た。頭上を飛び交う鳥たちの勢い、目の前にオレン
ジのグラデーションの美しい景色が広がり、非
現実的な光景は生涯忘れられない感動的な朝と
なりました。

P148-149
Izunuma and Uchinuma - Tome City, Miyagi
The calls of the birds showcasing their power and
strength were overwhelming — I had never heard
such loud cries. The energy of the birds flying
overhead, coupled with the spectacular orange
gradient spreading out before my eyes, created a view
that was out of this world. It was a glorious morning
and one I would remember for the rest of my life.

P150-151
北海道上川郡　ブルーリバー
「ブルーリバー」と呼ばれる「美瑛川」。雪の白と
コバルトブルーの川面のコントラストが幻想的な風
景を作り上げる、冬にしか見ることのできない美
景です。 橋上から撮影していますが、橋の反対
側には「白ひげの滝」があります。本当は近くに
ある「青い池」を撮影したかったのですが、凍っ
て雪に覆われていました。

P150-151
Blue River - Kamikawa District, Hokkaido
The Biei River is also known as the Blue River. The
vivid contrast of the white snow and the cobalt-
blue surface of the river creates a fantastic scenery
that only appears in the winter. This photo was
taken from a bridge, and Shirahige Falls is located
on the opposite side of the bridge. I originally
intended to photograph the nearby Blue Pond, but
it was frozen over and covered with snow.

P152
徳島県鳴門市　鳴門海峡・鳴門海峡大橋
四国の最北東端と淡路島門崎との間に位置する
「鳴門海峡」。鳴門海峡は、世界３大潮流のひ
とつで、潮流は日本一の速さを誇ります。また、
日本百景に選定されている迫力のある海峡です。
鳴門海峡大橋の海上遊歩道を歩きましたが、少
し怖さを感じました。

P152
**Naruto Strait and Naruto Kaikyo Bridge
- Naruto City, Tokushima**
Located between the northeastern tip of Shikoku
and Tosaki on Awaji Island, Naruto Strait is one
of the three greatest whirlpools in the world
and boasts the fastest tidal current in Japan. The
dynamic and powerful whirlpools of Naruto have
been selected as one of the 100 Landscapes of
Japan. I walked the pedestrian path on the bridge
and it felt a little scary.

P153, 154-155
鳥取県鳥取市　鳥取砂丘
広大な日本最大級の砂丘で、国の天然記念物に
指定されています。なかなか行けずにいましたが、
念願の「雪の砂丘」を撮影することができました。
その光景は、異世界と思ってしまうほど幻想的で
した。

P153, 154-155
Tottori Sand Dunes - Tottori City, Tottori
One of the largest sand dunes in Japan is a designated
National Natural Monument. I didn't have the
chance to visit for a while, but I was finally able to

capture the wintery dunes. The scenery was so
surreal that it felt like I was in another world.

P156
青森県弘前市　岩木山
標高1625mで青森県の最高峰の山。「津軽富士」
と呼ばれるだけあり、飛行機から初めて目にした
ときに富士山のような山があると思い、すぐさま撮
影しました。富士山が好きなこともあり、青森を旅
している最中は姿を見るたびに撮影していました。

P156
Mount Iwaki - Hirosaki City, Aomori
At 1,625 meters above sea level, it is the highest
mountain in Aomori Prefecture. Aptly nicknamed
Tsugaru Fuji, the mountain first appeared to me
from the plane. Its similarity to Mount Fuji intrigued
me, and I immediately started shooting. Coming
from my fondness for Mount Fuji, I took pictures of
Mount Iwaki whenever I saw it during my travels in
Aomori.

P157
秋田県仙北市　乳頭温泉郷
乳頭山の山麓に点在する「乳頭温泉郷」は、茅
葺き屋根の佇まいと銀世界に白い湯気が立ち上る
情感たっぷりの風景に魅了されます。まるで古い
時代にタイムスリップしたかのような雰囲気があり、
秘湯といわれる由縁が分かります。

P157
Nyuto Onsenkyo - Senboku City, Akita
Situated at the foothills of Mt. Nyuto, Nyuto
Onsenkyo is a quaint hot springs village dotted with
thatched-roof houses. White steam rising amidst
the snowy mountainscape creates an enchanting
atmosphere. It's as if you have stepped back in time
to a bygone era, and it is easy to see why it is called
a hidden hot spring resort.

P158
長野県長野市　戸隠神社
撮影当日の朝４時に起き、真冬の凍った道路を
運転し、吹雪いている深い雪の中を歩いてこの写
真を撮影。 地元の方曰く、「数日前まで雪がなかっ
たのでラッキーだね」と言われ、苦労が報われた
と思い、嬉しくなりました。一番過酷な撮影でし
たが、「痛みなくして得るものなし」を体感して成
長できました。

P158
Togakushi Shrine - Nagano City, Nagano
I woke up at 4 a.m., drove on icy roads, and walked
through snowy winds and deep snow to take this
picture at Togakushi Shrine in the middle of winter.
According to the locals, I was lucky because there
had been no snow until a few days earlier. I was
delighted that my hard work had paid off. It was
the toughest shoot ever, but it was a great growth
experience. As they say, "No pain, no gain."

P159, 160
青森県青森市　八甲田山
樹氷「スノーモンスター」を撮影に八甲田山の山
頂へ。ロープウェーを降りると凍てつく風が吹き荒
れ、おそらく人生で体感した中で一番の寒さでし
た。 手袋をしていなかったため、指がすぐにかじ
かんでシャッターボタンを押せず、無理やり親指
で押したほどです。

P159, 160
Hakkoda Mountains - Aomori City, Aomori
I went to the top of the Hakkoda Mountains to
photograph the frost-covered trees called snow

monsters. As I got off the ropeway, I was greeted
by fierce, freezing winds. It was probably the
coldest I had ever felt in my life. I wasn't wearing
gloves, so I immediately lost sensation in my fingers
and couldn't press the shutter. I had to resort to
using my thumb instead.

P161
山形県山形市　宝珠山立石寺からの眺め

P161
**The view from Hojusan Risshakuji Temple
- Yamagata City, Yamagata**

P161
山形県鶴岡市　羽黒山・五重塔
羽黒山は東北仏教文化の中心であり、この五重塔
は600年前に再建されたものですが、東北地方
最古の塔として国宝に認定されています。近くには
樹齢1000年の巨杉があり、杉並木の中に塔があ
ります。まるで、建てられた時代にタイムスリップし
たかのような感覚に陥る、とても厳かな場所です。

P161
**Five-storied Pagoda of Mount Haguro
- Tsuruoka City, Yamagata**
Hagurosan (Mount Haguro) is the center of the
Buddhist faith in the Tohoku region. Its five-storied
pagoda was reconstructed 600 years ago, making
it the oldest pagoda in the Tohoku region and a
registered National Treasure. Also near the tower
is a 1,000-year-old giant cedar tree. The pagoda
stands amidst a cedar forest, creating the illusion
that you have stepped back in time. The location
possesses an air of majestic solemnity.

P162-163
石川県金沢市　兼六園
日本三名園のひとつである「兼六園」。雪の兼六
園を撮影したくて行ったのですが雪は積もってお
らず、仕方がないので相倉、白川郷などを撮影し、
翌夜に金沢へ戻ると大雪警報が出て吹雪いていま
した。チャンスと思って滞在を延ばしたところ、翌
朝天気は回復し、この写真を撮影できました。実
に天気に恵まれました！

P162-163
**Kenrokuen Garden
- Kanazawa City, Ishikawa**
Kenrokuen Garden is one of the three most
beautiful gardens in Japan. I wanted to capture the
snowy garden, but there was no snow when I went
there. So instead, I headed for Ainokura village and
Shirakawa-go. I returned to Kanazawa the following
evening to a blizzard, and a heavy snow warning
had been issued. I extended my stay thinking this
was my chance. The weather had recovered the
following morning, and I was able to capture this
image. I was truly blessed with good weather!

P164-165
岐阜県大野郡　白川郷
世界遺産に登録されている、「白川郷」の合掌造
り集落。前日に大雪が降り、撮影当日も雪が降り
続いていたため、展望台からはうまく撮れず残念
でしたが、家が雪で覆われてしまったシーンを撮
影でき、感無量です。

P164-165
Shirakawa-go - Ohno District, Gifu
The village of Gassho-style houses in Shirakawa-
go is a registered World Heritage Site. It snowed
heavily the day before and continued on the day of
the shoot, so it was unfortunate that I could not

get a good shot from the observatory. However, I was able to capture some photos of the houses covered in snow, so I was deeply satisfied.

P166, 167

山形県山形市　宝珠山立石寺
車で向かっていると、突然ボタ雪が降り始めました。 天気予報では、雪が降ることをまったく報じられていなかったので驚きましたが、到着するとうっすらと雪が積もり、紅葉と雪の素晴らしい景色が目の前に広がっていました。

P166, 167

**Hojusan Risshakuji Temple
- Yamagata City, Yamagata**
As I was driving to the temple, it suddenly started to snow in large fluffs. I was taken by surprise because the forecast had not announced any snowfall. When I arrived, there was a thin blanket of snow, and a marvelous view of autumn leaves and snow spread out before my eyes.

P168

富山県南砺市　相倉合掌造り集落
約100〜350年前の合掌造りが立ち並び、日本の歴史的風景を今に残す世界遺産。ライトアップの時間より1、2時間早めに到着したため、撮影をしながら点灯まで雪の中を待っていると、辺りは人だかりに。思い通りの写真を撮影でき、寒い中早くから待っていた甲斐がありました。

P168

**Ainokura Gassho-style Village
- Nanto City, Toyama**
Thatched-roof houses built between 100 and 350 years ago line the streets of this World Heritage Site, preserving Japan's historical landscape. I arrived an hour or two before the light-ups. As I waited in the snow for the lights to come on, taking pictures in the meantime, a crowd started to gather in the area. I was able to photograph the image I had in mind, and it made the long wait in the cold worthwhile.

P169

長野県下高井郡　地獄谷野猿公苑
温泉につかるニホンザルの愛称「スノーモンキー」で有名。雪が降る中、猿たちが温泉につかっている姿を世界で唯一見ることができます。寒い中撮影をしていると一緒に温泉に入りたくなります。温泉の猿には近づくことができないため、撮影には望遠レンズがおすすめです。

P169

**Jigokudani Monkey Park
- Shimotakai District, Nagano**
The park is famous for its snow monkeys, a nickname for the Japanese macaques that bathe in hot springs. It is the only place in the world where you can watch monkeys relaxing in the natural bath as it snows. When you're taking photos in the freezing cold, you'll be tempted to join in the hot bath. Since you can't get close to the monkeys in the hot springs, a telephoto lens is recommended.

P170-171

北海道登別市　登別地獄谷
1万年前の活火山噴火により形成されたクレーターに点在する噴気口から噴気が立ち込める「地獄谷」。遊歩道が整備されており、地獄谷全体を探索できます。硫黄の匂いと立ち上る湯気、沸き立つ硫黄泉と別世界に来たような雰囲気と景観を楽しむことができます。

P170-171

**Noboribetsu Jigokudani
- Noboribetsu City, Hokkaido**
Jigokudani, or Hell Valley, is a crater formed by a volcanic eruption 10,000 years ago, with steam rising from numerous fumaroles scattered throughout. A pedestrian walkway allows visitors to explore the entire Jigokudani area. The sulfuric odors, rising steam, and bubbling springs create an otherworldly atmosphere and landscapes that are sure to amaze you.

P172

福島県会津若松市　大内宿
江戸時代に、会津若松市と日光のある今市市を結ぶ街道の宿場町として栄えました。約400年前の江戸時代の面影を残した茅葺き屋根の民家が街道沿いに立ち並びます。高台で出会った着物を着た美しい女性にモデルをしていただき、素晴らしい写真を撮影することができました。

P172

Ouchi-juku - Aizuwakamatsu City, Fukushima
Ouchi-juku flourished during the Edo period as a post town on the highway connecting Aizuwakamatsu City and Imaichi City, where Nikko is located. Lined up along the road are houses with thatched roofs, which still retain the original appearance of the Edo period from 400 years ago. I met a woman in a beautiful kimono on a hillside who modeled for me, and I was able to take some great photos.

P173

石川県金沢市　兼六園

P173

**Kenrokuen Garden
- Kanazawa City, Ishikawa**

P174

福島県会津若松市　祈りの里
・会津慈母大観音像
「祈りの里 会津村」内にある、高さ57mの巨大な仏像です。車で走っていると、存在感のある観音像が目に飛び込んできたのです。立ち寄ってみると、赤ちゃんを抱いた優しい顔の観音様が存在感を放っていました。

P174

**Aizu Jibo Dai-Kannon, Inori-no-Sato Aizumura
- Aizuwakamatsu City, Fukushima**
Located in the Inori-no-Sato, Aizumura, this giant 57-meter Kannon statue is the largest in the world. As I was driving, I caught a glimpse of an impressive statue of the goddess of mercy. When I stopped by, I found the gentle face of the Kannon holding a baby in her arms, radiating a powerful presence.

P175

山形県山形市　蔵王の朱い大鳥居
車を運転していると、巨大な鳥居が目に飛び込んできました。参拝客らを出迎える美しい大鳥居の朱色と白い雪のコントラストが美麗で、冬にしか見ることができない美しい日本の景色です。

P175

**Grand Red Torii Gateway of Zao
- Yamagata City, Yamagata**
As I was driving, a monumental torii gate jumped out at me. The splendid, vermilion-red gateway welcoming the worshippers stood in striking contrast with the white snow. It is a spectacular Japanese landscape that can only be seen in winter.

P176-177

大分県別府市　別府温泉
別府市内各地に温泉が数百もある、日本屈指の温泉街。街の至るところから湯気が立ち上るさまは、この街ならではの光景です。白く立ち上る湯気を撮影したくて、寒くなる冬まで待ちました。

P176-177

Beppu Onsen - Beppu City, Oita
Beppu City is one of the most prominent *onsen* resorts in Japan, with hundreds of hot springs located throughout the city. Steam rising up from all parts of the area is a unique spectacle. I waited until the cold winter season to capture the rising white steam, and the wait was definitely worth it.

P178

山梨県富士吉田市　本町2丁目商店街
昭和レトロな佇まいの商店街をバックに、迫力のある富士山。写真をInstagramに投稿すると、写真中央で犬を散歩されている方から「世界デビューさせてくれてありがとう」とメッセージをもらいました。後輩の方から連絡をもらったそうで、サプライズな出来事でした。

P178

**Honcho Ni-chome Shopping Street
- Fujiyoshida City, Yamanashi**
The majestic Mount Fuji stands in its splendor in the backdrop of the retro-style shopping street that takes us back to the Showa era. When I posted this photo on Instagram, I received a comment from the person walking the dog thanking me for their chance at a global debut. His friend had notified him, and his kind response was a pleasant surprise.

P179

東京都
東京スカイツリーから撮影した東京の写真です。東京は、建物が地の果てまで続く巨大な都市だというのが分かります。

P179

Tokyo
A picture of Tokyo taken from the Skytree. You will notice that Tokyo is a massive metropolis with buildings stretching to the ends of the earth.

P180-181

東京都
ドイツに帰る飛行機からの撮影。冬の朝で空気が澄み、雲ひとつない空。富士山と東京がすっぽり一枚の写真に収まる写真を撮影できました。飛行機撮影は難易度が高いのですが、完璧な写真を撮影できたと自負しています。

P180-181

Tokyo
A shot taken from a plane returning to Germany. It was a clear winter morning, and the sky was cloudless. I was able to capture the entirety of Mount Fuji and Tokyo within the frame. Aerial photography is extremely challenging, but I am proud to have succeeded in capturing the perfect photo.

P183

東京都新宿区　歌舞伎町
日本最大、東洋一の歓楽街といわれる「歌舞伎町」。ベルリンの森のそばに一年間住んだ後に新宿を訪れ、人の多さ、駅の複雑さ、ネオンの光、街の熱気に圧倒され、夢中で撮影しました。

P183
Kabukicho - Shinjuku Ward, Tokyo
Kabukicho is considered to be the largest entertainment district in Japan and the most notorious in the East. I made a visit to Shinjuku after living near the Berlin woods for a year. The sheer number of people, the complexity of the train stations, the neon lights, and the fervent energy of the city were overwhelming, and I enthusiastically shot away with my camera.

P184
神奈川県横浜市　生麦ジャンクション
ドイツの高速道路はシンプルで、直線道路が続くのですが、日本に帰国して久しぶりに見る首都高速道路は複雑で何層にも重なり、近未来的で目を奪われました。東京を撮り始めた初期の作品です。

P184
**Namamugi Junction
- Yokohama City, Kanagawa**
German highways are simple and continue in a straight line. However, the Metropolitan Expressway, which I saw for the first time in a while after returning to Japan, captivated me with its complex, multi-layered structure and futuristic appearance. This is one of my early works from when I first started documenting Tokyo.

P184
神奈川県横浜市　本牧ジャンクション
横浜マリンタワーから撮影した新山下、本牧エリアの夜景。高速道路を流れる車の光が闇夜に光る川のように見えたので、光の線を描くために長時間にわたる露光で撮影しました。

P184
Honmoku Junction - Yokohama City, Kanagawa
A night scene of the Shinyamashita and Honmoku area taken from the Yokohama Marine Tower. The car lights moving on the highway looked like a luminous river in the black night, so I spent hours photographing with long exposure to capture the light trails.

P185
東京都中央区　銀座・中央通り
銀座のメインストリート。日が暮れると、色とりどりのネオンサインと街灯、幾台ものタクシーのライトが光り輝きます。週末には歩行者天国になり、終日活気のあるエリアです。

P185
**Chuo-dori Street, Ginza
- Chuo Ward, Tokyo**
Ginza's main street. At nightfall, the avenue glitters with colorful neon signs, streetlights, and the lights from numerous cabs. On weekends, it becomes a pedestrian street bustling with activity throughout the day.

P186-187
東京都中央区　銀座・数寄屋橋交差点
晴海通りと外堀通りが交差するスクランブル交差点で、この辺りは再開発が進められ、以前とはだいぶ変わってしまいました。渋谷のスクランブル交差点とはまた違った街の空気です。

P186-187
**Sukiyabashi Crossing, Ginza
- Chuo Ward, Tokyo**
This is a crosswalk where Harumi-dori Street and Sotobori-dori Street intersect. This area has been redeveloped and has changed a lot since the past. The crossing carries a distinctive vibe that is a bit unlike the one in Shibuya.

P188
東京都渋谷区　渋谷駅地下鉄改札
毎日新しい進化を続ける渋谷。日本に帰国するたびに、渋谷の駅や街自体が複雑化していっていると感じます。地下鉄の駅が好きで、この改札はサイバーパンクな印象でとても格好良いです。

P188
**Subway ticket gates at Shibuya Station
- Shibuya Ward, Tokyo**
Shibuya is constantly evolving with new developments every day. Every time I return to Japan, it feels like Shibuya station and the city itself have become more and more complex. I like subway stations, and this ticket gate looked very cool with its cyberpunk feel.

P188
東京都港区　レインボーブリッジ
写真を始めた頃に撮影した作品で、当時は広角レンズと三脚がメインの機材でした。レンズの絞りを絞ると光がウニのようになる、光芒（こうぼう）という現象を知ったのがこの頃です。絞り羽の枚数が多いと光の線が増えるので、レンズの仕様にもこだわるようになりました。

P188
Rainbow Bridge - Minato Ward, Tokyo
I took this photo when I first started photography. At the time, my primary equipment was a wide-angle lens and a tripod. It was around this time that I learned about the starburst effect, a phenomenon in which lights appear like sea urchins when the aperture of the lens is stopped down. The more aperture blades you have, the more rays of light you get, so I became very particular about the specifications of my lenses.

P189
東京都渋谷区　渋谷
東京中で一番多く夜景を撮影したのが渋谷の街です。帰国するとまず、渋谷スクランブル交差点の喧騒を見に行ったものです。数年前は今より高い建物や展望施設がなく、撮影場所を探すのに悪戦苦闘していました。

P189
Shibuya - Shibuya Ward, Tokyo
Shibuya is where I photographed the most night views in all of Tokyo. Whenever I returned to Japan, I would first go to see the hustle and bustle of the Shibuya scramble crossing. A few years ago, there were no towering buildings or observation facilities as there are now, so it was a challenge to find the best photo locations.

P190-191
東京都
友人の東京夜景写真家と、ヘリコプターから東京の街を撮影しました。空気が澄んだ冬の日で、雲ひとつなく富士山まで見渡せました。撮影時間帯も完璧で長い間、東京の空撮をしたいという念願が叶った夜です。

P190-191
Tokyo
I photographed the city of Tokyo from a helicopter with my friend who is a Tokyo night photographer. It was a clear winter day with not a cloud in the sky, and we could see as far as Mount Fuji. The time of day was perfect for shooting, and this was the night I fulfilled a long-held dream of taking aerial photos of Tokyo.

P192
東京都千代田区　千鳥ヶ淵
ライトアップされた満開の桜と東京タワー。「千鳥ヶ淵」の桜は昼間も美しく、私の好きな桜スポットですが、夜景でも桜の魂が震えているような神秘的な姿が胸を打ちます。

P192
**Chidorigafuchi Moat
- Chiyoda Ward, Tokyo**
Illuminated cherry blossoms in full bloom and Tokyo Tower. The cherry trees along Chidorigafuchi Moat are beautiful in the daytime, and it is my favorite sakura blossom viewing spot. Even in the evening, the cherry blossoms appear as if their souls are reverberating with a mystical presence that pulls upon my heartstrings.

P193
東京都港区　お台場海浜公園
レインボーブリッジと東京タワーをバックにライトアップされた屋形船が並ぶ、東京ならではの夜景。夕暮れのお台場で、大都会でもこうした趣のあるシーンに遭遇できるのが東京の面白さです。

P193
Odaiba Seaside Park - Minato Ward, Tokyo
A unique Tokyo night view of illuminated *yakatabune* (traditional pleasure boats) with the Rainbow Bridge and Tokyo Tower in the background. What's intriguing about Tokyo is that in Odaiba at dusk, you can still encounter such atmospheric sights in the middle of a metropolis.

P194
大阪府大阪市　新世界
天下の台所、大阪。通天閣をバックに多くの飲食店がひしめきあい、熱気に溢れています。大阪の夜は、東京とはまた違ったアットホームな雰囲気で、楽しく撮影できるのが魅力です。

P194
Shinsekai - Osaka City, Osaka
Osaka has a reputation as the "best kitchen under the heavens." The Shinsekai (New World) district is bustling with excitement, where you'll discover restaurants and bars crammed in close quarters against the backdrop of the Tsutenkaku tower. The nightlife in Osaka is a bit different from that of Tokyo, with a more friendly and homey atmosphere, which I find charming because it makes shooting more enjoyable.

P195
大阪府大阪市　道頓堀
大阪の食い倒れ文化を象徴する「道頓堀」。数え切れないほどの飲食店、道頓堀川沿いはグリコの看板を筆頭にたくさんの看板とネオンで覆い尽くされており、きらびやかで活気があります。

P195
Dotonbori - Osaka City, Osaka
Dotonbori is the symbol of Osaka's eat-till-you're-broke food culture. The area is home to countless restaurants and bars, and the storefronts along the Dotonbori River are adorned with numerous neon lights and billboards, most notably the Glico Man sign, giving the place a glitzy and vibrant atmosphere.

P196
東京都新宿区　西新宿
雨の降る夜に撮影するのが好きです。この写真のように、ネオンライトや車のライトが濡れた路面に反射してドラマチックで近未来的な写真が撮れるからです。雨の夜はいつも終電まで撮影していました。

P196
**Nishi-Shinjuku
- ShinjukuWard, Tokyo**
I like to take pictures at night when it is raining. The reason is that I can capture dramatic and futuristic imagery, like this photo, in which the lights from the cars and neon signs reflect off the surface of the wet road. On rainy nights, I always stayed out to shoot until the last train.

P197
大阪府　心斎橋
雨降る繁華街。大阪で撮影していると、楽しいことのひとつは見知らぬ人々が気軽に声をかけてくれることです。このときも「お兄ちゃん、カメラ濡れるで」と傘を差し出してくれる方がいて、胸が熱くなりました。

P197
Shinsaibashi - Osaka
The downtown area in the rain. One of the fun things about shooting in Osaka is that strangers will come and casually chat with you. On this occasion, a person offered me an umbrella and said, "Hey bro, your camera is going to get wet." It was a heartwarming gesture.

P198
東京都新宿区　歌舞伎町
不夜城の「歌舞伎町」をバックに、大ガードの上を電車が行き来し、無数の車や人々が行き交う交差点。長時間露光で撮影しました。

P198
Kabukicho, Shinjuku - Shinjuku Ward, Tokyo
The intersection is bustling with countless cars and pedestrians as trains run back and forth above the large overpass against the sleepless Kabukicho district in the background. This image was captured with a long exposure.

P199
東京都渋谷区　渋谷スクランブル交差点

P199
**Shibuya Scramble Crossing
- Shibuya Ward, Tokyo**

P200
東京都江東区　お台場
各階に虹色のドアが並び、まるでゲームや映画のシーンに出てくるような近未来的なビル。カラフルなドア色とコンクリートのコントラストは、おしゃれでフォトジェニックです。

P200
Odaiba - Koto Ward, Tokyo
Each floor is lined with doors painted in all colors of the rainbow, giving this building a futuristic feel, like something out of a video game or movie scene. The colorful door panels against the concrete create a contrast that is stylish and photogenic.

P201
大阪府大阪市　裏天満ちょうちん通り
「浪花の台所」と呼ばれる、天満市場にあるユニークな通り。夜になると、1000 を超える提灯が照らされ、下町情緒のレトロで温かい雰囲気に心が温かくなります。

P201
**Uratenma Chochin-dori Street
(Lantern Street) - Osaka City, Osaka**
The Tenma Ichiba Market is also known as the kitchen of Naniwa (the former name for the area around Osaka city), and situated within the market is an alleyway like no other. At night, more than 1,000 lanterns light up the street, creating a warm and nostalgic downtown atmosphere. The coziness will surely lift your spirits.

P202
静岡県静岡市　薩埵峠
歌川広重の『東海道五十三次』に登場し、東海道一の絶景といわれる「薩埵峠（さったとうげ）」。富士山をバックに、東海道本線、国道1号線、東名高速道路が走ります。夜明けの風景を長時間露光で撮っています。

P202
**Satta-toge Pass
- Shizuoka City, Shizuoka**
Satta-toge appears in Utagawa Hiroshige's ukiyo-e series, the *Fifty-Three Stations of the Tokaido*, and is said to command the most spectacular view along the Tokaido Road. Here you see the JR Tokaido Main Line, National Route 1, and the Tomei Expressway running through the pass with Mount Fuji in the background. I took this long-exposure shot of the landscape at dawn.

P203
北海道斜里郡　天に続く道
知床ドライブで誰もが一度は走りたいと思う、全長約 28km の直線道路。道の先が " 天まで " つながっているように見えることから、「天に続く道」と呼ばれます。

P203
Road to Heaven - Shari District, Hokkaido
Stretching in a straight line for roughly 28 km, the Road to Heaven is a coveted destination for anyone who has been on the road in Shiretoko. Aptly named, the far end of the path appears to lead directly to the sky.

P204
東京都
青く輝く永代橋の後ろにそびえ立つ高層マンション群。ビルの裏手には、月島もんじゃストリートが広がります。高層ビルと昔ながらの木造住宅が共存して密集する光景も、東京ならではでしょう。

P204
Tokyo
A cluster of high-rise condominiums soars above the shimmering blue Eitai Bridge, and Tsukishima Monja Street stretches out behind these buildings. The coexistence of skyscrapers and old-fashioned wooden houses to form a dense community is also a sight that is distinctive of Tokyo.

P204
岡山県倉敷市　水島コンビナート
瀬戸内海に臨む、日本を代表する重化学コンビナートです。非現実的なコンビナートの夜景は、日本夜景遺産事務局選定の「日本夜景遺産」、日本三大夜景・夜景 100 選事務局選定の「夜景 100 選」にも選ばれています。

P204
**Mizushima Industrial Complex
- Kurashiki City, Okayama**
Located on the Seto Inland Sea, this is Japan's best-known heavy-chemical industrial complex. The otherworldly night view of the industrial complex

has been selected as a Night View Heritage of Japan by the Yakei-Isan Secretariat as well as one of the 100 Best Night Views of Japan by the Secretariat of the Three Major Night Views and the 100 Best Night Views of Japan.

P205
東京都　北十間川とスカイツリー
世界一の高さ 634m を誇る、自立式電波塔。東京オリンピックの特別ライティングを撮影に行きました。雲が多い夜で、スカイツリーに雲がかかった幻想的な瞬間を撮ることができました。

P205
Kitajukken River and Tokyo Skytree - Tokyo
Standing at 634 meters, Tokyo Skytree is the tallest free-standing broadcasting tower in the world. I went to shoot the special light-up in celebration of the Tokyo Olympics. It was an overcast evening, but I was able to capture a dramatic moment when the Skytree was draped in clouds.

P206-207
東京都
どこまでも広がる東京の夜景。隅田川と荒川に沿って、「首都の動脈」のようにも見える首都高速道路が縦横無尽に広がります。東京の大きさと複雑さには驚きを隠せません。

P206-207
Tokyo
The infinite nightscape of Tokyo. The Metropolitan Expressway spreads like the arteries of the capital city, winding in all directions along the Sumida River and Arakawa River. The sheer scale and intricacies of Tokyo never cease to amaze me.

P208-209
東京都
東京に住んでいたときは分かりませんでしたが、東京ほど果てなく大都市が広がっている場所は、世界に類を見ません。一つひとつの窓の光の中に、人々の生活と個々の人生があると思うと感慨深いです。

P208-209
Tokyo
I never realized this when I lived in Tokyo, but there is no other place in the world where a megacity spreads out as boundlessly as it does in Tokyo. It is deeply compelling to think that within the light of each window is the life of the people and their individual stories.

Special Thanks

Conny、Linus、Elly、Anita、Manfred、Martina、両親。
Friends and Family.

旅先や撮影時に出会い、ご協力いただいた皆様。
インスタグラムをフォローしていただいている皆様。
そして、公私ともにいつもお世話になり、サポートしていただいている皆様方。
いつも本当にありがとうございます。

写真集を出版するきっかけを作っていただき、
全力を注いでいただいた編集の篠谷様。
パイ インターナショナルの三芳会長、三芳社長、高橋様、
デザイナーの伊藤様、翻訳の Hiroko さん。
この度は素晴らしい写真集を制作していただき、
ありがとうございます。

Adobe Lightroom Team (Katrin、Pei、Ben)
Adobe Japan (三井様、吉本様、田中様)
キヤノンマーケティングジャパン （株） (新保様、小川様)
Sony Deutschland (Oliver)
Apple Deutschland
#Teampixel
CANDEO HOTELS (Felicia)
Chrome japan (関口様)
Edwin Europe (Olli)
INSPIRATION CULT
Jack Wolfskin Team (Kim、 Mokhtar、 宮城様、喜田様)
Leica Deutschland
Peace & After (森様)
MDLR(Marco)
SILAS (Yusaku さん、二瓶様)
Toraichi Concept （池田様、村上様)
Zanter Japan （薬師寺様)
ZUICA
Hotel Grand Phenix (田島様)

Anne、Alexa、Ben、Calvin、Chisa、
Espinas、Gen、Hikari、Kanna、Kohei、
Mitsuru、Nemo、Nishi、OMB、
Rhyme、Risa、Shingo、T.Iwai、Teddy、
U、Umi、Yui、Yuma、齋藤さん

Model: @kanna0123 @nanac0421 @saltybarbara

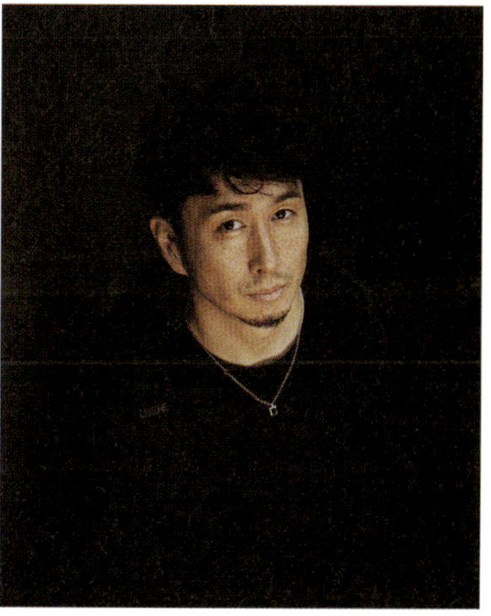

山田悠人

東京都出身。日本デザイナー学院グラフィックデザイン科卒業、広告制作会社勤務を経て、留学のためニューヨークに渡米。帰国後フリーランスデザイナーとして活動。2013年よりドイツの首都ベルリンに活動拠点を移し、写真家、映像クリエイターとしても活動を開始する。
デザイナーとしてのスキルを生かしたグラフィカルな写真表現を得意とし、拠点であるベルリン、出身地である東京を中心に国内外で作品展示を行う。近年は日本の美を世界に広めるため、精力的に日本を撮影するかたわら、広告写真や企業案件の撮影を手がける。Apple, Google などの企業がスポンサーとなり『Adobe Lightroom』のアンバサダーにも選出されている。
Website: yuto-yamada.com
Instagram: @tokio_kid

YUTO YAMADA

Yuto Yamada was born and raised in Tokyo. After completing the Graphic Design Course at Nippon Designers School, Yuto joined an advertising production company before moving to New York to pursue his studies. He became a freelance designer upon returning to Japan. In 2013, the creative relocated his base to Germany's capital city of Berlin, where he began is career as a photographer and videographer.
Yuto specializes in applying his design expertise to create an artistic style of photography. The artist holds exhibitions mainly in Berlin, where he is based, as well as in his native city of Tokyo, among other locations around the world. In recent years, he has been dedicating his talents to document the sights in Japan with an aim to communicate its beauty to the world, while also contributing his photography to advertisements and corporate projects. Yuto has been sponsored by companies such as Apple and Google and is an ambassador for Adobe Lightroom.

ジャパニズム
JAPANISM —— 世界に伝えたい、日本の美景 ——

2022 年 12 月 18 日　初版第 1 刷発行
2024 年 5 月 9 日　　　第 3 刷発行

著者：山田 悠人
アートディレクション：伊藤 修一
デザイン：伊藤 修一　紺田 達也
翻訳：米林 ひろこ（株式会社 LPH）
編集協力：宮沢 香奈
編集：篠谷 晴美

撮影協力
日本航空株式会社

制作進行：高橋 かおる（株式会社 パイ インターナショナル）

発行人：三芳寛要
発行元：株式会社 パイ インターナショナル
〒 170-0005 東京都豊島区南大塚 2-32-4
TEL 03-3944-3981
FAX 03-5395-4830
sales@pie.co.jp

印刷・製本　株式会社シナノ印刷